THE FINANCIAL SYSTEM IN
NINETEENTH-CENTURY BRITAIN

THE FINANCIAL SYSTEM IN NINETEENTH-CENTURY BRITAIN

Edited by

Mary Poovey

New York University

New York   Oxford

OXFORD UNIVERSITY PRESS

2003

Oxford University Press

Oxford   New York
Auckland   Bangkok   Buenos Aires   Cape Town   Chennai
Dar es Salaam   Delhi   Hong Kong   Istanbul   Karachi   Kolkata
Kuala Lumpur   Madrid   Melbourne   Mexico City   Mumbai
Nairobi   São Paulo   Shanghai   Taipei   Tokyo   Toronto

Copyright © 2003 by Oxford University Press, Inc.

Published by Oxford University Press, Inc.
198 Madison Avenue, New York, New York, 10016
http://www.oup-usa.org

Oxford is a registered trademark of Oxford University Press

Library of Congress Cataloging-in-Publication Data

The financial system in nineteenth-century Britain / edited by Mary Poovey.
     p. cm. — (The Victorian archives series ; 1)
     Includes bibliographical references and index.
     ISBN 0-19-516102-5 (cloth)—ISBN 0-19-515057-0 (pbk. : alk. paper)
       1. Finance—Great Britain—History—19th century.   I. Title: Financial system in
19th-century Britain.   II. Poovey, Mary.   III. Series.

  HG186.G7 F58 2003
  332′.0941′09034—dc21

                                                                    2002022463

Printing number: 9   8   7   6   5   4   3   2   1

Printed in the United States of America
on acid-free paper

Contents

Preface

This collection of primary documents is intended for undergraduates, graduate students, and scholars interested in the development of the modern financial system in Britain. While the documents collected here specifically concern financial institutions in nineteenth-century Britain, this volume also speaks to other topics of enduring interest: the development of a world system of financial credit and indebtedness; the various ways that financial relationships organize individuals' experiences of modern society, not to mention their personal lives; and the complex system of financial arrangements that informs so many Victorian novels and poems. Readers of this volume will discover how intricate familiar financial institutions were (and are) and how pervasive some concerns that now seem almost incomprehensible once were. The documents collected here, in short, reveal that the world of nineteenth-century financial institutions is both recognizably the ancestor of our own and a place whose byways are almost completely foreign to most modern readers.

In addition to the unprecedented growth in the financial sector, nineteenth-century Britain also witnessed an explosion in the number and kind of printed documents available to a larger and increasingly diverse body of readers. With the founding of the *Edinburgh Review* in 1802, a new kind of periodical was born. Four times a year, quarterlies like the *Edinburgh* published long, detailed discussions of contemporary issues for readers with sufficient education, leisure, and money to enjoy them. Meanwhile, the increased number and size of newspapers continued to provide reading material for Britons at nearly all levels of the social scale, and, after the taxes on paper and advertisements were abolished in the 1850s, dailies and weeklies became even more numerous, varied, and affordable. In the world of literature, expensive three-volume novels (the so-called triple-deckers) increasingly had to compete with serialized fiction, which was published either as individual monthly pamphlets or in magazines like Charles Dickens's *Household Words.* Whatever its format, this fiction tended to fill many pages—as did many of the century's great poems, such as Lord Tennyson's *The Princess,* Elizabeth Barrett Browning's

Aurora Leigh, and Robert Browning's *The Ring and the Book.* A surprising number of the thousands of pages that compose nineteenth-century periodicals, newspapers, and literature were devoted, directly or indirectly, to financial topics. These new forms of print culture, in other words, were made possible by the financial developments these selections represent, and they return obsessively to finance as a subject of increasing importance to readers at all levels of the social scale. It is one argument of this collection that we cannot understand the nineteenth-century developments in the British financial sector without recognizing the role that print culture played in these changes. By the same token, we cannot understand the voluminous writing nineteenth-century Britons produced unless we begin to grasp the details of the financial system that so intrigued them.

One of the aims of this collection is to introduce modern readers to part of the vast range of nonliterary printed material available to nineteenth-century readers. Another is to provide some sense of what it was like to read this material when it was originally published. Because the anthology format does not allow me literally to reproduce the form in which these articles were published—whether stand-alone pamphlet or article on a newspaper page or essay in a two-hundred-page quarterly—readers of this collection will experience mainly the length and complexity of many nineteenth-century discussions of finance. While length is not the only feature of their original format that matters, of course, reprinting almost all of these selections in their entirety does enable modern readers to see how nineteenth-century financial writers developed their arguments, how they circled back on familiar themes, and how they drew readers into the world they sought to describe by devices that also appeared in contemporary fiction, such as fictionalized autobiographies or the personification of household goods. Unlike most collections of primary documents, then, this volume does not rely heavily on extracts that isolate a single theme because it interests us. Instead, this collection asks modern readers to reexperience what reading about finance was like for many nineteenth-century Britons. This means that we need to develop the patience necessary to work through long selections, to cultivate the ability to recognize how what look like digressions actually fit together, and to discover how complexity adds to instead of simply obscures the single point an extract would preserve.

Nineteenth-century writing about finance is so extensive that this collection could easily have been expanded to a multivolume work. So much of this writing is now unavailable to most readers, moreover, that one might argue that a volume three times the size of this one would capture merely the tip of a rapidly disappearing iceberg. While there is much to be said for giving modern readers more of this crucial component of nineteenth-century British culture, there is also much to be said for making the subject manageable. In this collection, I have tried to include essays that provide enough detail to answer basic questions for readers new to this area. At the same time, I hope that these selections will provoke readers already familiar with some aspects of nineteenth-century finance to read more. To that end, I have included at the end of the volume a list of suggestions for further reading drawn from contemporary sources as well as secondary material. Whether one reads only the selections included here or pursues these leads further into nineteenth-century writing about finance, readers should take from this volume a better sense of how one of the most important components of modern society developed as one facet of a culture that is both like and unlike our own.

ACKNOWLEDGMENTS

A number of colleagues helped me find a way through the thicket of nineteenth-century writing about finance. For their advice and support, I would especially like to thank Christina Crosby, Elaine Freedgood, Nancy Henry, Steve Mihm, and Richard Sylla. To Timothy Alborn I owe a special debt, for without his suggestions, not to mention his financial guide to the *Wellesley Index of Victorian Periodicals,* my task would have been immeasurably more difficult. At various times and in various ways, Erik Bond and Eileen Bowman helped gather and collate these materials, and Joanna Holzman provided indispensable research assistance throughout the project. Joanna also researched and helped write the biographical entries about contributors. I thank all of these individuals for their help, and I can only hope that they feel rewarded, as I do, in knowing more about the hitherto mysterious world of nineteenth-century finance.

Chronology of the British Financial System

1600	East India Company chartered
1608	First Prices Current published in London
1619	First Bills of Entry published in London
1692	First Marine Lists published in London
1693	England establishes a permanent funded debt, known as the National Debt
1694	The Bank of England established
1696	*Lloyd's News* established
1697	First Exchange Rate Current published in London
	The Course of the Exchange established
1712	Stamp duty imposed on newspapers and advertisements
1720	South Sea Bubble (speculative mania); Bubble Act passed
1734	*Lloyd's List* founded
1776	Stamp duty raised
1780	Stamp duty raised
1789	Stamp duty raised
1797	The Bank of England suspends cash payments
1801	London Stock Exchange formally opens
1802	*Edinburgh Review* founded
1811	Industrial shares quoted on the London Stock Exchange for the first time
1816	England adopts the gold standard
	One-pound notes withdrawn
1817	First Mint issue of gold sovereigns
1821	Bank of England resumes cash payments
1823	London Stock Exchange opens Foreign Funds Market in Capel Court; Nathan Rothschild assumes prominence in foreign loans market
1824	Bubble Act repealed

1825	*London Times* publishes first "Money, Market, and City Intelligence" column
1825–26	First financial crisis of the nineteenth century: ninety-three banks in England and Wales fail
1826	Banking CoPartnership or Joint-Stock Bank Act passed, allowing banks with more than six partners to incorporate outside a sixty-five-mile radius of London
1832	J. R. McCulloch's *Dictionary of Commerce and Commercial Navigation* published
1832–34	Harriet Martineau's *Illustrations of Political Economy* published
1833	Bank Charter Act: makes Bank of England notes legal tender in England; repeals the Usury Law
	Joint-Stock Banks allowed to incorporate within London
1835	Foreign Funds Market and London Stock Exchange officially united
1836	Stamp duty decreased
1837	Financial crisis
	Telegraph invented
1839	Financial crisis
1843	*Economist* founded
1844	Act for the Registration, Incorporation, and Regulation of Joint-Stock Companies, creating the Registry Office
1844	*Banker's Magazine* launched
	Bank Charter Renewal Act, ending the Bank of England's monopoly over joint-stock incorporation and breaking the Bank into an issue department and a banking department
1845–46	Railway mania
1847	Financial crisis
1848	Suspension of the 1844 Bank Act
	Transgressions of George Hudson, the "railway king," revealed
	Gold discovered in Australia
1851	First submarine cable laid across the English Channel
1852	Gold discovered in California and Australia
1855	Stamp duty and advertisement tax abolished
1856	1844 Company Act repealed. New Company Law passed
	William James Robson, chief clerk in the transfer department of the Crystal Palace Company, sentenced to twenty years' transportation for embezzlement; Leopold Redpath, registrar of Great Northern Railway, convicted on embezzlement and transported for life
1857	Financial crisis

1858   Suspension of the 1844 Bank Act

1860   George Pullinger, chief cashier of the Union Bank of London, sentenced to twenty years' transportation for embezzlement

Anglo-international banks founded in London: Bank of Egypt, Ottoman Bank, London and Brazilian Bank, and the Anglo-Austrian Bank

1861   Paper duty abolished

Post Office Savings Banks established for small investors

1862   Consolidation Act passed, extending privileges of the 1856 Act to banks and insurance companies and establishing limited liability for corporations

1864   Bank of England admitted to the London Clearing House

1866   Financial crisis: collapse of Overend, Gurney, & Co.

London to New York submarine cable laid

1867   Suspension of the 1844 Bank Charter Act

Ticker tape machine introduced into London Stock Exchange

1870   London Institute of Accountants established

1870s   Foreign bills of exchange become more prevalent than inland (domestic) bills

1873   Bagehot's *Lombard Street* published

1877   Treasury bill created

1878   Financial crisis: City of Glasgow Bank collapses

Statist founded

Bank of England begins to use a double interest rate

Telephones first used in the London Stock Exchange

1879   Companies Act: eases the transition to limited liability for banks by establishing "reserve liability"—a fixed amount for which shareholders would be held responsible in case of liquidation

1880   Institute of Chartered Accountants in England and Wales established

1880s   Height of the bank amalgamation movement within England

1884   *Financial News* launched

1886   *Quarterly Journal of Economics* founded

Gold discovered in South Africa

1888   *Financial Times* launched

1890   *Economic Journal* founded

The merchant bank Barings nearly falls; London banks unite with the Bank of England to save the firm

1895   London School of Economics founded

1900   R. H. Inglis Palgrave's *Dictionary of Political Economy* published

Harry Marks sued for libel for fraudulent stock announcements in the *Financial News*

1903   Cambridge University establishes the Economics Tripos

1912   London Stock Exchange institutes minimum commission fees

1913   Outbreak of World War I transforms worldwide economic conditions

THE FINANCIAL SYSTEM IN
NINETEENTH-CENTURY BRITAIN

INTRODUCTION

As every reader of Victorian literature knows, nineteenth-century Britons were preoccupied with money. They brooded about how to get it, save it, and spend it, and they worried about where money comes from, why it incites so many crimes, and how the well-to-do can live on so little while the poor need so much. This preoccupation was both imaginative and practical. As nineteenth-century novelists and poets turned the national fixation into some of the most engaging fictions of the century, capitalists, bankers, and jurists were forging the financial institutions that enabled money to circulate, international trade to flourish, and Britain to become the richest and most powerful nation in the world.

The sheer number and variety of nineteenth-century writings about money and finance make these topics all but impossible for the modern reader to master. Then, too, the intricacy of nineteenth-century credit instruments, company legislation, and investment opportunities can frustrate readers who lack the time to consult business and financial history. This volume is intended to illuminate some of the most important components of the nineteenth-century British financial system and to explore how a variety of British citizens thought about it. While the selections included here do not cover every aspect of this system, much less every financial topic debated in the nineteenth century, they do provide the materials necessary to understand how the primary financial institutions of the period worked. They also show—sometimes in vivid detail—why the development of this system inspired both grandiose fantasies about success and acute anxieties about failure and fraud.

Before explaining how the nineteenth-century financial system worked, I need to make several general points. The first is that, at the institutional level, nineteenth-century finance functioned as a *system*. By this I mean that no single institution or group of institutions worked in isolation from others. Taken as a whole, the purpose of this system was to make capital available for purchasing goods, pursuing trade, or otherwise developing economic opportunities. To do so, the institutions that composed the financial system enabled individuals and banks to move capital from parts of the country where it was temporarily unemployed to parts of the country (or the world) where it was needed. At the end of the harvest season in agricultural areas, for example, farmers had more money than they could profitably invest. To help their clients generate revenue, country bankers would send money to the London banks in which they held accounts, and these banks would make the capital available to borrowers, such as industrialists, who needed more money than their local banks could supply. At each stage of this transaction, banks charged for their services, so that the original proceeds of good harvests not only generated interest for the investing farmer and capital for the industrialist but also revenue for the banks. At the beginning of the next agricultural season, when farmers needed money to plant new crops, the flow of capital would be reversed, with money traveling through the banking system from parts of the country where capital was available to the farmers who needed it.

As we will see in a moment, the financial system was far more complicated and geographically extensive than this simple model suggests, and it included many institutions in addition to banks. Crucially, moreover, the capital that financial institutions moved from investor to borrower did not typically take the form of literal coins or bank notes. Instead, the gold that stood behind the capital was represented by various kinds of paper documents that signified the lender's worth. Even more typically, these paper documents represented the *credit* the lender enjoyed as a consequence of his possessions, his potential for future earnings, or his reputation for honesty. This means that much of the wealth that fueled Britain's spectacular growth in the nineteenth century was never available for its possessors to touch or count, for the gold that composed the wealth was characteristically rendered unnecessary by the paper that represented it, while the capital that wealth signified was typically at work elsewhere, awaiting collection at some future date. These characteristics made capital seem completely different from land, which had been the primary form of wealth during most of the eighteenth century. Unlike land, which could be made to yield crops slowly, through the application of manual labor and agricultural improvements, capital could generate more of itself almost overnight, simply by being invested. Capital's ability to generate wealth through circulation, combined with its alternatively virtual and embodied states, were among the features that helped make money so imaginatively engaging to nineteenth-century Britons. Even as they occupied an everyday world increasingly filled with objects from all over the globe, more Britons measured their worth not simply by the acres (or square feet) that surrounded them but by this immaterial representative of a form of value that was always deferred.

I return to these matters in the pages below, but it is important to remember that all of the intricacies of the financial institutions I describe here contributed to most Britons' impression that, in its own way, capital was as substantial—as real—as land. No one doubted that money could fund the labor that produced real objects, of course, but as journalists and novelists explored the mysterious circulation of capital through institutions like banks or the Stock Exchange, they helped give capital imaginative substance for readers grappling with the emergence of a national and world credit economy. Especially in the beginning of this period, most Britons were willing to invest their coins and bank notes in bank accounts or shares only if they believed that the particular institution or individual they could actually see, like a local bank or London broker, belonged to a system that was both effective and trustworthy. Making this system seem trustworthy—making it imaginatively visible—was the work of the journalists and novelists who wrote about financial matters. Even when they were critical of parts of the financial system, like fraudulent clerks or mismanaged banks, writers who described how money was misappropriated and share prices manipulated were helping make these financial institutions work by representing the criminals as exceptions to a general rule of reliable transactions.

Before exploring the implications of the role played by writing in the development of the nineteenth-century financial system, it is important to note a second feature of the system as a whole. During the course of the nineteenth century, various parts of the financial system were developed or refined, but different kinds of institutions did not develop or change in the same ways or at the same rates. This means that, while the system as a whole developed in the course of the century, its various sectors developed at uneven speeds and not always toward a single end. It also means that even though the components of this system were always related to each other and need to be seen that way, it would be misleading to personify the system as a whole or to speak of an implicit logic that governed it.

Signs of this internal unevenness are visible everywhere in the histories of the individual institutions that composed the financial system. Just to take one example, even though the period is generally characterized by a tendency toward decreasing the role of government in economic matters like trade, in some financial sectors, like banking, national legislation increasingly dictated the terms under which new banks could be formed and old ones could operate. The Stock Exchange, by contrast, was regulated almost exclusively by its own Governing Committee, with no interference from Parliament—and, partly as a consequence, it provided almost no protection for investors. In some cases, the uneven development within the financial system reflects a society-wide ambivalence about the very terms in which value should be understood. The dramatic changes in bankruptcy legislation, for example, which alternated between imprisoning bankrupts and excusing their debts, and which mandated, then outlawed, then restored government supervision of settlements, suggests a pervasive uncertainty about whether an individual's financial failure should be treated as an ethical failure too. In some cases, the uneven development within the financial system reveals the power of established institutions relative to new ones. We see this in the privileges enjoyed by one joint-stock bank, the Bank of England, which was treated as the nation's official bank long before it became such by law in 1946. By contrast, new banks, especially the joint-stock banks that were permitted to form in London only after 1833, had to struggle against restrictions imposed by the directors of the Bank of England and the owners of private banks, who worked in concert to quell the competition that the new banks posed.

If it is possible for us to look back on the nineteenth-century financial scene and see it both as a system and as a set of dissimilar institutions, we also need to remember that neither of these views was consistently available to nineteenth-century Britons. For much of the nineteenth century, in fact, most British citizens could only grasp parts of the financial system and they could only see those parts through writing that was not always intended (or able) to give a comprehensive or accurate picture. In some cases, as with the London Stock Exchange, ordinary Britons could not visualize how the market worked because what they could read by journalists was limited to what the journalist could find out—and this was limited by the stockbrokers' desire to control information so as to limit competition from other brokers. In other cases, like that of some private banks, information was only erratically collected even for internal use, and, because thorough audits were not required for most of the century, such information, even when collected, was typically neither public nor systematic. In yet other cases, like that of fledgling companies, the information that was made public, in the form of the mandated prospectus, was sometimes blatantly false. As we will see, newspapers and periodicals were created during the period to open the mysterious world of finance to the public view, but even these were not always reliable, since newspapers depended on advertisements for income—and advertisers were often the very companies that might have been the targets of more skeptical reporting. For many parts of the financial sector, especially when fraud or mismanagement was involved, only parliamentary commissions, convened after extensive financial losses, could reveal how particular institutions worked. As the source of the most reliable—but also belated—information, these commission reports often helped journalists and novelists conjure what the public was struggling to understand.

It is critical to keep this last point in mind for two reasons. First, the lack of readily available information means that every piece of writing about finance in this period was an attempt to understand and interpret something that was only partially visible and constantly in a state of change. This means, in turn, that we should not read the selections included here as straightforward descriptions. Even the entries taken from dictionaries, like McCulloch's *Dictionary of Commerce and Commercial Navigation,* need to be read as *interpretive descriptions,* which are informed both by their authors' relative proximity to existing sources of information and by their own theoretical and political positions on issues that were often highly controversial and imperfectly understood. It follows from the interpretive nature of all writing about finance in this period that these selections cannot fully explain the meaning of episodes in Victorian literature that turn on financial issues. While the reader will surely acquire from the various selections on bills of exchange a clearer understanding of what Fascination Fledgby is doing with the "odd bills" he collects in Dickens's *Our Mutual Friend,* knowledge of what an accommodation bill is does not dispel the connotations of malice that cluster around this character or explain his relationship to the novel's other characters. The selections collected here will certainly make it easier for the student of Victorian literature and nineteenth-century history to recognize terms contained in other writing of the period, but treating these selections as simple background or as mere reference material would obscure one of the most fascinating aspects of all nineteenth-century writing about finance. Every instance of this writing—from McCulloch's *Dictionary* to Trollope's novels—needs to be viewed as part of a discursive system in which Britons constructed ideas about finance and money alongside the system of finance itself.

Now we come to the second reason why it is critical to remember the relative scarcity of reliable information in this period. Because the operations of the financial system are extremely sensitive to the circulation of information (or rumors), efforts to understand the system—to represent and dramatize its parts—could actually affect the system itself. This tendency is especially clear in the interaction between technology developed to speed the circulation of information and the development of innovative trading practices on the Stock Exchange. Thus, for example, when a telephone room was created in the London Stock Exchange in 1883, it became possible for London jobbers in constant telephonic contact with provincial markets to take advantage of price discrepancies, buying low and selling high in a new kind of transaction known as arbitrage. This mutually provocative interaction is also evident in the financial panics that punctuated the nineteenth century. These panics, which focused the public's attention on banks or discount houses, were often fueled by newspaper accounts that a particular house was overextended. In reporting the angry crowds milling about in Lombard Street, even a newspaper as staid as the *Times* could incite more worried investors to demand their money, and thus exacerbate the lenders' woes.

The financial system's extreme susceptibility to the influence of representations means that we need to read the selections collected here as participants in the financial system itself. We need to remember that unusually tight links bound the institutional and discursive systems in this area of nineteenth-century culture. We also need to understand that even the most neutral accounts of banking or the Stock Exchange, for example, could contribute to future legislation. The close relationship between efforts to understand finance and developments within financial institutions themselves means that reading these selections can open a window onto the dynamic of change within the nineteenth-century financial world. For this reason, I give special attention to the development of the financial press at the end of this introduction. It is important to know both what nineteenth-century Britons could know about financial institutions and how they came to know it.

The selections included in this book extend from the first decade of the nineteenth century through the first decade of the twentieth. The historical period I discuss in my introductory narrative covers a slightly longer period, from 1797, when the Bank of England suspended cash payments, to 1913, when World War I began to transform economic and financial and economic conditions around the world. Given the constraints of space, the prolixity of Victorian writing, and my decision to include as many complete essays as possible, these selections could not possibly cover the period or explore every part of the financial system. To some readers, the most notable omission may be political economy, which arguably represents one of nineteenth-century Britain's most important contributions to economic writing. I do not include selections from the major political economists for two reasons: First, I wanted to emphasize the operations of specific financial institutions rather than theories about them; and second, political economy has been extensively treated in recent secondary literature. Among the nineteenth-century financial institutions themselves, I have not been able to include materials that deal specifically with Scottish banks, the decimal currency, post office savings banks, or insurance. I deal with merchant banks, which specialized in international investment, only in passing, although the topic of international commerce recurs repeatedly in articles that acknowledge how extensively overseas trade and investment affected the financial well-being of Britons. The crucial issue of Britain's relationship to the colonies is addressed in several selections, especially those in Parts 1 and 2, although these essays do not discuss all of Britain's colonies. The rank of the authors represented here ranges across the spectrum of British classes, but, even though women were obviously affected by financial institutions, I have not included any selections by or specifically about women. Some of the most notable popularizers of political economy were women—Harriet Martineau and Mrs. Marcet, for example—but, as far as we can tell, the vast majority of specifically financial journalists were men. Novels like Elizabeth Gaskell's *Cranford* (1850) and George Eliot's *Middlemarch* (1870–72) enable us to see women's imaginative engagement with these subjects. The prevalence of financial topics in women's novels suggests that these matters were not far from women novelists' minds, even if few women contributed articles to the financial press.

Finally, I admit at the outset that I do not even try to answer the single most frequently asked question about money in this period: How can we translate nineteenth-century money amounts into modern equivalents? Despite several attempts to provide tables of equivalencies, I remain convinced that such tables are unreliable. I hold this conviction for several reasons, the most important of which is that changing social values made some commodities more desirable—and hence more costly—in some periods than in others. Comparing the cost of a single item across time would need to take into consideration this social factor, which is, for all intents and purposes, immeasurable. The desire to know what a certain price would mean to us seems to me to be just that— a desire to understand meaning, not equivalent value. The meaning of commodities, opportunities, and risk can only be derived from the discursive and institutional context in which writing about these things occurs. To understand meaning, such selections as the ones included here are a better guide than any numerical tables of approximate equivalents would be.

THE PRINCIPLE INSTITUTIONS OF THE NINETEENTH-CENTURY FINANCIAL SYSTEM

Currency and Credit Instruments

Pounds, shillings, and pence—which are typically represented by the figures £, s., and d.—are units of value, useful for all kinds of bookkeeping and accounting. In the nineteenth century, before the adoption of the decimal currency, 20s. equaled £1, and 12d. equaled 1s. The guinea, which was the only term that represented both an abstract measure of value and a physical coin, equaled 21s., or £1 1s. These values, in turn, were represented by a variety of physical instruments, ranging from coins, which (theoretically) embodied the precious metal to which the units of value referred, to written entries in ledger sheets, which (again theoretically) referred to the currency that embodied gold or silver. By the second decade of the century, coins made of gold, silver, and copper circulated in Britain. These included gold sovereigns (1 pound or 20 shillings), half-sovereigns (10 shillings), and guineas (21 shillings); silver shillings (12 pence), crowns (5 shillings), half-crowns ($2\frac{1}{2}$ shillings), sixpenny and threepenny pieces; and copper pence (1 penny), halfpence ($\frac{1}{2}$ penny), farthings ($\frac{1}{4}$ penny), and half-farthings ($\frac{1}{8}$ penny). A silver fourpenny piece was minted between 1836 and 1856, and in 1849, the silver florin, worth 2s., was minted for the first time. Guineas were not minted after

1813, even though the coins continued to circulate and prices continued to be quoted in this unit. After 1860, pence, half-pence, and farthings were minted in bronze instead of copper.

These coins did not constitute the bulk of English (not to mention British) currency, of course. Not only did Scotland and Ireland have their own coins, but, at the beginning of the nineteenth century, there were not enough gold, silver, and copper coins in circulation to pay wages and purchase goods. The shortage of coin was partly the result of the outflow of precious metal that had gone on throughout the eighteenth century. Because Britain's silver coins had been grossly undervalued for over a century, unscrupulous individuals had long been melting British coins and sending the metal out of the country for the higher price it could command abroad. The coins that remained in Britain were badly scarred, clipped, and worn, and, partly as a consequence, it was not unusual for eighteenth-century British shopkeepers to value coins by weight rather than face value. In 1816, Parliament began to rectify this situation. It adopted gold as the sole measure of value and declared gold coins to be legal tender for sums over £2; in 1817, the mint issued the first gold sovereigns; and, in 1819, Parliament lifted the restrictions on the export of coin and the bullion derived from melting coin. As a consequence, the state of the circulating coins gradually improved—at least until the late 1860s, when the government determined once again that the precious metal in the coins had been seriously eroded through use, and a new debate about recoinage began.

The shortage of coin that characterized the first decades of the nineteenth century also stemmed from the English government's war against France, which began in 1792–93. By 1794, the government's demand for funds exceeded the aggregate income of the country's entire population. Even more worrisome, the coin and bullion held by the Bank of England was reduced to an alarmingly low level. To address what was quickly becoming a national emergency, the Bank of England suspended cash payments early in 1797. This suspension meant that the Bank was no longer willing to exchange a citizen's worn coins for gold bullion, and it was no longer willing to back the paper notes it issued with gold. Almost immediately, gold and silver coins disappeared from domestic circulation, as they were hoarded in private coffers or hastened onto ships bound for other countries.

During the period known as the Restriction, which lasted until 1821, Britons had to conduct their financial transactions with a variety of kinds of paper, none of which—not even the notes issued by the Bank of England—was convertible to gold. This reliance on nonconvertible paper, along with the country's dependence on a system of borrowing known as the National Debt, further extended the network of credit and debt that was already well established in eighteenth-century Britain. In the eighteenth century, much of this credit was informal and local, as when a shopkeeper allowed a regular customer to run an account for months at a time. By the end of the century, this local credit had been integrated into a national network, and, when the Bank suspended payment in 1797, the possibility of avoiding debt disappeared as credit instruments became virtually the only available medium of exchange.

By the second decade of the nineteenth century, Britain was awash in paper money. To some, like the radical William Cobbett, the prevalence of paper meant that the nation had swindled the gullible poor, who had no choice but to accept rags in place of gold. To others, like J. R. McCulloch, one of the most prolific apologists for the credit economy, it meant that Britain could seize the lead in international finance. By and large, however, by the middle of the century, most Britons had become reconciled to paper money, for the Bank had made notes convertible once more in 1821, and, in 1844, it had bowed to the parliamentary mandate that a gold reserve back any notes issued beyond £14,000. In 1816, bank notes of less than one pound were withdrawn, and the Bank continued to issue paper money in denominations beginning with £5 notes. In 1833, Bank of England notes were made legal tender in England but not in Scotland, where local paper continued to circulate.

In addition to paper money, the system of British credit was based on other kinds of written promises to pay. These included simple promissory notes and I.O.U.s, cheques (or checks), various kinds of bills of exchange, and accommodation bills. After paper bank notes, bills of exchange were the most important credit instruments in nineteenth-century Britain. These bills had initially been developed by merchants in order to facilitate overseas trade, but, as early as the seventeenth century, merchants also began to use them within Britain both for trade and for financial purposes. In their original form, bills of exchange were agreements between merchants used to extend credit across geographical and currency boundaries. A merchant in England, for example, would accept as payment for goods to be delivered a bill of exchange from another merchant. The bill would typically be drawn on a London bank, thus allowing the merchant who sold the goods to receive payment in his local currency before the goods arrived at their destination. The merchant who purchased the goods, meanwhile, could defer payment to the bank that had guaranteed the bill until the date specified on the bill. Such bills were used for financial purposes (as opposed to trade) when brokers purchased them (and the debts they represented), then sold them, at a profit, to third-party financiers.

Unlike paper money, which represented and was backed by the issuing bank's resources, bills of exchange were secured by the goods a merchant actually possessed, the profits he was likely to receive through commercial trade, or the reputation he had earned through past transactions. In other words, a lender (typically a banker) would be willing to give the borrower bank notes for a bill of exchange (to "accept" the bill) only if he judged the borrower to be worth the risk of extending credit. To offset the risk that the borrower would not repay the loan by its due date, the lender charged the borrower interest for the credit extended. Typically, this interest, which was called the "discount," was exacted up front, when the lender accepted the bill. Accepting a bill of exchange was thus referred to as "discounting a bill." When a lender accepted a bill of exchange, he signed its face and wrote "accepted" beside his name. He then deposited the bill, alongside his other assets, in a secure place like a vault—assuming he did not intend to trade the bill in order to pay his own debt or to profit further from the debt the bill represented.

An acceptor of a bill could trade it because bills of exchange, like paper money, were fully negotiable instruments. Until the due date on the bill, one holder could pass it along to someone else as payment for goods or services or use it as an investment. When a second person agreed to take the bill as payment, he signed its back. This signature, called the "endorsement," also made the second holder responsible for the debt represented on the bill. Having endorsed the bill, the new recipient could then pass it along to another person, and so on, until the bill was due. Because bills represented indebtedness, moreover, it was possible to purchase bills (for less than their face value), then sell them to others whose business was to arrange loans between lenders and borrowers. When this financial use of bills became organized in the first quarter of the nineteenth century, it was known as the London discount market. The houses that composed this market were physically centered on Lombard Street, and thus the London discount market was known simply as Lombard Street.

When a bill of exchange fell due, the current holder either had to renew the bill, typically at a discount again, or pay the debt it represented. If the current holder was unable to pay the debt, the original lender or the financier who had purchased the debt could try to collect from every person who had endorsed the bill. For this reason, bills of exchange bound their various endorsers into a relationship of collateral indebtedness, and the circulation of bills extended the system of credit and debt through, but also beyond, networks of friends and relatives. This system of indebtedness was also mobilized when an individual wrote across the bottom of the bill "In case of need, apply to X and Co.," for this phrase signified the willingness of X and Co. to pay the bill on the day it was due. This is the kind of responsibility Caleb Garth assumes on Fred Vincy's behalf in *Middlemarch,* and Fred's inability to pay his debt explains the indebtedness that consumes the Garth family. Because every person who accepted a bill of exchange had to endorse the bill to make it negotiable, each bill carried its own history on its back in the signatures that appeared there. Bills of exchange were therefore not only instruments of exchange but also records of the credit and trading networks that tied one individual to another. As records of the loans and payments that linked various businessmen to each other, bills of exchange betrayed the very business transactions that many merchants wanted to keep secret. For this reason, some banks in particular were unwilling to sell (or "rediscount") their bills, since doing so disclosed the business histories of their clients.

As discounting, or bill broking, became an established business in the first two decades of the nineteenth century, brokers developed expertise in judging the quality of a given bill by the creditworthiness of its endorsers. Bills were more or less deeply discounted (that is, charged more or less interest for the extension of the loan) according to the signatures that appeared on their backs. Both lenders and borrowers tended to rely on the expertise of discount houses because no individual could possibly judge the creditworthiness of all the signatories of a bill. Bills were also discounted more or less deeply according to the time remaining before expiration, with bills that extended credit for a longer period being charged a higher interest rate than "short bills."

Bills of exchange resembled two other credit instruments common in nineteenth-century Britain, the accommodation bill and the check. Accommodation bills, which were also called "kites" (or "wind bills" in Scotland), were typically drawn for even amounts of money, for the largest sum allowed by the government stamp (which was required for all bills over the value of 40 s.), and for a long term. They were also usually presented for conversion into bank notes soon after they were drawn, and their parties, typically few in number, were often relatives, friends, or people who were unlikely to have legitimate business connections with each other. Bankers typically refused accommodation bills because they assumed that they were instruments of pure speculation. Check, by contrast, were legitimate credit instruments, drafts upon bankers payable to the bearer upon demand. Legally, they had to be drawn within fifteen miles of the bank on which they made a claim, and they had to be presented for payment at the bank within a "reasonable" period. In practice, this period was usually two days from the checks' date of issue. Postdating a check to make it function as a bill of exchange was punishable by a steep penalty. Checks were also used by banks, especially those in London, as a means of settling claims without incurring transaction costs or having to settle any amount over the balance due in cash. The use of checks for this last purpose had been facilitated by the establishment of the London Clearing House in 1773.

The extensive circulation of domestic (or inland) bills of exchange in nineteenth-century Britain enabled businesses to grow with borrowed capital, and the bills extended the local networks of credit centered on country bank loans to provincial borrowers across the nation (and, through foreign bills, across the globe). In the highly capitalized London discount market in place by 1825, discount houses functioned as the middlemen of the extensive and expanding British financial system. They purchased bills of exchange from provincial banks, as well as from merchants, industrialists, and businessmen, and they sold these bills to borrowers, having endorsed them, as every acceptor had to do. This kind of organized discount market required sufficient competition and agreement among the bill dealers to guarantee that there would be no marked differences among the prices different lenders charged. The presence of such a market, where bills changed hands every day, meant that the British system of credit and debt was flexible, always open to new participants, and virtually ubiquitous.

The combination of all these factors—an inadequate supply of full-weight coin, an elaborate array of written credit instruments, and an extensive system of credit and debt—meant that opportunities for fraud abounded in nineteenth-century Britain. At the beginning of the period in particular, before £1 notes were withdrawn, the forgery of small notes was commonplace. Coining and counterfeiting were also relatively easy. Certainly, these practices were common enough to inspire imaginative narratives, as we see in Sidney Laman Blanchard's "Biography of a Bad Shilling" (1851). Given the range of handwritten credit instruments that circulated, forgery could be practiced in numerous ways, from the bank clerk changing a "1" into a "9" or adding "one hundred" before the written amount on a check to John Sadlier's massive forgeries in the 1850s. Some bills that circulated were entirely "fictitious," in the sense that all or some of the endorsers' names were forged. After 1830, forgery was no longer a capital offense, but convicted forgers—especially those in the lower social ranks—were often sentenced to long prison terms or transported (before transportation was abolished in the 1860s). The period's literature is filled with instances of discovered forgers ending their lives rather than face transportation or imprisonment.

The National Debt and the London Stock Exchange

The National Debt, which was created in 1693, is a system of permanent, transferable debt. It allows the government to generate a continuing source of revenue by selling its debt, while it allows the holders of this debt to sell their investments when they need money, much as shareholders in a joint-stock company do. Before 1693, the English government had borrowed on a short-term basis, refinancing or redeeming the loans when they fell due. England created a funded debt to avoid the uncertainties of refinancing during its expensive, late seventeenth-century war with France. Wealthy individuals and joint-stock companies were initially willing to invest in the nation's debt because the government guaranteed regular interest payments and because investors could buy or sell their holdings at will. The success of the first issue of government debt was quickly followed by a series of private initiatives, in which joint-stock companies exchanged their shareholders' capital for government-issued debt. When the Bank of England was formed as a joint-stock company in 1694, for example, it paid over its entire capital of £1.2 million to the government in exchange for an interest payment of £50,000 every six months.

In 1749, the government consolidated most of its borrowings into a single loan, for which it paid a fixed rate of 3 percent annual interest. The quarterly interest that investors received for their investments was thus said to come from the "consols," or consolidated annuities. In addition to the funded debt, which was also known as "the funds," the government raised revenue through Exchequer Bills, which represented an unfunded debt whose interest varied according to market conditions. By 1750, the British government owed £78 million, 93 percent of which was permanently funded, as opposed to the £3.1 million of unfunded debt it had owed in 1691. By 1760, nearly 60,400 individuals held shares in the National Debt.[1]

The National Debt forms part of a larger securities market, which had existed in England from the sixteenth century. Before the eighteenth century, this securities market was small, for there were few joint-stock companies in which to invest and few investors with capital available for short-term loans. Before 1700, the basis of investment was land, not securities, and the principal object of finance was credit, not capital. When the government established the National Debt, investors were given the opportunity to buy and sell securities on a greatly expanded scale. As they began to do so, it became apparent that this kind of trading would benefit from a regular, rule-governed forum in which to transact business, as well as from experienced traders who could buy and sell for clients. The incentive to create these facilities was enhanced by developments within the banking system, for as more Britons began to deposit money in banks, banks had to find a short-term, interest-generating home for money that was not currently in use but might be demanded by depositors ("money at call"). Increasingly, banks found this home in the transferable securities of the National Debt. As a result, the continuous ebb and flow of individuals' funds into banks in London and the countryside generated an equally continuous tide of bank buying and selling in the securities market, especially in the popular, because virtually risk-free, government consols. Meanwhile, a similar dynamic was developing in the international domain. Having moved away from a system in which payment had to be in gold and goods had to be delivered when traded, European merchants increasingly turned to London's merchant bankers for the credit that enabled trade, and all parties in this network sought investment in the British securities market. Thus, what some contemporaries lamented as the instability of a securities market where buyers and sellers from all over the world engaged in continu-

---

1. See Ranald C. Michie, *The London Stock Exchange: A History* (Oxford: Oxford University Press, 1999), pp. 18–20.

ous trading at prices that mysteriously rose and fell was actually the hub of a highly flexible, international monetary system that indirectly benefited agricultural and industrial growth at home and directly facilitated trade between countries.

In order for any securities market to work efficiently, it has to guarantee that the sales and prices involved in trades will be honored. This guarantee, in turn, requires two, apparently antithetical arrangements: Barriers between buyers and sellers must be kept to a minimum so that participants can buy or sell at will; and participants have to be evaluated so that individual buyers and sellers—or their representatives—can trust their trading partners. Even though a securities market existed in eighteenth-century London, it did not attain this level of organization until the French Revolution disrupted the operations of London's two greatest financial rivals, Paris and Amsterdam, and redirected the flow of wealth and talent from those centers to London. Wanting to expand its war against France, the English Parliament simultaneously increased the available government securities by increasing the size of the National Debt. With money, foreign financial experts, and increased investment opportunities at their disposal, London traders organized themselves into a quasi-professional community. In January 1799 they declared that all traders had to pay a daily fee to attend the London Stock Exchange building, which had been erected in 1773 at the corner of Threadneedle Street and Sweetings Alley. On March 3, 1801, the London Stock Exchange formally came into existence, with a set of regulations designed to govern how business was conducted and who could buy and sell. The London Stock Market was soon housed in a new, enclosed building in nearby Capel Court.

The emergence of a closed market in securities dramatically altered the nature of the British and, by extension, the international money markets. Whereas the eighteenth-century British securities market had been open and unregulated, the closed London Stock Exchange was governed by rules that dictated who could trade and how trading could proceed. Before 1912, when a minimum commission was established, traders typically charged investors a standard commission of 0.125 percent (with 0.0625 percent available to bankers). Before 1845, when the hours were shortened by one, the Exchange usually opened at 10 A.M. and closed at 4 P.M. Stockbroking firms tended to be small, with five or fewer members, and some specialization developed within the securities industry, with brokers buying and selling exclusively for clients, while jobbers were willing to incur risk by buying for themselves, then reselling their shares. In 1850, the Committee that governed the Stock Exchange established eight settling days per year, when members were required to honor the commitments previously made. Throughout the first part of this period, membership of the Exchange continued to grow alongside the National Debt. Thus, in 1815, the Exchange had 541 members, when the Debt stood at 744.99 million pounds (92 percent funded); when the Debt peaked in 1819 at 844.3 million pounds (94 percent funded), membership in the London Stock Exchange stood at 737. After that year, the Debt did not continue to grow, but the number of Exchange members did, reaching 906 in 1851 and over 2,500 in 1883. The number of stockbrokers continued to increase because, beginning in 1811, the London Stock Market began to expand its securities beyond shares in the National Debt. The first industrial shares were quoted on the Exchange in 1811, and, in 1823, the London Stock Exchange annexed the business in foreign securities that had previously been conducted outside its walls. By the following year, an estimated 624 joint-stock companies, ranging from domestic canal and railway projects to foreign metal-mining companies, had joined the Exchange's domestic and foreign securities (representing principally Colombian, Chilean, Peruvian, Mexican, and Brazilian loans). Even though other securities markets existed in places such as Dublin and Manchester, the phrase "Stock Exchange" was increasingly used to refer only to the London Stock Exchange.

In 1825, the rapid expansion of the securities market came to an abrupt halt with the collapse of the speculative bubble in foreign shares. In this, the first of the nineteenth century's financial panics, the business in foreign funds dried up, money was in short supply, and terrified citizens filled the streets around the Exchange and the Bank. This kind of bank pressure, which was typically, although not always, sparked by overextended trading, occurred repeatedly in nineteenth-century Britain—in 1825–26, 1837, 1839, 1847, 1857, 1866, and 1878. For the money market as a whole, the panic of 1825–26 was a frightening sign of how fragile the entire financial edifice was, for during the winter ninety-three English and Welsh banks failed. For the London Stock Exchange, by contrast, the collapse produced at least one constructive result: In 1835, the previously separate Foreign Funds market was officially united with the Stock Exchange. Even though foreign funds continued to be viewed as more risky than government securities or joint-stock companies, investors' interest in loans to foreign countries revived in the mid-1830s, then again periodically during the century. Trading in joint-stock companies, meanwhile, continued to grow exponentially, especially after new company law was enacted in 1844.

Because joint-stock companies played an increasingly important role in nearly every aspect of British finance, it is important to understand what these companies were and how they could provoke such swings in the securities market. Essentially, joint-stock companies were publicly owned companies, whose shares could be bought and sold, typically on the London Stock Exchange, by individuals with no further involvement in the company's activities. As a form of company ownership, joint-stock incorporation constituted an alternative to the partnership, which was the typical company form in the eighteenth century. The distinction between a corporation and a partnership carried with it important legal and practical differences. A joint-stock corporation was a distinct legal entity, which was not dissolved if its membership changed. This meant both that a corporation could (and regularly did) outlive its founders and that it acted under law as a single body, which could sue and be sued in its corporate name. The assets of a corporation constituted its only security against debts, so that a member, having paid the capital to purchase shares, incurred no further liability for the corporation's losses. Legally, a partnership was not a single entity but a collection of individuals, each of whom was regarded as the fully accredited agent of the company as a whole. As sharers in the company's profits, each of these individuals was also regarded as fully liable for any losses the company incurred "to his last shilling and acre," as the partnership law stated. Practically, this meant that partners could be sued for transgressions the company committed, that they were at a legal disadvantage if they wanted to act against the other partners, and that, if a partner died, the ownership of the company could be at risk.

Until the 1840s, a joint-stock corporation could only be created by a private act of Parliament or an award of a royal charter. Not surprisingly, in the years before 1844, only a few companies, including the East India Company and the Bank of England, attained this status. Partnerships, by contrast, could be formed by any group of individuals willing to invest in and be liable for a company's losses. While partnerships could achieve the superior form of corporation, the process required an expensive and cumbersome legal application and was rare before the 1820s. Typically, the partners who formed a company knew each other well or were actual relatives, worked together, and were few in number. Investors in a joint-stock enterprise, by contrast, were not usually related, did not even have to know each other, and could number in the hundreds or even thousands.

In 1844, an act "for the Registration, Incorporation, and Regulation of Joint-Stock Companies" was passed, which simultaneously made it easier for companies to incorporate and enacted relatively stringent rules for doing so. The 1844 Act did not cover banks, which were legislated by the Banking Act of 1826, nor did it apply to railway companies, which still required a special act of Parliament for incorporation. In 1856, joint-stock incorporation was rendered easier still by the repeal of the 1844 Company Act and the passage of new legislation. This Act allowed a company to incorporate by simply submitting to the Registry Office a Memorandum of Association that was signed by as few as seven shareholders, each of whom might hold as little as one share. In 1857, the Joint-Stock Bank Act was repealed, and in 1862, a consolidating act was passed that extended the privileges of the 1856 Company Act to banks and insurance companies.

The 1856 Company Act and the 1862 Consolidation Act also granted limited liability to shareholders in corporations and joint-stock banks. With the restrictions on company formation eased and the financial liability of each shareholder limited to the amount of the investment, promoters rushed to incorporate new companies. Between 1844 and 1856, 966 companies had registered with the Registry Office, but, after the repeal of the 1844 Act, applications mushroomed, with nearly twenty-five hundred companies forming between 1856 and 1862 and an additional four thousand companies incorporating between 1862 and 1868. By the end of the century, approximately five thousand companies were incorporating each year.[2] This proliferation of companies had a dramatic impact on the London Stock Exchange, where a majority of company shares were bought, sold, and traded. Whereas in 1843, approximately £200 million were invested in the nine hundred companies quoted on the London Stock Exchange, in 1897, the paid-up capital for the almost twenty-four thousand incorporated companies amounted to £1,300,000,000. This figure represented about one-fifth of the nation's wealth and was more than double the combined investments of companies in France and Germany.[3] Between 1870 and 1914, the number of serious stockholders is said to have quadrupled; between 1853 and 1913, the number of securities quoted on the London Stock Exchange rose from under five hundred to over five thousand.[4] Growth in both the amount invested and the number of shareholders was facilitated by the issuing of shares in lower denominations (down from £50 or 60 in the 1840s to £1 in the 1880s) and by the revolution in communications technology that occurred in the second half of the century. The telegraph, which was invented in 1837, linked London to the major British cities by 1840, and by the 1890s, it was possible for a London broker to exchange share prices with a broker in Glasgow in two and one-half minutes. The first submarine cable was laid across the English Channel in 1851, making it possible for brokers to send international cables to Paris, then to other

2. George Robb, *White-Collar Crime in Modern England: Financial Fraud and Business Morality, 1845–1929* (Cambridge: Cambridge University Press, 1992), p. 15. See also H. A. Shannon, "The Limited Companies of 1866–1883," *Essays in Economic History: Reprints Edited for the Economic History Society,* ed. E. M. Carus-Wilson (London: Edward Arnold, Ltd., 1954), pp. 380–405.

3. Robb, *White-Collar Crime,* p. 28.

4. Michie, *The London Stock Exchange: A History,* pp. 72, 95. We should remember that the social class of investors remained relatively narrow. Based on a sample of eighty thousand shareholders from the years 1883 to 1907, one historian estimates that only about 1 percent of shares were held by working-class individuals, as opposed to 25 percent to 30 percent held by the gentry and aristocracy (who constituted only 1 percent or 2 percent of the population). Members of the middle classes held about 50 percent to 60 percent of all shares (Michie, *London Stock Exchange,* p. 72).

continental cities. In 1866, the London to New York submarine cable was laid, reducing transfer time from London to New York from sixteen days (in 1854) to twenty minutes. By World War I, information could travel from London to New York in only thirty seconds. By 1872, when telegraphic communication was established between London and Melbourne, one could say that a global securities market existed.

While the expansion of the British securities market meant increased investment opportunities for many, some radicals and members of the laboring poor continued to consider all investment schemes—most notably the National Debt—frauds perpetrated against the people. What passed as investment opportunities, after all, might also be ruses designed to transform a working man's wages into a capitalist's profit. After 1844, even people willing to embrace investment as a legitimate way to enhance a godly life began to worry that the Stock Exchange (if not the Debt) could generate as much evil as good. In that year, the Select Committee on Joint-Stock Companies revealed some of the unsavory practices that had characterized company management in the previous decade. The 1844 Company Act was intended to prevent such abuses, but subsequent decades proved it to be largely ineffective. In 1845–46, the so-called railway mania erupted, and in the frenzy to court investors, company promoters cultivated an arsenal of fraudulent practices that made it virtually impossible for investors to distinguish a legitimate company from one never intended to survive. Promoters issued misleading or even blatantly false advertisements for new companies; "rigged" the market by buying up, then reselling, the inflated shares; appointed "guinea-pig" directors (so called because they received a guinea for attending a board meeting); manufactured "dummy" investors to make up the requisite signatories; and decorated the prospectus's cover sheet with the names of "front-sheeters" (prominent men who might—or might not—have agreed to serve as the company's directors). The London Stock Exchange's Committee of General Purposes did not concern itself with the merits of the companies whose shares made its official list because it was too jealous of potential competition from outside brokers. As a result, investors were left to the mercy of the promoters who too often pushed companies only in order to "wind them up," or liquidate them. For the promoter, who profited not from the company's success but from its sale, winding up a company was often as profitable as promoting it in the first place.

Such fraud was not limited to the railway companies, of course, although the transgressions committed in the 1840s by George Hudson, the "railway king," were often cited as paradigmatic of company promotion gone criminal. After the 1856 passage of new company law, financial fraud almost certainly became more common still, with mismanaging company directors and embezzling clerks joining fraudulent promoters in the pantheon of iniquity. The degree of criminal activity is often tied to the rate of failure for the new companies, for many of these corporations were created exclusively to generate capital for the promoters. Of the seven thousand companies formed between 1844 and 1868, only twenty-nine hundred, or 42 percent, still existed in 1868. To contemporaries who read such financial exposés as D. Morier Evans' *Facts, Failures, and Frauds* (1859) or Malcolm Ronald Meason's *Seamy Side of Finance* (1886), such figures suggested that every public trade might be a risky speculation.

The Bank of England and the Banking System

As we have already seen, the Bank of England was one of a very few joint-stock incorporations founded by royal decree and granted special privileges in the late seventeenth century. As a profit-making joint-stock company, the Bank of England was initially run for the benefit of the mercantile community and for its shareholders in particular, not for the nation or the banking community. The Bank was not a central bank, and, although it held a virtual monopoly on the issue of notes within London and its surroundings, these notes were not legal tender in the eighteenth century and their circulation was largely confined to London and the southeast.

The eighteenth century also witnessed the gradual emergence of a banking system in England, with the number of provincial banks growing from only a handful in 1750 to nearly four hundred by the end of the century and six hundred by the mid-1820s. Modern historians agree that by 1826, a group of firms existed that offered sufficiently specialized services to be considered modern banks.[5] These firms were typically partnerships, but, with the number of partners limited by law to six, the banks were inherently unstable and dangerously subject to swings in the general economy. When times were good, the country banks tended to encourage business by advancing loans to the surrounding community, but when money was in short supply, the banks' contraction could cause businesses to fail. Banks in Scotland and, after 1820, in Ireland, were protected from some of the difficulties that English banks faced, for neither country was dominated by a single bank with a monopoly over joint-stock incorporation, as England was. As a consequence, Scottish and Irish banks could have more than six partners, thus increasing individual banks' resources, and they could form branches, thus extending liability beyond the partners who initially founded the bank.

The weakness of the English banking system became obvious in the financial panic of 1825 and 1826 when so many banks failed in England and Wales. As with subsequent nineteenth-century panics, this first money pressure began

---

5. Michael Collins, *Money and Banking in the U.K.: A History* (London: Croom Helm, 1988), p. 14.

with national prosperity, increasingly speculative investments (particularly in overseas mining ventures), and free lending by the Bank of England. By the end of 1825, when mining companies began to fail and loans fell due, England faced a dramatic shortage of domestic cash. By mid-December of 1825, with the shortage of cash provoking repeated runs on London and provincial banks, the rush to convert the country banks' notes to gold or to Bank of England notes began to threaten the reserves of the entire banking system. With the public losing confidence in the ability of the country banks to meet their obligations and London bankers unable to stem the rising panic, the Bank of England was forced to protect the convertibility of its own notes by lending freely. This practice helped quell the immediate panic, but the problems that the panic exposed prompted Parliament to enact two pieces of legislation intended to bolster the system. The first halted the issue of any bank notes of denominations under £5, and the second ended the Bank of England's monopoly over the joint-stock form. The latter, the Banking Co-Partnership or Joint-Stock Bank Act of 1826, permitted the formation of corporate banks outside a sixty-five-mile radius of London. In 1833, joint-stock banks were allowed to incorporate within London itself.

Unlike private banks, which drew their capital solely from the partners, joint-stock banks were publicly traded firms, which, like any corporation, could draw relatively small investments from a relatively large number of investors. The 1826 Joint-Stock Bank Act preserved the partnership law obligation that all partners in an incorporated bank be fully liable for the bank's losses, and this act probably initially helped keep the number of joint-stock banks low: in 1830, there were still only fourteen joint-stock banks in England. Both private banks and joint-stock banks were local concerns; typically they sought deposits from their clients, for which the joint-stock banks paid interest. In provincial areas, both kinds of banks also dealt extensively with both the London banks and the discount houses that formed the London money market. The latter in particular lent money to provincial banks when clients in various areas needed it and provided investment opportunities for provincial funds when cash was available. The London banks, meanwhile, held accounts for provincial banks on a fee-for-service basis. In this arrangement, the London banks helped the provincial banks meet financial claims when necessary, paying cash for notes, drafts, and bills drawn on or by the provincial firm, and buying or selling securities for the provincial banks.

During the first four decades of the nineteenth century the various pieces of a national banking system gradually began to come together in something resembling its modern form. Banking facilities remained unevenly distributed, but few sizable communities were located more than ten miles from a bank. Even though advocates for joint-stock banks in particular still had to overcome investors' suspicions about the liabilities of the corporate form, promoters continued to float, finance, and launch new banking companies. Like the securities market, the banking system was extended and enhanced partly by improvements in communication. Whereas banks had relied on stagecoaches to convey cash and news at the end of the eighteenth century, by the 1880s, railways enabled money transfers between London and Edinburgh in $8\frac{1}{2}$ hours and telegraphs conveyed financial information in a matter of minutes. This accelerated communication was important because provincial bankers relied on London agents for advice about investments, the creditworthiness of potential customers, and the implications of government policies. In an emergency and with reliable channels of fast information, an imperiled provincial bank could increase its cash reserve by drawing on a special deposit left with its London agent or by borrowing directly from a London bank or discount house.

The Bank of England also performed a critical role in consolidating the banking system. By the 1820s, the Bank had already become the repository of the nation's gold reserve, and it was quickly becoming the lender of last resort to the London banks. Provincial banks tended to borrow not from the Bank of England but from the London banks and discount houses, like the great Overend, Gurney, & Co. These discount houses borrowed from the Bank if money was available nowhere else. After 1826, when the Bank of England began to open provincial branches, some country banks did borrow directly from these branches and some even held cash reserves at the Bank. By and large, however, the role played by the Bank of England in the national system was indirect and focused on the London heart of the money market. Because all banks were dependent on the London money market, the Bank could influence national monetary policy by adjusting its lending rates to the London discount houses. By so doing and by superintending the nation's gold reserves, the Bank could generally act as a buffer against monetary shocks and help keep the system growing even when individual banks failed.

By allowing incorporation, the 1826 Joint-Stock Banking Act did solve some of the problems that had caused so many private banks to fail, but the law did not really address the weakness inherent in the joint-stock form. The legislation did not establish regulations to dictate the rights and responsibilities of shareholders in the new banks, nor did it establish the denomination of shares, the amount that had to be paid up on shares, the nature or frequency of required audits, or even the legal status of the banks. Like other joint-stock companies floated during the middle of the nineteenth century, joint-stock banks continued to be subject to fraudulent promotion, and because they were also vulnerable to fluctuations in the country's overall monetary conditions, they continued to fail in numbers alarming enough to keep the public wary of banks. Between 1840 and 1866, banks failed more frequently than any other type of company. Of the 291 banks established between 1844 and 1868, only

49, or 16 percent, were still in operation at the later date. Despite this alarming rate of failure, however, the number of joint-stock banks continued to grow, especially after the 1860s. In 1850, there were 99 incorporated banks with 575 offices in England, as opposed to 327 private banks with 518 offices. Between 1862 and 1866, the number of joint-stock banks increased by over one-half, and there was something like an 80 percent increase in note and deposit liabilities. During this same four-year period, the number of private banks remained stagnant, and their liabilities rose by less than one-fifth. By the late 1870s, private banks' share in the number of banking offices and in the overall deposit and note liabilities was less than one-third of the national total.[6]

If the 1826 legislation deprived the Bank of England of its monopoly over the corporate form, then another piece of legislation had equally far-reaching effects on the Bank's place in the overall banking system. In 1844, partly to curb the stock speculation fueled by readily available money, Parliament renewed the Bank's Charter by enacting new privileges and imposing new responsibilities. The Bank Charter Act of 1844 conferred upon the Bank new rights for issuing currency, and it fixed the maximum value of notes that other banks could issue, thus encouraging the eventual disappearance of commercial bank notes and helping to make Bank of England notes, which were declared legal tender (in England) in 1833, the only paper money that was as good as gold. As the same time, however, the 1844 Bank Charter Act also split the Bank into two parts and deprived the Bank of its ability to exercise discretion over the volume of the nation's currency. After 1844, the Bank was composed of an Issue Department that issued notes, and a Banking (or Deposit) Department that managed the government's accounts, paid cheques, made loans, discounted bills, and generally conducted the ordinary business of a bank. The Issue Department, which was the main target of the 1844 legislation, was allowed to issue £14 million in notes based on a reserve of government securities, but any notes beyond this amount had to be backed by a 100 percent reserve of gold and silver bullion. In essence, this stipulation meant that the Bank's note issue could only be increased if the cash reserve in the Bank rose.

The 1844 Bank Charter Act was one of the most controversial pieces of financial legislation of the century. Opponents charged that it did not allow enough flexibility in note issue to accommodate the nation's growing monetary needs, and supporters responded that only the Act's mandated reserve kept the Bank from printing too much paper money. To a certain extent, subsequent events proved that the Act's critics were right, even though the charge that the Act allowed for insufficient flexibility did not target the heart of the

---

6. Collins, *Money and Banking,* pp. 68–74.

problem. The technicalities of the Act actually allowed the Bank some discretion in adjusting the ratio between reserve and circulating notes, but the Bank Charter Act still proved intolerably rigid. In three periods of monetary pressure—1847, 1857, and 1866—the Bank Charter Act had to be suspended temporarily. To be more precise, at the height of the pressure in each of these years Parliament gave permission for the Bank to suspend the Act, but in each case, news that the Bank would be allowed to issue more notes than the Act allowed was sufficient to avert the crisis that would actually have triggered suspension.

After the 1825–26 panic, the most serious threat to the banking system— and to Britain's financial system as a whole—was posed by the panic of 1866, when the City's most important discount house, Overend, Gurney, & Co., failed, taking with it ten important banks. Overend, Gurney, & Co. had been in operation since 1805. Like the other London discount houses, its role was to evaluate and discount bills of exchange and other requests for loans presented by individuals and, most importantly, by provincial, London, and foreign banks. A hub for the flow of capital from lenders to borrowers and a buffer that protected the Bank of England from the demands of other banks, Overend, Gurney, & Co. constituted a critical piece of the overall financial system. As the repository of public trust in the system, moreover, Overend, Gurney, & Co. served a symbolic function that was almost as important as its fiscal role. When the venerable house collapsed on May 10, 1866, it sparked a panic that threatened the entire system. There were runs on London and provincial banks; at the height of the panic, the Bank of England lent over £4 million in a single day; and the Bank's reserves fell to £3 million. The century's third suspension of the 1844 Bank Act helped quiet the public's fears, although aftershocks of the collapse continued to be felt throughout the financial community.

The suspicion about banks expressed in the first half of the century by radicals like William Cobbett and R. J. Richardson was not altogether unwarranted, therefore, for, before the 1870s, banks and discount houses were too often unreliable repositories for one's money. In the last third of the century, however, the industry instituted measures intended to guarantee stability, and the Bank of England gradually accepted its role as lender of last resort and governor of the discount rate. In 1879, English bankers formed the Institute of Bankers, which sponsored a rigorous course of professional training for bank employees, issuing certificates to successful candidates. By 1900, membership in the Institute numbered four thousand and certification was considered essential to success in the industry.[7] Similar professional organizations were formed in Scotland in 1875 and in Ireland in 1898.

---

7. Robb, *White-Collar Crime,* pp. 71–74.

The stabilization of the banking industry was further insured by the amalgamation movement, which began in Scotland in the 1830s and peaked in England in the 1880s and 1890s. In this movement, the number of separate banking companies decreased dramatically, while the number of branches escalated, primarily through mergers and takeovers. Thus, Scotland reduced its banks from thirty-six in 1830 to seventeen in 1850, and England reduced its separate banking companies from six hundred in 1825 to seventy in 1913. The amalgamation movement was epitomized by the situation in London, which was dominated in 1918 by only five banks, the so-called Big Five of Barclays, Lloyds, the National Provincial, the Midland, and the Westminster banks.[8]

The Bank of England also helped stabilize the banking system as a whole. Inevitably, the role of bankers in the money market is correlated to fluctuations in the general economy. When the economy is expanding, as it was in the mid-1830s and early 1860s, the number of requests for loans increases, and bankers are more inclined to lend because money is readily available. In periods of economic downturn, by contrast, borrowers typically seek fewer loans, money becomes more expensive, and bankers tend to be more cautious. In the century's periods of recession—1825–26, 1837, 1839, 1847, 1857, 1866, and 1878—economic downturns were accompanied, if not intensified, by runs on banks which, in the worst cases, led to bank failures. In 1864, when the Bank of England was admitted to the London Clearing House, conditions were established for a national check-clearing system, which enabled banks from all over England to draw on accounts at the Bank to settle debts among themselves. (Similar clearinghouses were set up in Scotland in 1865 and in Dublin in 1845.) The Bank's ability to affect the money market was further enhanced by actions that occurred in the 1890s. The Usury Law, which set the maximum interest rate any bank could charge at 5 percent, had been repealed by the Bank Charter Act of 1833, and periodically throughout the century the Bank of England raised its discount rate above that figure. Until other banks were forced to tie their rates of discount to the Bank's, however, such raises had little effect. By the last decade of the century, the Bank had learned to use open market operations to influence the entire money market. When the Bank increased its own discount rate, it also reduced the supplies of money available to discount houses. Finding themselves short of funds, the discount houses then borrowed from the Bank at this new higher rate, and, in order to protect their own profits, they passed the rate increase along to the provincial and commercial banks that discounted bills with them. The commercial banks then raised their rates as well, and potential borrowers tended to decrease in number. Acting as the ultimate source of capital, the Bank was able to use this

---

8. Collins, *Money and Banking,* pp. 78–79.

chain of interdependent financial institutions to affect many more borrowers than just its own clients, and it also deployed its own discount rate to stabilize overall market conditions. The Bank had begun to use a double interest rate system as early as 1878, setting one rate—the Bank rate—at the minimum price at which the Bank was willing to discount for the money market in general and another—its private rate—at a more commercially competitive level for its regular customers. By the end of the century, even though the Bank of England was still not a central bank, the Bank rate was generally recognized as the best index to conditions in the short-term money market.[9]

Finding Out about Finance

In theory, at least, one institution that could have helped allay the public's fears about the financial system was the press. Indeed, if the frequently made claim that publicity was a greater deterrent to crime than legislation had had any validity, the press should have been able to protect the investing public from the financial fraud that was endemic by the 1840s. But the relationships among the press, the public, and the financial community were more complicated than the equation of publicity and morality suggests. On the one hand, every part of the financial system depended on the press's ability to circulate ever-more voluminous amounts of information at ever greater rates of speed. On the other hand, however, the individuals who collected and circulated this information did not always benefit either from getting the information right or from telling everything they knew. This curious relationship between the financial community and the press, in which secrecy and misinformation were sometimes considered more valuable than accuracy, meant that the members of the public could not always find out what they wanted to know or know when they could trust what they read. Because the relationships among public curiosity, representations of finance, and the operations of finance themselves were so uneven and complex, it is important to understand not only how the financial press developed in this period but also the agendas that might have informed the various kinds of writing developed to inform—or mislead—the British public.

The financial press had its origin in Antwerp and Venice in the sixteenth century, with the publication of the market prices of commodities, or prices current. Such papers began to be published in London as early as 1608, and, by 1716, a London merchant would have been able to subscribe to seven weekly or semiweekly business newspapers, at a cost of more than £6 annually, to find out the latest available information about ships, cargoes, prices,

---

9. Collins, *Money and Banking,* pp. 182–92.

and exchange rates.[10] Until the 1670s, this information was published under license from the Crown, and, from 1685 until the Licensing Act expired, financial information was strictly monitored by the national government. When the Act terminated in 1695, individuals actually involved in trade began to circulate financial news in the form of newssheets, many of which originated at coffeehouses like Lloyd's, which established *Lloyd's News* in 1696. By 1697, *Lloyd's News* (soon to be renamed *Lloyd's List*) was joined by another financial newspaper, *The Course of the Exchange, and Other Things,* issued by Jonathan's Coffeehouse. Both of these papers were single sheets, printed in columns on either one or both sides.

Financial information briefly became financial news in the boom years of 1719–20, as interest in South Sea stock began to sweep the nation. With the collapse of the South Sea Bubble, financial news became less prominent, but by the 1740s, public interest in the subject revived. By the end of the century, "remarks on trade" had become a staple of nearly every London and provincial newspaper, and London papers also carried lists of bankrupts, the prices of commodities and stocks, and shipping news. Even more important was the introduction into British papers of what one historian has termed "business opinion." Beginning in earnest in the 1780s, journalists began to use newspapers as a forum to discuss commercial subjects, such as the desirability of exporting wool. By the end of the century, the literate public was accustomed to reading about financial and commercial topics in their local papers—a fact, it has been suggested, that contributed to the emergence of political economy in the second half of the eighteenth century.[11]

The development of the financial press, like the delivery of commercial news more generally, is inextricable from the history of various taxes, which were imposed by the British government to control the dissemination of all kinds of information and opinion. The stamp duty on newspapers, initially imposed in 1712, was increased in 1776 and 1789, finally coming to rest at 2d. per page, with advertisements taxed at 3s. apiece. These costs, which figured in the cover price, put newspapers beyond the reach of many Britons, including members of the urban artisan classes, whom the government suspected of political sedition.[12]

One effect of these prohibitive taxes was to increase the likelihood that a newspaper would be read aloud to multiple listeners. In 1812, Robert Southey

10. John J. McCusker and Cora Gravesteijn, *The Beginnings of Commercial and Financial Journalism: The Commodity Price Currents, Exchange Rate Currents, and Money Currents of Early Modern Europe* (Amsterdam: NEHA, 1991), p. 291.
11. Wayne Parsons, *The Power of the Financial Press: Journalism and Economic Opinion in Britain and America* (New Brunswick: Rutgers University Press, 1989), p. 18.
12. Stephen Koss, *The Rise and Fall of the Political Press in Britain: The Nineteenth Century* (Chapel Hill: University of North Carolina Press, 1981), p. 32.

registered the anxiety this practice could conjure in middle-class Britons. "Where one who can read is to be found, all who have ears can hear," Southey complained in "On the State of the Poor, the Principle of Mr. Malthus's Essay on Population, and the Manufacturing System."

> The weekly epistles of the apostles of sedition are read aloud in tap-rooms and pot-houses to believing auditors, listening greedily when they are told that their rulers fatten upon the gains extracted from their blood and sinews; that they are cheated, oppressed, and plundered. . . . These are the topics which are received in the pot-house, and discussed over the loom and the lathe: men already profligate and unprincipled, needy because they are dissolute, and discontented because they are needy, swallow these things when they are getting drunk, and chew the cud upon them when they are sober. The lessons are repeated day after day, and week after week. If madder be administered to a pig only for a few days, his bones are reddened with its dye; and can we believe that the bloody colouring of such "pigs' meat" as this will not find its way into the system of those who take it for their daily food?[13]

When the stamp duty was finally repealed in 1855, it was partly because the strategy of limiting access to news through taxation was widely acknowledged to have failed.

By the early nineteenth century, economic opinion appeared regularly in newspapers, often in the form of letters by such prominent figures as John Ramsey McCulloch and David Ricardo. By that time, the *Edinburgh Review* was also bringing lengthy and often quite theoretical discussions of economic subjects to middle-class readers and members of Parliament. Although the *Edinburgh Review,* like the other quarterlies, was relatively expensive, it was surprisingly widely read. It is estimated, for example, that in 1814 the *Edinburgh Review* reached an audience of about fifty thousand within a month of each issue's publication. As a point of comparison, the circulation of the *Times* was about ten thousand in 1834 (although it is impossible to estimate how many people read each issue).[14]

The substantial articles published in the *Edinburgh Review* were probably most successful in familiarizing readers with the terminology of political economy, not in popularizing the nuances of its doctrines. Most of the articles in the *Edinburgh Review* sought to make economic concepts seem critical to the discussion of political and social issues by presenting a picture in which economics were inseparable from the problems of the day. By the 1820s, this

---

13. Quoted in Kevin Gilmartin, *Print Politics: The Press and Radical Opposition in Early Nineteenth-Century England* (Cambridge: Cambridge University Press, 1996), p. 102.

14. Parsons, *The Power of the Financial Press,* p. 20; Ruth Dudley Edwards, *The Pursuit of Reason: "The Economist," 1843–1993* (Boston: Harvard Business School Press, 1993), p. 15.

picture of a complex interplay between economic and social issues began to be challenged by newspaper reporting that was paradoxically both more narrowly financial and more generally cultural in nature. Sparked by the dramatic growth in stock investment in the early part of the decade, writing about financial issues began to be a regular part of London and provincial newspapers in the 1820s. Unlike the dry tables of market information previously published, however, this new financial journalism treated the City as a distinct culture, which writers assumed would be intrinsically interesting to readers. The first such reports had appeared in 1818 in the Sunday papers, but they only became commonplace in 1821, when W. I. Clement took over the *Morning Chronicle* and decided to make City coverage a daily news item. In 1825, the *Times* followed suit, introducing a money column entitled "Money, Market, and City Intelligence," which was typically written by the newspaper's financial editor, Thomas Massa Alsanger. Having declared its political independence by refusing government subsidies in 1802, the *Times* led the way in providing reports of the City that were entertaining, generally reliable, and sometimes sharply critical, even of advertisers. In the 1840s, for example, Alsanger repeatedly warned readers that the speculative railway bubble would eventually burst, even though the *Times,* like other newspapers, carried numerous advertisements for new railway companies.[15]

In addition to the political economic theory published in the quarterlies and the newspapers' daily City reports, from 1843 British readers also had access to a weekly periodical designed to show the relationship between economic theory and business matters. This weekly was the *Economist.* Founded by James Wilson and initially an organ of the Anti-Corn Law League, the *Economist* published articles intended to promote free trade, political reform, and the ideas of the Classical Political Economists. From its first issue, however, the weekly tended to detach its financial and economic information from the political agenda it presumably advocated, and the link between the free-trade organization and the weekly became increasingly more attenuated as trade restrictions were abolished in the late 1840s and 1850s.

The first issue of the *Economist* cost 6d., which priced it above the daily newspapers but considerably below the quarterlies. By 1845, the paper had a circulation of 2,894, a figure that peaked at 4,483 in 1847, then leveled off to about 3,500.[16] The importance of the periodical far outstripped its circulation figures, however. In articles that have been described as a new kind of economic journalism, the *Economist* developed a style of writing that encouraged readers not only to think that economic issues might be related to politics but also to see their everyday lives in terms that combined economic reasoning,

---

15. Parsons, *Power of the Financial Press,* pp. 22–23.
16. Edwards, *Pursuit of Reason,* p. 35.

practical business matters, and political considerations.[17] According to Walter Bagehot, who began to write for the paper in 1857, the *Economist* launched "the economic age," for it was a great "belief-producer" that made the members of the growing middle class feel like they belonged to a single, if complex, community.[18] Bagehot himself was one of the period's most respected writers on economic, commercial, and financial issues. During the eighteen years in which he wrote for the weekly—from 1857 through 1875—Bagehot came to be considered "the greatest interpreter of commercial sentiment and economic ideas of his day." As such, Bagehot provided a public persona and a voice for capitalism, commerce, and economic theory, much as J. R. McCulloch had done before him.[19]

The period in which Bagehot wrote for the *Economist* also saw the repeal of the stamp duties that had long kept newspaper prices high. In one sense, the campaign to repeal these taxes expressed the anxieties about working-class politics that we have already seen in Southey's comment. In another, this campaign was simply the logical extension of the free-trade movement spearheaded by the Anti-Corn Law League. Even though the stamp duty had been reduced in 1836 from 4d. to 1d., the "tax on knowledge" seemed increasingly indefensible, for restricting the press was considered by many even more detrimental to national progress than restricting trade. After the Corn Law was repealed in 1846, supporters of the stamp duties increasingly lost ground. In June 1855, the stamp duty and the advertisement tax were both officially abolished (the latter having been practically discontinued in 1853), and in 1861, the final remaining "tax on knowledge," the paper duty, was ended.

The period of Bagehot's ascendancy at the *Economist* also witnessed the proliferation of book and pamphlet publications about money matters and the City in particular. Journalists like David Morier Evans and Ronald Laing Meason collected and republished articles that originally appeared in newspapers and periodicals, making them accessible to readers who did not subscribe to the periodicals themselves. These journalistic treatments of financial activities, frauds, and schemes often drew upon conventions familiar to nineteenth-century readers of novelists like Charles Dickens and Wilkie Collins. Cast as nonfictional but highly stylized autobiographies, romances, or exposés, these books and pamphlets purported to take readers into the recesses of the Stock Exchange and the Bank of England and into the boardrooms of fraudulent companies. With novelists also drawing upon financial plots to organize short stories and novels, the line between factual reporting and fiction sometimes proves difficult to establish in this writing.

17. Parsons, *Power of the Financial Press,* p. 26.
18. Parsons, *Power of the Financial Press,* pp. 27, 25.
19. Parsons, *Power of the Financial Press,* p. 28.

In 1863, Bagehot recruited William Newmarch to write for the *Economist.* Newmarch's arrival marked another important turning point in financial journalism, for Newmarch's interest in statistics anchored the periodical's commitment to relate economic opinion to facts in the increasingly mathematical practice of statistics. The use of statistics made financial reporting seem more scientific, and it also permitted readers to chart long-term tendencies in prices and values for the first time. Building on work conducted independently by Newmarch and the political economist Stanley Jevons, the *Economist* became the first paper regularly to publish a price index. Such indices, along with the tabulated percentage changes of volumes and values that began to appear in the financial press in the 1880s, allowed financiers and politicians to track the fluctuations of trade and thus to identify as "cycles of trade" the booms and busts that had previously seemed to occur without warning.[20]

The success of the *Economist* spawned several imitators, the most important of which was the *Statist,* founded by Sir Robert Giffen and Thomas Lloyd in 1878. The emphasis on statistics that Newmarch had brought to the *Economist* was even more pronounced in the *Statist,* where statistics also began to be placed in the service of investment advice. This trend—away from the discussion of economic ideas toward investment advice—marked the beginning of the end of journalists' efforts to engage their readers in considered analyses of economic issues. With papers like the *Economist* and the *Statist* devoting more space to detailed and technical accounts of the stock exchange and the money markets, readers were encouraged to think of finance as the most significant component of the economy and to consider themselves primarily investors or capitalists. This emphasis tended to narrow what counted as economic news to mere financial information and it encouraged readers to think of the financial sector as separable from the political and social issues to which earlier political economists had linked their discussions of commerce and trade.[21]

The narrowing of economic news to market information had its counterpart in the withdrawal of economic analysts from continuous involvement in political debates. After about 1870, developments within economic theory tended to be driven by exchanges among specialists rather than social or political events, and, with the founding of the *Quarterly Journal of Economics*

---

20. Edwards, *Pursuit of Reason,* pp. 277–79. Edwards quotes Judy Klein's assessment of this development: "The first use of statistics was for financiers to compare one week's values with another, but the same data connected in a longer series could also be used by 'public men' to give clues to the causes of economic fluctuations—hence tracking ups and downs of trade, and the tendency for good years to follow bad years in succession, produce the notion of 'cycles of trade' " (*History of Practical Dynamics and Time Series Analysis,* quoted. p. 279).

21. Parsons, *Power of the Financial Press,* pp. 31–32.

in 1886 and the *Economic Journal* in 1890, economic theorists had vehicles for pursuing these exchanges in terms more technical than would have been welcomed by a "General Newspaper" like the *Economist*. In 1890, economists established their first professional society, the Royal Economics Society; five years later, their discipline was powerful enough to found its own university, the London School of Economics; and in 1903, one of the oldest British universities, Cambridge University, signaled the importance of the discipline by establishing the Economics Tripos.

The increasing specialization of economics as a discipline does not mean that financial information stopped selling papers, of course. Indeed, with the repeal of the stamp and paper duties, Britain witnessed an explosion in the number of financial newspapers. Most of these were dailies aimed at investors and speculators, not weeklies in the mold of the *Economist*. The two most significant financial dailies were the *Financial News,* which was founded by Harry Marks in 1884, and the *Financial Times,* launched in 1888. The success of these papers, which were merged into the *Financial Times* in 1945, reflected the enormous growth in securities trading, which, in turn, reflected the dramatic increase in the number of companies floated after the passage of permissive company law. With the Governing Committee of the Exchange devoted to increasing the volume of trade, not protecting investors, and the daily money articles of papers like the *Times* providing no clear investment advice, members of the investing public eagerly sought guidance. This was what Harry Marks set out to provide. Drawing upon his newspaper experience in America, Marks devised a paper that brought both "Yankee bounce" and the kind of sensational journalism pioneered by W. T. Stead in the *Morning Chronicle* to the delivery of financial news. Marks's paper, whose complete title proclaimed that it was "Devoted to the Interests of the Investors," published not only general articles and editorials promoting particular companies, but also two sections devoted to readers' inquiries: "The Voice of the Public" and an "Answers to Correspondents" column.

Marks is also credited with inventing two new sources of newspaper revenue: selling advertising space to companies for extended reports of their meetings, and charging companies for the space occupied by a share price quotation.[22] While these charges may have helped finance the paper (whose early circulation was probably only a few thousand), they also contributed to the perception that the *Financial News* was too invested in promoting its advertisers. On July 16, 1884, for example, the paper published on one page a large prospectus for the Western Australia Mortgage & Mercantile Agency

---

22. Dilwin Porter, "A Trusted Guide of the Investing Public: Harry Marks and the *Financial News, 1884–1916,*" in *Speculators and Patriots: Essays in Business Biography,* ed. R. P. T. Davenport-Hines (London: Frank Cass and Co., Ltd., 1986), p. 7.

Company, presumably paid for by the company, and, on another page, it printed a glowing report of the company's prospects, which was theoretically an unbiased account.[23] By 1890, such practices inspired charges of libel when a disgruntled investor demonstrated that Marks had previously owned shares in the Rae (Transvaal) Gold Mining Company, which his newspaper had aggressively promoted. Having used his paper's puffs to drive up share prices, Marks had sold his investments through various dummy vendors. Although he avoided a prison sentence, Marks's reputation was blackened by this suit and the adverse publicity it provoked.

The ethical ambiguity that surrounded puffing one's advertisers was not limited to the *Financial News*. Indeed, by 1913, the *Economist* was considered the only financial newspaper above reproach. Even Charles Duguid, who served as assistant editor of the *Economist* from 1890 to 1892, was held to indulge in morally dubious practices while he was financial editor for the *Morning Post*—even though Duguid had gone on record as stating that "the first qualification of the City editor is integrity, the second integrity, and the third integrity." Integrity may have been the ideal, but the importance of raising revenue for a financial newspaper, together with the money market's long tradition of withholding as much information as it made public, made it all but impossible for newspapermen to avoid the appearance of impropriety.[24]

CONCLUSION

It is difficult to know whether the ethical ambiguities that surrounded the financial press after 1884 were the inevitable products of the way this journalism was financed. Certainly, until 1908, when public companies were required to publish balance sheets, British law did little to promote public access to accurate information about the companies whose shares were traded on the Exchange. Only in 1939, with the passage of the Prevention of Fraud Act, did the London Stock Exchange support legislation that might assist investors. Whatever the reasons for the practices that journalists like Marks developed—and they were no doubt numerous—it is clear that the financial dailies were not able to achieve the kind of analytic distance available to weeklies like the *Economist,* whose writers continued to try to explain and contextualize events in the financial world. Even contributors to the *Economist,* of course, could neither know everything that went on in the City nor publish everything they knew. With only partial access to financial information and, in most cases, even less preparation in the sophisticated mode of analysis increasingly necessary to understand what they could read about,

23. David Kynaston, *The Financial Times: A Centenary History* (London: Viking, 1988), p.12.
24. Porter, "A Trusted Guide," p. 12.

most members of the nineteenth-century investing public must have relied on other kinds of journalism—not to mention novels and stories—to track their money managers and to fantasize about the social status that money could obviously confer.

With the advantage of hindsight, we can know more about the nineteenth-century financial system than most of its participants could, but much valuable information is still lost to us forever because records were imperfectly collected and the desire for secrecy or drama too often influenced those who wrote about the system. This unavoidable mix of clarity and obscurity may make establishing a perfect picture of the past impossible. Nevertheless, it makes representations of the financial system all the more intriguing, for it encourages us to read selections like the ones collected here as generically ambiguous—as gestures toward accuracy that nevertheless draw many of their most effective conventions from some of the literary forms that flourished in the nineteenth century: melodrama, romance, the detective story, and sensationalism.

CURRENCY AND CREDIT INSTRUMENTS

The selections contained in these three chapters address some of the most important issues associated with the circulating currency, the concept of money, and the international effects of the gold discoveries in the second half of the century. Three of these essays—Cobbett's "Paper against Gold," McCulloch's dictionary entry on the "Substitution of Notes for Coins," and Robert H. Patterson's "Gold and Social Politics"—take up the issue of paper money, either to defend it, as McCulloch and Patterson do, or to expose the fraud it perpetrates against the people, as Cobbett attempts to do. Two of the selections describe bills of exchange, with McCulloch focusing on distinguishing between paper money and bills and Rae describing how a banker can discriminate between "good" paper and "bad." Blanchard's "Biography of a Bad Shilling," like Patterson's "Gold and Social Politics," explores the implications of the concept that value is not intrinsic to the instrument that represents it, but Blanchard's whimsical account of the career of a counterfeit coin explores the frauds that individuals practice on each other, while Patterson is primarily concerned with the political and moral improvement that even arbitrary forms of value confer upon the world. Patterson, Sidgwick, and Ameer all recognize that financial arrangements within Britain form part of an international network. They implicitly argue that British readers should be alert to events occurring elsewhere, for discoveries of gold in Australia, the fall of the gold value of the rupee, and various ways of defining "money" affect the well-being of all British citizens, whether they realize it or not.

These selections also represent a range of nineteenth-century modes of publication and readerships. Cobbett's "Paper against Gold" was published as a cheap weekly newssheet, then reprinted (in 1815) in pamphlet form. Its intended audience included members of the working class, the poor, and urban artisans. McCulloch's *Dictionary of Commerce and Commercial Navigation* was initially published in 1832, then reissued, each time in expanded form, in 1848, 1859, 1869, and 1871, by which edition it contained over fifteen hundred pages. In the preface to the second edition, McCulloch notes that the first printing of the *Dictionary* was two thousand copies and that it sold out in less than nine months. In the preface to the first edition, he describes the audience he wanted to reach: "merchants, traders, ship-owners . . . and shipmasters" as well as readers in "all classes." The compendious *Dictionary* contains numerous engraved maps and numerical tables, as well as the kind of descriptive articles represented here.

George Rae's "Bills of Exchange" is taken from a volume published primarily for practicing bankers in 1885. (A small portion of this work was published anonymously in 1850.) His use of the fictional setting of the "quiet country town in Oxborough" suggests that by the 1880s it was still possible to write in a nontechnical way about what was rapidly becoming a professional occupation (the English Institute of Bankers was established in 1879). Sidney Laman Blanchard's "Biography of a Bad Shilling" was published in Charles Dickens's popular weekly magazine, *Household Words,* which was launched in 1850. The magazine contained topical journalism, essays, short fiction, and poetry, and cost 2d. per issue.

The last three selections contained in this part appeared in three of the great nineteenth-century reviews. Unlike magazines, which tended to be miscellanies of various kinds of short pieces, relatively inexpensive, and published as frequently as every week, reviews contained lengthy critical articles and literary reviews, often punctuated with long extracts from the book under consideration. Reviews were more expensive than magazines, they often bore the distinguishing stamp of their editor, and many of the earliest (and most famous) were published only four times a year. The three reviews represented here were all launched in the wake of the success of the *Cornhill,* which was edited by William Thackeray beginning in 1860. *Blackwood's Edinburgh Review* was created by William Blackwood in 1863; its best-known editors were Gibson Lockhart and John Wilson. The *Fortnightly Review,* established in 1865 and edited by John Morley, was founded on a policy of signed reviews, thus departing from the tradition (maintained by *Blackwood's* until well into the twentieth century) of anonymity. *Nineteenth Century,* founded in 1877 and edited by James Knowles, was the first review to publish only signed articles. The review took full advantage of the star power of its contributors by printing their names on each issue's cover.

The essays in the third part require a little additional contextualization, for the abstract concept of "money" is not as self-explanatory as are currency and counterfeiting. The concept of money performs three functions in modern ideas about the economy: as a means of payment, it is a medium of exchange; as a standard of value and a device for record-keeping, it is a unit of accounting; as a store of value, it is a means of holding wealth. The various debates about money represented here engaged all three functions of money. The debate in which Henry Sidgwick was engaged—the debate about how to define money—looks like a relatively simple question about bookkeeping, although it actually had important repercussions for people who wanted to identify a reliable bank for everyday use. This debate turned on how a banker should define bank money and the bank's "reserves." Should the bank's money include the credits extended to borrowers, which would presumably come back as cash, and the debts the bank owed, which would someday need to be repaid? Should bank money include only the bank's gold reserve, the value of its partners' assets, or the value represented on the bills and checks it held? As contemporaries debated this question in the press, they addressed two issues at once: the theoretical question of how money should function as a repository of value, and the practical question of whether investors should trust banks not to fail.

The debate to which Patterson and Ameer were contributing turned on the complex relationship between prices, currency, and the precious metals that backed currency. Britain had embraced the gold standard in 1816, which means that from that date it valued its coin and currency strictly in terms of gold, but this valuation did not mean that the prices of commodities and services remained steady. A series of good harvests could cause the price of bread to fall (unless kept high by tariffs), and the discovery of a new supply of gold could cause the prices of everything to rise. This already complicated set of relationships was further clouded by Britain's relation to her colonies, some of which (like Australia) were the sites of important gold discoveries, and others of which (like India) based their currencies on silver. When the value of silver fell against gold, as it began to do after the first Australian gold discoveries in 1848, the value of India's local currency (the rupee) fell dramatically. At the end of his essay, Ameer refers to the vanishing possibility that the European nations would adopt a bimetallic standard of value (that is, one based on both gold and silver), but he concludes by recommending that India adopt the gold standard, as Germany, Holland, the Scandinavian countries, France, Switzerland, and Belgium had done in the 1870s.

CHAPTER ONE

COINS AND CREDIT INSTRUMENTS

WILLIAM COBBETT
⊠⊠⊠

PAPER AGAINST GOLD

LETTER I

Appointment of the Bullion Committee—Main points of the Report—Proposition for the Bank to pay in two Years—To merit the appellation of a Thinking People, we must shew that our Thinking produces Knowledge—Go back into the History of Paper Money—Definition of Money—Increase of Paper—What is the cause of this Increase?—Origin of the Bank of England—How it came to pass that so much Paper Money got afloat—Increase of Bank Notes wanted to pay the increase of the interest on the National Debt—Progress in issuing Bank Notes from 20 to 1 Pounds—Suspicion awakened in 1797 which produced the Stoppage of Gold and Silver Payments at the Bank of England.

Gentlemen,

During the last session of parliament, a Committee, that is to say, ten or twelve members, of the House of Commons, were appointed to inquire into the cause of the high price of Gold *Bullion,* that is, Gold *not coined;* and to take into consideration the state of the circulating medium, or money, of this country. This Committee have made a *Report,* as they call it; but, it is a great

William Cobbett, "Paper against Gold," Letter I (August 30, 1810). London: W. Molineux, 1817.

book, that they have written, and have had printed; a book much larger than the whole of the New Testament. Of this Report I intend to enter into an Examination; and, as you have recently felt, and are still feeling, some of the effects of Paper-Money, I think it may not be amiss, if, upon this occasion, I address myself to you. I have introduced myself to you without any ceremony; but, before we part, we shall become well acquainted; and, I make no doubt, that you will understand the distinction between Paper-Money and Gold-Money much too well for it to be in the power of any one ever again to deceive you; which understanding, will, in the times now fast approaching, be of great utility to all those amongst you, who may have the means of laying up money, however small the quantity may be.

The Committee above-mentioned, which, for brevity's sake, I call the Bullion Committee, sent for several persons, whom they examined as *witnesses,* touching the matter in question. There was SIR FRANCIS BARING, for instance, the great loan-maker, and GOLDSMIDT, the rich Jew, whose name you so often see in the news-papers, where he is stated to give grand dinners to princes and great men. The *Evidence* of these, and other money-dealers and merchants, the Bullion Committee have had printed; and, upon this evidence, as well as upon the Report itself, we shall have to make some remarks.

The result of the Committee's inquiries is, in substance, this; *that the high price of gold is occasioned by the low value of the paper-money; that the low value of the paper-money has been occasioned* (as, you know, the low value of apples is) *by the great abundance of it; that the only way to lower the price of the gold is to raise the value of the paper-money, and that the only way to raise the value of the paper-money is to make the quantity of it less than it now is.* Thus far, as you will clearly see, there was no conjuration required. The fact is, that, not only do these propositions contain well-known, and almost self-evident truths; but, these truths have, during the last two or three years, and especially during the last year, been so frequently stated in print, that it was next to impossible that any person in England, able to read, should have been unacquainted with them. But, having arrived at the conclusion, that, in order to raise the value of the paper-money, *its quantity must be lessened;* having come to this point, the rest of the way was more difficult; for, the next object was, to point out *the means of lessening the quantity of the paper-money,* and this is an object, which, in my opinion will never be effected, unless those means include the destruction of the whole mass.

Not so, however, think the Gentlemen of the Bullion Committee. They think, or, at least, they evidently wish to make others think, that it is possible to lessen the quantity of the paper-money, and to cause guineas to come back again and to pass from hand to hand as in former times; they would fain have us believe, that this can be done without the total destruction of the paper-money; and, indeed, they have actually recommended to the House of Commons to pass a Law to cause the Bank in Threadneedle Street, London, commonly called the Bank of England *to pay its notes in real money,* at the END OF TWO YEARS from this time. Two years is a pretty good lease for people to have of this sort. This Bank *promises to pay on demand.* It does this upon the face of every one of its notes; and, therefore, as a *remedy* for the evil of want of gold, to propose, that this Bank should *begin* to pay in two years' time, is something, which I think, would not have been offered to the public in any age but this, and, even in this age, to any public except the public in this country. The notes of the Bank of England bear, upon the face of them, a promise that the Bankers, or Bank Company, who issue the notes, will *pay* the notes upon *demand.* Now, what do we mean by *paying* a note? Certainly we do not mean, the giving of *one note for another note.* Yet, this is the sort of payment, that people get at the Bank of England; and this sort of payment the Bullion Committee does not propose even to begin to put an end to in less than *two years* from this time.

Gentlemen; we, the people of this country, have been persuaded to believe many things. We have been persuaded to believe ourselves to be "the *most thinking* people in Europe;" but to what purpose do men think, unless they arrive at useful knowledge by thinking? To what purpose do men think, if they are, after all their thinking, to be persuaded, that a Bank, which has not paid its promissory notes in gold for *thirteen years and a half,* will be able to pay them in gold at the end of *fifteen years and a half,* the quantity of the notes having gone on regularly *increasing?* If men are to be persuaded to believe this, to what purpose do they think? But, before I proceed any further in my remarks upon the Report of the Bullion Committee; before I proceed to lay before you the *exposures* now made by the labours of this Committee; the facts now become *evident* through this channel; the *confessions* now made by these members of the House of Commons: before I proceed to lay these before you, and to remark upon the remedies, proposed by the Committee, it will be necessary for me to go back into the *history of the paper-money;* because, without doing this, I shall be talking to you of things, of which you will have no clear notion, and the reasonings, relating to which, you will, of course, not at all understand. It is a great misfortune, that any portion of your time, should be spent in reading or thinking about matters of this kind; but, such is our present situation in this country, that every man, who has a family to preserve from want, ought to endeavour to make himself acquainted with the nature, and with the probable consequences, of the paper-money now afloat.

Money, is the *representative,* or the *token* of property, or *things of value.* The money, while used as money, is of no other use; and, therefore, a bit of lead or of wood or of leather, would be as good as gold or silver, to be used as money. But, if these materials, which are every where found *in such abundance,* were to be used as money, there would be so much money made that there would be no end to it; and, besides, the money made in one country would, however there enforced by law, have no value in any other country. For these reasons *Gold* and *Silver,* which are amongst the most *scarce* of things, have been, by all the nations that we know any thing of, used as money.

While the money of any country consists of nothing but these scarce metals; while it consists of nothing but gold and silver, there is no fear of its becoming *too abundant;* but if the money of a country be made of lead, tin, wood, leather, or paper; and if any one can make it, who may choose to make it, there needs no extraordinary wisdom to foresee, that there will be a great abundance of this sort of money, and that the gold and silver money, being, in fact, no longer of any use in such a state of things, will go, either into the hoards of the prudent, or into the bags of those, who have the means of sending or carrying them to those foreign countries where they are wanted, and where they will bring their value.

That a state of things like that here spoken of, does now exist in this country, is notorious to all the world. But while we are all acquainted with the fact, and while many of us are most sensibly feeling the *effects,* scarcely a man amongst us takes the trouble to inquire into the *cause:* yet, unless the cause be ascertained, how are we to apply, or to judge of a *remedy?* We see the country abounding with paper-money; we see every man's hand full of it; we frequently talk of it as a strange thing, and a great evil; but never do we inquire into the cause of it.

There are few of you who cannot remember the time, when there was scarcely ever seen a bank note among Tradesmen and Farmers. I can remember, when this was the case; and, when the farmers in my country hardly ever saw a bank note, except when they sold their hops at Weyhill fair. People, in those days, used to carry little bags to put their money in, instead of the pasteboard or leather cases that they now carry. If you look back, and take a little time to think, you will trace the gradual increase of paper-money, and the like decrease of gold and silver money. At first there were no bank notes under 20 pounds; next they came to 15 pounds; next to 10 pounds: at the beginning of the last war, they came to 5 pounds; and, before the end of it, they came down to 2 and to 1 pounds. How long it will be before they come down to parts of a pound, it would, perhaps, be difficult to say; but in Kent, at least, there are country notes in circulation to an amount so low as that of seven shillings. It is the *cause* of this that is interesting to us; the cause of this change in our money, and, in the *prices* of goods of all sorts and of labour. All of you who are forty years of age can remember, when the price of the gallon loaf used to be about ten pence or a shilling, instead of two shillings and sixpence or two shillings and ten pence, as it now is. These effects strike you. You talk of them every day; but the *cause* of them you seldom, if ever, either talk or think of: and it is to this cause that I am now endeavouring to draw your attention.

You have, during the last seventeen years, seen the quantity of paper money rapidly increase; or in other words, you have, day after day, seen less and less of gold and silver appear in payments, and, of course more and more of paper-money. But, it was not till the year 1797, that the paper-money began to increase so very fast. It was then that the *two* and *one* pound notes were first made by the Bank of England. It was then, in short, that paper-money became completely predominant. But, you will naturally ask me, "what was the cause of *that?*" The cause was, that the Bank of England *stopped paying its notes in gold and silver.* What! stop paying its notes? Refuse to pay its *promissory notes?* The Bank of England, when its notes were presented, *refuse to pay them?* Yes: and, what is more, an Act of parliament brought in by Pitt, was passed, to protect the Bank of England against the legal consequences of such refusal. So that, the people, who held promissory notes of the Bank, and who had, perhaps, given gold or silver for them, when they went to the Bank for payment, were told, that they could have no gold or silver, but that they might have other notes, *more paper,* if they pleased, in exchange for the paper they held in their hands and tendered for payment. From that time to this, the Act of parliament, authorising the Bank of England to refuse to pay its notes in gold and silver, has been in force. At first it was passed for *three months;* next till the parliament should meet again; then it was to last to the end of the *war;* then, when *peace* came, it was continued just for a year, till things should be settled; then, as things were not quite settled, it was continued till parliament should meet again; and, as this present war had begun by that time, the act was made to continue till *six months after the next peace.*

The *reasons* given upon the different occasions, it will be very material to notice; for, it is this stoppage in the payment of gold and silver at the Bank of England upon which the whole question turns. Every thing hangs upon this; and, when we come to examine that part of the Report which treats of the Bank's reviving its payments in gold and silver, we shall find it of great use to us to recur to the *reasons,* the divers, the manifold reasons that were given, at different times, for suspending those payments. Since that suspension took place, you have seen the gold and silver disappear; you have seen, the paper has supplied the place of gold; paper-money makers have set up all over the kingdom; and might not this well happen, when, to pay paper-money nothing more than paper-money was required? But, the *reasons* given for this measure of suspension; the reasons given for the passing of an Act of Parliament to protect the Bank of England against the demands of its creditors are seldom recurred to, though, as you will presently see, without recurring to those reasons, and without ascertaining the *true* cause of the passing of that Act of Parliament, we cannot form so good a judgment relative to the *remedy* now proposed; namely, that of the Bank of England's reviving its payments in gold and silver. This is the remedy, which the Bullion Committee propose; and, you will say, a very good remedy it is; a very good remedy indeed; for people who have, for so long a time, not paid their notes in gold and silver, to begin to pay their notes in gold and silver, is a very good remedy; but, the thing to ascertain, is, *can the remedy be applied?* This is the question for us to discuss. It required nobody to tell us, that *paying in gold and silver* would be an effectual remedy for the evils arising from *not paying in gold and silver;* but, it required much more than I have yet heard to convince me, that to pay again in gold and silver *was possible.*

The chief object of our enquiries being this: *Whether it be possible without a total destruction of all the paper money, to restore gold and silver to circulation amongst us;* this being the chief object of our enquiries, we should first ascertain *how the gold and silver was driven out of circulation* and had its place supplied by a paper-money; for, unless we get at a clear view of this, it will be next to impossible for us to reason satisfactorily upon the means of bringing gold and silver back again into circulation.

Some people suppose, that paper *always* made a part of the currency, or common money, of England. They seem to regard the Bank of England as being as old as the Church of England, at least, and some of them appear to have full as much veneration for it. The truth is, however, that the Bank of England is a mere human institution, arising out of causes having nothing miraculous, or supernatural, about them; and that both the institution and the agents who carry it on, are as mortal as any other thing and any other men, in this or in any other country. THE BANK, as it is called, had its origin in the year 1694, that is, a hundred and sixteen years ago; and it arose thus: the then King, WILLIAM III, who had come from Holland, had begun *a war* against France, and, wanting money to carry it on, an act was passed (which act was the 20th of the 5th year of his reign) to invite people to make voluntary advances to the government of the sum of 1,500,000 pounds, and for securing the payment of the interest, and also for securing the re-payment of the principal, *taxes* were laid upon beer, ale, and other liquors. Upon condition of 1,200,000*l.* of this money being advanced, within a certain time, the subscribers to the loan were to be incorporated; and, as the money was advanced in due time, the incorporation took place, and the lenders of the money were formed into a trading Company, called "THE GOVERNOR AND COMPANY OF THE BANK OF ENGLAND." Out of this, and other sums borrowed by the government in the way of mortgage upon the taxes, there grew up a thing called the *Stocks,* or the *Funds* (of which we will speak hereafter); but the Bank Company remained under its primitive name, and as the *debt* of the nation increased, this Company increased in *riches* and in consequence.

Thus, you see, and it is well worthy of your attention, the Bank had its rise *in war* and *taxation.* But, we must reserve reflections of this sort for other occasions, and go on with our inquiries how *gold and silver have been driven out of circulation* in this country, or, in other words, how it came to pass that so much paper-money got afloat.

The Act of Parliament, which I have just referred to, points out the manner in which the Bank Company shall carry on their trade, and the articles in which they shall trade, allowing them, amongst other things, to trade in gold, silver, bills of exchange, and other things, under certain restrictions; but, as to what are called *bank notes,* the Company was not empowered to issue any such, in any other way, or upon any other footing, than merely as *promissory* notes, for the amount of which, in the coin of the country, they were liable to be sued and arrested. Having, however, a greater credit than any other individuals, or company of individuals, the Bank Company issued notes to a greater amount; and, which was something new in England, they were made payable, not to any *particular person,* or his *order,* and not at any *particular time;* but to the *bearer,* and on *demand.* These characteristics, which distinguished the promissory notes of the Bank of England from all other promissory notes gave the people greater confidence in them; and as the Bank Company were always ready to pay the notes in Gold and Silver, when presented for payment, the notes became, in time, to be looked upon as being as good as gold and silver. Hence came our country sayings:—. *"As good as the Bank;" "As solid as the Bank;"* and the like. Yet the Bank was, as we have seen, merely a company of mortal men, formed into an association of traders; and their notes nothing more than written promises to pay the bearer so much money in gold or silver.

We used to have other sayings about the Bank, such as, *"As rich as the Bank;" "All the gold in the Bank;"* and such like, always conveying a notion, that the Bank was a *place,* and a place, too, where there were great heaps of money. As long as the Company were ready and willing to pay, and did actually pay, their notes in gold and silver, to all those persons who wished to have gold and silver, it is clear that these opinions of the people, relative to the Bank, were not altogether unfounded; for, though no bit of paper, or of any thing which has no value in itself, can be, in fact, so good as a bit of gold; still, if it will, at any moment, whenever the holder pleases, bring him gold or silver to the amount written upon it, it is very nearly as good as gold and silver; and, at the time of which we are speaking, this was the case with the promissory notes of the Bank Company. But, it must be evident, that though the Company were ready, at the time now referred to, to pay their notes in gold and silver, they had never in their money-chests a sufficiency of gold and silver to pay off *all* their notes, if they had been presented all at once. This must be evident to every man; because, if the Bank Company kept locked up as much gold and silver as their notes amounted to, they could get nothing by issuing their notes, and might full as well have sent out their gold and silver. A farmer, for instance, who is generally using a hundred pounds of money to pay his workmen, might lend the hundred pounds and get interest for it, if he could persuade his workmen to take promissory notes of his own drawing, instead of money, and, if he were sure, that these promissory notes would not be brought in for payment; but if this was not the case, he would be compelled to keep the hundred pounds in his drawer ready to give to those who did not like to keep his promissory notes; and, in such case, it is clear, that the money would be of no use to him, and that he might full as well have none of his notes out.

Just so with the Bank Company, who, at no time, could have in hand gold and silver enough to pay off *all* their notes at once; nor was this necessary as long as the people regarded those notes as being equally good with gold and silver. But, it is clear, that this *opinion of the goodness* of the Company's notes, or rather, the *feeling of confidence,* or, still more properly perhaps, the *absence of all suspicion,* with respect to them, must, in a great degree, depend upon the *quantity* of notes seen in circulation, compared with the quantity of gold and silver seen in circulation. At first, the quantity of notes was very small indeed; the increase of this quantity was, for the first twenty years, very slow; and, though it became more rapid in the next twenty years, the quantity does not appear to have been large till the war which took place in 1755, before which time the Bank Company put out no notes under 20 pounds in amount. Then it was that they began to put out 15 pound notes, and afterwards, but during the same war, 10 pound notes. During all this time, loans, in every war, had been made by the government. That is to say, the government had borrowed money of individuals, in the same way as above-mentioned, in the year 1694. The money thus borrowed was never payed off, but was suffered to remain at interest, and was, as it is now, called the NATIONAL DEBT, the interest upon which is annually paid out of the taxes raised upon the people. As this debt went on increasing, the bank-notes went on increasing, as, indeed, it is evident they must, seeing that the interest of the Debt was, as it still is and must be, *paid in bank-notes.*

It is not simply the quantity of bank-notes that are put into circulation, which will excite alarm as to their solidity; but, it is that quantity, if it be great, *compared with the quantity of gold and silver,* seen in circulation. If, as the bank-notes increased, the circulating gold and silver had increased in the same proportion; then, indeed, bank-notes would still have retained their usual credit; people would still have had the same confidence in them. But, this could not be. From the nature of things it could not be. The cause of the increase of the bank-notes, was, the increase of the interest upon the National Debt; and, as it grew out of an operation occasioned by poverty, it would have been strange indeed had it been accompanied with a circumstance, which would have been an infallible indication of riches.

Without, however, stopping here to inquire into the cause of the coin's not increasing with the increase of paper, suffice it to say, that such was the fact.

Year after year we saw more of bank-notes and less of gold and silver; till, in time, such was the quantity of bank-notes required to meet the purposes of gold and silver in the payment of the interest of the still increasing Debt, and in the payment of the taxes, many other banks were opened, and they also issued their promissory notes. The Bank Company's notes, which had never before been made for less sums than 10 pounds were, soon after the beginning of PITT's war, in 1793, issued for *five pounds,* after which it was not to be supposed, that people could have the same opinion of bank-notes that they formerly had. Every part of the people, except the very poorest of them, now, occasionally, at least possessed bank-notes. Rents, salaries, yearly wages, all sums above five pounds, were now paid in bank-notes; and, the government itself was now paid its *taxes* in this same sort of currency.

In such a state of things it was quite impossible that people should not begin to perceive, that gold and silver was better than bank-notes; and that they should not be more desirous of possessing the former than the latter; and, the moment this is the case, the banking system must begin to tremble; for, as the notes are payable to the *bearer,* and payable on *demand,* it is very certain, that no man, with such a preference in his mind, will keep in his possession a bank-note, unless we can suppose a man so absurd as to keep a thing, of the goodness of which he has a suspicion, while, for merely opening his mouth or stretching forth his hand, he can exchange it for a thing of the same nominal value, and of the goodness of which it is impossible for him or any one else to entertain any suspicion. "Public Credit," as it has been called, but, as it may more properly be called, "*The credit of bank-notes,*" has been emphatically denominated, "SUSPICION ASLEEP." In the midst of events like those of 1793 and the years immediately succeeding; in the midst of circumstances like those above-mentioned, relating to the bank-notes, it was impossible that SUSPICION should sleep any longer. The putting forth of the 5 pound bank-notes appears to have rouzed it, and, in the month of February, 1797, it became broad awake. The stoppage of payment on the part of the Bank Company was the immediate consequence; but, a particular account of that important event, which totally changed the nature of all our money transactions, and which will, in the end, produce, in all human probability, effects of the most serious nature, must be the subject of a future Letter. In the mean while I am,

Your Friend,
Wm. Cobbett.
State Prison, Newgate,[1] Thursday:
30th August, 1810.

---

1. William Cobbett was imprisoned for two years (1809–11) in Newgate Prison for his protest against the flogging of English militiamen by German mercenaries. [Ed.]

J. R. McCULLOCH
❧❧

SUBSTITUTION OF NOTES FOR COINS

Notwithstanding the precious metals are in many respects admirably fitted to serve as media of exchange, they have two very serious drawbacks, viz., their cost, and the difficulty and expense of carrying them from place to place. If no bank notes circulated in the United Kingdom, it might be fairly assumed that from 35,000,000 to 40,000,000 more sovereigns would be required for the public accommodation than at present, including in those now employed the reserves held by the bankers: and the expense of such a currency, taking it at 37,500,000*l.* and the rate of profit at 6 per cent., with an allowance of 1 per cent. for wear and tear and loss of coins, would be at least 2,625,000*l.* a-year. But the inconvenience attending the use of a currency consisting wholly of gold would be a much greater drawback on its employment than its cost. The weight of 1,000 sovereigns exceeds 21 lbs. troy; so that were there nothing but coins in circulation, the conveyance of large sums from place to place to discharge accounts would be a very laborious process, and even small sums could not be conveyed without considerable difficulty. Hence it is that most commercial and civilised nations have fabricated a portion of their money of less costly and heavy materials, and resorted to various devices for economising the use of coin. Of the substitutes for the latter hitherto suggested, paper is in all respects the most eligible. When governments are sufficiently powerful and intelligent to enforce the observance of contracts, individuals possessed of written promises from others that they will pay certain sums at specified periods begin to assign them to those to whom they are indebted; and when those by whom such obligations are subscribed are persons of whose solvency no doubt can be entertained, they are readily accepted in payment of the debts due by one individual to another. But when the circulation of obligations or bills in this way has continued for a while, individuals begin to perceive that they may derive a profit by issuing them in such a form as to fit them for being readily used as a substitute for money in the ordinary transactions of life. Hence the origin of bank notes or paper money. An individual in whose wealth and discretion the public have confidence being applied to for a loan, say of 5,000*l.,* grants the applicant his

J. R. McCulloch, "Substitution of Notes for Coins," "Distinction between Bills of Exchange and Paper Money." From "Bank—Banking": Section I: "General Principles in Regard to Paper Money and Banking." *A Dictionary Practical, Theoretical, and Historical of Commerce and Commercial Navigation.* 1832; rev. ed. London: Longmans, Green, and Co., 1871. Pp. 86–87, 87–88.

bill or note payable on demand for that sum on his receiving adequate security for its repayment with interest. Now, as this note passes, in consequence of the confidence placed in the issuer, currently from hand to hand as cash, it is quite as useful to the borrower as if he had obtained an equivalent amount of gold; and supposing that the rate of interest is 4 per cent., it will yield, so long as it continues to circulate, a revenue of 200*l*. a year to the issuer. A sense of the advantages that might, in this way, be derived from the circulation of bills or notes led to the formation of banks for their regular issue. Those who issue such notes, coin as it were their credit. They derive the same revenue from the loan of their written promises to pay certain sums that they would derive from the loan of the sums themselves; and while they thus increase their own income, they at the same time contribute to increase the wealth of the society. Besides being incomparably cheaper, bank notes are also incomparably more commodious than a metallic currency. A bank note for 1,000*l*. or 100,000*l*. may be carried about with as much facility as a single sovereign. It is of importance, too, to observe, that its loss or destruction, whether by fire, shipwreck, or otherwise, would be of no greater importance, in a public point of view, than the loss or destruction of as much paper. No doubt it might be a serious calamity to the holder; but to whatever extent it injured him, it would proportionally benefit the issuer, whereas the loss of coin is an injury to the holder without being of service to anyone else; it is, in fact, so much abstracted from the wealth of the community.

DISTINCTION BETWEEN BILLS OF EXCHANGE AND PAPER-MONEY

Under the phrase paper-money or paper-currency, we do not include bills of exchange, or bills issued by bankers, merchants, and others, and payable some time after date. Such bills perform, in some respects, the same functions as money; and have, in consequence, been frequently regarded in the same light as bank notes. But this is quite improper: for though there are many points in which a bill of exchange and a bank note closely resemble each other, there are others in which there is a distinct and material difference between them. A note bears to be payable on demand; it is not indorsed by a holder on his paying it away; the party receiving has no claim on the party from whom he received it, in the event of the failure of the issuers. Practically speaking, this is the fact; but a person paying away a bank note is liable to be called upon for repayment, should the bank fail before it was in the power of the party to whom it was paid, using ordinary diligence, to present it. The responsibility seldom exceeds a couple of hours, and can hardly in any case exceed a couple of days. In practice it is never adverted to; and everyone is thus encouraged, reckoning on the facility of passing it to another, to accept bank paper, "*even though he should doubt the ultimate solvency of the issuer.*"[1] Bills, on the contrary, are almost all drawn payable at some distant period; and those into whose hands they come, if they be not in want of money, prefer retaining them in their possession, in order to get the interest that accrues upon them. But the principal distinction between notes and bills is, that every individual, in passing a bill to another, has to indorse it, and by doing so makes himself responsible for its payment. "A bill circulates," says Mr. Thornton, "in consequence chiefly of the confidence placed by each receiver of it in the last indorser his own correspondent in trade; whereas the circulation of a bank note is owing rather to the circumstance of the name of the issuer being so well known as to give it an universal credit." Nothing, then, can be more inaccurate than to represent bills and notes in the same point of view. If A pay to B 100*l.* in satisfaction of a debt, there is an end of the transaction; but if A pay to B a bill of exchange for 100*l.*, the transaction is not completed; and in the event of the bill not being paid by the person on whom it is drawn, B will have recourse upon A for its value. It is clear, therefore, that a great deal more consideration is always required, and may be fairly presumed to be given, before anyone accepts a bill of exchange in payment, than before he accepts a bank note. The note is payable on the instant, without deduction—the bill not until some future period; the note may be passed to another without incurring any risk or responsibility, whereas every fresh issuer of the bill makes himself responsible for its value. Notes form the currency of all classes, not only of those who are, but also of those who are not engaged in business, as women, children, labourers, &c., who in most instances are without the power to refuse them, and without the means of forming any correct conclusion as to the solvency of the issuers. Bills, on the other hand, pass only, with very few exceptions, among persons engaged in business, who are fully aware of the risk they run in taking them. There is plainly, therefore, a wide and obvious distinction between the two species of currency; and it cannot be fairly argued, that because Government interferes to regulate the issue of the one, it should also regulate the issue of the other. To use the words of Lord Mansfield,[2] "Bank notes are not, like bills of exchange, mere securities or documents for debts, nor are so esteemed, but are treated as money in the ordinary course and transactions of business, by the general consent of mankind; and on payment of them, whenever a receipt is required, the receipts are always given as for money, not as for securities or notes."[3]

---

1. Henry Thornton (1760–1815), author of *Enquiry into the Nature and Effects of Paper Credit of Great Britain* (1802). [Ed.]
2. Follower of John Wilkes, Lord Mansfield (1733–1821) was Lord Chief Justice in the 1770s. [Ed.]
3. Joseph Chitty (1776–1841), author of *A Treatise on Bills of Exchange* (1799). [Ed.]

GEORGE RAE

BILLS OF EXCHANGE

> Amongst many roses some thistles grow, some bad weeds and enor-
> mities, which much disturb the peace of this body politick, eclipse
> the honour and glory of it, fit to be rooted out and with all speed to
> be reformed.
>
> —*Anatomy of Melancholy.*[1]

The bill of exchange is the highest form of banking security. As such, it even
excels Consols, in one respect;—its principal sum is not subject to depreciation; it will be paid in full when it reaches maturity; whereas an equal sum invested in Consols would yield on realization simply the price of the day. The
price may have advanced, it is true, but it is equally possible that it may have
receded. A bill, moreover, is unsurpassed in facility of transfer. The mere signature of the indorser transfers all property in the instrument to you as effectually, as if the transfer were embodied in a conveyance of the regulation
length on lawyers' vellum.

If the first bill of exchange had been framed by a leading conveyancer, reduced to shape in a committee of the whole House, and had suffered periodical amendment at the hands of the Legislature ever since, it becomes a curious speculation what complexity of form and measure of length this simplest
of documents would have attained by this time. Fortunately for the commercial interests of the human race, it has escaped this ordeal, and remains to us
an instrument altogether matchless in brevity of form, facility of transfer and
simplicity of title. There is no difficulty in settling the title to a bill of exchange. You have but to assure yourself that the indorser is none other than
himself and the point is settled. And you can with equal promptness and ease
render the document inalienable, except by your own act and deed, by the
simple process of specially indorsing it to the Bank, whereby you render it
useless plunder to a thief.

At a previous stage of this correspondence, we sought to analyse the class
of bills which you would chiefly meet with, in a quiet country town like
Oxborough.

George Rae, "Bills of Exchange." *The Country Banker, His Clients, Cares, and Work from an
Experience of Forty Years.* 1885; rev. ed. London: John Murray, 1930. Pp. 243–56.
1. Study of despondency by Robert Burton (1577–1640). [Ed.]

We have now to glance at the varieties of paper with which you may have to deal, in the populous and busy commercial town where your Bank has its head-quarters, when you come to rule as its Manager in chief.

In the first order of merit, come bills bearing the names of banks or banking houses, as drawers, acceptors or indorsers, together with other names of high standing. These bills stand A I in the estimation of the discount market, and the fanciful speak of them as gilt-edged. Then we have "remittance paper"—bills drawn by houses abroad on banks, or correspondents in England. Then comes "inland drawn" paper—bills drawn by the shippers of goods on the agents in England of the houses abroad, to whom the goods are shipped. Anon we come upon brokers' paper—bills drawn by importers against commodities placed in brokers' hands for sale. Then we reach the immense class of bills arising out of our manifold trades and industries, which pass under the term of "trade paper": and finally, we have a nondescript class, of limited amount, consisting of promissory notes or loan-bills; such as those of Bowdler on Starkey, and the like.

Your largest holding of paper will, no doubt, consist of trade bills, the features of which we discussed at length in a former letter, and of which we took for an average sample the draft of Cartridge on Booker & Co.

Next in probable amount will come your holding of "brokers' bills,"—a description of paper unknown to Oxborough—drawn by the owner of produce upon the broker in whose hands he has placed it for sale. The bill is usually accompanied by the written undertaking of the broker to apply the proceeds of the merchandise in payment of the bill, and to hold the produce meanwhile duly insured against fire. When this undertaking is supplemented by a warehouse warrant, shewing that the merchandise has been transferred into the name of the Bank, no safer transaction could well be offered you.

But the legal transfer of the property into the name of the Bank is indispensable, if absolute security is to be insured. If this is not done, neither the owner nor the Bank has control over the produce or commodity advanced upon. In that respect they have to trust entirely to the integrity of the broker. It is rarely that this trust is abused, but it has been in certain flagrant instances; and this kind of malversation will always be a possibility, where the transaction is not fortified by a warehouse-warrant in the name of the Bank.

It is difficult to understand why this should not be done in every case, on principle; unless we are to concede that the borrower of money has a greater claim to be the holder of the commodity borrowed upon, than the Bank which lends the money; a contention which is clearly untenable, not to say ridiculous. By all laws of reason and business usage, the lender of money is held to be the natural holder of the property advanced upon.

You question whether leading brokers will take this view of the matter. If so, all that need be said is, so much the worse for the leading brokers; because they will thus divert such business into the hands of less substantial people, who will not be deterred by sentimental scruples from giving business validity to business transactions.

With respect to bills drawn, indorsed, or accepted by banks, at home or abroad, of undoubted means and stability, and bearing other names of high standing, there will be no difficulty of selection. They will turn into bank notes of their own accord, as they fall due, and you will be without a care or anxiety in respect of them.

Bills drawn by houses abroad on their correspondents in England against actual shipments of merchandise to this country, and known to banks and bill-brokers as remittance paper, are frequently drawn upon banks or houses of the highest mercantile standing, and are in high repute and favour in the discount market.

As between this class of bills, and those drawn by English shippers on the agents in England of houses in India, China, or elsewhere abroad, there is this difference: in the case of remittance paper, the bills are drawn against value on its way to this country; in the other, the bills are drawn against value which is leaving this country for distant parts of the globe. A bill drawn against value which will be in hand before the bill falls due, obviously rests on a different basis from a bill drawn against commodities which, at the maturity of the bill, are being realized in the distant markets of the East or West.

It may chance, however, unless due caution has been exercised by your predecessor in office, that bills are to be found in your portfolio which do not come strictly within any of the above definitions. We have seen that even in quiet humdrum Oxborough, bills may be fabricated and set afloat against values purely fictitious.

But bills may be drawn against values only too ponderous. Bills, for example, are sometimes drawn against ships or steamers in the course of construction. Where the acceptor is a man of sufficient means himself, or where he has an 'ownery' for the vessels, from whom he is able to collect the money needful to meet the bills as they mature, there is little to be said: but if his ownery is not in hand,—if it consists of persons who owe their existence for the most part to a hopeful imagination,—he will not be able to meet his acceptances at maturity; and if the builder cannot take them up, the bills will have to be renewed, whilst additional ones may have to be drawn, to provide the wherewithal to complete the vessel and send her to sea.

What may next happen is problematical; she may prove a lucky ship, or she may prove to be the reverse: but in either event, the native element of vessels thus launched and sent to sea, is manifestly paper. They float as much on bills as on the ocean wave; and the outcome to the discounters of such paper—as witness the experiences of Overend, Gurney & Co.—is frequently more disastrous than exhilarating.

It is not the province of banking to discount bills, the proceeds of which are to provide the acceptors with fixed capital. A man may properly be drawn upon against goods, produce, or commodities which he is turning over in his business from day to day; but not against his buildings or machinery. These are not floating capital. He cannot meet his acceptances with factories or fixtures, buildings or machinery. These represent his fixed capital, and are provided by himself out of his own means, or they ought to be. In any case, they are no basis to run bills of exchange upon; neither are vessels in course of construction, or navigating the high seas.

A ship-owner, or ship's husband, may properly be drawn upon for sails, or cordage, or stores supplied to his ships, because there is a tangible fund in his incoming freights to meet this class of marine paper: but when he accepts against the hull of a ship, he passes the recognized limits of negociable value, and his paper becomes discredited in the estimation of the bill market.

KITE-FLYING

We have thus far dealt with bills drawn against "value" actually given by the drawers and received by the acceptors of the bills; although we have not found the value of approved quality in every case. Nevertheless, we have found a value of some kind, underlying and forming the basis of each transaction. Every genuine bill of exchange is in fact the presentment and voucher of a mercantile or trading transaction, which has actually passed between the parties to the instrument. But we have yet to speak of certain bills of more nebulous quality—bills drawn and accepted against values received which have no existence—bills which have their origin and exclusive base in the predatory instincts of their makers. You have met, as we have seen, with an obvious "kite" or two at Oxborough; but the character of this class of bill is not always so apparent: there are diversities of kites, as of other things.

When Mr. Julius Webber tenders for discount his draft on Wefton & Co., and you already hold certain drafts of theirs upon him, both being customers of your Bank, and both in the same line of business, you will not only look askance at the proffered transaction, but will naturally desire to know the basis on which the bills already afloat are supposed to rest. You will be vehemently assured, no doubt, that actual value has passed in every case. When Wefton & Co. run short of a certain class of goods, the friendly Webber lets them have some of his, and draws against them; similarly, when his stock requires "assortment" they, with equal courtesy, furnish the needful and draw upon him therefor with equal promptitude. Nothing, they will assure you, could be more regular than their drawings upon each other.

In a certain sense—possibly not; but when two firms in the same trade take to exchanging goods with each other, and to drawing bills against the total of each exchange, instead of for the difference only, it is manifest that such bills have no more real foundation to rest upon, than if the same bale of goods were shuttlecocked backwards and forwards between the parties, whensoever either of them was moved with the desire to draw.

Let us suppose that Webber has bills running on Wefton & Co. for, say, £1500, for which he has sold and delivered them goods of equal value; and that Wefton & Co. have drafts running upon him for a similar amount, and for which they have supplied him with actual value in goods. It is clear that by these operations they have raised £3000, without thereby adding a shilling of value to their respective stocks in trade. It is further manifest that by this financial hocus-pocus, bills might be set afloat to an amount, not merely equal to, but largely in excess of their combined stocks in trade,—if banks could be found incautious enough to discount paper of this light and airy description.

And there are other methods of kite-flying, equally plausible, more difficult of detection, and only a shade less censurable.

A. has imported a cargo of produce,—value, say, £5000, which he sells to B., who buys it on speculation, and re-sells it also on speculation to C., who disposes of it to D., a wholesale dealer; who finally parts with it to the trade, and draws upon the smaller buyers against sales. Now, if bills are drawn at every stage of the process, as they may easily be, a single cargo might thus be used as a base to set afloat bills to three or four times its value. The proceeds of each bill ought, in strictness, to be applied, as soon as the bill is drawn, to take up and cancel the previous one; but this is not the usage. As a rule, A., B., C., and D., will prefer to have £5000 each to play with for a few months, and their respective bankers meanwhile will be the holders of £20,000 in bills, three-fourths of which amount have gone for the time being into other forms of commercial speculation.

There is yet another description of paper against which you have to be on your guard. The drawer and acceptor of the bills may both be respectable English firms; and there may be nothing on the face of the bills to suggest irregularity. The drawer is an importer of the produce or commodity which it is the special business of the acceptors, his brokers, to deal in and dispose of, and everything seems fair and above-board; until some day, to your amazement, both firms give way together. You then discover that the bills were drawn, not against produce or commodities in the hands of the acceptors, but to provide the drawer with means to make advances to growers abroad, in anticipation of problematical crops.

You further find, that the parties have been carrying this speculative game on for years, and that the frequent result of such trading has followed, and brought both concerns to grief. You have been an unconscious instrument in effecting your own heavy loss, and abetting them in their own undoing. You have been treating as genuine commercial paper a series of flagitious kites.

Your excuse is, that the bills had every appearance of validity. There was respectability at both ends, and probability in the ostensible transactions; but unhappily there was a want of candour. The bills, in every case, purported to be drawn as against so much value in hand and not against so much value in expectation. Had they been so drawn, it is needless to observe that they would never have seen the inside of your bill-case.

The polite moralist may draw a distinction betwixt the fabrication of bills of this description and the vulgar game of thimble-rig; but the banker who finds himself hocussed by such paper is apt, in his rage, to think that in dealing with a professed trickster, he would at least have the advantage of being on his guard.

You ask how you are to detect such paper when offered? By the simple process of requiring, as in the case of other brokers' paper, that the acceptors shall hypothecate and transfer to the Bank the commodity against which the bills are drawn. By a resolute enforcement of this necessary condition, you will avoid being the holders, henceforth, of bills drawn against crops in expectancy and values in the air.

But if we would know one of the causes of recurring panic and widespread banking loss, we have to look at methods of kite-flying, practised at higher levels and on areas of wider range than are accessible to the Webbers and Weftons, or the Bargoods and Laxeys of trade; whose offences, compared with those of the larger practitioners of the craft, dwindle to petty larceny.

More than once during the current half century, bills have been drawn by certain large houses of the period on each other, against merchandise purporting to be on its way either to England or to English houses abroad, to the extent of millions—merchandise which had no existence beyond its fraudulent inscription on the face of fictitious bills.

The credit given to these houses was not made to rest on the homely principles on which banking at Oxborough is conducted. The credit given was not based upon an intimate knowledge of the parties themselves, their habits of life, their business capacities, their liabilities and their resources; but was accorded with lavish hand, in ignorance of these essential facts and regardless of the conclusions to which they might point.

Neither would there seem to be much ground for hope that matters will be different in the future, so long as the engagements which any mercantile house may come under, in excess of its capital, are subject to no law of control, beyond what the house may see fit to impose upon itself. Limits are assigned to other things. We breathe and move in a labyrinth of legal and moral restraint; but there is no limit, in law or equity, to the most baleful expansion of commercial credit. In the progress of each decade, it grows and spreads unseen, until its presence, like the fire-damp, becomes known only by explosion.

If the paper of each house were to centre in any one bank or discount house, some limit might be put to this fertile source of banking misfortune; but this is impracticable. Such paper is scattered throughout the country; here a little, there a little; each banker knowing how much he himself holds, but knowing nothing of the aggregate paper afloat of each house. In this ignorance, he hugs himself with the belief that his few thousands on a house worth its plum, are as safe as the bank notes in his till—a form of delusion from which, every ten years or so, he has a rude awakening.

I protested five and thirty years ago, that the then recent losses on this pernicious brood of "kites," were sufficient to strike bankers dumb—but they would appear to have had the more serious effect of striking certain of our number blind. We have lived to witness developments of the bill system of 1847, and of other so-called forms of banking, on a scale of magnitude, in comparison with which the figures of that time shrink into abject insignificance. The practitioners of that early period were as pigmies, compared with the leviathan operators of a later time.

One cause, which has rendered the manufacture and negociation of such bills practicable, still exists. The intense competition for so-called high-class paper among London and other banks and discount houses, is still such as to enable any astute and speculative firm to have discount facilities in half-a-dozen different quarters at the same time.

Now, one old-fashioned rule of country banking was, and still is, to require that a man shall have only one banker, and to close his account if it is discovered that he has two; and you will do well to adhere in all cases to this prudential rule in respect of your own customers. How can you know, with any approach to exactitude, what a man is doing, or how his affairs stand, if he is transacting a portion of his business elsewhere? The very fact of his doing so excites a suspicion that he has some reason for withholding certain of his operations from your cognizance. When you lend him money, and discount his bills, you have a right to know the whole of his banking transactions; otherwise you may awake some day to the knowledge, that he has been availing himself of facilities elsewhere, by means of which he has succeeded in effectually deluding you as to his real position.

And you will find that some of the discount establishments in London afford such facilities to parties whom they know to be customers of country banks. Even with money of your Bank lying with them at call, they hold themselves at liberty to compete against you, with your own customers, for discounts, at your very doors. It is not a neighbourly policy, nor altogether a wise one; it is a question whether it even "pays." The broker who should practise this sort of competition would have no ground for complaint, if he found the money placed with him at call or short notice by the bank competed against, taking to itself wings to seek a more friendly custodian.

Would it not be a better way, even as a question of profit and loss, for a London bill broker gradually to limit the discount business coming to him from the provinces to the bills of Country banks seeking re-discount? The same volume of country paper would still have to seek London for discount; but then, all such paper would reach the brokers through the medium of bankers on the spot. The broker would thus have the assurance that the bills had been selected by those who had unrivalled means of judging of their regularity and safety; and this assurance would be substantiated by the indorsements of the banks. A broker's chances of loss on country paper would thus be reduced to vanishing point. If such a policy were gradually adopted—if London discounters of bills were gradually to close the door against all country business, except that coming to them from Country banks, or from provincial houses having no local bankers, the "fast" firms of the future would find themselves pulled up by their bankers, long before their liabilities could reach the monstrous figures of the recent past.

By dealing direct with provincial customers, the discount broker no doubt obtains a rate of discount slightly in excess of what he would obtain, if the bills came to him through a Country bank and under its indorsement. But if against the fractional advantage of profit thus realized during, say, the last ten years, were weighted the losses on such transactions; who can doubt on which side the balance of advantage would incline?

You ask how a Country banker, under the existing order of things, can best guard himself against danger in furnishing his bill-case with its necessary quota of first-class paper? You say that if enquiry had been made as to the position of any one of the large houses which have failed during the last quarter of a century, the answer, up to the very eve of their failure, would in all likelihood have been that their credit was beyond question. That is true, and because it is true, I would submit that a country bank had best secure its first-class paper through a first-rate discount house, and under its guarantee. This would render the operation safe beyond the reach of doubt, and would be doing by the bill brokers as you would have them do by you; you would thus avoid meddling with their business, as you would have them abstain from interference with yours.

Let us suppose that you choose instead, to select your first-class paper on the strength of your own judgment, and thereby gain a quarter per cent. per annum on each transaction. On a bill for £5000, having three months to run, your gain will be £3 2s. 6d., and no more. This will be the extent of your gain, by working without the light of a broker's experience, or the substantial backing of his guarantee.

Let it be the result of a discount business thus personally conducted, that the bill becomes a loss—a contingency which would not be without precedent—and the gain of £3 2s. 6d. for the sake of which you have risked so much, will seem pitiful indeed. Beware of these petty allurements of gain, which are as calculated to swallow dividends up, every now and then, as to enlarge them. "I was caught by a morsel," was the mournful reflection of the fish in the adage.

When you have completed the investigation of your bill-case and made a synopsis of its contents, and would know the financial value of the whole,—deduct from the total, the amount of your promissory notes and loan bills, and all paper of dubious quality, if you hold any, and the difference will be the result required. In other words, the amount remaining in your bill-case, after this deduction is made, will represent the net amount of negociable paper which you hold—that is to say, the total of your bills available for re-discount in case of need.

What proportion of unmarketable paper it may be prudent for you to hold at any time, must be determined by the same laws which guide you in fixing the limits of your other forms of asset.

In constructing your balance-sheet, we assumed that the whole of the £1,190,000 in bills of exchange were of negociable quality. These, added to your cash and Consols, represent a total of readily available resources, equal to 80 per cent. of your deposits—a position of undeniable strength. But, if certain of your bills are not negociable, this percentage will have to be reduced: if you hold unmarketable paper to the extent of say £300,000, the percentage would drop from 80 to 68—and your financial barometer would indicate a fall of 12 degrees. The amount you hold of promissory notes or loan bills may, therefore, be an important item, in estimating from time to time the general strength of your position.

The degree of that strength, it may be well to note, is always to be measured by the proportion which your fusible assets bear to your liabilities to the public. Your cash in hand and at call may be regarded as assets in actual fusion: your Consols and negociable bills as fusible into cash in a high degree; your promissory notes and loan bills as in-fusible, within any exact time; and the bulk of your overdrafts as opposing an obstinate resistance to fusion, whatever heat of application may be brought to bear upon them.

CHAPTER TWO

COUNTERFEIT COINS

SIDNEY LAMAN BLANCHARD
⊗⊗⊗

A BIOGRAPHY OF A BAD SHILLING

I believe I may state with confidence that my parents were respectable, notwithstanding that one belonged to the law—being the zinc door-plate of a solicitor. The other, was a pewter flagon residing at a very excellent hotel, and moving in distinguished society; for it assisted almost daily at convivial parties in the Temple.[1] It fell a victim at last to a person belonging to the lower orders, who seized it, one fine morning, while hanging upon some railings to dry, and conveyed it to a Jew, who—I blush to record the insult offered to a respected member of my family—melted it down. My first mentioned parent—the zinc plate—was not enabled to move much in society, owing to its very close connexion with the street door. It occupied, however, a very conspicuous position in a leading thoroughfare, and was the means of diffusing more useful instruction, perhaps, than many a quarto, for it informed the running as well as the reading public, that Messrs. Snapples and Son resided within, and that their office hours were from ten till four. In order to become my progenitor it fell a victim to dishonest practices. A "fast" man unscrewed it one night, and bore it off in triumph to his chambers. Here it was included by "the boy" among his numerous "perquisites," and, by an easy transition, soon found its way to the Hebrew gentleman above mentioned.

Sidney Laman Blanchard, "A Biography of a Bad Shilling." *Household Words* 2 (January 1851): 420–26.

1. A term for the four Inns of Court in London (the Inner and Middle Temples, Lincoln's Inn, and Gray's Inn), which housed legal societies that had the exclusive right of admitting people to practice at the bar. [Ed.]

The first meeting between my parents took place in the melting-pot of this ingenious person, and the result of their subsequent union was mutually advantageous. The one gained by the alliance that strength and solidity which is not possessed by even the purest pewter; while to the solid qualities of the other were added a whiteness and brilliancy that unadulterated zinc could never display.

From the Jew, my parents were transferred—mysteriously and by night—to an obscure individual in an obscure quarter of the metropolis, when, in secrecy and silence, I was *cast,* to use an appropriate metaphor, upon the world.

How shall I describe my first impression of existence? how portray my agony when I became aware *what I was*—when I understood my mission upon earth? The reader, who has possibly never felt himself to be what Mr. Carlyle[2] calls a "sham," or a "solemnly constituted impostor," can have no notion of my sufferings!

These, however, were endured only in my early and unsophisticated youth. Since then, habitual intercourse with the best society has relieved me from the embarrassing appendage of a conscience. My long career upon town—in the course of which I have been bitten, and rung, and subjected to the most humiliating tests—has blunted my sensibilities, while it has taken off the sharpness of my edges; and, like the counterfeits of humanity, whose lead may be seen emulating silver at every turn, my only desire is—not to be worthy of passing, but simply—to pass.

My impression of the world, on first becoming conscious of existence, was, that it was about fifteen feet in length, very dirty, and had a damp, unwholesome smell; my notions of mankind were, that it shaved only once a fortnight; that it had coarse, misshapen features; a hideous leer; that it abjured soap, as a habit; and lived habitually in its shirt-sleeves. Such, indeed, was the aspect of the apartment in which I first saw the light, and such the appearance of the professional gentleman who ushered me into existence.

I may add that the room was fortified, as if to sustain a siege. Not only was the door itself lined with iron, but it was strengthened by ponderous wooden beams, placed upright, and across, and in every possible direction. This formidable exhibition of precautions against danger was quite alarming.

I had not been long brought into this "narrow world" before a low and peculiar tap, from the outside of the door, met my ear. My master paused, as if alarmed, and seemed on the point of sweeping me and several of my companions (who had been by this time mysteriously ushered into existence) into some place of safety. Reassured, however, by a second tapping, of more marked peculiarity, he commenced the elaborate process of unfastening the

---

2. Thomas Carlyle (1795–1881). Social critic and author born in Scotland, author of *Sartor Resartus* (1833–34), *The French Revolution* (1837), and *Chartism* (1839). [Ed.]

door. This having been accomplished, and the entrance left to the guardian-ship only of a massive chain, a mysterious watchword was exchanged with some person outside who was presently admitted.

"Hollo! there's two on you?" cried my master, as a hard, elderly animal entered; followed somewhat timidly by a younger one of mild and modest aspect.

"A green un as I have took under my arm," said Mr. Blinks (which I presently understood to be the name of the elder one) "and werry deserving he promises to be. He's just come out of the stone-pitcher, without having done nothing to entitle him to have gone in. This was it: a fellow out at Highbury Barn collared him, for lifting snow from some railings, where it was a hang-ing to dry. Young Innocence had never dreamt of anything of the kind—bein' a walking on his way to the work'us—but beaks being proverbially otherwise than fly, he got six weeks on it. In the 'Ouse o' Correction, however, he met some knowing blades, who put him up to the time of day, and he'll soon be as wide-awake as any on 'em. This morning he brought me a pocket-book, and in it eigh—ty pound in flimsies. As he is a young hand, I encouraged him by giv-ing him three pun' ten for the lot—it's runnin' a risk, but I done it. As it is, I shall have to send 'em all over to 'Amburg. Howsomever, he's got to take one pund in home made; bein' out of it myself, I have brought him to you."

"You're here at the nick o' time," said my master, "I've just finished a new batch—"

And he pointed to the glittering heap in which I felt myself—with the dif-fidence of youth—to be unpleasantly conspicuous.

"I've been explaining to young Youthful that it's the reg'lar thing, when he sells his swag to gents in my way of business, to take part of it in this here coin." Here he took *me* up from the heap, and as he did so I felt as if I were growing black between his fingers, and having my prospects in life very much damaged.

"And is all this bad money?" said the youth, curiously gazing, as I thought, at me alone, and not taking the slightest notice of the rest of my companions.

"Hush, hush, young Youthful," said Mr. Blinks, "no offence to the home coinage. In all human affairs, everythink is as good as it looks."

"I could not tell them from the good—from those made by government, I should say"—hastily added the boy.

I felt myself leaping up with vanity, and chinking against my companions at these words. It was plain I was fast losing the innocence of youth. In jus-tice to myself, however, I am bound to say that I have, in the course of my sub-sequent experience, seen many of the lords and masters of the creation behave much more absurdly under the influence of flattery.

"Well, we must put you up to the means of finding out the real. Turtle from the mock," said my master. "It's difficult to tell by the ring. Silver, if it's at all cracked—as lots of money is—don't ring no better than pewter: besides, people can't try every blessed bit o' tin they get in that way; some folks is offended if they do, and some ain't got no counter. As for the colour, I defy anybody to tell the difference. And as for the figgers on the side, wot's your dodge? Why, wen a piece o' money's give to you, look to the hedges, and feel 'em too with your finger. When they ain't quite perfect, ten to one but they're bad 'uns. You see, the way it's done is this—I suppose I may put the young 'un up to a thing or two more?" added Mr. Blinks, pausing.

My master, who had during the above conversation lighted a short pipe, and devoted himself with considerable assiduity to a pewter pot—which he looked at with a technical eye, as if mentally casting it into crown pieces,—now nodded assent. He was not of an imaginative or philosophic turn, like Mr. Blinks. He saw none of the sentiment of his business, but pursued it on a system of matter of fact, because he profited by it. This difference between the producer and the middle-man may be continually observed elsewhere.

"You see," continued Mr. Blinks, "that these here '*bobs*' "—by which he meant shillings—"is composed of a mixter of two metals—pewter and zinc. In coorse these is first prigged raw, and sold to gents in my line of bis'ness, who either manufacturs them themselves, or sells 'em to gents as does. Now, if the manufacturer, is only in a small way of bis'ness, and is of a mean natur, he merely casts his money in plaster of Paris moulds. But for nobby gents like our friend here (my master here nodded approvingly over his pipe), this sort of thing won't pay—too much trouble and not enough profit. All the top-sawyers in the manufactur is scientific men. By means of what they calls a galwanic battery a cast is made of that particklar coin selected for himitation. From this here cast, which you see, that there die is made, and from that there die impressions is struck off on plates of the metal prepared for the purpose. Now, unfortunately, we ain't got the whole of the masheenery of the Government institootion *yet* at our disposal, though it's our intention for to bribe the Master of the Mint (in imitation coin) some of these days to put us up to it all—so you see we're obliged to stamp the two sides of this here shilling, for instance (taking *me* up again as he spoke), upon different plates of metal, jining of 'em together afterwards. Then comes the *milling* round the hedges. This we do with a file; and it is the himperfection of that 'ere as is continually a preying upon our minds. Any one who's up to the bis'ness can tell whether the article's geniwine or not, by a looking at the hedge; for it can't be expected that a file will cut as reg'lar as a masheen. This is reely the great drawback upon our purfession."

Here Mr. Blinks, overcome by the complicated character of his subject, subsided into a fit of abstraction, during which he took a copious pull at my master's porter.

Whether suggested by the onslaught upon his beer, or by a general sense of impending business, my master now began to show symptoms of impatience. Knocking the ashes out of his pipe, he asked "how many bob his friend wanted?"

The arrangement was soon concluded. Mr. Blinks filled a bag which he carried with the manufacture of my master, and paid over twenty of the shillings to his *protégé*. Of this twenty, *I* was one. As I passed into the youth's hand I could feel it tremble, as I own mine would have done had I been possessed of that appendage.

My new master then quitted the house in company with Mr. Blinks, whom he left at the corner of the street—an obscure thoroughfare in Westminster. His rapid steps speedily brought him to the southern bank of the "fair and silvery Thames," as a poet who once possessed me, (only for half-an-hour), described that uncleanly river, in some verses which I met in the pocket of his pantaloons. Diving into a narrow street, obviously, from the steepness of its descent, built upon arches, he knocked at a house of all the unpromising rest the least promising in aspect. A wretched hag opened the door, past whom the youth glided, in an absent and agitated manner; and, having ascended several flights of a narrow and precipitate staircase, opened the door of an apartment on the top story.

The room was low, and ill-ventilated. A fire burnt in the grate, and a small candle flickered on the table. Beside the grate, sat an old man sleeping on a chair; beside the table, and bending over the flickering light, sat a young girl engaged in sewing. My master was welcomed, for he had been absent, it seemed, for two months. During that time he had, he said, earned some money; and he had come to share it with his father and sister.

I led a quiet life with my companions, in my master's pocket, for more than a week. At the end of that time, the stock of good money was nearly exhausted, although it had on more than one occasion been judiciously mixed with a neighbour or two of mine. Want, however, did not leave us long at rest. Under pretence of going away again to get "work," my master—leaving several of my friends to take their chance, in administering to the necessities of his father and sister—went away. I remained to be "smashed" (passed) by my master.

"Where are you going so fast, that you don't recognise old friends?" were the words addressed to the youth by a passer-by, as he was crossing, at a violent pace, the nearest bridge, in the direction of the Middlesex bank.

The speaker was a young gentleman, aged about twenty, not ill-looking, but with features exhibiting that peculiar expression of cunning, which is popularly described as "knowing." He was arrayed in what the police reports in the newspapers call "the height of fashion,"—that is to say, he had travestied the style of the most daring dandies of last year. He wore no gloves; but the bloated rubicundity of his hands was relieved by a profusion of rings, which—even without the cigar in his mouth—were quite sufficient to establish his claims to gentility.

Edward, my master, returned the civilities of the stranger, and, turning back with him, they agreed to "go somewhere."

"Have a weed," said Mr. Bethnal, producing a well filled cigar case. There was no resisting. Edward took one.

"Where shall we go?" he said.

"I'll tell you what we'll do," said Mr. Bethnal, who looked as if experiencing a novel sensation—he evidently had an idea. "I tell you what—we'll go and blow a cloud with Joe, the pigeon-fancier. He lives only a short distance off, not far from the abbey; I want to see him on business, so we shall kill two birds. He's one of us, you know."

I now learned that Mr. Bethnal was a new acquaintance, picked up under circumstances (as a member of parliament, to whom I once belonged, used to say in the House) to which it is unnecessary further to allude.

"I was glad to hear of your luck, by-the-bye," said the gentleman in question, not noticing his companion's wish to avoid the subject. "I heard of it from Old Blinks. Smashing's the thing, if one's a presentable cove. You'd do deuced well in it. You've only to get nobby togs and you'll do."

Mr. Joe, it appeared, in addition to his ornithological occupations, kept a small shop for the sale of coals and potatoes; he was also, in a very small way, a timber merchant; for several bundles of firewood were piled in pyramids in his shed.

Mr. Bethnal's business with him was soon despatched; although not until after the latter had been assured by his friend, that Edward was "of the right sort," with the qualification that he was "rather green at present;" and he was taken into Mr. Joe's confidence, and also into Mr. Joe's upstairs sanctum.

In answer to a request from Mr. Bethnal, in a jargon, to me then unintelligible, Mr. Joe produced from some mysterious depository at the top of the house, a heavy canvas bag, which he emptied on the table, discovering a heap of shillings and half-crowns, which by a sympathetic instinct, I immediately detected to be of my own species.

"What do you think of these?" said Mr. Bethnal to his young friend.

Edward expressed some astonishment that Mr. Joe should be in the line.

"Why, bless your eyes," said that gentleman; "you don't suppose I gets my livelihood out of the shed down stairs, nor the pigeons neither. You see, these things are only dodges. If I lived here like a gentleman—that is to say, without a occupation—the p'lese would soon be down upon me. They'd be obleeged to take notice on me. As it is, I comes the respectable tradesman, who's above suspicion—and the pigeons helps on the business wonderful."

"How is that?"

"Why, I keeps my materials—the pewter and all that—on the roof, in order to be out o' the way, in case of a surprise. If I was often seed upon the roof, a-looking arter such-like matters, inquisitive eyes would be on the look out. The pigeons is a capital blind. I'm believed to be dewoted to my pigeons, out o' which I takes care it should be thought I makes a little fortun—and that makes a man respected. As for the pigeon and coal and 'tatur business, them's dodges. Gives a opportoonity of bringing in queer-looking sackfuls o' things, which otherwise would compel the '*spots*'—as we calls the p'lese—to come down on us."

"Compel them!—but surely they come down whenever they've a suspicion?"

"You needn't a' told me he was green," said Mr. Joe to his elder acquaintance, as he glanced at the youth with an air of pity. "In the first place, we takes care to keep the vorkshop almost impregnable; so that, if they attempts a surprise, we has lots o' time to get the things out o' the way. In the next, if it comes to the scratch—which is a matter of almost life and death to us—we stands no nonsense."

Mr. Joe pointed to an iron crowbar, which stood in the chimney-corner.

"I ses nothing to criminate friends, you know," he added significantly to Mr. Bethnal, "but *you* remember wot Sergeant Higsley got?"

Mr. Bethnal nodded assent, and Mr. Joe volunteered for the benefit and instruction of Edward an account of the demise, and funeral of the late Mr. Sergeant Higsley. That official having been promoted, was ambitious of being designated, in the newspapers, "active and intelligent," and gave information against a gang of coiners; "Wot wos the consequence?" continued the narrator. Somehow or another, that p'leseman was never more heered on. One fine night he went on his beat; he didn't show at the next muster; and it was s'posed he'd bolted. Every enquiry was made, and the 'mysterious disappearance of a p'leseman,' got into the noospapers. Howsomnever, *he* never got anywheres."

"And what became of him?"

Mr. Joe then proceeded to take a long puff at his pipe, and winking at his initiated friend, proceeded to narrate how that the injured gang dealt in eggs.

"What has that to do with it?"

"Why you see eggs is not always eggs." Mr. Pouter then went on to state that one night a long deal chest left the premises of the coiners, marked outside, 'eggs,' for exportation. They were duly shipped, a member of the firm being on board. The passage was rough, the box was on deck, and somehow or other somebody tumbled it overboard."

"But what has this to do with the missing policeman?"

"The chest was six feet long, and——."

Here Mr. Bethnal became uneasy.

"Vell," said the host, "the firm's broke up, and is past peaching up, only it shows you my green un what we *can* do."

I was shaken in my master's pocket by the violence of the dread which Mr. Joe's story had occasioned him.

Mr. Bethnal, with the philosophy which was habitual to him, puffed away at his pipe.

"The fact o' the matter is," said Mr. Joe, who was growing garrulous on an obviously pet subject, "that we ain't afeerd o' the p'lese in this neighbourhood, not a hap'orth; *we* know how to manage them." He then related an anecdote of another policeman, who had been formerly in his own line of business. This gentleman being, as he observed, "fly" to all the secret signs of the craft, obtained an interview with a friend of his for the purpose of purchasing a hundred shillings. A packet was produced and exchanged for their proper price in currency, but on the policeman taking his prize to the station house to lay the information, he discovered that he had been outwitted. The rouleau contained a hundred good farthings, for each of which he had paid two pence half-penny.

"Then, what is the bad money generally worth?" asked Edward, interrupting the speaker. "As a general rule," was the answer, "our sort is worth about one-fifth part o' the wallie it represents. So, a sovereign—(though we ain't got much to do with gold here—that's made for the most part in Brummagem)—a 'Brum' Sovereign—may be bought for about four-and-six; a bad crown piece for a good bob; a half-crown for about fippence; a bob for two pence half-penny, and so on. As for the sixpenny's and fourpenny's, we don't make many on 'em, their wallie bein' too insignificant." Mr. Joe then proceeded with some further remarks for the benefit of his protégé;—

"You see you need have no fear o' passing this here money if you 're a respectable looking cove. If a gentleman is discovered at anythink o' the kind, its always laid to a mistake; the shopman knocks under, and the gentleman gives a good piece o' money with a grin. And that's how it is that so much o' our mannyfactur gets smashed all over the country."

The visitors having been somewhat bored, apparently, during the latter portion of their host's remarks, soon after took their departure. The rum-and-water which Mr. Joe's liberality had supplied, effectually removed Edward's scruples; and on his way back, he expressed himself in high terms in favour of "smashing," considered as a profession.

"O' course," was the reply of his experienced companion. "It ain't once in a thousand times that a fellow's nailed. You shall make your first trial to-night. You've the needful in your pocket, hav'n't you? Come, here's a shop—I want a cigar."

Edward appeared to hesitate; but Mr. Joe's rum-and-water asserted itself, and into the shop they both marched.

Mr. Bethnal, with an air of most imposing nonchalance took up a cigar from one of the covered cases on the counter, put it in his mouth, and helped himself to a light. Edward, not so composedly, followed his example.

"How much?"

"Sixpence."

The next instant the youth had drawn *me* from his pocket, received sixpence in change, and walked out of the shop, leaving me under the guardianship of a new master.

I did not remain long with the tobacconist: he passed me next day to a gentleman, who was as innocent as himself as to my real character. It happened that I slipped into the corner of this gentleman's pocket, and remained there for several weeks—he, apparently, unaware of my existence. At length he discovered me, and one day I found myself, in company with a *good* half-crown, exchanged for a pair of gloves at a respectable looking shop. After the purchaser had left, the assistant looked at me suspiciously, and was going to call back my late owner, but it was too late. Taking me then to his master, he asked if I was not bad. "It don't look very good," was the answer. "Give it to me, and take care to be more careful for the future."

"I was slipped into the waistcoat pocket of the proprietor, who immediately seemed to forget all about the occurrence."

That same night, immediately on the shop being closed, the shopkeeper walked out, having changed his elegant costume for garments of a coarser and less conspicuous description, and hailing a cab, requested to be driven to the same street in Westminster in which I first saw the light. To my astonishment, he entered the shop of my first master:—how well I remembered the place, and the coarse countenance of its proprietor! Ascending to the top of the house, we entered the room, to which the reader has been already introduced,—the scene of so much secret toil.

A long conversation, in a very low tone, now took place between the pair, from which I gleaned some interesting particulars. I discovered that the respectable gentleman, who now possessed me, was the coiner's partner,—his being the "issue" department, which his trade transactions, and unimpeachable character, enabled him to undertake very effectively.

"Let your next batch be made as perfectly as possible," I heard him say to his partner. "The last seems to have gone very well: I have heard of only a few detections, and one of those was at my own shop to-day. One of my fellows made the discovery, but not until after the purchaser left the shop."

"That, you see, will 'appen now and then," was the answer; "but think o' the number on 'em as is about, and how sharp some people is getting—thanks to them noospapers, as is always a interfering with wot don't concern 'em. There 's now so much of our metal about, that it 's almost impossible to get change for a suff'rin nowhere without getting some on it. Every body's a-taking of it every day; and as for them that 's detected, they 're made only by the common chaps as ain't got our masheenery,"—and he glanced proudly at his well-mounted galvanic battery. "All I wish is, that we could find some dodge for milling the edges better—it takes as much time now as all the rest of the work put together. Howsomever, I've sold no end on 'em in White-chapel and other places, since I saw you. And as for this here neighbourhood, there 's scarcely a shop where they don't deal in the article more or less."

"Well," said Mr. Niggles (which, I learned from his emblazoned door-posts, was the name of my respectable master), "be as careful about these as you can. I am afraid it 's through some of our money that that young girl has been found out."

"Wot, the young 'ooman as has been remanded so often at the p'lese court?"

"The same. I shall know all about it tomorrow. She is to be tried at the Old Bailey, and I am on the jury as it happens."

Mr. Niggles then departed to his suburban villa, and passed the remainder of the evening as became so respectable a man.

The next morning he was early at business; and, in his capacity of citizen, did not neglect his duties in the court, where he arrived exactly two minutes before any of the other jurymen.

When the prisoner was placed in the dock, I saw at once that she was the sister of my first possessor. She had attempted to pass two bad shillings at a grocer's shop. She had denied all knowledge that the money was bad, but was notwithstanding arrested, examined, and was committed for trial. Here, at the Old Bailey, the case was soon despatched. The evidence was given in breath-less haste; the judge summed up in about six words, and the jury found the girl guilty. Her sentence was, however, a very short imprisonment.

It was my fortune to pass subsequently into the possession of many per-sons, from whom I learnt some particulars of the after-life of this family. The father survived his daughter's conviction only a few days. The son was de-tained in custody; and as soon as his identity became established, charges were brought against him, which led to his being transported. As for his sis-ter—I was once, for a few hours, in a family where there was a governess of her name. I had no opportunity of knowing more; but—as her own nature would probably save her from the influences to which she must have been subjected in jail—it is but just to suppose, that some person might have been found to brave the opinion of society, and to yield to one so gentle, what the law calls "the benefit of a doubt."

The changes which I underwent in the course of a few months were many and various—now rattling carelessly in a cash-box; now loose in the pocket of some careless young fellow, who passed me at a theatre; then, perhaps, tied up carefully in the corner of a handkerchief, having become the sole stock-in-hand of some timid young girl. Once I was given by a father as a "tip" or pres-ent, to his little boy; when, I need scarcely add, that I found myself ignomin-iously spent in hardbake ten minutes afterwards. On another occasion, I was (in company with a sixpence) handed to a poor woman, in payment for the making of a dozen shirts. In this case I was so fortunate as to sustain an entire family, who were on the verge of starvation. Soon afterwards, I formed one of seven, the sole stock of a poor artist, who contrived to live upon my six companions for many days. He had reserved me until the last—I believe because I was the brightest and best-looking of the whole; and when he was at last induced to change me, for some coarse description of food, to his and my horror I was discovered!

The poor fellow was driven from the shop; but the tradesman, I am bound to say, did not treat me with the indignity that I expected. On the contrary, he thought my appearance so deceitful, that he did not scruple to pass me next day, as part of change for a sovereign.

Soon after this, somebody dropped me on the pavement, where, however, I remained but a short time. I was picked up by a child, who ran instinctively into a shop for the purpose of making an investment in figs. But, coins of my class had been plentiful in that neighbourhood, and the grocer was a sagacious man. The result was, that the child went figless away, and that I—my edges curl as I record the humiliating fact—was nailed to the counter as an example to others. Here my career ended and my biography closes.

CHAPTER THREE

MONEY

ROBERT H. PATTERSON
❧❧❧

GOLD AND SOCIAL POLITICS

In the spring of 1854 there was discovered in Australia one of the richest "placers," or gold-beds, even of that most auriferous country. The spot was a deep ravine, formed by the Buckland River, enclosed by steep mountain-sides which excluded every breath of wind. It was autumn in Australia, though spring here. The air in the ravine was stagnant, and the scorching sun made it intensely hot during the day, while at night the temperature fell to a piercing cold; so that the sojourners in the ravine were alternately in an oven and an ice-house. Moreover, as the gold-beds lay in the channel of the river, the miners worked up to their waists in water. To this gold-field of surpassing richness hundreds of adventurers flocked in feverish haste; but disease, like the fabled dragons and griffins of old, kept horrid sentry over the buried treasures. A peculiar fever, of the typhoid character, was the natural denizen of the spot; besides which, the gold-seekers suffered severely from eye-blight, owing to the concentrated blaze of the sunshine reflected from the steep sides of the ravine, and moreover were at all times grievously tormented by clouds of flies. Bad diet and want of vegetables aggravated the diseases natural to the place and to the kind of work; and in the strangely interesting accounts which then reached us, we read of onions selling at six shillings a pound; and cabbages, which we buy here for a penny, were so precious that they were cut up and sold by weight—from half-a-crown to four shillings the pound being readily paid for them. Physic, or what passed for it, rose in price in a still more

Robert H. Patterson, "Gold and Social Politics." *Blackwood's Edinburgh Magazine* 44 (October 1863): 499–520.

startling manner—Holloway's pills selling at one shilling each, or a guinea per box! It was a valley of death. "Constitutions that had borne the hardships of other fields broke down here," wrote an eyewitness of the scene; "and hundreds have perished, dying unattended and unknown. The little levels between the stream and the base of the mountain-wall, for ten miles along the valley, are so thickly studded with graves that the river appears to run through a churchyard." One new-comer, wiser than the rest, having counted eleven corpses carried past his tent during the dinner-hour of his first working day, and thinking that even gold may be purchased too dearly, left the place instantly. Many abandoned it after a somewhat longer trial. But the greater number, fascinated by the unusual richness of the gold-beds, remained in defiance of disease, and "took their chance,"—with what result the numerous graves of the valley testify to this day.

It was a scene "to point a moral or adorn a tale." Had some wandering spirit from another planet looked down upon that valley of death, or upon many other striking incidents of the gold-fever of the last dozen years; if he had seen men in myriads rushing across oceans and continents to the gold-fields of California and Australia, waste places in the uttermost parts of the earth; if he had beheld them toiling in the gulches of the mountains amidst all manner of hardships and disease, beset with extremes of weather, exhausting work, exorbitant prices, and lawless society, he must have said to himself, "Surely mankind have some mighty end in view, when so many myriads come here to toil and suffer with such feverish energy and extraordinary endurance." Yet the yellow substance which these crowds so eagerly seek after, what could it do for them? They could not eat it or drink it,—it was neither food, medicine, nor clothing: it was simply a metal of unusual weight and ductility, and exhibiting a yellow lustre. And were this wandering spirit to show a piece of the yellow metal to one of the natives of the country, and ask its use, the savage would tell him that it served to make rings for wearing in the nose and ears, or on other parts of the body, by way of ornament, but otherwise was of no account,—it could neither head an axe for him nor point a spear. In fine, were this planetary sage, following the track of the gold-ships, to proceed to Europe, and the abodes of civilisation, to see what is made of the metal which men seek for with so great eagerness, he would find that the getting of it is so expensive that (unlike iron and lead) it is of no use in the necessary commodities of life, and only figures as a costly means of ornament and decoration. He would find it, in fact—so far as the arts of life are concerned—closely allied in character to gems and precious stones, the exorbitant prices given for which show how much barbarism still lurks under the cloak of civilisation.

But this inquiring spirit would soon see also another side to the question. Were he to go into our banks, our marketplaces, our counting-houses, he would speedily comprehend the object for which we mortals seek gold, and prize it so much. If he were to visit the great monetary emporium in Thread-needle Street, with its busy throng of customers ceaselessly depositing or withdrawing the yellow metal, and thereafter were to watch for half an hour the gay crowds who go a-shopping in Regent Street, he would see that this metal is the recognised symbol of Property, into which we can convert our wealth, whether it be of land, houses, or merchandise, and store it up in little space, and reconvert it into any kind of property at pleasure. He would see, too, that by common consent nearly one-half of the entire civilised population of the earth take this view of the matter, and have made this yellow metal in-dispensable to them, by decreeing it to be the substance out of which shall be made the counters with which men buy and sell, and reckon up the gains of material existence. But what of the other half of the civilised world? Here the doubts of our planetary sage would begin anew: for he would see that this en-throning of gold as a special and almost sacred metal is, after all, a purely ar-bitrary proceeding, and that civilised mankind are divided on this question into two rival and hostile camps. Six hundred millions of the human race (constituting fully two-thirds of the civilised population of the globe), in China, India, and Japan, and in Asia generally, repudiate the peculiar value at-tached to the yellow metal by their Western brethren, and exalt a shining white metal into a like conventional importance. If gold reigns in the West, silver rules in the East. And what of that outer world, those regions beyond the pale of civilisation which still occupy so large a portion of the earth's surface? There, among the uncivilised races of the world—in Africa, in parts of Amer-ica, and among the multitudinous islands of the Pacific—we find that the counters in which men condense their gains and carry on the commerce of life are little shells picked up on the sea-shore; or else, that counters are dispensed with altogether, and trade is managed by simple barter.

Barter is the fundamental basis of commercial transactions; bullion is an accessory—most convenient, but very costly. In countries which have not the advantage of wealth and civilisation, an ox is bartered for so many sheep, a gun for so many skins of the beaver or tusks of the elephant, &c. But, among wealthy and civilised nations, the consumers have so many and such various wants, and, owing to the division of labour, each worker produces so little that is of use to himself, that simple barter becomes too cumbrous a process in wholesale transactions, and utterly impracticable in shopping, and other forms of retail business. Civilisation, therefore, has to pay for the infinite lux-uries of life and subdivision of labour, which are its boast and enjoyment, by introducing a class of objects—counters or "currency"—the only use of which is to facilitate the exchange of commodities in buying and selling; and, secondarily, by representing value in little bulk, to admit of the gains of life being reckoned and possessed in less cumbrous form than houses and land, herds of cattle, or ships and merchandise. It is a form of wealth established for the purpose of representing all the other forms; and which, intrinsically worthless of itself, derives its value from the other kinds of property of which it is the acknowledged representative. Gold and silver are the articles which civilised mankind have chosen as the prime materials out of which these counters of commerce and of life's gains shall be made. And in order to procure the material for these counters, hundreds of thousands of human beings proceed to the uttermost parts of the earth, encamp in the wilderness, and suffer in an aggravated form hardships, privations, and death,—toiling, as in that valley of the Buckland River, in pursuit of the yellow dross in which civilised man insists upon counting up his gains. The cost of their conveyance to the distant gold countries, the cost of their living in a region where everything is very dear, owing to the distance from which it must be brought, and the extra profit which is needed before men will go so far and suffer so much—these constitute the price which civilisation pays for its money-counters. It is a heavy price: and each ounce of gold represents so much labour withdrawn from agriculture and other industrial pursuits, which minister directly to the necessities and comforts of mankind.

The European nations are in the van of the world—they are the chiefs of civilisation; and if grand old Milton in his day spoke disdainfully of the pomp which delights in "*barbaric* pearl and gold," regarding it as a foible of the East, it is not to be thought that any sensible man of our day will ascribe the great value of gold to its mere attractiveness as an ornament. Doubtless it was its fitness for ornamentation which first, in the world's infancy, led men to attach value to gold. But this cause of the value of gold has long ago become quite subsidiary; indeed, it now only maintains itself in consequence of the metal having acquired a new and greater value from an entirely different source. To have imparted a conventional value to an article for the sake of making it a medium of exchange, would have been very difficult in early times (though it was accomplished at Carthage), and quite impossible beyond the limits of a single community. Instinctively, therefore, and doubtless unconsciously, Civilisation availed itself of the high value which earlier times had attached to gold as an ornament, as a basis for giving to that metal an equal value of a civilised and really useful kind. Civilisation found that gold, from its wide acceptance or negotiability, its scarcity, portability, and divisibility, would make an excellent material for supplying counters for trade; and these counters, of course, became thereafter condensed wealth—a convenient form in which wealth might be stored. The great value, therefore, now ascribed to gold, and which makes men seek for it all over the world, arises from the fact that it constitutes Money. But what is Money? What is the characteristic of this something which imparts a peculiar value to gold, and which disperses civilised mankind into the wildernesses of the world to search for the yellow metal? Every one knows that money is a good thing to have, and that there is no doing without it,—that it is used in buying and selling,—that men get it by giving in exchange for it labour or goods, and in exchange for it supply themselves with the comforts or luxuries of life. But what constitutes Money? Is money, like the pearl and the diamond, and some other prized articles, a thing which man must necessarily take from the hand of Nature? Or can he not make it for himself? And if so, what conditions are necessary for its production and circulation? Of what substances can money be made? and how do these substances come to be recognised as symbols of value?

The currency of the world includes many kinds of money. Gold, silver, copper, iron, in coins or by weight—stamped leather, stamped paper, wooden tallies—shells of various kinds—pieces of silk, or strips of cotton-cloth, of a fixed size and quality—are, or have been, all in use among mankind as forms of currency, as convenient and negotiable forms or representatives of property. Many of these kinds of money are simultaneously in use in the same country. Gold, silver, copper, and stamped paper coexist as different forms of money in the currency of Europe and America; gold, silver, copper, and shells in India; silver, copper, and pieces of silk in China; copper, cotton-strips, shells, and the silver dollar in various parts of Africa. Sparta had a currency of iron,— Carthage of stamped leather, like our paper money,—China, under the dynasty of Kublai Khan, of paper money and stamped leather together.[1] There is ample variety in the substances out of which money is made,—metals, shells, cloth, leather, paper; and, moreover, every country shapes these substances, or such of them as it uses, in a different form from the others. What, then, is Money? We need not seek a definition in the intrinsic qualities of the substances out of which money is made; for there is not a single intrinsic quality which is common to them all. The generic quality which constitutes money is manifestly something extrinsic to these substances—some quality superimposed upon or attributed to them, or at least to the shape which they assume as currency.

If English merchants send out sovereigns to China, the Chinese will not receive these coins as money—nor any other kind of gold coins. Gold is not money in the Celestial Empire: one-third of the human race (nearly one-half of the civilised population of the globe) there refuse to accept the yellow metal as currency. In like manner, if the Chinese or Hindoo merchant were to send payment of a large sum in his silver coins to this country, it would be ex-

---

1. Sir John Maundeville, speaking of the Emperor of China in the fourteenth century, says:— "This Emperour makethe no money but of lether emprented, or of papyre. And of that money is som of gretter prys, and som of lesse prys, aftre the diversitie of his statutes. And whan that money hathe ronne so longe that it begynnethe to waste, than men beren it to the Emperoures tresorye, and than thei taken newe money for the old. And that money gothe thorghe out all the contree, and thorghe out all his provynces. For there and beyond hem, thei make no money nouther of gold nor of sylver."—*Travels of Sir John Maundeville* (edit. 1839), p. 239.

tremely embarrassing to the English merchant. Even if a man in this country seek to discharge a debt in our own silver coins, the creditor is entitled to refuse payment in such a form. Silver is not money—is not a legal tender—in this country, save to the extent of forty shillings. Above that amount, it is simply bullion: it is no more money than brass or tin or platinum is. Again, we laugh when a semicivilised people propose to pay us for our manufactures in sea-shells, or some other form of non-metallic currency; but we find some of those people not less averse to receive our gold and silver coins which we regard as the perfection of currency. Barbarous tribes, again, will sell to us their produce for coloured glass beads and suchlike valueless trinkets, in preference to money or other articles which in our estimation are infinitely more valuable. We see, then, that the substances which some nations, even though civilised, regard as the best, if not as the only standard form of money, other nations refuse to acknowledge or accept as money at all. Moreover, even when different nations use the same substance as money, it sometimes happens that they differ widely in the relative value which they attach to these substances.

A few years ago, when the trade with Japan was opened by Lord Elgin's mission, our merchants were surprised to find that the Japanese appraised gold and silver very differently from us; so that a sovereign, a napoleon, or any other piece of gold, whether in coin or as bullion, was esteemed by the Japanese equal to only about one-fourth of the quantity of silver which the same amount of gold represents in Europe. A not less curious monetary fact may be cited from China. Half-a-dozen kinds of silver coin are current at Shanghai—five kinds of the dollar and the Indian rupee; but a few years ago only one of these coins, the old Spanish Carolus dollar, was a legal tender. In consequence of this, although the intrinsic value of all the dollars was nearly alike, the old Carolus dollar (which is becoming scarce) was worth 7s., whereas the others were barely worth 5s. A difference of 40 per cent! The only reason for the preference was, that the Carolus dollar was the one which was best known to the Chinese merchants, and in which, accordingly, they had most confidence. This state of matters was remedied in the autumn of 1855, when, after duly assaying the different coins, the Chinese Superintendent of Customs published a proclamation informing the people of the true state of the case, and ordering that after a certain date all the six different coins should pass current, according to their respective intrinsic values, which he announced.

Such are some of the differences of value, and limitations of circulation, which Opinion, or Law as the expression of Opinion, imposes upon the various forms of money. But the case is wider than this. The States of Europe have in some respects almost become a common-wealth, but the currency of one state will not circulate in another. The English sovereign, indeed, is readily taken in payment in some parts of the Continent; but even it does not *circu-*

late—no more than napoleons will circulate in England. They are strange to the people, who are suspicious of them, and (as foreign coins are never a legal tender in any country) refuse to receive them as money. Still more so is this the case with paper money. Although the coins of one country will not circulate in another, gold and silver are recognised as the raw material of money all over Europe and America, and are valued accordingly; but paper money, out of its own country, may be said to carry no value at all. Bank of England notes, indeed, which have the same prestige over other kinds of paper money which the sovereign has over other coins, may be cashed without difficulty in Paris, and at no greater charge than is made for converting sovereigns or half-crowns into French money. Convince a Continental money-changer that the English bank-note is genuine, and he will give you cash for it as readily as for our metallic money: although, of course, there is this difference, that coins can be tested anywhere, whereas bank-notes cannot, and in foreign countries can only be received as genuine out of confidence in the person who presents or endorses them. But even in the same country there is often a limitation to the circulation of some kinds of money. The sovereign—though a legal tender, and (save in some sequestered parts of the Highlands) readily accepted when offered in payment—hardly circulates in Scotland,—the Scotch preferring paper money, as the best known to them, as in their opinion the more safe and convenient form of currency, and also as the cheapest. Scotch bank-notes, again, are not a legal tender in the other parts of the kingdom. In England, too, there are many provincial banks the notes of each of which circulate readily in the district where the issuing bank is situated, but are looked upon with suspicion elsewhere: they will not circulate widely, simply because they are a kind of money with which the public at large are not familiar, and in which, accordingly, they have not confidence.

Of all forms of money silver is the most widely recognised, and, therefore, holds the first place in the currency of the world. It is the standard money of China, with a population of 400,000,000, and of India, with a population of 160,000,000. It is also recognised as money all over Europe and America,—indeed, silver still constitutes the greater portion of the currency of the Continent; and in the outlying and half-barbarous parts of the world silver will be accepted where gold coins would be refused. Gold at present holds the second place in the currency of the world. But unless new silver-mines are found, the recent discovery of the gold deposits in California and Australia will, by making gold more abundant and more cheap, tend to wrest the supremacy from silver and give it to gold,—by inducing the European and American States to make all the necessary additions to the metallic portion of their currency in the latter metal. Next in amount of circulation to gold and silver money comes paper money. In this country, the paper money issued under legal restrictions by the banks amounts to about £40,000,000 sterling (the gold and silver money, whether in circulation or kept in reserve by the banks, amounting probably to more than twice as much). In France, although banking is much less developed than in this country, the amount of paper money is nearly as great as it is here. In Russia and Austria it is also very large—not owing to banking, which in both countries is still in its infancy, but owing to an actual dearth of the precious metals. Paper money has the widest range in value of all kinds of money. It is also the cheapest and most portable. You could carry twenty or thirty £1000 Bank of England notes in your waistcoat pocket; whereas it would take a couple of the strongest porters to carry the same amount in gold for a hundred yards. At the same time, as has been seen in Russia and Austria, you may have paper notes in circulation of as small amount as the smallest silver coin. The gamut of paper money, if we may so speak, goes far higher than that of gold money, and ranges down to the lowest reach of silver money. In fact, in the form of bills of exchange—which, however, are not a legal tender, and, therefore, not money in the strict sense of the word—paper money plays the most important part of all in carrying on the trade and commerce of the world. It may also be used as a substitute for all the other kinds of money—if under proper restrictions, with perfect safety and great economy. And in modern times it has always been had recourse to, with more or less prudence and advantage, by nations who in exceptional times find themselves in a temporary deficiency of metallic money.

Coming back, then, to our starting-point, "What is Money?" let us observe what is the one quality which all these kinds of money have in common, and which suffices to exalt each of them into a more or less widely recognised representative of wealth. Between gold, cowrie-shells, and paper, there is not a single point of resemblance. But the quality which gives to these and other substances their circulating power as money is one and the same: it is simply the agreement on the part of nations, or parts of nations, to recognise those substances, either of themselves or when presented in certain forms, as representatives of wealth. It is an agreement on the part of communities, or of large sections of the population of the globe, to regard these substances or articles as a medium in which wealth can be condensed, and to make of them counters with which the game of life may be carried on, and property be transmuted at pleasure from one form into any other. The quality which constitutes currency, therefore, is extrinsic to the material of which currency is made, and becomes imparted to any articles which a nation or nations may agree to recognise as tokens of value.

That paper notes or stamped leather possess no intrinsic value will be at once admitted; but, almost universally, it will be asserted that gold is money entirely because of its intrinsic value. Now—passing over the important fact that one-half of the civilised population of the globe do not attach to gold the value which we do—let us ask, How does gold acquire the peculiar value which we attach to it? It will be answered, "Owing to the great amount of labour required for its production." But how is it that so costly an amount of labour is devoted to its production? An article may be rare, yet valueless: it must be *scarce* before it becomes valuable. There are many things as difficult to find or produce as gold, which nevertheless are but little sought for, because for the finding or production of them no one will give sufficiently high wages. Before a thing can become valuable, there must not only be a difficulty in its production, but a great demand for it: because, unless there be a great demand for it, the price offered for it will be inadequate to induce men to encounter the difficulties or undergo the hardships inseparable from its production. What, then, causes the great demand for gold? *Because one-half the world requires it for currency.* And thus the circle of reasoning comes back to our starting position, that the peculiar value of gold arises from its having been so widely adopted as Money. Demonetise gold, and what would follow? Probably three-fourths of all the gold in use among mankind is employed as money; and if the Western world were, for the sake of uniformity, to adopt the currency of the East, and resolve that gold should not be received as money any longer, would not the value of gold fall immensely? The moment the news reached California and Australia, would not the mines be abandoned, and the workers betake themselves to other occupations,—feeling of a surety that, now gold was demonetised, the world had already more than enough of the yellow dross, and that henceforth no man would give a dollar for a whole ounce of it. Silver would be immensely increased in value, and gold would descend from its high estate to the rank of an ordinary metal. Thenceforth gold would only be used for ornaments, plate, and gilding—if, indeed, the comparative abundance of the metal for these purposes, owing to its demonetisation, would not make it too common to be a fitting ornament of the wealthy. It is the value, not the beauty, of the yellow metal that makes it so much prized nowadays in ornaments. It is not merely as barbaric toys and gewgaws that people wear it in chains and rings and other personal ornaments, and load their tables with it as plate; but because it is condensed wealth. It is the display of wealth which constitutes the chief charm of golden plate and ornaments; and if gold were no longer to be condensed wealth, but simply a metal like the others, we might safely reckon that its dethronement as money would tend rather to diminish than to increase the demand for it as an ornamental luxury.

Money is the expression of wealth—the voucher of accumulated gains—a "universal language" of property all over the civilised world. It is an *Open Sesame* which everywhere admits us into the enjoyment of other men's goods or labour. Unlike houses or horses or hounds, or food and clothing, or works of art, or articles of merchandise, money is of no use in itself—only as a means of getting other things. To borrow the language of the schoolmen, the value of money is *in posse*—that of other articles *in esse:* the one is merely potential, the other is essential. Money is a useless thing for ever doing useful things—a valueless thing for ever purchasing things of value. Like the electric fluid, money is undynamic when at rest: it is only when in motion, passing in purchase from one owner to another, that its great power is manifested. But that power, we repeat, is merely imputed to it, in order to facilitate the business of life: and if all the world could act together as easily as a single community can do, we might say of every form of money, "A breath can make it, as a breath has made." All the various forms of currency depend for their peculiar value simply upon Opinion, or conventional agreement; and their value is (chiefly in some cases, entirely in others) extrinsic, not intrinsic—a something imparted to them by the consent of the people among whom they circulate. In short, currency of every kind is essentially dependent upon credit—using that word in its amplest sense. Negotiability is the grand point—and that depends upon agreement. Accordingly, the more widely the credit of any coin or note is recognised, the more extensive will be its circulation, the greater its acceptability, and the higher its rank as a form of money.

These considerations, of course, render it doubtful whether mankind are right in the value which they continue to attach to gold as the prime form of money. We shall leave Posterity, with its superior advantages, to answer that question: content to believe that, in the actual circumstances of the world, the monetary system which has been established could not have been very different from that which exists. High as is the price which civilisation pays for the convenience of money, the investment, on the whole, has been a good and profitable one. The invention of money lies at the base of all material civilisation. Division of labour is the grand characteristic of material civilisation; but there could not be any great subdivision of labour without money. Before the industrial classes of a community will devote themselves each to a separate pursuit, a means must have been found by which the produce of each is made readily exchangeable for the goods of any of the others. Money does this. A man who has only an ox to barter, will find it difficult to supply his wants. He will find it difficult to apportion it correctly among his various tradespeople—grocer, baker, tailor, shoemaker, landlord, &c.—even supposing that all these dealers need beef at once. But let him first convert the ox into money, and thereafter he can purchase all that he wants with rapidity and ease. Money is a reservoir of power, immediately available, and for any purpose. It is wealth condensed and mobilised. Its effective force is as much superior to an equal amount of property in other forms, as a mobilised and concentrated army is to an equally numerous crowd of common men. If there were no money—no conventional means of storing up accumulated gains in an instantaneously negotiable form—how long would be the time, and how cumbrous the preparations, requisite to prepare an expedition, to get up a railway company, or to accomplish any great project? What would require the co-operation of thousands, and consequently great preliminary delay, in times of pure barter, can with money be accomplished at once. Secure the aid of a single great capitalist, and forthwith the streams of power flow in all directions simultaneously, each becoming transmuted into different objects—labour, stores, implements, raw material, or directing genius. The conversion of power is direct and instantaneous. By means of money, human power can strike its *coups* on the instant. Prove an object desirable, an enterprise profitable, and the man who holds his property in the form of money can accomplish the object or engage in the enterprise with the speed of the telegraph.

But the world-wide results of the invention of money in facilitating all the branches of human industry, and promoting friendly intercommunication between different nations and countries, will best appear in the next stage of our inquiry, which relates to the effects of the recent gold-discoveries on the world at large.

The first phenomenon attendant upon the gold-discoveries has been the great Emigration—the transfer of large masses of population from their old seats to new ones,—the vast and sudden spread of civilised mankind over the earth, making deserts and waste places to bloom, cities to rise amid the solitude, and seas, whose virgin waters had hardly been stirred by a single prow, to grow white with the sails of golden argosies. The regions where these gold-beds have been found were in the utmost ends of the earth—regions the most secluded, the most isolated from the seats of civilisation. California and the adjoining auriferous provinces of the Pacific, are separated from eastern America by an almost impassable and then unexplored chain of mountains and expanse of desert plains; yet no sooner was gold found in the Sacramento river than immigrants came pouring over the passes of the Rocky Mountains, voyaging in tedious and perilous course round Cape Horn, and rushing in such numbers across the Isthmus of Darien as to convert that neck of the New World into a highway between the two great oceans of the world. Australia was, if possible, a still more isolated quarter of the globe; and, if no new attraction had come into play, it would have remained for generations a slow-moving cityless country of pastoral settlers. But the attraction of gold has rapidly changed the scene, and opened a brilliant future for that vast island-continent, of whose glories we only see the beginning. Already the European race is making a new world for itself at the Antipodes. Nor do the triumphs of gold, as an agent affecting the destinies of the world, stop here. Hardly noticed as yet, but certain to attract another rush of emigration before long, is the auriferious region of Siberia, which Humboldt affirmed to stretch right across northern Asia, from the Ural Mountains to Kamtschatka and the bleak solitudes of "Oonalaska's shore." Here again is one of the vast solitudes of the earth; yet, ere many years have passed, we shall see the wizard Gold drawing all men after him, peopling with civilised men the heart of Upper Asia—establishing cities and peaceful communities where once roamed the ruthless cavalry of the Golden Horde—and bringing back mankind, after long and devious wanderings, to settle in maturity in the region that was the cradle of our race. The corresponding region of the New World—the American Siberia— the desolate zone which intervenes like an unbridged chasm between Canada and British Columbia, already begins to be affected from a similar cause; and the reported discovery of gold on the eastern side of the Rocky Mountains, on the head-waters of the Saskatchewan river, will mightily contribute to people that solitude also, and to extend British settlements in unbroken line from the Atlantic to the Pacific. Lastly, but not less surely, the passion for gold will, at no distant time, carry bands of adventurers into the heart of Africa, that greatest waste place of the earth. If famous in old times as "the fierce mother of lions," Africa was not less famous as a gold-country; and we believe that the *auri sacra fames* will be the first agency that will give a great impulse to the invasion of that continent by the European race, and lead bands of daring adventurers up the watery highways of the Nile and the Niger to search the gold-beds of the interior, and pitch their tents beneath the shadowless Mountains of the Moon.

Such is the mighty influence which gold is exerting upon the condition of the earth. Let us now mark the chain of effects, and the nature of those effects, which the gold-discoveries are producing upon the condition of mankind. The demand for gold, as the prime material of money, is so great that the wages of the gold-diggers in California and Australia are, on the average, four times greater than the class of skilled workmen can make at home. In consequence they spend four times as much. In other words, for every £1 of goods which they consumed at home, they now consume £4. Their consuming power has been quadrupled, and the result is, that they give four times as much employment to other men. Hence, not only are these emigrants benefited by the gold-diggings, but the population which they have left at home is likewise benefited. Not only is the labour-market at home thinned, but there is more employment than before. The profits of the gold-diggers keep more ships on the sea, and give more employment to the producers alike of the luxuries and of the necessaries of life. Nor is this all. For not only is a new and lucrative trade created between the gold-countries and the old seats of civilisation, but commerce in all directions obtains a mighty impulse, increasing the area of Employment and the comforts of mankind all over the world.

These are happy effects of the gold-discoveries. And they are political as well as social. When nations are prosperous, they are contented. Suffering is the great parent of revolution. We believe that never yet was a country convulsed by political revolution, save where the outbreak had been preceded by a period of general distress. The distress, so widespread and apparently mysterious, which overspread our own country for twenty years before the passing of the Reform Bill,[2] as well as for several years afterwards, was the agency which gave to that long crisis its exasperation and serious political perils; and (if this were the place for such a discussion) it could be shown that the most potent cause of that widespread distress was the continuously increasing scarcity of the precious metals, in consequence of the great decrease in the produce of the American mines. Now, happily, the position is reversed. Gold is abundant, wages are rising, employment has increased, and the people are contented. Nor is this benefit confined to our own country. All Europe feels the happy change, and especially France and Germany. Look at the state of Europe in 1820, 1830, and 1848, and in a lesser degree in the intervals of troubled peace which lay between those crises of discontent; and say whether the last ten years, in regard to political contentment, do not appear to belong to a wholly different epoch. The old seats of civilisation, which appeared to be sinking under the weight of over-population, were suddenly thinned of their swarms; room was made for a new growth of population, and that new increase is growing up under circumstances of unexampled prosperity. France under a military despotism has benefited in this respect (considering the lesser action of the gold-discoveries upon her) as much as England under freedom and free-trade. Let neither Government boast itself overmuch, and attribute to mere legislative measures a happy result, in which future ages will see clearly the merciful hand of overruling Providence. We are proud of our country and of our statesmen and of our Queen; but for the height of this great blessing let us give God the glory.

The remarkable increase which has of late years taken place in the commerce of the world is generally attributed to the adoption of the principles of free-trade in this country, and to the relaxation of tariffs which is now taking place abroad. Unquestionably there is truth in this view; but it is far from being the whole truth. Every great movement of mankind is due to a concurrence of influences, rather than to a single one. Whatever may have been the initial cause of the great increase of international trade during the last fifteen years (during which time our export-trade has *more than doubled*), it is important to observe that the commencement of the increase was contemporaneous with the discovery of the Californian gold-mines. That discovery at once, and even before its material effects began to operate, gave a moral impulse, an impulse of excitement and hope, to the trading world. And it is very evident that the great expansion of trade which has since occurred could not

---

2. The Reform Bill was passed into law in June 1832. It made the property qualifications of borough voters uniform throughout England and, in the process, disenfranchised dozens of small boroughs. It did not confer universal male suffrage, as working-class radicals wanted. [Ed.]

possibly have taken place if the new gold-mines had not been discovered. The most prominent feature of that expansion has been the increased trade between Europe and America on the one hand, and the East on the other. That trade has in all ages been a peculiar one. The constant absorption of the precious metals by the East has attracted attention, and given rise to much speculation, for at least a century and a half. The explanation is, that India and China have hitherto been non-importing countries. And to this day the exports from these countries are largely in excess of their imports. We yearly consume a large portion of their produce, while they take comparatively little of our goods. Such a trade can only be carried on when Europe possesses an abundant supply of the precious metals; and it could never have been carried on to the extent which we have witnessed of late years, if the new gold-mines had not rendered the precious metals in Europe not only abundant, but superabundant. In 1851, after free-trade had been for several years established in this country, and when the produce of the Californian gold-mines had just begun to operate, the exports of silver to the East from Great Britain and the Mediterranean ports only amounted to £1,716,000. But from that time our trade with the East increased rapidly, and the balance against us, which had to be paid in the precious metals, underwent a corresponding increase. So much so, that in the twelve years which have since elapsed, the balance of trade which we have paid to the East in the precious metals has amounted to about £120,000,000, showing an average of £10,000,000 a-year.[3] But for the new gold-mines such payments on our part would have been impossible; yet without such payments the trade could not have been carried on. Before the gold-discoveries came to our aid, to have attempted to export even half the present average amount of bullion to the East would have so tightened the money market (in other words, would have so reduced the amount of loanable money) as speedily to stop the trade. The rate of discount would have risen to such a height as to leave no adequate margin of profits on the articles exported: indeed we should have been fortunate if our whole trade had not been involved in the calamities of a monetary crisis. In present circumstances, on the contrary, this drain of bullion is of itself an advantage, and our increase of trade with the East, while adding to our wealth, is relieving Europe of a portion of the precious metals of which we have no need, and which it is advantageous to get rid of. Had all this bullion remained in Europe, the value of gold would have already fallen greatly; in consequence, the mines would be less

---

3. This year (owing partly to the cotton crisis), our trade with the East is assuming gigantic proportions. Our imports, during the first six months of 1863, from the East (including £8,000,000 from Egypt, but exclusive of Australia and the Mauritius) amount to upwards of £35,000,000, or more than a third of our whole imports during the six months, which amount to within a fraction of £100,000,000.

resorted to, emigration would be already declining, the expansion of commerce and increase of employment would be checked, and the prosperity of the Golden Age—instead of continuing, as we trust, for several generations—would be all over in a few years. The prosperity of the world depends upon the continuance of this drain of bullion to the East. Without it, the effect of the gold-discoveries would be but local and evanescent; with it, the whole world will be partakers of the blessing,—the Golden Age may last for a hundred years,—and, as the result of the ever-widening commerce, all nations both of East and West will be drawn together in bonds of mutual interest and sympathy, which will remain as a happy legacy after the Angel of Gold has again disappeared from the scene.

Such are the effects upon the world at large which the new gold-mines are producing, and are calculated to produce. They constitute the most powerful lever by the action of which the world can be moved, human progress hastened, and human prosperity increased. Let us now consider these gold-discoveries in another and narrower aspect. Let us ask, as a question of purely monetary science, what good do we derive from the new mines? It is obvious that an addition to the currency of a country is not necessarily a benefit. If the country be already adequately supplied with money, every addition is a positive loss. If the currency of a country be increased from £50,000,000 to £100,000,000, while the productions of that country and the demand for money remain as they were, the hundred millions will do no more than the fifty millions,—only, all prices, wages, rents, &c., will be doubled in amount. The prices which a farmer or manufacturer gets for his goods will be increased, but so also, and in similar proportion, will be the amount of his outlay in rents and taxes, &c. It is like adding equally to both sides of an equation. It would be a sheer waste of money. The labour which produced these extra fifty millions would be as much lost as if that amount of gold had been sunk in the sea. A case like this, however, never occurs in the actual world. It would only be possible if the country in question were absolutely isolated from the rest of the world,—and hardly even then: for the mere influx of increased supplies of gold is found to give an impulse of hopefulness and energy which of itself tends to create more trade, and consequently more need for money.

Any sudden derangement of prices, whether caused by a rise or by a fall in the value of the precious metals, is bad; for it involves a transference of wealth from one section of the community to another, without any fault on the one side or merit on the other. A farmer, for example, who has taken his farm on a twenty years' lease, at a time when the ordinary price of wheat is 60s. a quarter, would lose greatly if prices (owing to a change in the value of money) were suddenly to fall to 40s., and would gain greatly if they were to rise to 80s.; while the landlord would equally gain in the first event, and lose in the second. True, there would be no loss to the community at large; what one man lost another would gain: but it would be a taking from those who rightfully had, and giving to those who had no claim to get. Moreover, it generally happens (on the principle of "lightly come, lightly go") that those who get money in such a way squander it, or at least do not turn it to such good account as those to whom it belonged. So far as experience goes, however, it is doubtful whether any great change of value ever can take place suddenly. We think it cannot. It is as gradual operations that these alterations in the value of money fall to be regarded and discussed; and this limitation at once strips such movements of their necessarily injurious character. Nevertheless, at all times such movements exercise a mighty influence upon the fortunes of States, or of mankind at large; and their social effects vary immensely according as they are produced by a rise in the value of the precious metals, or by a fall.

During the last eighteen hundred years we have had experience of monetary changes of both kinds. For fifteen centuries after the Christian era, the precious metals became gradually more scarce; chiefly, doubtless, owing to the widening area of civilisation, and the consequent increase of trade. In the sixteenth century, a mighty change took place, owing to the enormous amount of the precious metals obtained by ruthless conquest in the New World, and by the discovery and working of the gold and silver mines in Peru and Mexico. Ere long, however, as population and trade increased, the opposite tendency again commenced; money gradually became scarce, and, despite the alleviation caused by the invention of banking and paper money, "hard times" set in, and were felt with especial intensity in the period between 1810 and 1840, after which latter year the produce of the Ural mines began to compensate in some degree the almost total stoppage of the working of the American mines. Once more a change has taken place, and the discovery of the rich mines of California, Columbia, and Australia has commenced a period when money will again become not only plentiful but redundant. It is important to note the social effects which take place during these different epochs.

In times like the present, when the value of the precious metals is falling, the effect of the change is to benefit the many at the expense of the few. Mortgages and all money-contracts which extend over a long period, are lessened in value; for in the course of twenty years, £1000 becomes worth no more than (say) £800 was at first. Such creditors, who are necessarily capitalists or wealthy men, lose, and their debtors gain. But it is on the Government expenditure of a country that the change is most felt. The pressure of the Government debt is lightened, and the taxation necessary to provide for it is virtually reduced. The same amount of taxation, indeed, may be raised, but that amount represents a much smaller value than before, and accordingly is less felt by the people. It is also to be remembered that a large portion of the Government expenditure in all countries, including Government salaries of all kinds, are fixed payments—money contracts which extend over a long period; and as these decline in value, the national burdens are lightened in this way also. Trade likewise increases, with the increased facilities for carrying it on which an abundance of the precious metals affords; and with more trade there is more employment, and consequently increased prosperity among the working classes. On the other hand, in periods when the precious metals are becoming scarce—in other words, when the value of money is rising—the opposite of all this takes place. Mortgages, long leaseholds, and money-contracts of all kinds, weigh more heavily upon those whom they affect; and the pressure of taxation—though no more taxes be raised than before—is seriously augmented. It was this pressure of Government taxation which wrought such havoc in Italy and some other provinces of the Roman empire under some of the emperors. The value of money was rising, yet the Imperial expenditure could not be reduced so as to comport with the altered state of affairs; and towns and provinces were called upon to pay their old amount of taxation, although the value of that amount had largely increased. Under the pressure of this taxation whole districts became depopulated, and large masses of the population became pauperised. Periods when the precious metals are becoming scarce are always times of more or less national distress and discontent. In modern times, when the people take part in the government, political discontent arises, and a cry is raised for retrenchment and reform. This was notably the case in our own country in the period between 1810 and 1830, though the cause was never suspected. Had the real source of the national distress been perceived, there would doubtless have been more moderation and discretion on the part of the people, and the crisis would certainly have been met by wiser measures on the part of the Government.

Now, the first effect of the recent gold-discoveries was to save us, and Europe at large, from the hard times which had been in operation, and which, but for these discoveries, must have gone on increasing in severity. Although the produce of the Ural mines, discovered in 1830, tended to check the increasing rise in the value of money, its counteracting effects would soon have wholly disappeared under the steady increase of population and trade. The recent enormous expansion of trade, indeed (as we have shown), could never have taken place at all, if no new mines had come into play; but even the ordinary increase of population and trade would soon have made money so scarce as to land the working-classes in this country, as well as in the States of the Continent, in no little distress, productive, it is to be feared, of great political discontent.

This has been the negative advantage of the new gold-discoveries upon the social condition of Europe. Their positive effects are not fully developed, but we already see enough of them to be able to appreciate their general character. By giving us an abundance of the precious metals wherewith to trade with those countries which will not accept payment for their goods in ours, the new gold-mines have given an immense facility to commerce, and consequently greatly increased the production of all articles suited for the foreign markets. And more commerce means more employment, more profits, more comfort. The trade with India and China is the one which has most benefited by this new facility; but even in our trade with the countries of Europe, the new gold-supplies have been of great advantage. The balance of trade between one country and another has always to be paid in the precious metals; and when these metals are scarce, every nation has to be careful lest the balance against it should necessitate a greater export of the precious metals than is compatible with its own monetary wants. For, as bitter experience has proved, even a temporary drain of the precious metals—a few months' absence of a few millions of gold—is sufficient to derange our whole currency, and to produce a diminution of credit, which causes a commercial crisis and paralysis of trade. So far, then, from thinking with M. Chevalier and Mr Cobden[4] that the new gold-supplies will render commercial crises more frequent than before, we hold the very opposite opinion.

These benefits—alike the negative and the positive—arising from the gold-discoveries, are so manifest that no reasonable man can call them in question. It is considered doubtful, however, whether the new gold-supplies have as yet produced any alteration in the value of money, as indicated by a rise of prices. For our own part, we entertain no doubt that this change of value, though slight, is perceptible, and that the effects consequent upon such a change are already coming into play. Manufactures vary so much in the quantity produced, and in the cost of production, that the prices at which they sell constitute no sure basis for determining whether or not there has been a change in the value of money. The new materials of manufactures, and the staple articles of food, which cannot be so easily multiplied, will show it much sooner. But land, which is a fixed quantity, is always the first commodity to be affected by a change in the value of money; and although rent (owing to the normal increase of population and wealth) always tends to rise in an old and prosperous country like England, still the rise of rents in this country has recently been so great, rents (both of farms and of house-property) have taken so rapid a spring upwards, as cannot be adequately accounted for except on the supposition that money has sensibly fallen in value. It is in the great seats of industry and wealth—London, Paris, Glasgow, Liverpool, New York—that a rise of prices most quickly shows itself; but in these times of railway communication, the change soon extends to all parts of the country. Whether the value of money has been depreciated to the extent of 10 per cent, as Mr.

4. Richard Cobden (1804–65) was a Manchester industrialist who helped organize the Anti-Corn Law League to lobby for repeal of grain tariffs. [Ed.]

Jevons[5] maintains, we cannot assert with much confidence in the correctness of our opinion.[6] But a change is perceptibly taking place; and it is all the better for us that the change is slow and gradual. At present we are experiencing all the advantages of an increase of the precious metals, with a minimum of disadvantages—in fact, with no perceptible drawback at all. In the fullest sense of the word we may be said to be *enjoying* a rise of prices: the rise is so gentle, and the benefits of the new gold-supplies so widespread and substantial.

Hitherto, at least, our fears have been disappointed, and our best hopes more than realised. A sudden change, even in a good direction, is an evil in monetary affairs. And such a change was fully expected and predicted by some of the best authorities in those matters. The circumstance which has falsified these predictions is of itself one of the happiest features of the times. The great increase of commerce which has taken place was not foreseen, nor its consequences calculated; yet it is to that increase that we owe our escape from a sudden change in the value of money. That increase has not only created more employment for money in Europe, but it has drained off the surplus of precious metals in payment of the large trade-balances which necessarily accumulate against us in the course of an extended commerce with the East. These trade-balances could not, it is true, be paid in gold—what the East wants, and will alone accept, is silver: but silver in sufficient amount was easily procured in Europe—especially from the currency of France, and its place was supplied by gold, of which we were obtaining such large supplies, and which is the superior metal of the two for coinage. Thus, as gold flows into Europe, silver flows out; and thus our increased commerce with the East proves to us a double blessing,—at once increasing employment, and averting any great change in the value of money. It is a waste-pipe by which nothing is wasted. It is a channel by which we not only rid ourselves of a surplus of the precious metals, but turn them to most profitable account.

Thus far, we believe, we have been treading upon firm ground. We have been dealing with facts,—the accuracy of which, no doubt, may be contested, but which we believe to be substantially correct. But the next step takes us beyond the region of certainty into the fields of speculation. The future is a mist,

5. William Stanley Jevons (1835–82), economist and logician. Author of *Theory of Political Economy* (1871) in which he presented political science as a mathematical science. [Ed.]

6. In India the influx of the precious metals has been followed by an extraordinary rise in prices. As one consequence of this, the Bombay Government has just appointed Commissioners to report on the subject, with a view to ascertain what addition must be made to the salary of Government officials. When so great a change in the value of money is taking place, we may congratulate ourselves that Lord Canning's hasty decree for the sale of waste lands and redemption of the land-tax was not adopted by the Home Government, and that the Perpetual Settlement as yet applies only to Lower Bengal. [George Canning (1770–1827), a Conservative, served as foreign secretary 1822–27.]

in which we may grope our way, but where there are no sure land-marks to guide us. In attempting to calculate the future effects of the new supplies of gold upon the value of money, the very first basis of the calculation is unascertainable. No one can form any well-founded estimate of the amount of the precious metals in use among mankind. Such estimates, indeed, have been hazarded, but it is mere guess-work. All that we can ascertain with even approximate accuracy is the amount of the addition to the precious metals which has taken place since the end of the fifteenth century. That amount is estimated by M. Chevalier at two thousand millions sterling (£2000,000,000). And, judging from the change of prices, this addition is said to have reduced the value of the precious metals to about one-sixth of what it was prior to the discovery of America. But a change of prices is, in this case, no safe test; for the coinage of almost every country in Europe has been altered since the end of the fifteenth century. The names of the coins may remain, but the amount of gold or silver which they contain has been altered. For example, in our own country, under Henry VII., the pound weight of gold was coined into £22, 10s. sterling, and the pound weight of silver into £1, 17s. 6d. But in the following reign, Henry VIII.'s (A.D. 1509–30), the coin was immensely reduced in value, so that at the end of his reign the pound weight of silver was coined into £7, 4s. In the reign of Elizabeth (1558–1603), the value of the coinage was raised again, so that the pound weight of gold was coined into £36 sterling, and the pound weight of silver into £3. Doubtless it was the influx of the precious metals from the New World that enabled Elizabeth to make this partial restoration of the coinage; nevertheless it is to be observed that the English coinage under Elizabeth fell short in the quantity of bullion which it contained of the same coins under Henry VII. by more than one-third; so that £36 sterling in the time of Elizabeth would buy no more wheat than £22, 10s. did in the time of her grandfather, although the purchasing power of gold was as great in the later period as in the earlier. Nor did the reduction of the value of the coinage end with Elizabeth. On the contrary, it has continued in steady process down to 1817; the pound weight of gold being now coined into £46, 14s. 6d. sterling, and the pound weight of silver into £3, 6s.; so that, supposing prices had remained *really* the same, yet in appearance they must have doubled since the end of the fifteenth century—£46 sterling at the present day containing no more gold than £22 did in the time of Henry VII. We think these facts throw doubt on the various estimates which have been founded upon the change of prices since the discovery of America. Indeed, it seems an extraordinary thing, if money really became so redundant during the last three centuries, that the English Government should have continued steadily reducing the value of our coins—trying to make the same amount of gold and silver go farther than before. The same process has taken place on a still greater scale in the coinage of France. And notwithstanding all this, currency became so scarce, that paper money was invented to supply the deficiency; and banking also was introduced as another means of economising the currency. These are facts which do not appear reconcilable with the current opinion as to the great depreciation which has taken place in the value of the precious metals; and whatever depreciation may actually have occurred must be ascribed not merely to the American mines, but also in some degree to the introduction of paper money, bank-checks, and commercial bills, by which so large a portion of mercantile transactions are now carried on.

Moreover, even if we could accept the current opinion as to the depreciation of the precious metals since the fifteenth century, it is of importance to observe, that we cannot safely infer from this that a similar addition to the stock of the precious metals, spread over a similar period, will now produce a similar effect. At the time of the discovery of America (in 1492), the greater portion of the traffic in Europe was conducted by simple barter. Rents and suchlike obligations, and to some extent even revenue, were then discharged by payments in kind. And the same process has continued in a lessening degree even in the most advanced countries of Europe almost to our own times. It is obvious that if this process of barter had still continued in use to the same extent as in 1492, the fall in the value of money would have been very much greater than it has been; and that the gradual supplanting of payments in kind by money-payments has tended to uphold the value of money by producing a wider demand for it. In fact, then, in judging of the future, we have to estimate not only the probable amount of the precious metals which will be thrown into the market within a given time, but also the probable increase in the demand for them. And this increased demand will depend upon three things—namely, upon the increase of population, upon the increase of trade (which implies increased production), and upon the extent to which the use of money will supplant the process of barter throughout the world. But these two latter elements may almost be considered as one, for they are to a great extent mutually dependent.

In forecasting the future, therefore, one has to deal with two distinct considerations. Firstly, the probable amount of the future supplies of the precious metals; and, secondly, the probable amount of the demand for them. Neither of these considerations, in the present state of our knowledge, lead us to any definite conclusions. If we could judge of the new mines by what has taken place in regard to the old ones, we should conclude that the new supplies of the precious metals will last for a very long time. The annual produce of the silver-mines of Potosi, which were first worked in 1545, amounted, at the end of the sixteenth century, to about £2,000,000; and though thereafter it began to decline, it still amounted at the end of the eighteenth century to about £800,000. These mines are all in a single mountain. The annual produce of the Mexican mines, some of which were worked before the end of the sixteenth century, continued to increase steadily, partly owing to the opening of new mines; so that the produce of the mines, which was only £1,800,000 at the commencement of the eighteenth century, rose to £6,400,000 in 1795, and continued at that amount till their working was stopped by the revolt of Mexico against Spain in 1810. But it is manifest that the case of these old mines is very different from that of the new ones. The new mines are worked by a vastly more numerous body of men than the old ones. Instead of a few gangs of labourers, we have a whole population at work. We have also mining apparatus of all kinds, which multiplies the power of the workers, and enables them to exhaust a vein or gold-bed much more rapidly and cheaply than they could otherwise do. And, lastly, our facilities of locomotion and knowledge of geology enable us to discover new mines much more easily and quickly than in former times. Hence we may infer that the mines at present in operation will be exhausted far more quickly than similar mines were when worked by the Spaniards. But this does not settle the question. Firstly, because we have no reliable information of the extent of the auriferous districts of California and Australia; though, so far as we can judge, these districts are immensely vaster than any which were known to the Spaniards. To all appearance, the present number of workers may find profitable employment in the auriferous districts of Australia, California, Oregon, and British Columbia, for a century to come. Moreover, there are other regions known to be rich in the precious metals—especially in the north-western provinces of Mexico, in South America,[7] and in Siberia—which, in all probability, will begin to be worked even before the present mines fail. In fact, the Siberian mines will be supplied with labour from an independent source—namely, from China—and will make no draft upon the labour market of Europe and America, which furnishes almost all the emigrants to the mines of California and Australia.

Of course, if the value of gold were to experience a great fall, such an event, whenever it occurred, would lessen the number of emigrants to the gold-fields, and the produce of the mines would decline. But as the wages of the gold-diggers are at least four times higher than the wages of skilled labourers in this country, the fall in the value of gold would require to be very great before it materially lessened the number of workers at the mines—especially as there is

---

7. The silver mines of South America have as yet hardly begun to be worked. Major Rickards, inspector of mines in the Argentine Republic, in his newly published 'Mining Journey Across the Great Andes,' describes one silver-bearing district (eighteen leagues W.S.W. from San Juan), which extends over ninety miles in length. The quality of the ore, as proved by the analysis of 100 samples by Major Rickards, besides seven assays made in London, is remarkably fine; and of the abundance of the precious metal we may judge from the Major's statement, that within the space of 1000 yards square, "There are upwards of twenty mines open, on distinct veins, some of them enormously rich; and in every direction, for miles and miles in circumference, the hills are a perfect network of metallic veins,—yet I consider the district almost virgin."

in every community a class of men to whom the excitement and gambling character of gold-seeking has a peculiar attraction. Indeed, M. Chevalier states that there are men who labour at gold-finding (witness the gold-washers of the Rhine), though they make only 15d. or 20d. a-day.

All present indications, however, are against the supposition that there will be any sudden fall in the value of gold. Demand will tread closely upon the heels of supply—if not actually keep pace with it. Apart from increase of population, which is facilitated by the means of emigration, there never was a time when the circumstances of mankind were so favourable for an increase in the demand for currency.[8] We stand on the threshold, indeed we have already entered the vestibule, of an epoch when commerce and international relations will obtain an expansion undreamt of before. During the last thirty years, steam-navigation and railways have given to mankind facilities of locomotion which have immensely extended the sphere of human action, and have made each man a denizen of the world rather than merely of his own country. And now Gold comes to give wings to these inventions, and to carry them, and commerce along with them, into every civilised region of the earth. The flood of the precious metals which came across the Atlantic in the sixteenth century was poured only into Europe—or, rather, merely into part of Europe—into Spain, France, England, Italy, and part of Germany. But now the flood pours into every part of Europe and of America, and the surplus flows off rapidly to the other regions of the globe. Not even yet have the precious metals the whole world for a market—for a large portion of mankind, and notably the population of the African Continent, still remain in a state of barbarism which dispenses with the money required for international trade. But if we restrict our view merely to India and China, we find in the vast population of those countries, numbering nearly six hundred millions, a field for the absorption of the precious metals greater than all Europe presented in the sixteenth century. With India we may almost say that we had no commerce at all, till the new gold-mines gave us the means of prosecuting that commerce in earnest; and with the far vaster population of China our commerce is only in its infancy. We have been making railways in India, and we shall make many more; and every such enterprise sends the cost of it, in the form of specie, out of Europe to the scene of operations. Tea-planting, also, and many other kinds of investment opened to Europeans by the recent Act for the sale of waste lands, are attracting capital from this country to our empire in the East. And our native fellow-subjects in India, stimulated by the increase of

---

8. Besides the causes mentioned in the text for an increased absorption of the precious metals, we may also observe that the employment of gold in ornamentation and plate will experience a great increase: just as it decreases in times when gold is scarce, and is in unusual request in the form of money.

employment, and by the contagion of English spirit and ideas, will soon follow in our path, and by their increased energy and trade will cause an increased absorption of the precious metals to supply their deficiency of currency. In China the field is still vaster; and in sober truth, it would require the imagination of a poet to do justice to the triumphs which there await civilisation. Amongst the Chinese, as much as amongst any nation in the world, the people are industrious, and every man is anxious to better his condition. Every man in these four hundred million souls has an eye to business, a love for trade; they but wait for the quickening touch of European energy and science to enter upon a new career of livelier and more expansive action. Before long, ere ten years are over, the ships of the West will be whitening with their sails or darkening with their smoke the broad stream of the Yangtse-kiang, one of the noblest river-highways in the world, and the great artery of China; and from its banks the commerce and money of Europe will penetrate into the heart of the Celestial Empire. At present, metallic money is very scarce in China—so much so that the opium-trade was opposed by the Imperial Government chiefly on account of the export of silver which it occasioned. Domestic trade is shackled by the cumbrous process of barter; and foreign trade on an extensive scale is impossible till the nation has provided itself with a larger stock of the precious metals. Australia, also, has to be provided with railways, spanning the island-continent from Melbourne and Sidney to the Gulf of Carpentaria; and South America is still an undeveloped continent. Or, turning from these wide fields for the absorption of the precious metals as money, and looking only at our own Continent, do we not find even here a growth of civilisation which will require no small amount of metallic currency to aid its development? In Germany, to this day, payments in kind are in use to a considerable extent. Austria, with her vast undeveloped resources, is also deficient in the sinews of trade. And the whole of Russia, with her sixty millions of people, is virtually an undeveloped region. All these countries have yet to provide themselves with an adequate metallic currency; and even in the most advanced countries, such as England and France, the increase of trade and employment will suffice to enable them to absorb some of the new supplies of gold without occasioning any rapid decline in the value of money.

We attach importance to these considerations as indicating that no great and sudden fall in the value of money is to be expected. But that a fall will come, steadily and surely, we firmly believe. Let it but be gradual and slow, and no well-wisher to humanity, and to the masses of our own people, will have reason to complain. We cannot expect to have the stimulus of the gold-discoveries, and the great facilities which they supply for an expansion of commerce, without experiencing an alteration in the value of money. A rise in the value of money crushes the many to the benefit of the few—and, speaking generally, the nonproducers at the expense of the producing classes. A fall in the value of money does the reverse: and now the bees are benefiting at the expense of the drones. The more slow and unfelt the change, the better. In truth, if a fall in the value of money be spread over a long period, the loss is little felt by any particular owner of money. Government stock, railway debentures, and suchlike investments, are constantly changing hands; and if their fall in value be gradual, the loss of each holder of them is merely fractional. Leases, in like manner, are being constantly renewed. And unless the change in the value of gold prove much more rapid than there is at present reason to expect, the hardships which the change will inflict on money-holders will not be greatly felt, and to a considerable extent will be avoidable. As a national concern, and as affecting the world at large, the new gold-supplies cannot but be regarded as a great benefit. By producing increased trade and employment, they are improving the condition of the masses of the population in every country which they affect;[9] and by breaking down the barriers of isolation, and drawing all nations into mutual relationship, they are elevating the condition of mankind at large, and speeding the progress of civilisation in every quarter of the globe.

Paper-money is the most civilised of all forms of currency, and we have no wish to see its sphere of operation diminished. It is a form of money which costs nothing, and which is perfectly adequate to constitute the domestic currency of a country. At present it is of no use in carrying on foreign trade,—except in the form of bills of exchange, which are not properly speaking money, because not a legal tender. In one respect, the use of paper-money will be checked, because the new supplies of gold will render further issues of notes by the banks unnecessary. But in another form we may expect it to extend. Banking is being adopted every year more widely in Europe; and it is easy to see that a time is coming when bank-checks will gradually acquire an inter-

---

9. A volume of the *Population Tables,* compiled from the English census returns of 1861, has just been published, which demonstrates very strikingly that the years subsequent to 1851 have been a time of social prosperity and comfort. From the statistics contained in this volume we learn, that while the increase of the entire population of England and Wales in the ten years 1851–1861 was below 12 per cent, and the increase in the total number of females was below 13 per cent, the increase in the number of wives was above 15 per cent. In 1851 there were 3,015,634 married women in England and Wales; in 1861 there were 3,488,952. The proportion of children to a marriage, and the increase of population, are greatly affected by the age at which marriage takes place; and it appears that early marriages, as always happens in times of prosperity, have been on the increase. The number of wives who were under 25 years of age when the census was taken in 1851 was 290,034; but in 1861 the number had risen to 350,919, an increase of more than a fifth. Marriages increased in the ten years, and celibacy declined. The adult bachelors, men of 20 and upwards, fell from being 30.28 per cent of all the adult males in 1851 to be only 27.67 per cent in 1861, and the adult spinsters from 28.32 per cent of all the adult females in 1851 to 26.72 per cent in 1861. Of the women of the age of 20 and upwards, therefore, 28 in every 100 were without husbands in 1851, not 27 in 100 in 1861. Or, taking none but persons in the prime of life, 20 and under 40 years of age, 45 in 100 of the men of this age were bachelors in 1851, but only 42 in 1861; and of the women 41 in 100 were spinsters in 1851, but only 39 in 1861.

national value,—when a Bank of Europe will be established, whose notes will pass current with the banks of all countries, and which will be employed by these banks (as Bank of England notes are with us) in settling the balances due to one another.

Very probably, as an alteration in the value of money becomes apparent, the great capitalists and money-dealers will endeavour to place further restrictions upon the issue of paper-money by the banks, in order that an additional amount of sovereigns may be required to fill the vacuum, and consequently be absorbed without acting upon prices. Any such attempt ought to be strenuously resisted. There are forty millions sterling of bank-notes in use amongst us; and to replace these with gold would cost the country £40,000,000, besides at least £3,000,000 for loss of interest and tear-and-wear. It would be a backward step in civilisation, and also a sacrifice of the interests of the many for those of a few. Possibly—though we hardly think probably—an attempt will be made to alter the standard of value, so as to prevent any depreciation taking place in the value of consols—in other words, to prevent any lightening of the National Debt. We are surprised that M. Chevalier and Mr. Cobden should have counselled such a course. It is now obvious that the change in the value of money will be far more gradual than these gentlemen anticipated, and that the circumstances will not be such as to justify any intervention on the part of the Government. But even if the change threatened to be great and rapid, it must be borne in mind that about one-half (£400,000,000), of the National Debt was contracted in a currency lower in value by 30 or 50 per cent than it became a few years afterwards, in consequence of the Bank Act of 1819. If, then, the holders of the Government Stock which represents the National Debt had their property increased from one-fourth to one-half within ten years, they have no reason to complain if, by the natural course of events, their property should become depreciated to a like extent by a far more gradual and protracted process.

We have already indicated very fully the many social benefits which the new supply of the precious metals is calculated to confer on the population of our own and of other countries. But there is one political consequence of the gold-discoveries which is deserving of especial notice. These gold-discoveries will, of themselves, produce an extension of the suffrage, on an important scale, and in as desirable a form as any Reform Bill could devise. If, as we believe, a rise of prices is in progress—producing alike a rise of wages and an increase of house-rents—it is easy to see that this change will elevate a new class into the possession of the franchise. We believe that houses which were rented at £8 in 1848, as a general rule, are now rented at £10, which secures the franchise for the occupiers; and this rise of rents, we believe, will steadily progress. Indeed, in an old and rich country like ours, where population, trade, and wealth are steadily increasing, there is a tendency even in ordinary times for rents to advance,—producing, of course, a corresponding extension of the franchise. Taking the case of England, in the nineteen years before the new gold-supplies came into play, we find (from Dod's "Electoral Facts") that between 1832 and 1851 the registered electors for boroughs increased one-half, and those for counties more than one-third, while the total population increased less than one third. The figures stand thus:—

	1832.	1851.
Registered electors (for both boroughs and counties), ...	619,213	874,191
Total population, ...	13,091,005	16,819,017

These figures show that in England, in the nineteen years subsequent to the Reform Bill, the electors increased one-sixth faster than the population. The case of Ireland, owing to the great social and political changes which took place in that country in the same period, is valueless: nevertheless, as a matter of fact, we may state that between 1832 and 1851, while the population had decreased about one-seventh, the registered electors had more than doubled in number. Scotland in many respects furnishes a safer test than either England or Ireland, as there has been no disturbance as regards the increase of its population, and also inasmuch as it has no forty-shilling freehold franchise, by means of which factitious additions can be so easily made to the constituencies. And the statistics for Scotland show, that whereas population in the nineteen years subsequent to 1832 increased less than one-fourth, the electors increased more than one-half. The following are the figures:—

	1832.	1851.
Population, ...	2,365,114	2,870,784
Electors, ...	64,444	97,777

Here, then, we have a gradual and great extension of the franchise even in ordinary times. And even if no perceptible depreciation of money (*i.e.,* rise of prices and rents) were to take place in consequence of the vast increase of the precious metals, the immense increase of commerce, employment, and wealth, consequent upon the gold-discoveries, would of itself carry on this natural extension of the franchise in a double ratio. We think, then, that the small minority of "advanced" Liberals, who bewail the failure of Lord Russell's[10] vast projects of Parliamentary Reform, may take comfort, seeing that, gradually and surely, a virtual lowering of the franchise is taking place sufficient to satisfy the desires even of the most ardent believer in the wisdom of the masses.

Halcyon periods of unbroken quiet and prosperity are of rare occurrence and of brief duration in the history of any country. There is always a shadow—

10. John Russell (1792–1878). Member of Parliament who introduced the Reform Bill into the House of Commons in 1831. [Ed.]

always a drawback. Wars and calamities we may expect in the future, as we have met them in the past. Nevertheless there are times when the social condition of a people improves with a rapidity and to an extent which are exceptional in its history. Such a period, we believe, this country—and in some degree the whole civilised world—has now entered upon; and the chief agent (though of course not the only one) in producing this period of prosperity is the new and great supply of the precious metals, which enables every country to extend its foreign commerce to a degree impossible before, and, by means of that commerce, to obtain more employment for its people, and increased profits for its traders and capitalists. Every one has been surprised that so great a calamity as the Cotton Famine has weighed upon us so lightly; but if we look into the case thoughtfully, we shall see that the great mitigator of the calamity has been the increase of our trade with foreign countries, which but for the gold-discoveries we had not the means of carrying out. Providence sometimes sends hard times upon the world; now it sends prosperity,—a prosperity, indeed, not uncheckered, but apparently more full of promise and of social advantages than any which the world at large has yet witnessed.

HENRY SIDGWICK

WHAT IS MONEY?

Professor Jevons, in his excellent little book on "Money," tells us that the ingenious attempts that have been made to define money "involve the logical blunder of supposing that we may, by settling the meaning of a single word, avoid all the complex differences and various conditions of many things, requiring each its own definition." Without denying that this blunder has been sometimes committed, I think it misleading to suggest, as Mr. Jevons does, that the attempt to define a class-name necessarily implies a neglect of the specific differences of the things contained in the class. Indeed, when he goes on to say that the many things which are or may be called money—"bullion, standard coin, token coin, convertible and inconvertible notes, legal tender and not legal tender, cheques of various kinds, mercantile bills, exchequer bills, stock certificates, &c."—"require each its own definition," he apparently maintains the rather paradoxical position that it is logically correct to give

---

Henry Sidgwick, "What Is Money?" *Fortnightly Review* 31; n. s. 25 (April 1879): 563–75.

definitions of a number of species, but logically erroneous to try to define their common genus. It is easy to show that several at least of these more special notions present just the same sort of difficulties when we attempt to determine them precisely as the wider notion "money" does. For instance, the distinction between bullion and coin seems at first sight plain enough; but when we ask under which head we are to classify gold pieces circulating at their market value in a country that has a single silver standard, we see that it is not after all so easy to define coin. The characteristic of being materially coined—that is, cut and stamped by authority—though it has always been combined in our own experience with the characteristic of being legal tender, is capable of being separated from it; so that we have to choose between the two in our definition. So again, we may ask, what makes a coin a token? Does a seignorage sufficient to cover the expense of coining have this effect? If not, why not? and what further difference is required between the value of coin and the value of the metal contained in it? Similarly, we may inquire whether by calling notes convertible it is merely meant that their issuer has promised to convert them into coin on demand, or whether a belief is affirmed that he would so convert them if required? If the latter alternative be chosen, it must be evident that the legitimacy of such a belief must depend upon the nature and extent of the provisions made by the issuer for meeting demands of coin; so that in order to define convertibility precisely we shall have to determine what provisions are adequate, and whether all possible demands should be provided for or only such as may reasonably be expected. Then further, how shall we treat the case—which used to be common in the United States[1]—of notes for which coin will almost certainly be paid if demanded, but not without a serious loss of good-will to the demander? In short, we cannot escape the proverbial difficulties of drawing a line, if we attempt to use any economic terms with precision; and instead of seeing in these difficulties—as Professor Jevons seems to do—a ground for not making the attempt, I venture to take an exactly opposite view of them. I think that there is no method so convenient for bringing before the mind the "complex differences and various conditions" of the matters that it is occupied in studying, as just this effort to define general terms. The gain derived from this process (as I have urged in a previous paper[2]) is quite independent of its success. We may find that the reasons for drawing any proposed line between money and things rather like money are balanced and indecisive. But since such reasons must consist in statements of the important resemblances and differences of the things that we are trying to classify, the knowledge of them must be useful in economic reasoning, whatever definition we may ultimately adopt.

1. See Prof. F. A. Walker's book on "Money," c. xxi. pp. 481–2.
2. See the *Fortnightly Review* for February, 1879.

Let me then raise once more the vexed question—What is money? But first, we must observe that when proposed in this form the problem is fundamentally ambiguous; as it blends the two quite distinct questions, (1) What *do* we call money? and (2) What *ought* we to call money? I am inclined to think that the "intellectual vertigo," which has been said to attack all writers who approached this "fatal theme," may be partly traced to the want of a clear separation between these two very different issues, and the different methods of discussion respectively appropriate to each. The first point has obviously to be settled entirely by reference to the current use of language. In fact it is not strictly an economic question at all, but a linguistic one; only it is a linguistic question which it requires a certain amount of economic knowledge to answer satisfactorily. For though we have all of us something to do with money, most of us are even painfully conscious that our acquaintance with it is very limited. We commonly recognise that there are certain classes of persons, bankers, merchants, writers of city articles, &c., who are especially occupied in considering and discussing money and its relations from a practical point of view. Hence it is their use of the term which we shall naturally begin by investigating. If there is any one who ought to know what is meant by money, they ought to know.

At the very outset of our inquiry a curious phenomenon presents itself. There seems to be a tolerable accord among our monetary experts[3] in England, at the present time, as to the answer that ought to be given to the question What is money? when they directly attempt to answer it; at any rate, the extent to which they differ is inconsiderable in comparison with the extent of their agreement. Unfortunately the answer so given is in palpable discrepancy with their customary use of the term when they are not trying to define it; and this discrepancy is not of a minor kind, but as fundamental as can well be conceived. When the question is expressly raised they have no doubt that by money they mean what they also call currency, that is, coin and bank-notes. They see the need of distinguishing the latter as paper money or paper currency; and they recognise the existence of a narrower definition which restricts the term money to coined metal, on the view that bank-notes are mere promises to pay money, which ought not to be confounded with money, however currently they may be taken for it. But they are disposed to reject this view as a heresy; and though the narrower sense is that adopted by several economists of repute, I imagine that it would be regarded as at least old-fashioned by practical men; except so far as the word is quite technically employed in relation to the details of banking business. Again, our authorities allow that there is a certain resemblance between bank-notes and bills of exchange, letters of credit, promissory notes

---

3. I may refer the reader, for example, to Tate's "Cambist," Seyd's "Bullion and the Foreign Exchanges," Nicholson's "Science of Exchanges," &c.

issued by private persons, &c.; but though they may perhaps regard these lat-ter as constituting an "auxiliary currency," they do not consider them to be cur-rency in the strictest sense, and therefore do not call them money. The only im-portant point on which their utterances are doubtful or conflicting is the question whether notes issued by private banks and not made legal tender should be considered as money; the importance of this question, however, so far as England is concerned, is continually diminishing. But when bankers and merchants, or those who write for them, are talking of "money" in the sense in which, generally speaking, they are most practically concerned with it—of money which (or, more strictly, the temporary use of which) is continually val-ued and bought and sold in the money market, which is sometimes scarce and dear and at other times cheap and plentiful—they speak of something which must be defined quite differently. For though coin and bank-notes form a spe-cially important part of money-market money, they certainly cannot constitute the whole of it in any country where deposit-banking is fully developed and payment by cheques customary; and in England, at present, they do not con-stitute even the greater part of it.

What has just been said will appear to some of my readers a truism. But there are probably more to whom it will appear a paradox; and for the sake of these latter it will be well to pause and illustrate pretty fully this use of the term money. For this purpose I shall take Bagehot's *Lombard Street*[4] as my author-ity. I do this not merely on account of the marked popularity of this little book, which is now in its sixth edition; but because Bagehot united practical and the-oretical qualifications for dealing with this subject, such as have rarely been combined in any single man. He was himself a banker; he was, as editor of the *Economist,* in the habit of writing for bankers and merchants, so that "he that went by rail" might read; while, at the same time, he was a master of abstract economic theory, thoroughly acquainted with the criticisms that theorists have passed on the common language and ways of thinking of dealers in money. Hence we may be sure that his sense of the term money is deliberately chosen; not, perhaps, as the sense he would have adopted if he had assumed the lin-guistic liberty of a purely theoretical writer, but, at any rate, as a sense which he found so fixed in the ordinary thought and discourse of his readers as to ren-der it inexpedient for him to try and modify it.

What, then, is the money of Lombard Street, the possession of which makes England "the greatest moneyed country in the world"? The answer is very simple. It is a commodity of which the greater part exists only in the shadowy form of what is sometimes called bankers' credit, but may be more

---

4. Walter Bagehot's book, published in 1873, that contains a description of the City and ap-peals to the Bank of England to accept responsibility for the operations of the money mar-ket. [Ed.]

definitely conceived as bankers' obligations to pay money on demand; such credit or obligations being not even embodied in bank-notes. It is true that Bagehot never says that he means this by money, but there are many passages in which it is clear that he can mean nothing else. Take, for example, the following:—

> Every one is aware that England is the greatest moneyed country in the world; every one admits that it has much more immediately disposable and ready cash than any other country. But very few persons are aware how much greater the ready balance—the floating loan-fund, which can be lent to any one for any purpose— is in England than it is anywhere else in the world. A very few figures will show how large the London loan-fund is, and how much greater it is than any other. The known deposits—the deposits of banks which publish their accounts—are, in

London (31st December, 1872)	£120,000,000
Paris (27th February, 1873)	13,000,000
New York (February, 1873)	40,000,000
German Empire (31st January, 1873)	8,000,000

> And the unknown deposits—the deposits in banks which do not publish their accounts—are in London much greater than those in any other of these cities. The bankers' deposits of London are many times greater than those of any other city—those of Great Britain many times greater than those of any other country.

Here Bagehot clearly regards these bankers' deposits as "immediately disposable and ready cash," or, as he afterwards calls it, "money-market money." If, then, we ask ourselves where and in what form this money exists, it must be evident that, at any given time, most of it exists only in the form of liabilities or obligations, acknowledged by rows of figures in the bankers' books; and that it is transferred from owner to owner, and thus fulfils all the functions of a medium of exchange, without ever changing its form. Most of us, no doubt, have had a vague impression that these figures in bankers' books "represent" sovereigns or bank-notes; which, though they are not actually in the banker's possession, have yet passed through his hands, and exist somewhere in the commercial world. But I need hardly say to any one who has read *Lombard Street* that this cannot be Bagehot's view; since the main drift of that book is to bring prominently forward the fact that, in consequence of the "one-reserve system" upon which English banking is constructed, but little of this immense "loan-fund which can be lent to any one" could possibly be presented in the shape of coin or bank-notes. Of course some portion of the money lent by London bankers is continually taken from them in this shape. But a little reflection on the mode in which it is borrowed and used will show how comparatively small this portion is. Such loans are chiefly made to traders, either directly by the bankers or through the agency of the bill-brokers; and when a trader borrows from his bank, he almost always does so by having the loan placed to his credit in his banker's books, and drawing against it by cheques; and the effect of such cheques, for the most part, is not to cause the money to be produced in the form of coin or notes, but merely to transfer it to some other person's account at the same or some other bank. The bank-notes and gold are merely the small change of such loans; and it is only when money is lent to manufacturers and farmers, who have large sums to pay in wages, that the amount of this change bears even a considerable proportion to the whole loan. It may seem that when cheques on one bank are paid into another, material money must pass between bank and bank. But by the system of the Clearing House the mutual claims of the different banks are set off against each other; so that, even when the balance daily due from each bank to others was paid in notes, the amount of these required was very small in proportion to the amount of liabilities transferred; and now no notes are commonly needed at all, as such balances are paid by drafts on the Bank of England, where the other banks keep the main part of their reserves.

But we may reach the same result more briefly by means of a few statistics, which I may conveniently take from Mr. Inglis Palgrave, whose *Notes on Banking* were published almost contemporaneously with Bagehot's book.[5] Mr. Palgrave estimates the whole amount of deposits held by English, Scotch, and Irish banks (exclusive of the discount-houses) on the 12th of March, 1873, at about 486 millions, the liabilities of the London banks alone being about 179 millions: while he estimates the metallic circulation of the whole kingdom in 1872 at about 105 millions, and the note circulation at 43 millions. If we consider that more than 10 millions of notes and coin, on the average, were kept as reserve by the Bank of England, and that the provincial banks require a considerably larger proportion of coin for their daily business than the London banks, we shall require no elaborate proof to convince us that the greater part of the "unequalled loan-fund" of Lombard Street can never emerge from the immaterial condition of bankers' liabilities.

The difficulty, indeed, is not to prove this, but rather to explain why this obvious truth is overlooked, or even implicitly denied in so much of what is said and written about money.[6] Even Bagehot frequently uses language which suggests that what banks receive on deposit and lend to traders and manufac-

5. Robert Henry Inglis Palgrave (b. 1827). Economic writer and compiler of the *Dictionary of Political Economy* (1900). [Ed.]
6. A special exception has to be made in favour of Mr. McLeod, whose *Theory of Banking* contains, so far as I know, the first clear and full exposition of the nature and functions of bankers' deposits. In saying this, I must guard myself against being understood to approve of Mr. McLeod's general treatment of economics. [Henry Dunning McLeod (1821–1902). Author of *The Elements of Banking* (1877).]

turers is entirely legal tender, coin or bank-notes. Take, for example, a passage (p. 142) where he is arguing that the rise in general prices in 1871 was due partly to "cheap money":—

> It might be said at first sight that so general an increase must be due to a depreciation of the precious metals. . . . . . And, indeed, there plainly is a diminution in the *purchasing power* of money, though that diminution is not general and permanent, but local and temporary. The peculiarity of the precious metals is that their value depends for unusually long periods on the quantity of them which is in the market. In the long run, their value, like that of all others, is determined by the cost with which they can be brought to market. But for all temporary purposes, it is the supply in the market which governs the price, and that supply in this country is exceedingly variable.

One cause of this variation, he goes on to explain, which operates during the depressed period that follows a commercial crisis, is that the

> savings of the country increase considerably faster than the outlet for them. A person who has made savings does not know what to do with them. And this new unemployed saving means additional money. Till a saving is invested or employed it exists only in the form of money: a farmer who has sold his wheat and has £100 'to the good,' holds that £100 in money, or some equivalent for money, till he sees some advantageous use to be made of it. Probably he places it in a bank, and this enables it to do more work. If £3,000,000 of coin be deposited in a bank, and it need only keep £1,000,000 as a reserve, that sets £2,000,000 free, and is for the time equivalent to an increase of so much coin.

This passage certainly suggests that "saving," as actually performed in England at present, consists either in depositing coin with a banker, or at least in doing something which has the same effect as depositing coin; and that the business of a banker normally consists in lending about two-thirds of the coin thus paid in to him. But it must be evident that what each of us chiefly deposits when he saves is represented by cheques, dividend warrants, &c.; and that by these he merely transfers to his own banker the obligations towards himself that other bankers have incurred, together with the right of collecting corresponding sums of money from these other bankers. And the total effect of this process on the aggregate of banks cannot possibly be to increase directly the amount of "loanable money;" it can only influence this indirectly, so far as the saving diminishes the amount of legal tender which the bankers' customers require for their expenditure from day to day, and by thus increasing the proportion which the bankers' notes and coin bear to their liabilities, induces them to extend the latter. No doubt, to a certain extent, increased saving leads to a direct transfer of coin and bank-notes from the circulation to the bankers' cash-boxes; and this is especially the case with *provincial* saving, which is largely performed by farmers and retail tradesmen. Still, the phenomenon of cheap money in Lombard Street, for which Bagehot is trying to account, should be explained by reference rather to a decrease in the demand for loans than to any positive increase in the supply of loanable money directly caused by the process of saving.

I need hardly say that I do not attribute to such writers as Bagehot any settled misapprehension of the real nature of what they call money. But I think that their language is apt to mislead persons less familiar with the facts; and that it further has some tendency to confuse their own reasonings. Thus even Bagehot seems hardly aware that he uses the phrase "ready cash" in two different significations. In one sense, as we saw, England is said to have "much more ready cash" than any other country. That is, she has much more of the immaterial money which exists in the form of bankers' obligations to render material money if required. For of this latter, as he goes on to explain, England has comparatively little; the amount of our "cash in hand" (in this sense) "is so exceedingly small that a bystander almost trembles at its minuteness compared with the immensity of the credit that rests upon it." The truth is that the same thing presents itself to him in the opposite characters of credit and cash, according to the point of view from which he regards it. When he is considering possible crises and collapses of credit, the difference between bankers' liabilities and their means of meeting them becomes only too palpable; so that the latter, as "cash in hand" is naturally contrasted with the former. But in ordinary times "book-money," as I have called it, is generally preferred as a medium of exchange to gold or bank-notes, involving as it does not only less trouble but less apparent risk; since a man is more afraid of having his gold or notes stolen, than he is of his banker breaking. Since, then, each depositor is aware that he only leaves his money in its immaterial condition for his own convenience, and that he can convert any portion of his bankers' liabilities into gold or notes at will, he naturally comes to conceive the former as "ready cash" no less than the latter.

In this way we may partly explain the paradox which I noticed at starting, that money is expressly defined by most of those who write about it in a manner which implicitly excludes the greater part of the medium of exchange, which (as they are aware) is commonly lent and borrowed under the name of money in England. But a further explanation may be found in the view which influential economists have taken of the current commercial use of the terms money and the value of money. This view contains, or at least suggests, an important element of truth; but the statement of it, which I find (e.g.) in Mill's treatise, seems to me seriously misleading, and indeed calculated to shroud the whole matter in an impenetrable fog of confused thought.

Mill begins his chapter on the Value of Money[7] by "clearing from our path a formidable ambiguity of language," by which, as he explains, money is commonly confounded with capital.

> When one person lends to another, . . . what he really lends is so much capital; the money is the mere instrument of the transfer. But the capital usually passes from the lender to the receiver through the means either of money, or of an order to receive money, and at any rate it is in money that the capital is computed and estimated. Hence, borrowing capital is universally called borrowing money; the loan market is called the money market . . . and the equivalent given for the use of capital, or, in other words, interest, is not only called the interest of money, but, by a grosser perversion of terms, the value of money.

Now, I do not deny that there is an ambiguity in the phrase, value of money; but there seems to me a second equally serious ambiguity in the language that Mill uses in exposing the first. No doubt, when the value of money is mentioned in Lombard Street, it is not the purchasing power of money, measured in commodities, that is intended; but neither is it exactly the rate of interest, as Mill elsewhere uses this phrase, *i.e.* the average annual return to capital, subtracting insurance for risk and wages of management. It is, in fact, the value of the temporary use, not of capital generally, but of money in particular; estimated, as other values are commonly estimated, in terms of money. It is quite true that people often speak of the interest paid for the use of capital in other forms, as the "interest of their money;" but they are aware that it is money invested, and I do not think they really confound this with ready money. They must know that the interest of invested money, or capital generally, may vary comparatively little, while the price paid for the use of ready money is fluctuating through all the stages of a financial crisis; rising perhaps as high as ten per cent., and then falling as low as two per cent. But even if we admit that what is called interest of money should often be rather termed interest of capital, it is still misleading to say that by borrowing money we really mean borrowing capital; since, as Mill elsewhere observes, "loanable capital is all of it in the form of money," and therefore the antithesis is obviously inappropriate.

The truth is that Mill, in his account of Money and Credit, is rather too much influenced by his desire to guard against two errors. In the first place he wishes to dispel completely the illusory assumption, which he regards as the basis of the old Mercantile System,[8] that "wealth consists solely of money." Whether this illusion ever did really "overmaster the mind of every politician

---

7. *Polit. Econ.* b. iii. c. viii. [John Stuart Mill's (1806–73) influential *Principles of Political Economy,* first published in 1848.]
8. A term used by Adam Smith and subsequent political economists for the system of economic theory and legislation based on the idea that money alone constitutes wealth. [Ed.]

in Europe," I do not now inquire; perhaps we inevitably exaggerate the errors of our predecessors in the intellectual struggle that rids us of them; at any rate the doctrine is now happily defunct. But there is a more subtle confusion of the same kind which Mill also effectively exposes; the tendency to infer increase of wealth from what is merely increase of money, and to imagine that we are all better off when we have only got "more counters to reckon with." In the laudable effort to crush this fallacy, Mill is occasionally led to depreciate unduly the importance of money, and to speak of it as if it were not really "wealth" or "capital" at all; intermittently forgetting that "money being the instrument of an important public and private purpose is rightly regarded as wealth," and, since it is indispensable to the most effective production, as capital also. Thus, he tells us that "there cannot be a more insignificant thing than money, except in its character as a contrivance for sparing time and labour." It is not so much *what* is here said that is misleading, as the tone in which it is said. We might with equal truth affirm that there cannot be a more insignificant thing than a steam-engine, except in its character as a contrivance for generating and applying steam-power. But Mill's sentence certainly suggests that money is something that we could easily do without; whereas his real aim is not to depreciate the economic importance of the function of money, but merely to urge that this function will be no better fulfilled by a larger amount than by a smaller; provided that our habits and customs of distribution and exchange are duly adapted to the smaller amount. Similarly, the statement that "when one person lends to another, what he transfers is not the mere money, but a right to a certain value of the produce of the country, to be selected at pleasure," is unsatisfactory, though it is in a sense incontrovertible. A man only borrows money in order to buy something else, or to pay for something already bought; but what he actually borrows is money, and it is essentially inexact to represent him as borrowing anything else. The bad effects of this inexactness are, indeed, latent so long as we are dealing with metallic money; for when commodities are bought and sold for hard coin, it is impossible to ignore the fact that they are transferred by means of an instrument which is equal in value to the wealth that it is used to transfer. But when bankers' credit is the medium of exchange, it is easier to let this fact drop out of sight; and Mill continually does so. Thus he speaks contemptuously of an "extension of credit being talked of. . . . as if credit actually were capital," whereas it is only "permission to use the capital of another person." Now, in a certain rather strained way, we might say this of gold coin; its function is to "permit" or enable its owner to obtain and use other wealth. And it is only in this sense that Mill's statement is true of the credit or liabilities which a banker lends to his customers, whether in the form of notes, or under the rather misleading name of "deposits." This credit, no doubt, is a comparatively fragile and perishable instrument for transferring wealth; like the magic money of the Arabian

Nights, it is liable to be turned by a financial crisis into "worthless leaves" of written or printed paper: still, so long as it is commonly accepted in final settlement of debts, it has not only precisely the same function as gold coin, but also precisely the same market value; viz. the interest or discount that is paid for the use of it. And probably those who have "talked of credit as capital" have never meant to imply more than this.

At the same time, as I said, there is an element of truth suggested by the statement that "borrowing money is really borrowing [other] capital;" and it is an element all the more important to bring out, as it is inevitably ignored in most of what is written about the money market. It is true that the existence of these vast amounts of bankers' credit depends on the concomitant existence of corresponding amounts of wealth of other kinds, which are transferred by means of it. While it is needful for clearness of thought to insist that the "loanable capital" of Lombard Street is merely money—in the wider sense above explained,—and most of it immaterial money, it is no less necessary for completeness of view to bear in mind that this immaterial money is only kept in being by the continued exercise of its function. There would not actually be these millions of it in London, if London were not the greatest emporium in the world, and therefore a centre through which many more millions' worth of commodities is continually passing.[9]

Let us now sum up briefly the different uses of "money" which we have found to be more or less current. We may conveniently arrange them in order, according to their width of meaning. First will come the narrowest use, which is also the earliest, to denote coined metal. Next there is the sense universally recognised in the definitions now given by monetary experts, which includes besides coin such "paper money" as is "legal tender." Thirdly, there is the wider use which such experts sometimes, though not most commonly admit, in which bank-notes that are not legal tender are taken in. Fourthly, there is the still wider signification, which we have found to be current in the language of Lombard Street, though it is not often expressly recognised, according to which bankers' liabilities not represented by notes constitute the larger part of the so-called money. All these four—metallic money, paper money of both kinds, and "book money"—have the same exchange value, are lent and borrowed for the same interest or discount, and in ordinary times are currently accepted in final settlement of all debts—except, of course, the debts of bankers. It is by this latter characteristic especially that "book money" is distinguished from other kinds of credit which are not regarded as "money in

---

9. In saying this, I do not mean to ignore the possibility that London might remain a banking centre, even after the greater part of its trade had passed to other cities. But this could only occur in a more highly developed state of international trade than the present, and such a development would not be possible, if London had not previously been a great centre of trade.

hand;" in particular from bills of exchange, since the liabilities represented by these, though they may serve as a medium of exchange no less than bankers' liabilities, are always ostensibly to be liquidated at some definite time; hence they are not looked on as finally settling transactions, and so are not commonly regarded as money. The same remark applies to exchequer bills, as these are not absolutely convertible into legal tender to the amount they nominally represent, except at certain definite times. For similar reasons cheques are not commonly held to be money, though they perform some of the functions of money, since a transaction settled by cheque is not finally completed until the cheque has been paid in and money transferred from the drawer's banking account to that of the presenter of the cheque at the same or some other bank. In the case of cheques, however, there is the further difference that the cheques themselves do not exactly "circulate," though the liabilities transferred by means of them do. Still less, again, are securities, such as Government bonds or railway debentures or shares, regarded as ready money, since there is no time at which they are convertible into coin for a fixed amount: when taken in liquidation of a debt they must always first be sold like any other goods, or at least estimated at a continually varying market value; though, no doubt, as being more conveniently carried and kept, and more readily exchanged than most commodities, they are better fitted for taking the place of money. We have, however, had occasion to notice a lax usage by which such bonds and shares are often spoken of as "money;" but here, as was said, the notion of "invested" money seems to be always implied. In this fifth signification money is almost, as Mill says, a synonym for wealth, but yet not quite, for we do not apply the term to landed estates or pictures in a picture-gallery; we confine it, in fact, to wealth that is readily negotiable, and of which the current value is more or less definitely known.

It is now time to consider the second question originally raised, "What ought we to call money?" But I must hasten to say that I have no pretension to answer this dogmatically. I should be quite content to accept any of the denotations above given; or indeed, since there are undoubted disadvantages in rejecting any established use of language, I am quite willing to adopt them all at once, and to change from one to the other according to the nature of the subject, provided only the change be clearly announced. What most concerns us is that we should not give weak reasons for adopting any particular denotation of the term; that we should not misapprehend the nature or importance of the characteristics by which we distinguish money from what is not money. Thus if we restrict the term, in the old way, to coined metal, we must at least not do so because metallic money alone has "intrinsic value;" since it is not the difference in the source of the value of coin, confusedly expressed by the word "intrinsic," which is practically important, but the difference in its range and permanence. It is not because coin is made of a more expensive material that it is a better money than notes; but because it could be used as a medium of exchange over a wider area, and because its value is not liable to sudden destruction through the insolvency of the issuer, nor to sudden diminution in consequence of excessive issues. And it should be borne in mind that these distinctions are not absolute; there is no reason why we should not have an international circulation of bank-notes; and the progress of science and industry might so enlarge the supply of gold as to make it easy for a wise and stable government to devise a paper currency of more durable value than gold coin would then be, if still issued as at present. So again, I have no objection to define money by the characteristic of being "legal tender;" provided we do not imagine that it is this legal tender alone that becomes "scarce" or "abundant," and consequently "cheap" or "dear," in what we shall still have to call the money market. Only in this case it will be well also to remember that the notes of the Bank of England, though in a certain sense "legal money," are not so in the sense most important to the political economist; since their legal currency would cease, if the Issue Department ceased to give gold for them, and therefore could hardly be effective in sustaining their value, if this ever came to be seriously doubted. No doubt the quality of these notes is unique; in the severest crisis they would be taken as readily as gold. But this is not due to the fact that they are legal tender, but to the special provision made for maintaining their convertibility; and perhaps even more to the general belief that the credit of the English Government is practically pledged to maintain it. And here again it must be observed that the unique position of the Bank of England has a practically equal effect in sustaining the currency of the liabilities of its banking department: in the worst of panics every one has considered "money deposited" with the Bank of England as safe as its bank-notes in his own strong chest.

Hence it seems to me that, in relation to English finance, the definition of money that includes bank-notes generally, and excludes the rest of bankers' liabilities, is the least acceptable of all; since it ignores the profound distinction that separates the credit of the Bank of England from the credit of all other banks, while it unduly emphasizes the more superficial distinction between the liabilities of provincial banks that are transferred by notes and the liabilities of the London joint-stock banks that are transferred by cheques. No doubt there is actually an important difference between the working of the cheque-system and that of the note-system; since cheques do not circulate as notes do; the receiver of a cheque commonly pays it in without delay, and thus selects the banker whose liabilities he consents to take as money, whereas the receiver of a note usually exercises no such choice. But this is not the ground which I find most frequently given for drawing a broad line between notes and deposits; but rather such trivial reasons as that deposits cannot be "currency" because they do not pass "from hand to hand," as though the mere physical transmission were the important fact, and not the transfer of the ownership of bankers' liabilities.

Again, suppose we adopt the widest meaning of "money" which we have found to be current in Lombard Street, and include bankers' liabilities, whether represented by bank-notes or not, we shall still be excluding that other kind of "currency" of which the material is merchants' credit, represented by bills of exchange. We shall have, therefore, to bear in mind carefully that bills of exchange—so far as they still circulate among traders, and are not at once discounted—perform the main function of money, in being a medium for transferring commodities. And finally, for some purposes it would be convenient to extend the denotation of money still farther, and define it as any commonly accepted medium of exchange, so as to include bills of exchange, as the "paper money of commerce," as well as bullion, its metallic money. But if we do this we must not forget that what is most important to the buyer of commodities is, that the seller should take what he offers in exchange, and not that other people should take it. Now there are other valuable articles besides bills of exchange—as, for instance, Government bonds—which are more convenient for transmission than bullion; hence, if foreigners will take them in payment for the goods they have sold, as is now more and more the case, they will fulfil this important function of money better than the noblest metal. In short, whatever course we adopt, we shall find that definitions are not talismans for simplifying the complex relations of facts, but merely instruments by which, when we have thoroughly analysed any part of the complexity, we may fix in our thought some of the most important results of our analysis.

ALI AMEER

THE RUPEE AND THE RUIN OF INDIA

AN impression seems to prevail in certain quarters that the fall in the gold value of silver affects only the European officials in India, and that an attempt to restore the rupee to anything like its old value would be prejudicial to the people of the country. This fallacious idea owes its origin, no doubt, to an imperfect acquaintance with the condition of the masses, and I therefore propose to show how the depreciation of the rupee in relation to gold affects the population at large. With the wealthy rajah, the rich *mahajan,* and the flourishing pleader I have no concern; when the general weal is in the balance, their in-

Ali Ameer, "The Rupee and the Ruin of India." *Nineteenth Century* 33 (March 1893): 515–24.

terests are of little weight. The general population of India may, for the purposes of my remarks, be divided into two classes, agricultural and non-agricultural. The non-agricultural portion, speaking roughly, forms about one-third of the entire body of inhabitants. Of the so-called agricultural classes, the largest portion, or more than three-fourths, are mere labourers, and are consequently classified as such in all Government statistics.

The first question to consider, therefore, is how the fall in the gold value of the rupee affects the non-agricultural classes and the urban population of India. In connection with this, one circumstance which furnishes a remarkable index to the popular feeling is worthy of note. Throughout the country there is an opinion prevalent among the masses that the Queen's rupee does not possess the same 'blessing' as the old coins bearing the King's effigy. This opinion is loudly expressed among themselves, and often to outsiders when the fear of the police or of the penal code is not present to their minds; but the idea has a strong hold over them, and is a frequent topic of bewailment. The feeling, no doubt, is an ignorant expression of the fact that the purchasing power of the rupee has declined, that it does not go as far to relieve their wants as before. In their ignorance they are unable to apprehend the causes of this decline, and are led to ascribe it somehow to the British rule. They would not be far wrong in supposing that were it not for the lethargy which hangs over the counsels of Government the distress would be neither so acute nor so prolonged.

Coming back to the question, How does the fall in the gold value of the rupee affect the people in general? we find that within the last twenty years the incomes of the wage-receiving classes have for the most part remained stationary, whilst the prices of food-grains have risen by leaps and bounds. Among the wage-receiving classes I include the underpaid 'ministerial' clerks of Government, the not overpaid clerks in the employ of private individuals or companies, and people in the like condition.

Taking Bengal first, we find that in 1873 the monthly wages of the agricultural labourers varied from Rs.3 in the Behar districts to Rs.10 in Chittagong, giving on the average Rs.5 over the whole province. In the North-Western Provinces the average wages amounted to Rs.4 a month, in the Punjab to Rs.5, in the Madras Presidency to Rs.3. Of a horse-keeper, in Bengal, the average wages were Rs.5; of a common mason or blacksmith, Rs.9. In 1878 the average wages of the agricultural labourer in Bengal were Rs.5; in the North-West, Rs.4; in the Punjab, Rs.6. Of a horse-keeper the average wages during this year in Bengal were Rs.5; of a common blacksmith or carpenter a little over Rs.9. From 1883 to 1888 there was no substantial variation in the wages; in 1891 there was, if anything, a reduction.[1] In towns like Calcutta, Patna, Cawnpore, Meerut,

---

1. These averages are struck from figures in Government statistics. I have not given the fractions.

Bombay, and Kurrachee some slight increase is shown, but the variation is so small as to be of very little account in the consideration of the general question. For example, in Calcutta the average of wages of a common mason or carpenter or blacksmith between 1873 and 1880 is given as Rs.13 3a. 1⅕p.; between 1881 and 1885, Rs.12 8a. 9⅗p.; between 1886 and 1892, Rs. 14 and a fraction. In Patna the average wages during the same periods were Rs.6 10a. 6p. Rs.6 12a. 6p., Rs.7 4a. 4p., and Rs.7 8a. Of the agricultural labourer the average wages in Patna were Rs.3 8a, Rs.3 14a., Rs.4 8a., Rs.4 8a., and so forth.

A reference to the wage rates in some of the industrial and other establishments may also prove useful. At the Mirzapore East Indian Railway station the maximum wage of a blacksmith in 1866 was Rs. 10, in 1892 it was the same, although it had a slight rise for some years in the interval. The minimum of Rs.8 has always remained the same. The carpenter's wage in 1892 was the same as in 1870, viz. Rs.10. In private establishments, such as collieries, no change in the monthly wages rates is perceptible. It would be useless to multiply examples for what I have stated above, that, in spite of little variations here and there, the bulk of the wage rates in Bengal have remained stationary.

As regards the clerks, &c., in the employ of Government, or of private individuals, or companies, railway, trading and banking, it is notorious that their incomes have not varied for the last twenty years, and those of the professional classes (among whom I might mention the country *mookhtears* and the native doctors) have fallen, whatever the cause of the fall may be.

During this period of time the fluctuation in the gold value of the rupee has been as follows:—

Year	Average rate for Rupee		Year	Average rate for Rupee	
	s.	d.		s.	d.
1872	1	11¼	1882	1	8
1873	1	10¾	1883	1	7½
1874	1	10¼	1884	1	7½
1875	1	10	1885	1	7¼
1876	1	9½	1886	1	6¼
1877	1	8½	1887	1	5½
1878	1	8¾	1888	1	5
1879	1	7¾	1889	1	4½
1880	1	8	1890	1	6
1881	1	8	1891	1	4½

In March 1892 it stood at 1*s.* 3¼*d.;* a slight reaction raised it to 1*s.* 4⅛*d.;* since then it has declined steadily, and now stands at 1*s.* 2⅔-½*d.*

Whilst, as shown already, the earnings of the wage-receiving classes have practically remained stationary, the price of the food-grains has gone on increasing steadily in inverse proportion to the rapid declension in the gold value of the rupee.

In 1873 the average retail price in Bengal of common rice was R.1 10a., and of *ballam* rice Rs.1 14a. per maund; in 1878, which was an abnormal year, the price of the first rose to Rs.3 5a. 4p.; in 1883 it fell to Rs.2; in 1888 it rose to Rs.2 1a.; in 1891 to Rs.2 9a. 4p. Of other food-grains the prices varied as follows:—

		Rs.	a.	p.				Rs.	a.	p.
Wheat,	1873 3		11	3		Grain,	1883 2		2	7
"	1878 4		0	7		"	1888 2		4	6
"	1883 3		1	3		"	1891 2		4	9
"	1888 3		12	3						
"	1891 3		15	9						

Millet sold in 1873 at R.1 5a. 4p. per maund, in 1892 for Rs.2 5a. 8p., and is now sold for Rs.2 8a.

In January 1893 the retail price of common country rice had risen to Rs.3 13a. per maund, and of *ballam* rice to Rs.4 8a. The table hereunder shows the prices of other food-grains at the beginning of the current year, taking a general average from three different places:—

Table showing Prices of Food-grains and Salt, January 1893

			Rs.	a.	p.
Table rice (1st class),	per maund 6			4	0
Common country rice	"	 3		13	0
Ballam rice	"	 4		8	0
Grain	"	 2		12	0
Millet	"	 2		8	0
Wheat	"	. . . . 4 6 0 to 4		12	0
Pulse (Arhar).	"	 3		8	0

When we consider that among the labouring classes the average number of adults composing a household is three, and among classes slightly better off five, it will be seen how heavily the rise in the price of food-grains presses upon these people. They are, in fact, on the verge of starvation, and the majority of them have to be satisfied with one meal a day.

The intimate connection between the fall in the gold value of the rupee and the abnormal rise in the prices of food-grains is self-evident. It is in fact admitted, and a claim is based upon it by the speculative exporter that no attempt should be made to remedy the evil.

It is said that the agricultural classes have gained by the depreciation of the rupee, and it is urged that the export trade in India in grains and cereals of all kinds derives its chief impetus from the falling exchange and is beneficial to the agriculturist because he sells so much more! I shall not pause to inquire whether an export trade in food-grains factitiously fostered and maintained by the fall in the gold value of silver is beneficial to the people; nor shall I dwell on the fact that whatever impetus the export trade in grains has received from the fall in the exchange has resulted to the benefit of the small body of the produce brokers and exporters, who are now vociferously clamouring to prevent any interference to rehabilitate the rupee. The genuine export trade of India owes its development to causes wholly independent of the depreciation of silver. The Suez Canal, increased facilities of transport, immense reduction in the freight of goods, the construction of railways and roads, have combined to develop this trade. Were it left to these natural agencies for its development, the rise in the price of food-grains would have been balanced by the decline, owing to the same causes, in the prices of other necessaries of life. But the fall in the rupee has intensified the evil and accentuated the burden upon the people. The produce broker and the exporter are, no doubt, able with their sovereign to buy sixteen rupees' worth of goods, but how far that benefits the producer or the agriculturist I shall now proceed to examine. If, instead of theorising, we would only take the trouble to inquire for ourselves into the question of this hypothetical benefit, we would find that the bulk of the profit due to increased prices of food-grains goes into the pocket of the exporter; in another case, when the grain remains for consumption in the country, to that of the wholesale *mahajans* and the retail dealers. In Bengal, the producer himself estimates his profit as four annas to ten annas per maund over the old prices that existed before the 'cyclone,' which takes us back to the year of grace 1864.

But let us look to the other side of his account. For the agriculturist also, all over the country, the necessaries of life other than what he himself grows— the clothes which he wears, the oil which he burns, the salt for himself and his cattle, &c.—have become dearer. And, what is more, his rent is enhanced because he obtains more for his produce. Under a rule of peace and equal laws, free from the danger, generally speaking, of illegal exactions or forced contributions, with the developing resources of the country, the people had immense and potential opportunity of prosperity, had it not been for the terrible curse of a depreciated currency. Careful inquiry would show that no benefit accrues to any section of the people, agriculturist or non-agriculturist. If the former wears an aspect of comparative prosperity, it is due to fairly good harvests and the immunity he has enjoyed for the last few decades from illegal exactions and 'cesses.' The fall in the rupee only helps in his being deprived of his just prices. You might as well give him sixteen eight-anna pieces for, say, five maunds of rice, and call the coins rupees. That is just what is allowed to take place under the glamour of theories promoted and propounded by self-interest.

The native Indian employés above the rank of mere clerks, whether in the service of Government or private individuals and firms, with fixed salaries, which have not, in the majority of cases, altered for the last twenty years, are equally sufferers. The income of the bulk of them varies from Rs. 50 to Rs. 100 a month. Had the rupee retained its original value this would represent 5*l.* to 20*l.* a month; at present these figures barely represent 3*l.* and 12*l.* respectively. Only few get more than Rs. 200 a month. When it is considered that the household of a fairly well-to-do inhabitant of India consists of a number of poor relatives and dependents; that the cost of living, schooling, clothing, &c., has increased all round, there will be no difficulty in understanding how the struggle for existence is becoming harder for even this class of people. The education of boys is becoming dearer every day, resulting from a variety of causes too numerous to detail; many youths, chiefly from amongst the sons of Government officials, are sent to England to acquire that training, discipline, and culture which are conspicuous by their absence from the educational institutions of this country. Can it be said with any approach to truth that the fall in the gold value of the rupee does not affect these people with fixed salaries and a number of mouths to feed, children to educate, and some position to maintain in their society?

The native trader, the native banker, the native merchant (if their own statements, repeatedly made, are to be relied on), are half-ruined. Trade is disorganised, and business transactions generally in a most unsatisfactory condition. Nobody can say with certainty what the morrow may bring forth; nobody can properly forecast his gain or his loss; nobody can safely engage in any enterprise with any reasonable assurance of a fair outturn.

I have thus far endeavoured to show, albeit imperfectly, how the fall in the gold value of the rupee affects the people of India. How it affects the Government, the official and professional classes of Europeans, and those Indians who, from choice or necessity, desire to give their children a European education, are matters beyond controversy. The position of the Government may be described in one sentence: it is on the verge of veritable bankruptcy. Its vaunted surpluses have turned into deficits, ever growing. All new productive work practically stopped, expenditure reduced to what is absolutely needful, the mournful admission of helplessness implied in the quiet appropriation of the Famine Insurance Fund, furnish a clear and unmistakable indication of what is impending unless the Government awakens from its lethargic condition and abandons the laissez-faire course which has marked its policy throughout in dealing with the currency question.

The Indian Government has, from the necessities of the situation, to meet large sterling liabilities in England by payments in the coin in which it realises its revenue. So long as India is a dependency of the British Crown she has to remit to England each year a certain number of pounds sterling in discharge of her liabilities. The question whether this burden is right or proper is not relevant to the present issue. Not even the wildest Home-ruler would suggest that cutting India adrift from England, even if it were possible, would be for the benefit of this country. Now, as the revenue is collected in rupees, it is evident that in making the payment in sterling her loss or gain would be determined by the gold value of the silver coin. This is so obvious that it is unnecessary to dwell further on the subject. In 1843 the exchange was 2s. $0\frac{1}{4}d$.; in 1853, 2s. $1\frac{1}{4}d$.; in 1863, 2s. $0\frac{3}{4}d$.; in 1872, as already mentioned, it was 1s. $11\frac{1}{4}d$.; at the close of 1892, 1s. $2\frac{2}{3}-\frac{1}{2}d$. In the course of twenty years, from 1872 to 1891, as pointed out by a competent authority, the Indian Government has lost fully sixty-seven millions sterling over its remittances to England. This enormous sum, which might have been profitably spent in developing the resources of the country, in making railways, roads, canals, and opening up tracts still inaccessible to the outer world, in effecting reforms or reducing taxation, in providing means to prevent or to minimise famines, in constructing defensive fortifications on a threatened frontier, might, so far as any benefit to India is concerned, or for the matter of that to anybody else, have just as well been thrown into the sea.

As regards the threatening deficit, the local *Englishman,* in its issue of the 7th of January, had an interesting and instructive article, from which I venture to quote one or two passages to enforce my own remarks. After giving a table showing the surpluses and deficits each year from 1879 to 1890, it proceeds thus:—

> The surplus estimated for 1892–93 has, as the public is aware, been turned into a deficit of Rx. 1,600,000.[2] The net result of fourteen years of Indian finance is, therefore, a surplus in seven years of the period amounting to Rx. 11,192,000, and a deficit in seven other years amounting to Rx. 12,124,000, the deficit thus exceeding the surplus by Rx. 932,000, or, say, one crore.

Then, after referring to the circumstances which led to the reimposition of the taxes that had been reduced by Sir Evelyn Baring,[3] to the imposition of

---

2. The figures represent tens of rupees.
3. Sir Evelyn Baring, Lord Cromer (1841–1917), served as the British consul-general and high commissioner of Egypt from 1883–1907. He supported balancing the Egyptian budget. [Ed.]

new taxes, and to the various economies effected to make the two ends meet, the article in question runs thus:—

> We find, then, that after the recovery of the finances from the effects of the war with Afghanistan we had down to 1884 a period of prosperity, which has been followed since then by a time of stress and strain. The period of prosperity was coincident with a relative steadiness in the exchanges. From 1878–79 to 1884–85 the average annual rate of exchange varied between 19·96d. and 19·308d., the decline in seven years being under 3½ per cent. Beginning with 1885, the rupee tumbled headlong down the abyss, and with its downward progress we have had a period of increasing financial pressure, in which it has been necessary to impose heavy additional taxation, to deprive the local Governments of the means for carrying out material improvements, to restrict the progress of railway construction, to starve the administration generally, to suspend the Famine Insurance Grant, and to hunt unsuccessfully in every hole and corner for cheeseparings in the way of savings. It is not, however, a mere coincidence that the period of prosperity went with the steadiness of the rupee. We have given above the statement of the Ministers responsible for the finances, that the coincidence was more than a coincidence—that it was cause and effect.

In the course of fourteen years, whilst taxation has increased by four crores annually, the public debt has increased by twenty. A huge deficit for the present financial year is inevitable, and another, probably much larger, for the ensuing year is equally certain. How is this to be met? There is no margin for further taxation; practically the produce broker and exporter, the real gainers by the present state of things, the zemindars, who possibly have profited a little in consequence of increased rental from the ryots, are beyond the range of taxation. Any addition to the income-tax will be received with grave dissatisfaction. Is the country to be allowed to go to ruin, the people to starve, the official classes driven to the verge of insolvency, to satisfy theories or to fill the pockets of a small class of people?

The Viceroy, in his reply to the address of the planters of Coorg, made a statement, which, I submit, ought to form the keynote of the financial policy of Government. His Excellency observed:—

> No fortuitous advantage which any particular trade may for a time derive under a falling exchange can be allowed to weigh against the general injury and loss resulting to the trade of the Indian empire as a whole from fluctuations and uncertainty in the rate of exchange. . . . It will, perhaps, be sufficient if I say that, as the Indian empire does most of its commercial business with countries in which a gold standard obtains, it appears to me that it would be for the general advantage that India should be provided with a currency of which the gold value would no longer be subject to the fluctuations which have for some years past un-

settled our commercial system and discouraged the investment of capital in this country.[4]

The wonder is that, in spite of the unhesitating terms in which the enunciation was made, no action has yet been taken to carry it into effect. As regards the official classes of Europeans, it is indisputable that they have suffered severely by the loss on exchange. They are paid in a depreciated coinage, whilst almost everything they have to pay for, either directly or indirectly, is paid for in gold. Stores, wines, clothing, the schooling of their children, and the cost of living for their families at home, has all to be disbursed in sterling. The loss affects every grade and every class—the man who has a salary of fifteen hundred rupees a month, and the small sergeant of police who gets barely a hundred.

The extent of the hardship entailed upon the official classes can be gauged from the fact that many men holding offices hitherto considered as well paid have been compelled to withdraw their children from school, bring out their daughters to India, and send the sons to the Continent for that education which the falling rupee will not allow them to obtain in England. In a country like India, where influence depends a great deal on prestige, it is idle to expect an ill-paid official, Indian or European, can either command or maintain his position, and it will be the fault of Government if its poorly-paid servants get entangled in straits which in most civilised countries are regarded as detrimental to the public interests.

The professional classes are in exactly the same predicament; the fee of the doctor or of the lawyer, paid in rupees, has not increased. As in the case of service holders, though their earnings have lessened in value the expenses have increased in an inverse ratio. In neither case is there any compensation. The small trader who imports his goods from Europe has to pay for them in gold, and in order to compensate himself has to raise his own prices proportionately in silver, at the risk of losing customers whose diminishing incomes furnish little inducement for much outlay. The merchant and the banker appear to be little better off. One can now understand the angry discontent which pervades the official classes of Europeans, high or low. To suggest that the proper remedy for this evil is for the English to make a permanent home in the plains is to ignore the lessons derivable from the past. The fate of the Mahommedan conquerors of India ought to be a warning to those who discourage occasional home visits to Europe.

It is almost unnecessary to repeat the fact that a few years' existence without change of climate or scene robs English women of their vitality and reduces them almost into the condition of permanent invalids. Visits to Europe,

---

4. The *Pioneer,* November 15, 1892.

or, as a *dernier ressort,* to the hills, are matters of life and death to them. Children of European parentage do not thrive in the hills beyond a certain age, and even if they did, education in the proper sense of the term, with the same discipline and training as in Europe, is not to be had. The hill schools under European management are mere makeshifts, to be resorted to only in dire straits. The necessity of a European training has forced itself even into the minds of a large number of Indians, who, although themselves without English education, appreciate the benefits that accrue therefrom.

The Manchester Chamber of Commerce recently gave expression to a somewhat strange sentiment, viz. that any attempt to introduce a gold standard or to improve the currency of India would involve a serious political danger. The weight of this opinion may be fairly discounted. Speaking with some sense of responsibility and with some acquaintance with the condition of the people, in my opinion it would be a serious political blunder to let the rupee stand at its present low value, or to allow it to sink lower. "The rupee and not the Congress will drive the British out of India," was a remark once made to me by a member of the National Congress. The idea is by no means chimerical. If the present state of things is allowed to continue much longer, there can be little doubt that sooner or later the number of Europeans in the civil and military employ of Government will be considerably reduced. Few Englishmen will care to take up almost a life-long service in India upon the pittance into which the fairly good salaries of former days have turned, nor would parents be willing to invest money in the training of their sons for the Indian service. Under the apprehended circumstances, the unwillingness of Europeans to come out to India, or of Indians trained in Europe to take service under Government, will promote the employment of men trained in the country, but whether that will be for the advantage of the State is a matter for question.

To my mind, it would be an evil day for India when, from a permanent reduction in the emoluments of officers in the civil and military employ of Government, the agency which has been the making of India is either withdrawn or its efficiency impaired.

Another disastrous effect of the fall in the rupee, which is likely to be far-reaching and permanent in its character, is that it stops all influx of capital from outside. Capitalists in gold countries will not invest in securities in silver countries, because they have no confidence in the value of silver in relation to gold, and consequently, while money flows freely to foreign gold countries, it is denied to the British dependency of India. A currency which fluctuates from day to day, and the value of which depends upon the smartness of foreign speculators, hardly leaves room for any safe calculation. The result of this is that many of the projects for the development of the resources of the country have either to be abandoned or to be postponed until better times.

My object is not to suggest any theory for the solution of a difficulty which may certainly be regarded as the life-problem of India, and the gravity of which is recognised by all classes of people. My sole aim is to dispel the illusion that the fall in the rupee affects only the official classes and benefits the country at large. If Holland could devise a means for the protection of its colonies from a ruin such as is threatening India, surely it is possible for the talented men at the helm here and in England to find a remedy for the evil. Had the Brussels Conference resulted in an agreement for universal bimetallism our problem would have been solved and our difficulties would have disappeared; but as it is evident that there is no prospect of the dual standard being adopted by England for many years to come, the only remedy for India is to change her standard of value from silver to gold, closing her mints to the free coinage of silver, and retaining the silver currency as token-coinage, fixing the rupee at, say, 1*s*. 6*d*.

The change can be made without any of the risks of economic loss or political danger predicted by the Manchester bimetallists, and should be carried out without further delay. I venture to predict that if India's standard of value is brought into line with the standard in England, the country's progress and prosperity during the next twenty years will be such as has never before been recorded in the annals of Indian history.

TWO

THE NATIONAL DEBT AND THE
STOCK EXCHANGE

The first two selections attempt to make the National Debt imaginable for readers to whom it was, at best, a set of meaningless numbers. Like William Cobbett, the anonymous compiler of "Facts for Enquirers" and the Scotsman W. E. Aytoun consider the Debt an imposition against the people. Like Cobbett as well, these two writers composed their attacks on the Debt during one of the century's principal economic downturns. Whereas Cobbett wrote his "Paper against Gold" during a decade of monetary uncertainty, before England adopted the gold standard and the Bank of England resumed gold payments, these journalists wrote during the "Hungry 'Forties," when crops failed, the price of bread rose, and poor and often unemployed workers agitated for more political rights. With sympathies that are Tory rather than radical, Aytoun explicitly emphasizes politics in his historical account of the Debt, vehemently accusing the Whig "moneyed interest" of profiting from the Debt. By contrast, the anonymous compiler of "Facts" only implies his more radical political position by allowing the outlandishness of his examples to speak for themselves. The series of which this article was a part originally appeared in the most important Chartist newspaper, the *Northern Star,* edited in Leeds by Feargus O'Connor. "Facts for Enquirers" was then reprinted in another Chartist newspaper, the *English Chartist Circular,* which, like the *Northern Star,* campaigned for extending the franchise and other rights for working men.

"Stockbroking and the Stock Exchange" and Alexander Innes Shand's "Speculative Investments" pick up a concern also expressed in Aytoun's

123

essay—the worry that the entire stock trade provided opportunities for gambling and speculation. The literature of the period is filled with efforts to distinguish legitimate investment from self-indulgent speculation, and these two contributions are typical in failing to draw a stable line between the two. They are also typical in yoking concerns about speculation with a host of other worries: anxieties about the role that Jewish financiers play in the stock market, fears that the Limited Liability Acts have increased criminal opportunities, concerns that rumor has an undue effect on share prices, and doubts about the honesty of newspapers' City editors, who reported on but also influenced fluctuations in the market. Both of the articles were composed in the aftermath of parliamentary commissions convened to explore fraudulent companies and the panic of 1866, and the details they supply about the London Exchange and the transgressions it permitted derive largely from the commissions' reports. *Fraser's Magazine for Town and Country,* as the title suggests, was a miscellany that contained essays as well as learned articles. Founded in 1830, it enjoyed particular popularity under the editorship of J. A. Froude.

The last three articles in this part consider some of the effects of the English financial system on the colonies, especially India. All published in the last three decades of the century, after the price of silver had begun to fall relative to gold, these essays reveal that the overall optimism that characterized the economic expansionism of the 1850s and 1860s could not survive the arrival of bleaker economic times. India became a source of particular concern because, as Bagehot and Fawcett suggest, England's application to that country of "modern" financial ideas, like a permanent funded debt and an income tax, had signally failed to consider India's own unique cultural and economic conditions. As English journalists began to recognize the poverty of the "jewel in the Empire's crown," as India was popularly called, they urged legislators to save the special relationship between the two countries. Neither Bagehot nor Fawcett (nor Ameer, who published the article contained in Part 1 in 1893) wanted England to liberate India. Only Karl Marx, composing *Das Kapital* in exile in London, identified a systematic set of links connecting various nations' adoptions of permanently funded debts, a worldwide network of credit, the rise of manufacturing and trade protectionism, slavery, and the dependent status of a colony like India. The first volume of *Capital* was translated into English by S. Moore and E. Aveling in 1887. I discuss the *Economist,* where Bagehot's essay appeared, in the Introduction.

CHAPTER FOUR

HISTORY AND MAGNITUDE OF THE DEBT

ANONYMOUS

FACTS FOR ENQUIRERS
The National Debt

The returns lately published by order of the House of Commons, relative to the Public Debt of this country, state that the Unredeemed Capital of the Public Funded Debt was on

Jan. 5, 1828,	Jan. 5, 1831,	Jan. 5, 1841,
£777,476,892	£757,486,996	£766,371,725

That the amount of Exchequer Bills outstanding in the same years was respectively,

£27,546,150	£27,271,650	£22,271,050

(The second amount, including the issue under the Act of 11 George IV., cap. 26, to pay off the proprietors of Four per Cent. Annuities, amounting on the 5th of January, 1831, to £1,662,000.)

Anonymous, "Facts for Enquirers: The National Debt." *Hobson's Poor Man's Companion,* rpt. *English Chartist Circular: The Temperance Record for England and Wales* 2: 53 (1843): 4.

That the amount of Terminable Annuities, whether for lives or years, was for these years respectively,

£2,610,754	£3,297,375	£4,114,211

That the sums required to defray the Charge of the Interest and Management of the permanent public debt during these periods were—

£25,779,115	£24,377,379	£24,442,303

And that the sums paid or required to defray the interest on Exchequer Bills for these years were—

£873,246	£675,000	£818,046.

[The weight of the National Debt, in gold, amounts to 14,088,475lbs. or 6,289 tons. 9 cwt., 13lbs,; in silver to 266,666,666lbs., or 119,047 tons. 12 cwt., 1 qr. 14lbs. To transport this debt across the seas, in gold, it would require a fleet of twenty-five ships, of 250 tons burthen each. To carry the debt by land, would require 12,580 one-horse carts, each being loaded with half a ton of gold. These would extend in one unbroken line $35\frac{1}{2}$ miles. If conveyed by soldiers, and every soldier were to carry 50lbs. weight in his knapsack, it would require an army of 281,069 men. Eight hundred millions of sovereigns piled one upon another, or formed into one close column, would extend 710 miles. If this column were commenced at the Lizard, or extreme point of Cornwall, and continued northward, it would reach ten miles beyond John o' Groat's house, at the extreme point of Scotland. The same number of sovereigns laid flat, in a straight line, and touching each other, would extend 11,048 miles, or more than once and three quarters round the moon. Eight hundred millions of one pound notes sewed together, would cover a turnpike road 40 feet wide and 1,052 miles long, or from the Land's end to John o' Groat's house, and nearly half way back again. If the notes were sewed together end to end, they would form a belt long enough to go four times round the world, or sixteen times round the moon. Supposing for a moment such a thing possible as that we could procure silver in sufficient quantity to pay off the debt, it would require to bring it to England, a fleet of 476 ships of 250 tons each. To carry it to the bank of England, in one-horse carts, each containing half a ton of silver, it would take 238,095. These ranged in one unbroken line, would extend 676 miles, or from the Land's end to within twenty-four miles of John o' Groat's house.]—*Hobson's Poor Man's Companion.*

W. E. AYTOUN

THE NATIONAL DEBT AND THE STOCK EXCHANGE

It is curious to remark that the Stock Exchange cannot be said to have had any period of minority. It leaped out at once full-armed, like Minerva from the brain of Jupiter. All the arts of *bulling* and *bearing,* of false rumours, of expresses, combinations, squeezings—all that constitute the mystery of Mammon, were known as well to the fathers of the Alley, as they are to their remote representatives. Nay, it would almost appear that the patriarchal jobber had more genius than has since been inherited. William's retinue did not consist only of mercenaries and refugees.[1] Hovering on the skirts of his army came the sons of Israel, with beaks whetted for the prey, and appetites which never can be sated. *Vixere fortes ante Agamemnona*—there were earlier vultures than Nathan Rothschild.[2] The principal negotiators of the first British loan were Jews. They assisted the Stadt-holder with their counsel, and a Mephistopheles of the money-making race attached himself even to the side of Marlborough.[3] According to Mr. Francis:[4]—

> The wealthy Hebrew, Medina, accompanied Marlborough in all his campaigns; administered to the avarice of the great captain by an annuity of six thousand pounds per annum; repaid himself by expresses containing intelligence of those great battles which fire the English blood to hear them named; and Ramilies, Oudenarde, and Blenheim, administered as much to the purse of the Hebrew as they did to the glory of England.

It has been estimated, upon good authority, that from fifteen to twenty per

W. E. Aytoun, "The National Debt and the Stock Exchange." *Blackwood's Edinburgh Magazine* 66 (December 1849): 655–78 (excerpt).

1. King William, also known as William of Orange, who ruled England 1688–1702. William, a nephew of Charles II and James II, was a stadholder in the Dutch Republic when he agreed to invade England in 1688 in order to save the country from James II's Catholicism. His victory is known (to supporters) as the Glorious Revolution. [Ed.]
2. (1777–1836). Jewish financier who came to Manchester from Frankfurt in the 1790s. By 1822, he had established his prominence in the market of foreign loans through loans to Prussia, Russia, and Latin American countries. By that time, the monetary value of his London finance house was over a million pounds. [Ed.]
3. John Churchill, the first duke of Marlborough (1650–1722). Soldier-diplomat and the power behind the throne during the reign of Queen Anne (1702–14). Won victory at Bleinheim (the Low Countries) for the first English victory in Europe since the Middle Ages. [Ed.]
4. John Francis. Permanent official at the Bank of England and author of many books about the City, including *The History of the Stock Exchange,* which Aytoun is reviewing in this essay. [Ed.]

cent. of every loan raised in England, has, directly or indirectly, found its way to the coffers of those unconscionable Shylocks; so that it is small wonder if we hear of colossal fortunes coexisting with extreme national depreciation and distress. We might, indeed, estimate their profits at a much higher rate. Dr. Charles Davenant,[5] in his essay on the *Balance of Trade,* written in the earlier part of the last century, remarked—"While these immense debts remain, the necessities of the government will continue, interest must be high, and large premiums will be given. And what encouragement is there for men to think of foreign traffic (whose returns for those commodities that enrich England must bring no great profit to the private adventurers) when they can sit at home, and, without any care or hazard, get from the state, by dealing with the exchequer, fifteen, and sometimes twenty, thirty, forty, and fifty per cent.? Is there any commerce abroad so constantly advantageous?" We apprehend not. Capital is defined by the economists as the accumulation of the savings of industry. Such men as Rothschild have no doubt been industrious, but not according to the ordinary acceptation of the term. Their industry is of a wholesale kind. It is confined to a resolute and systematic endeavour to avail themselves of the savings of others; and we need hardly state that, in this pursuit, they have shown themselves most eminently successful.

The remarkable change which took place in the monetary system of England, under the auspices of William, could not, of course, have been effected without the concurrence of parliament. That body had certainly no reason to charge him with neglect of their interests. The representatives of the people for the first time began to understand, that there might be certain perquisites arising from their situation as men of trust, which could be made available to them, provided they were not too scrupulous as to the requirements of the crown. The mastiff which had bayed so formidably at James[6] and his predecessors, because none of them would deign to cajole him, became at once amenable to a sop. Mr. Macaulay[7] should have written: "The revolution of 1688 did not introduce the practice of regularly summoning parliaments; what it introduced was the practice of regularly bribing them." Mr. Francis, though an apologist of King William, who, as he thinks, was compelled to act thus from imperious necessity, is not blind to this stigma on his memory. He also believes that the settled animosity between England and France, which has caused so many wars, and led to such an extravagant expenditure of blood

---

5. (1656–1714). Late seventeenth-century author of economic treatises who argued that the market was driven by its own self-regulating dynamic. Published *An Essay on the East-India Trade* (1696) and *Discourses on the Publick Revenues* (1698). [Ed.]

6. King James II, Stuart monarch of England 1685–88. A convert to Roman Catholicism, James was ousted from power by William of Orange in 1688. [Ed.]

7. Thomas Babbington Macaulay (1800–59). Whig historian and Member of Parliament who opposed Chartists' demand for universal male suffrage. [Ed.]

and treasure, is mainly to be attributed to the persevering efforts of William of Orange. The following summary is of much interest:—

> The parliamentary records of William's reign are curious. The demands which he made for money, the hatred to France which he encouraged, and the frequent supplies he received, are remarkable features in his history. Every art was employed; at one time a mild remonstrance, at another a haughty menace, at a third the reproach that he had ventured his life for the benefit of the country. The bribery, during this reign, was the commencement of a system which has been very injurious to the credit and character of England. The support of the members was purchased with places, with contracts, with titles, with promises, with portions of the loans, and with tickets in the lottery. The famous axiom of Sir Robert Walpole[8] was a practice and a principle with William; he found that custom could not stale the infinite variety of its effect and that, so long as bribes continued, so long would supplies be free. Exorbitant premiums were given for money; and so low was public credit, *that of five millions granted to carry on the war, only two and a half millions reached the Exchequer.* Long annuities and short annuities, lottery tickets and irredeemable debts, made their frequent appearance; and the duties, which principally date from this period, were most pernicious.

These things are elements of importance in considering the political history of the country. They explain the reason why the great bulk of the nation never cordially supported the new succession;[9] and why, for the first time in English history, their own representative house lost caste and credit with the commons. Fifty years later, when Charles Edward[10] penetrated into the heart of England, he met with no opposition. If the inhabitants of the counties through which he passed did not join his standard, they thought as little of making any active opposition to his advance; thereby exhibiting an apathy totally at variance with the high national and independent spirit which in all times has characterised the English, and to be accounted for on no other ground than their disgust with the new system which, even then, had swollen the amount of taxation to an extent seriously felt by the commonalty, and

---

8. Sir Robert Walpole (1676–1745). Whig who rose to power with the collapse of the South Sea Bubble in 1720. Dominated English politics in the 1720s and 1730s as First Lord of the Treasury. [Ed.]

9. Reference to the succession that saw William of Orange take the throne from James II. This was called a "new succession," even though William was connected to the House of Stuarts, because William was said to have usurped the throne from James. William's kingship was also controversial because he allowed the Whigs and the moneyed interests to gain power. After the deaths of William and then his sister-in-law, the childless Queen Anne, the throne passed out of the House of Stuarts to the German Hanoverians (George I) because this was the nearest Protestant branch of the Stuarts. [Ed.]

10. Charles Edward Stuart (Bonnie Prince Charlie or the Pretender). Son of James II, Charles Edward Stuart landed in Scotland in 1745 in an unsuccessful attempt to overthrow George I and to regain the throne for the Stuarts. [Ed.]

which had so corrupted parliament that redress seemed hopeless within the peaceful limits of the constitution. The proclamation issued by the prince, from Edinburgh, bore direct reference to the funded debt, and to the notorious ministerial bribery; and it must have found an echo in the hearts of many, who began to perceive that the cry of civil and religious liberty is the standard stalking-horse for every revolution, but that the result of revolutions is too commonly an imperative demand upon the people for a large augmentation of their burdens, backed too by the very demagogues who were the instigators of the violent change. In this crisis,[11] the moneyed interest, which William had so dexterously created, saved the new dynasty—less, certainly, from patriotism, than from the fear of personal ruin.

It is a memorable fact that, from the very first, the Tory party opposed themselves strenuously to the creation and progress of the national debt. It is well that those who, in our own times, bitterly denounce the system which has landed us in such inextricable difficulties, and which has had the effect of rearing up class interests, irreconcilably opposed to each other, in once united England, should remember that for all this legacy we are specially indebted to the Whigs. Except by Tory ministers, and in one case by Walpole, no attempt has been made to stem the progress of the current; and this consideration is doubly valuable at this moment, when it is proposed, by a vigorous effort, to make head against the monster grievance, and, by the establishment of an inviolable sinking-fund, to commence that work which liberal and juggling politicians have hitherto shamefully evaded. It is more than probable that "the moneyed interest" will throw the whole weight of their influence in opposition to any such movement; unless, indeed, they should begin already to perceive that there may be worse evils in store for them than a just liquidation of their claims. Matters have now gone so far as to be perilous, if no practicable mode of ultimate extrication can be shown. Real property cannot be taxed any higher—indeed, the landowners have claims for relief from peculiar burdens imposed upon them, which in equity can hardly be gainsaid. The property and income-tax, admittedly an impolitic impost in the time of peace, cannot remain long on its present footing. To tax professional earnings at the same rate as the profits of accumulated capital, is a manifest and gross injustice against which people are beginning to rebel. There is no choice left; except between direct taxation and a recurrence to the system which we have abandoned, of raising the greater part of our revenue by duties upon foreign imports. The former method, now openly advocated by the financial reformers, is, in our opinion, a direct step towards repudiation. Let the fundholders look to it in time, and judge for themselves what results are likely to accrue from such a

---

11. The 1745 invasion of Charles Edward Stuart, also known as the Forty-Five. [Ed.]

The National Debt and the Stock Exchange 131

policy. One thing is clear, that if no effort should be made to redeem any portion of the debt—but if, on the contrary, circumstances should arise, the probability of which is before us even now, to call for its augmentation, and for a
corresponding increase of the public revenue, the financial reformers will not
be slow to discover that the only interest hitherto unassailed must submit to
suffer in its turn. The Whigs are now brought to such a pass, that they cannot
hope to see their way to a surplus. We shall have no more of those annual re-
missions of duties, which for years past have been made the boast of every
budget, but to which, in reality, the greater part of our present difficulties is
owing. Had a sinking fund been established long ago, and rigidly maintained,
and at the same time the revenue kept full, the nation would ere now have been
reaping the benefit of such a policy. We should have had the satisfaction of
seeing our debt annually diminishing, and the interest of it becoming less;
whereas, by the wretched system of fiddling popularity which has been pursued, the debt has augmented in time of peace, the annual burdens absolutely
increased, ruinous competition been fostered, and internal jealousies excited.
The Whigs, who arrogate for themselves, not only now but in former times,
the guardianship of the liberties of Britain, have taken especial pains to conceal the fact that they were, in reality, the authors of our funding system, and
the bitterest opponents of those who early descried its remote and ruinous
consequences. Their motives cannot be concealed, however it may be their interest at the present time to gloss them over. Lord Bolingbroke[12] thus exposes
their occult designs, in his *Letters on the Use of History.*

> Few men, at the time (1688), looked forward enough to foresee the necessary
> consequences of the new constitution of the revenue that was soon afterwards
> formed, nor of the method of funding that immediately took place; which, absurd
> as they are, have continued ever since, till it is become scarce possible to alter
> them. Few people, I say, saw how the creation of funds, and the multiplication of
> taxes, would increase yearly the power of the Crown, and bring our liberties, by
> a natural and necessary progression, into more real though less apparent danger
> than they were in before the Revolution! The excessive ill husbandry practised
> from the very beginning of King William's reign, and which laid the foundation
> of all we feel and fear, was not the effect of ignorance, mistake, or what we call
> chance, *but of design and scheme in those who had the sway at the time.* I am not
> so uncharitable, however, as to believe that they intended to bring upon their
> country all the mischiefs that we who came after them experience and apprehend.
> No: they saw the measures they took singly and unrelatively, or relatively alone
> to some immediate object. The notion of attaching men to the new government,
> by tempting them to embark their fortunes on the same bottom, was a reason of

---

12. Henry St. John, viscount Bolingbroke (1678–1751). Tory who struggled for power at the
end of Queen Anne's reign but lost out as moderates and Hanoverians won. [Ed.]

state to some; the notion of creating a new, that is, a moneyed interest, in opposition to the landed interest, or as a balance to it, and of acquiring a superior interest in the city of London at least, by the establishment of great corporations, was a reason of party to others; and I make no doubt that the opportunity of amassing immense estates, by the management of funds, by trafficking in paper, and by all the arts of jobbing, was a reason of private interest to those who supported and improved that scheme of iniquity, if not to those who devised it. They looked no further. Nay, we who came after them, and have long tasted the bitter fruits of the corruption they planted, were far from taking such alarm at our distress and our dangers as they deserved.

In like manner wrote Swift,[13] and Hume,[14] and Smith;[15] nor need we wonder at their vehemence, when we direct our attention to the rapid increase of the charge. William's legacy was £16,400,000 of debt, at an annual charge to the nation of about £1,311,000. At the death of Queen Anne, the debt amounted to fifty-four millions, and the interest to three millions, three hundred and fifty thousand—being nearly double the *whole revenue* raised by King James! The total amount of the annual revenue under Queen Anne, was more than five millions and a half. Under George I., singular to relate, there was no increase of the debt. At the close of the reign of George II., it amounted to about a hundred and forty millions; and, in 1793, just one hundred years after the introduction of the funding system in Britain, we find it at two hundred and fifty-two millions, with an interest approaching to ten. Twenty-two years later, that amount was more than trebled. These figures may well awaken grave consideration in the bosoms of all of us. The past is irremediable; and it would be a gross and unpardonable error to conclude, that a large portion of the sum thus raised and expended was uselessly thrown away; or that the corruption employed by the founders of the system, to secure the acquiescence of parliament, was of long continuance. On the contrary, it is undeniable that the result of many of the wars in which Britain engaged has been her commercial, territorial, and political aggrandisement; and that bribery, in a direct form, is now most happily unknown. The days have gone by since the parliamentary guests of Walpole could calculate on finding a note for £500 folded up in their dinner napkins—since great companies applying for a charter, were compelled to purchase sup-

---

13. Jonathan Swift (1667–1745). Dean of St. Patrick's and Tory satirist. Author of *Tale of a Tub* (1704), Gulliver's *Travels* (1726), and *A Modest Proposal* (1729). [Ed.]
14. David Hume (1711–76). Scottish philosopher and economic theorist. Author of *An Inquiry Concerning Human Understanding* (1748) and *Essays Moral, Political, and Literary* (1741). [Ed.]
15. Adam Smith (1723–90). Scottish philosopher and economic theorist. Author of *A Theory of Moral Sentiments* (1759) and *The Wealth of Nations* (1776). The latter is generally accepted as the foundational text of Classical Political Economy. [Ed.]

port[16]—or when peace could only be obtained, as in the following instance, by means of purchased votes:—"The peace of 1763," said John Ross Mackay, private secretary to the Earl of Bute, and afterwards Treasurer to the Ordnance, "was carried through, and approved, by a pecuniary distribution. Nothing else could have surmounted the difficulty. I was myself the channel through which the money passed. With my own hand I secured above one hundred and twenty votes on that vital question. Eighty thousand pounds was set apart for the purpose. Forty members of the House of Commons received from me a thousand pounds each. To eighty others I paid five hundred pounds a-piece." Still we cannot disguise the fact, that a vast amount of the treasure so levied, and for every shilling of which the industry of the nation was mortgaged, never reached the coffers of the state, but passed in the shape of bonuses, premiums, and exorbitant contracts, to rear up those fortunes which have been the wonder and admiration of the world. Nor is it less palpable that the fortunes so constructed could not have had existence, unless abstracted from the regular industry of the country, to the inevitable detriment of the labourer, whose condition has at all times received by far too little consideration. Add to this the spirit of public gambling, which, since the Revolution, has manifested itself periodically in this country—the sudden fever-fits which seem to possess the middle classes of the community, and, by conjuring up visions of unbounded and unbased wealth, without the necessary preliminary of labour, to extinguish their wonted prudence—and we must conclude that the funding system has been pregnant with social and moral evils which have extended to the whole community. Before we pass from this subject—which we have dwelt upon at considerable length, believing it of deep interest at the present point of our financial history—we would request the attention of our readers to the following extract from the work of Mr. Francis, as condemnatory of the policy pursued by recent governments, and as tending-to throw light on the ultimate designs of the Financial Reform Associations. It is quite possible that, in matters of detail, we might not agree with the writer—at least, he has given us no means of ascertaining upon what principles he would base an "efficient revision of our taxation;" but we cordially agree with him in thinking that, as we presently stand, the right arm of Great Britain is tied up, and the Bank of England, under its present restrictions, in extreme jeopardy at the first announcement of a war. [. . .]

Turn we now from the national debt to its eldest offspring, the Exchange. Marvellous indeed are the scenes to which we are introduced, whether we

---

16. Reference to joint-stock companies seeking monopoly status through a Crown-granted charter. Examples of eighteenth-century chartered companies include the Bank of England, the East India Company, the South Sea Company, and the Royal African Company. [Ed.]

read its history as in the time of William of Orange, enter it at the period when the South Sea bubble[17] had reached its utmost width of distension, or tread its precincts at a more recent date, when railway speculation was at its height, and the Glenmutchkin at a noble premium. John Bunyan[18] could not have had a glimpse of it, for he died in 1688: nevertheless his Vanity Fair is no inaccurate prototype of its doings. No stranger, indeed, may enter the secret place where its prime mysteries are enacted: if any uninitiated wight should by chance or accident set foot within that charmed circle, the alarm is given as rapidly as in Alsatia when a bailiff trespassed upon the sanctuary. With a shout of "Fourteen hundred fives!" the slogan of their clan, Jew, Gentile, and proselyte precipitate themselves upon the rash intruder. In the twinkling of an eye, his hat is battered down, and amidst kicks, cuffs, and bustling, he is ejected from the temple of Mammon. But, lingering in the outer court and vestibule, we can gain some glimpses of the interior worship; imperfect, indeed, but such as may well deter us from aspiring to form part of the congregation.

The creation and transferable character of public funds, necessarily involved the existence of a class of men who deal in such securities. That class multiplied apace, and multiplied so much that, after a time, the commissions exigible for each bona fide transaction could not afford a decent subsistence for all who were engaged in the business. People who buy into the stocks with a view to permanent investment, are not usually in a hurry to sell; and this branch of the profession, though, strictly speaking, the only legitimate one, could not be very lucrative. Gambling was soon introduced. The fluctuations in the price of the funds, which were frequent in those unsettled times, presented an irresistible temptation to buying and selling for the account—a process by means of which a small capital may be made to represent fictitiously an enormous amount of stock: no transfers being required, and in fact no sales effected, the real stake being the difference between the buying and the selling prices. But, the natural fluctuations of the stocks not affording a sufficient margin for the avarice of the speculators, all sorts of deep-laid schemes were hatched to elevate or depress them unnaturally. In other words, fraud was resorted to, from a very early period, for the purpose of promoting gain. The following may serve as an example:—

The first political hoax on record occurred in the reign of Anne. Down the Queen's road, riding at a furious rate, ordering turnpikes to be thrown open, and

---

17. The stock mania of 1720 that resulted from a combination of the lure of exotic trade and political intrigue. In their attempt to convert national debt into company stock, the directors of the South Sea Company promoted the company's stock with promises of an indefinite rise in share price. The boom lasted from February until September, when the bubble burst. The collapse of the Company opened the door for Robert Walpole's rise to power. [Ed.]

18. John Bunyan (1620–88). Author of *Pilgrim's Progress.* [Ed.]

loudly proclaiming the sudden death of the Queen, rode a well-dressed man, sparing neither spur nor steed. From west to east, and from north to south, the news spread. Like wild fire it passed through the desolate fields where palaces now abound, till it reached the City. The train-bands desisted from their exercise, furled their colours, and returned home with their arms reversed. The funds fell with a suddenness which marked the importance of the intelligence; and it was remarked that, while the Christian jobbers stood aloof, almost paralysed with the information, Manasseh Lopez and the Jew interest bought eagerly at the reduced price.

The whole thing was a lie, coined by the astute Hebrews, who then, as now, accumulated the greater part of their money in this disgraceful and infamous manner, and doubtless had the audacity even to glory in their shame. A more ingenious trick was played off in 1715, when a sham capture was made in Scotland of a carriage and six, supposed to contain the unfortunate Chevalier St. George. The news, being despatched to London, instantly elevated the funds, "and the inventors of the trick laughed in their sleeves as they divided the profit." Modern jobbers will doubtless read these records with a sigh for the glory of departed times, just as a schoolboy bitterly regrets that he was not born in the days of chivalry. Universal rapidity of communication, and the power of the press, have rendered such operations on a large scale almost impossible. The electric telegraph has injured the breed of carrier pigeons,[19] and more than half the poetry of fraudulent stock-jobbing has disappeared.

The range of the jobbers speedily extended itself beyond the comparatively narrow field presented by the funds. Exchequer bills with a variable premium were invented and brought into the market, a large and lucrative business was done in lottery tickets, and even seats in Parliament were negotiated on the Stock Exchange. Joint-stock companies next came into play, and these have ever since proved an inexhaustible mine of wealth to the jobbers. Nor were they in the least particular as to the nature of the commodity in which they dealt. Thomas Guy, founder of the hospital called after his name, acquired his fortune by means similar to those which are now made matter of reproach to the Jews of Portsmouth and Plymouth. It is a curious feature in the history of mankind, that money questionably amassed is more often destined to pious uses than the savings of honest industry. The conscience of the usurer becomes alarmed as the hour of dissolution draws nigh.

His principal dealings were in those tickets with which, from the time of the second Charles,[20] the seamen had been remunerated. After years of great endurance,

---

19. Between 1837 and 1840 carrier pigeons were used to transport financial information between London and Paris. The practice ended with the invention of the "winged messenger," the electric telegraph. [Ed.]

20. King Charles II, who ruled from 1660–85. [Ed.]

and of greater labour, the defenders of the land were paid with inconvertible paper; and the seamen, too often improvident, were compelled to part with their wages at any discount, which the conscience of the usurer would offer. Men who had gone the round of the world like Drake, or had fought hand to hand with Tromp, were unable to compete with the keen agent of the usurer, who, decoying them into the low haunts of Rotherhithe, purchased their tickets at the lowest possible price; and skilled seamen, the glory of England's navy, were thus robbed and ruined, and compelled to transfer their services to foreign states. In these tickets did Thomas Guy deal, and on the savings of these men was the vast superstructure of his fortune reared. But jobbing in them was as frequent in the high places of England as in 'Change Alley. The seaman was poor and uninfluential, and the orders which were refused payment to him were paid to the wealthy jobber, who parted with some of his plunder as a premium to the treasury to disgorge the remainder.

But frauds and injustice, even when countenanced by governments, have rarely other than a disastrous issue to the state. So in the case of those seamen's tickets. That the wages due to the sailor should have fallen into arrears during the reigns of Charles and of James, need excite little surprise, when we remember that the revenue in their day never exceeded two millions annually. But that the abuse should have been continued after the revolutionary government had discovered its easy method of raising subsidies—more especially when ample proof had been given of the danger of such a system, by the want of alacrity displayed by the English seamen when the Dutch fleet burned our vessels in the Thames and threatened Chatham—is indeed matter of marvel, and speaks volumes as to the gross corruption of the times. So infamous was the neglect, that at length the sailors' tickets had accumulated to the amount of nine millions sterling of arrears. Not one farthing had been provided to meet this huge demand; and in order to stay the clamours of the holders,—not now mariners, but men of the stamp of Thomas Guy,—Parliament erected them into that body known as the South Sea Company,[21] the transactions of which will ever be memorable in the commercial history of Great Britain.

The existence of this company dates from the reign of Queen Anne; but for some years its operations were conducted on a small scale, and it only assumed importance in 1719, when exclusive privileges of trading within certain latitudes were assured to it. We quote from Mr. Doubleday[22] the follow-

---

21. A monopoly founded in 1711 by the Tory government as a rival to the Bank of England. The Company was chartered to trade with the Spanish colonies in the Caribbean. In 1720, the government allowed the Company to take over three-fifths of the national debt, a provision that led to the investing mania known as the South Sea Bubble. [Ed.]
22. Thomas Doubleday (1790–1870). Whig poet, dramatist, radical politician, and political economist who advocated political reform. [Ed.]

ing particulars, which utterly eclipse the grandeur of modern gambling and duplicity.

> As soon as the act had fairly passed the Houses, the stock of the company at once rose to *three hundred and nineteen per cent.;* and a mad epidemic of speculative gambling seemed, at once, to seize the whole nation, with the exception of Mr. Hutchison, and a few others, who not only preserved their sanity, but energetically warned the public of the ultimate fate of the scheme and its dupes. The public, however, was deaf. The first sales of stock by the Court of Directors were made at three hundred per cent. Two millions and a quarter were taken, and the market price at once reached *three hundred and forty*—double the first instalment according to the terms of payment. To set out handsomely, the Court voted a dividend of ten per cent. upon South Sea Stock, being only a half-yearly dividend, payable at midsummer, 1720. To enable persons to hold, they also offered to lend half a million on security of their own stock; and afterwards increased the amount to a million, or nearly so. These bold steps gained the whole affair such an increase of credit, that, upon a bare notice that certain irredeemable annuities would be received for stock, upon terms hereafter to be settled, numbers of annuitants deposited their securities at the South Sea House, without knowing the terms! About June, when the first half-yearly dividend was becoming due, the frenzy rose to such a pitch, that the stock was sold at *eight hundred and ninety per cent.* This extravagance, however, made so many sellers, that the price suddenly fell, and uneasiness began to be manifested; when the Directors had the inconceivable audacity to propose to create new stock at *one thousand per cent.,* to be paid in ten instalments of one hundred pounds each. Strange to relate, this desperate villany turned the tide again, and, to use the words of Anderson, 'in a few days the hundred pound instalment was worth *four hundred!*'

We invariably find that the success, whether real or pretended, of any one scheme gives rise to a host of imitations. If any new company, whatever be its object, is started, and the shares are selling at a premium, we may look with perfect confidence for the announcement of six or seven others before as many days have elapsed. This is, of course, partly owing to the cupidity of the public; but that cupidity could not manifest itself so soon in a tangible form, but for the machinations of certain parties, who see their way to a profit whatever may be the result of the speculation. Amidst the ruin and desolation which invariably follow those seasons of infuriated and infatuated gambling, to which we are now almost habituated, such men preserve a tranquil and a calm demeanour. And no wonder: they have reaped the harvest which the folly of others has sown. At the hottest and most exciting period of the game, they have their senses as completely under control as the sharper who has deliberately dined on chicken and lemonade, with the prospect of encountering afterwards an inebriated victim at Crockford's. They may play largely, but they only do so while their hand is safe; the moment luck changes, they sell out, and leave the whole loss to be borne by the unfortunate dupes, who, believing in their deliberate falsehoods, still continue to hold on, trusting to the advent of those fabulous better times which, in their case, never can arrive. It has been so in our own times, and it was so when the South Sea bubble was expanding on its visionary basis. Multitudes of minor schemes were projected, subscribed for, and driven up to an exorbitant premium. The shares of really solid companies participated in the rise, and mounted correspondingly in the market. The nominal value of all the sorts of stock then afloat was computed at no less than five hundred millions; being exactly double the estimated value of the whole lands, houses, and real property in the kingdom!

The collapse came, and brought ruin to thousands who thought that they held fortune within their grasp. The history of the downfall is not less suggestive than that of the rapid rise. It has had its parallel in our days, when the most rotten and unsubstantial of companies have brazened out their frauds to the last, doctored accounts, declared fictitious dividends, and threatened with legal prosecution those who had the courage and the honesty to expose them.

> The minor bubbles burst first, when the South Sea schemers were foolish enough to apply for a *scire facias* against their projectors, on the ground that *their* schemes injured the credit of the grand scheme. This turned quondam allies into furious enemies. The *scire facias* was issued on 13th August 1720, when the downfall began: and Mr. Hutchison saw his predictions completely fulfilled. The South Sea villains, in sheer desperation, declared a *half-yearly dividend of thirty per cent.* due at Christmas, and offered to guarantee fifty per cent. per annum for twelve years! They might as well have declared it for the thirtieth of February. Everything was done to prop the reputation of the directors, but all was in vain; and when the stock fell at last to one hundred and seventy-five, a panic ensued, and all went to the ground together, totally ruining thousands, and nearly dragging the Bank and East India Company along with it. [. . .]

It would, we apprehend, be impossible to find any one who will advocate gambling upon principle; though a multitude of excellent persons, who would shrink with horror were the odious epithet applied to them, are, nevertheless, as much gamblers as if they were staking their money at *rouge-et-noir* or *roulette.* The man who buys into a public stock with the intention of selling in a week or a fortnight, in the expectation of doing so at an advanced price, or the other who sells shares which he does not possess, in the confident belief of a speedy fall, is, in everything save decency of appearance, on a par with the haunter of the casino. He may, if he so pleases, designate himself an investor, but, in reality, he is a common gamester. This may be a hard truth, but it is a wholesome one, and it cannot be too often repeated, at a time when general usage, and yielding to temptation, have perverted words from their ordinary significance, and led many of us to justify transactions which, when tried by the standard of morality, and stripped of their disguise, ought to be unhesitatingly condemned. "He that loveth gold shall not be justified," said the son of Sirach. "Many have sinned for a small matter; and he that seeketh for abundance will turn his eyes away. As a nail sticketh fast between the joinings of the stones, so doth sin stick close between buying and selling." This spirit, when it becomes general in the nation, cannot be otherwise than most hurtful to its welfare, since it diverts the thoughts of many from those industrial pursuits which are profitable to themselves and others, and leads them astray from that honourable and upright course which is the sure and only road to wealth, happiness, and esteem. This has been, to a certain extent, acknowledged by government, even within our own time. The pernicious effect of the lotteries, originally a state device, upon the morals and condition of the lower classes, as testified by the vast increase of crime, became at length so glaring, that these detestable engines of fraud were suppressed by act of parliament. They still linger on the Continent, as most of us have reason to know from the annual receipt of documents, copiously circulated by the Jews of Hamburg and Frankfort, offering us, in exchange for a few florins, the chance of becoming proprietors of several chateaux on the Rhine, with boar-forests, mineral springs, vineyards, and other appurtenances. We presume, from the continuity of the circulars, that Israel still finds its dupes; but we never happened, save in one of Charles Lever's[23] novels, to hear of any person lucky enough to stumble on the ticket which secured the right to Henkersberg, Bettlersbad, or Narrenstein. The extent to which lottery gambling was carried in this country seems to us absolutely incredible. Derby sweeps were nothing to it. [. . .]

A new discovery was presently made, which had a serious effect upon trade. Money-prizes were discontinued, and shopkeepers, parcelling out their goods, disposed of them by lottery. As a matter of course, this business, commenced by disreputable adventurers, proved most injurious to the regular dealer. People refused to buy an article at the regular price, when it might be obtained for next to nothing. They were, however, utterly wrong, for the staple of the prize goods, when inspected, proved to be of the most flimsy description. Tickets in the state lotteries became the subject of pawn, and were so received by the brokers, and even by the bankers. Suicide was rife; forgery grew common; theft increased enormously. Husbands and fathers saw their wives and children reduced to absolute starvation, and weeping bitterly for bread, and yet pawned their last articles of household furniture for one more desperate chance in the lottery. Wives betrayed their husbands, and plundered them for the same purpose. Servants robbed their masters; commissions and offices were sold. Insurance was resorted to, to accommodate all classes. Those who had not money to pay for tickets might insure a certain number for a small sum, and thus obtain a prize; and so lottery grew upon lottery, and the sphere was indefinitely extended. It was not until 1826 that this abominable

---

23. Charles Lever (1806–72). Novelist and friend of Thackeray and Trollope. Author of numerous novels, including *Tom Bourke* and *Maurice Tiernay*. [Ed.]

system was finally crushed. The image of the vans, placards, and handbills of Bish is still fresh in our memory; and we pray devoutly that succeeding generations may never behold a similar spectacle.

It would be in vain for us, within the limits of an article, to attempt even the faintest sketch of the speculative manias which, from time to time, have affected the prosperity of Great Britain. Some of these have been quite as baseless as the South Sea bubble, and may be directly traced to the agency and instigation of the Stock Exchange. Others were founded upon schemes of manifest advantage to the public, and even to the proprietary, if cautiously and wisely carried out; but here again the passion for gambling has been insanely developed, and encouraged by those who sought to make fortunes at the expense of their dupes. There is at all times, in this country, a vast deal of unemployed capital, which, in the cant phrase, "is waiting for investment," and which cannot well be invested in any of the ordinary channels of business. The fact is, that within the area of Britain, it has been long difficult for a capitalist to select a proper field of operation; and the tendency of recent legislation has materially increased the difficulty. The country, in fact, may be considered as entirely *made*. Agricultural improvement, on a large scale, which implied the possession of a tract of unprofitable country, was considered, even before the repeal of the corn laws,[24] as no hopeful speculation. Since that disastrous event, the chances have naturally diminished; and we suspect that, by this time, very few people have any faith in Sir Robert Peel's[25] proposal for establishing new colonies in Connaught. When we find the Whig Lord Monteagle denouncing free trade as the bane of Ireland, we may be sure that few capitalists will sink their funds in the western bogs, hoping that they may appear again in the shape of golden grain which may defy the competition of the fertile valleys of America. We have quite enough of factories for all the demand which is likely to come for years: instead of building new ones, it is always easy, if any one has a fancy for it, to purchase abandoned mills at a very considerable discount; but we do not find such stock eagerly demanded in the market. Foreign competition has extinguished several branches of industry to which capital might be profitably applied, and materially injured others; so that moneyed men really are at a loss for eligible investment. This want has been felt for a long time; and the uncertain polity of our ministers, with regard to colonial affairs, has undoubtedly had an injurious effect upon the prosperity of these dependencies. We have annihilated much of the capital invested in the West Indies, and have withdrawn a great deal more. It is long since Adam Smith urged the propriety and the policy of identifying some of our

---

24. The repeal, in 1846, of protective tariffs on grain. This is generally equated with the triumph of a doctrine of free trade in England. [Ed.]

25. Sir Robert Peel (1788–1850). Leader of the Tory party and prime minister 1841–46. Sponsored the Bank Charter Act of 1844 and the repeal of the Corn Laws in 1846. [Ed.]

more important colonies with Great Britain, by the simple process of incorporation, thus extending materially the field of the capitalist upon security equal to that which he can always command at home. Such an opportunity is at this moment afforded by Canada; but it seems that we will rather run the risk of seeing Canada merge in the United States than make any sacrifice of our pride, even where our interest is concerned. A considerable deal of capital has gone to Australia; but we suspect, from late events, that the future supply will be limited.

Before the railways opened to capitalists a channel of investment which appeared exceedingly plausible, and which was, in a great measure, guaranteed by the result of experiment, vast masses of realised wealth accumulated from time to time. Upon these hoards the members, myrmidons, and jobbers of the Stock Exchange, cast a covetous eye: they whispered to each other, in the language of King John—

> *Let them shake the bags*
> *Of hoarding abbots; angels imprisoned*
> *Set thou at liberty: the fat ribs of peace*
> *Must by the hungry now be fed upon:*
> *Use our* commission *in its utmost force.*

Acting upon this principle, they made their business to find out new channels of investment—an easier task than the discovery of a northwestern passage in the arctic regions—and to represent these in all the glowing colours which are peculiar to the artists of 'Change Alley.

The year 1823 was remarkable for the commencement of an epidemic which proved, in its effects, even more disastrous than the South Sea delusion. It would be tedious to enumerate or discuss the causes which led to this sudden outburst; some of them have been indirectly traced to the operation of Sir Robert Peel's famous Currency Act of 1819, which fettered the Bank of England, whilst it left the country bankers free to issue unlimited paper, and to the respite of the smaller notes which had been previously doomed to extinction. Whatever may have been the cause, speculation began and increased at a rate which was quite unprecedented. All kinds of ridiculous schemes found favour in the public eye: nothing was too absurd or preposterous to scare away applicants for shares. Mining, building, shipping, insurance, railway, colonising, and washing companies were established: even an association for the making of gold was subscribed for to the full amount, and doubtless a balloon company for lunar purposes would have been equally popular. This period was marked by the apparition of an entirely new animal in the precincts of the Stock Exchange. Bulls, bears, and even lame ducks, were creatures coeval with its existence; but the "stag," in its humanised form, first appeared in 1823. The following sketch might pass for a view of Capel Court some two-and-twenty years later:

The readiness with which shares were attainable first created a class of speculators that has ever since formed a marked feature in periods of excitement, in the dabblers in shares and loans with which the courts and crannies of the parent establishment were crowded. The scene was worthy the pencil of an artist. With huge pocket-book containing worthless scrip: with crafty countenance and cunning eye; with showy jewellery and threadbare coat; with well-greased locks, and unpolished boots; with knavery in every curl of the lip, and villany in every thought of the heart; the stag, as he was afterwards termed, was a prominent portrait in the foreground. Grouped together in one corner, might be seen a knot of boys, eagerly buying and selling at a profit which bore no comparison to the loss of honesty they each day experienced. Day after day were elderly men with huge umbrellas witnessed in the same spot, doing business with those whose characters might be judged from their company. At another point, the youth just rising into manhood, conscious of a few guineas in his purse, with a resolute determination to increase them at any price, gathered a group around, while he delivered his invention to the listening throng, who regarded him as a superior spirit. In every corner, and in every vacant space, might be seen men eagerly discussing the premium of a new company, the rate of a new loan, the rumoured profit of some lucky speculator, the rumoured failure of some great financier, or wrangling with savage eagerness over the fate of a shilling. The scene has been appropriated by a novelist as not unworthy of his pen. "There I found myself," he writes, "in such company as I had never seen before. Gay sparks, with their hats placed on one side, and their hands in their breeches' pockets, walked up and down with a magnificent strut, whistling most harmoniously, or occasionally humming an Italian air. Several grave personages stood in close consultation, scowling on all who approached, and seeming to reprehend any intrusion. Some lads, whose faces announced their Hebrew origin, and whose miscellaneous finery was finely emblematical of Rag Fair, passed in and out; and besides these, there attended a strangely varied rabble, exhibiting in all sorts of forms and ages, dirty habiliments, calamitous poverty and grim-visaged villany. It was curious to me to hear with what apparent intelligence they discussed all the concerns of the nation. Every wretch was a statesman; and each could explain, not only all that had been hinted at in parliament, but all that was at that moment passing in the bosom of the Chancellor of the Exchequer."

The sketch is not over-coloured. No one can have forgotten the sudden swarm of flesh-flies, called from corruption into existence during the heat of the railway mania, and the ridiculous airs of importance which they assumed. A convulsion of this kind—for it can be styled nothing else—does infinite injury to society: for the common greed of gain too often breaks down the barriers which morality, education, and refinement have reared up, and proves that speculation, as well as poverty, has a tendency to make men acquainted with strange companions.

There were, however, features in the mania of 1823 which distinguish it from every other. The joint-stock companies established for domestic bubble purposes engrossed but a limited share of the public attention; though the extent of that limitation may be estimated by the fact, that five hundred and thirty-two new companies were projected, with a nominal subscribed capital of £441,649,600. Of course only a mere fraction of this money was actually put down; still the gambling in the shares was enormous. The greater part of the capital actually abstracted from the country went in the shape of foreign loans, of which there were no less than twenty-six contracted during that disastrous period, or very shortly before, to an amount of about fifty-six millions. On sixteen of these loans interest has ceased to be paid. We find among the borrowers such states as Chili, Buenos Ayres, Colombia, Guatemala, Gunduljava, Mexico, and Peru, not to mention Greece, Portugal, and Spain, countries which have set to Europe a scandalous example of repudiation. Most of these loans purported to bear interest at the rate of six per cent., and some of them were contracted for at so low a figure as 68; nevertheless, with all these seeming advantages, it appears marvellous that people should have lent their money on such slender security as the new republics could offer. [. . .]

Those foreign loans, and the drain of bullion which they occasioned, speedily brought on the crisis. It was a very fearful one, and for the second time, at least, the Bank of England was in danger. It was then that mighty establishment owed its safety to the discovery of a neglected box of one pound notes, which, according to the evidence of Mr. Harman, one of the principal directors, saved the credit of the country. The coffers of the bank were exhausted, almost to the last sovereign; and but for that most fortunate box, cash payments must have been suspended in December, 1825, a position of affairs the issue of which no human intelligence could predicate. Subsequent legislation has not been able to guard us against the possibility of a similar recurrence. All that has been done is to insure the certainty of an earlier and more frequent panic, and to clog the wheels of commerce by rendering discounts impracticable at periods when no speculation is on foot. But as far as regards the stability of the Bank of England, under our present monetary laws, no provision has been made, in any way commensurate to the additional risk occasioned by the absorption of the twenty millions and upwards lodged in the savings-banks, all which must, when required, be repaid in the precious metals; and in case of any convulsion, or violent alarm, it is clear that such a demand would be made. The experience of 1832 has clearly demonstrated how the fate of a ministry may be made to depend upon the position of the establishment in Threadneedle Street.

It is perhaps not to be wondered at that, in a commercial country like ours, wealth should command that respect and homage which, in other times, was accorded to the possessors of nobler attributes. We make every allowance for the altered circumstances of the age. High and heroic valour, as it existed before, and undoubtedly still does exist, has not the same field for its display as in the days when Christendom was leagued against the Infidel, or even in those, comparatively later, when contending factions made their appeal to arms. Our wars, when they do occur, are matters of tactics and generalship; and physical courage and daring has ceased to be the path to more than common renown. Where most are loyal, and no treason is at hand, loyalty is no conspicuous virtue. Those who are distinguished in the walks of literature and science need not covet adulation, and very seldom can command it. Their fame is of too noble and enduring a quality to be affected by ephemeral applause; and it is good for them to work on in patience and in silence, trusting for their reward hereafter. The substantiality of wealth, the power and patronage which it commands, will inevitably make its possessor more conspicuous in the eyes of the community, than if he were adorned with the highest mental attributes. All things are measured by money: and when money is acknowledged as the chief motive power, he who knows best how to amass it cannot fail to be the object of attention. But the marked and indiscriminate homage which is paid to wealth alone, without regard to the character of the possessor, or the means through which that wealth has been acquired, is, in our estimation, a feature disgraceful to the age, and, were it altogether new, would justify us in thinking that the spirit of independence had declined. We shall hold ourselves excused from illustrating our meaning by making special reference to a recent but striking instance,[26] in which wealth suddenly acquired, though by most iniquitous means, raised its owner, for a time, to the pinnacle of public observation. We prefer selecting from the pages of Mr. Francis the portrait of a man whose character displayed nothing that was great, generous, benevolent, or noble; whose whole life and whole energies were devoted to the acquisition of pelf; whose manners were coarse; whose person was unprepossessing; whose mind never ranged beyond its own contracted and money-making sphere; and who yet commanded, in this England of ours, a homage greater than was ever paid to virtue, intellect, or valour. Such a man was Nathan Meyer Rothschild, the famous Jew capitalist.

Originally from Frankfort, this remarkable man came over to England towards the close of last century, and commenced operations in Manchester, where he is said to have speedily trebled his first capital of £20,000:—

This, says Mr. Francis, was the foundation of that colossal fortune which afterwards passed into a proverb; and in 1800, finding Manchester too small for the mind which could grapple with these profits, Rothschild came to London. It was the period when such a man was sure to make progress, as, clear and compre-

---

26. Possibly a reference to George Hudson, the "Railway King," who was responsible for extensive frauds in the 1840s. [Ed.]

hensive in his commercial views, he was also rapid and decisive in working out the ideas which presented themselves. Business was plentiful; the entire Continent formed our customers; and Rothschild reaped a rich reward. From bargain to bargain, from profit to profit, the Hebrew financier went on and prospered. Gifted with a fine perception, he never hesitated in action. Having bought some bills of the Duke of Wellington at a discount—to the payment of which the faith of the state was pledged—his next operation was to buy the gold which was necessary to pay them, and, when he had purchased it, he was, as he expected, informed that the government required it. Government had it—but, doubtless, paid for the accommodation. "It was the best business I ever did," he exclaimed triumphantly; and he added that, when the government had got it, it was of no service to them until he had undertaken to convey it to Portugal.

Rothschild was, in fact, a usurer to the state, as greedy and unconscionable as the humbler Hebrew who discounts the bill of a spendthrift at forty per cent. and, instead of handing over the balance in cash to his victim, forces him to accept the moiety in coals, pictures, or cigars. His information was minute, exclusive, and ramified. All the arts which had been employed on the Stock Exchange in earlier times were revived by him, and new "dodges" introduced to depress or to raise the market.

One cause of his success was the secrecy with which he shrouded all his transactions, and the tortuous policy with which he misled those the most who watched him the keenest. If he possessed news calculated to make the funds rise, he would commission the broker who acted on his behalf to sell half a million. The shoal of men who usually follow the movements of others sold with him. The news soon passed through Capel Court that Rothschild was bearing the market, and the funds fell. Men looked doubtingly at one another; a general panic spread; bad news was looked for; and these united agencies sank the price two or three per cent. This was the result expected; and other brokers, not usually employed by him, bought all they could at the reduced rate. By the time this was accomplished, the good news had arrived; the pressure ceased; the funds rose instantly; and Mr. Rothschild reaped his reward.

The morality of the ring has sometimes been called in question; but we freely confess, that we would rather trust ourselves implicitly to the tender mercies of the veriest leg that ever bartered horse-flesh, than to those of such a man as "the first baron of Jewry"—a title which was given him by a foreign potentate, to the profanation of a noble Christian order.

Such were the doings of Rothschild; let us now see him in person. "He was a mark for the satirists of the day. His huge and somewhat slovenly appearance; the lounging attitude he assumed, as he leaned against his pillar in the Royal Exchange; his rough and rugged speech; his foreign accent and idiom, made caricature mark him as its own; while even caricature lost all power over a subject which defied its utmost skill. His person was made an object of ridicule; but his form and features were from God. His mind and manners were fashioned by circumstances; his acts alone were public property, and by these we have a right to judge him. No great benevolence lit up his path; no great charity is related of him. The press, ever ready to chronicle liberal deeds, was almost silent upon the point; and the fine feeling which marked the path of an Abraham Goldsmid, and which brightens the career of many of the same creed, is unrecorded by the power which alone could give it publicity."

Mr. Disraeli,[27] in some of his clever novels, has drawn the portrait of a great Jew financier in colours at once brilliant and pleasing. His Sidonia,[28] whilst deeply engaged in money-making pursuits, is represented as a man of boundless accomplishment, expanded intellect, varied information, and princely generosity. He is the very Paladin of the Exchange—a compound of Orlando and Sir Moses Montefiore. The extravagance of the conception does not prevent us from admiring the consummate skill of the author, in adapting his materials so as to elevate our ideas and estimate of the Hebrew idiosyncrasy. Sidonia is as much at home in the palace as in the counting-room; his great wealth ceases to be the prominent feature, and becomes the mere accessory of the polished and intellectual man; avarice never for one moment is permitted to appear; on the contrary, the prodigality of the munificent Hebrew is something more than Oriental. We may refuse to believe in the reality of such a character, which implies a combination of the most antagonistic pursuits, and a union of mental attributes which could not possibly coexist; but, this difficulty once surmounted, we cannot challenge the right of so eminently gifted an individual to take his place among the true nobility of the earth. We fear, however, that such a phœnix of Palestine has no existence, save on paper. Certain it is, that Rothschild was not the man; and yet Rothschild, in his day, commanded as much homage as the novelist has claimed for Sidonia. Great is the power of money! Princes feasted with him; ambassadors attended him to the tomb; and yet, for all we can learn, he was not equal, in moral worth, to the meanest pauper in the workhouse. He would at times give a guinea to a street beggar, not for the object of relieving his wants, but to enjoy the joke of seeing him run away, under the apprehension that the donor had been mistaken in the coin. His wealth was gained by chicanery, and augmented by systematic deceit; and yet attend to the words of the chronicler:

> Peers and princes of the blood sat at his table; clergymen and laymen bowed before him; and they who preached loudest against mammon, bent lowest before the

27. Benjamin Disraeli (1804–81). Tory member of Parliament and prime minister (1874–80). Disraeli was also a novelist who published *Coningsby* (1844) and *Sybil* (1845). [Ed.]
28. The sympathetic Jewish character in Disraeli's *Coningsby* (1844). [Ed.]

mammon-worshipper. Gorgeous plate, fine furniture, an establishment such as many a noble of Norman descent would envy, graced his entertainments. Without social refinement, with manners which offensive in the million, were but *brusque* in the millionnaire; he collected around him the fastidious members of the most fastidious aristocracy in the world. He saw the representatives of all the states in Europe proud of his friendship. By the democratic envoy of the New World, by the ambassador of the imperial Russ, was his hospitality alike accepted; while the man who warred with slavery in all its forms and phases, was himself slave to the golden reputation of the Hebrew. The language which Mr. Rothschild could use when his anger overbalanced his discretion, was a license allowed to his wealth; and he who, when placed in a position which almost compelled him to subscribe to a pressing charity, could exclaim, "Here write a check—I have made one—fool of myself" was courted and caressed by the clergy, was fêted and followed by the peer, was treated as an equal by the first minister of the crown, and more than worshipped by those whose names stood foremost on the roll of a commercial aristocracy. His mode of dictating letters was characteristic of a mind entirely absorbed in money-making; and his ravings, when he found a bill unexpectedly protested, were translated into mercantile language before they were fit to meet a correspondent's eye. It is painful to write thus depreciatingly of a man who possessed so large a development of brain; but the golden gods of England have many idolaters, and the voice of truth rarely penetrates the private room of the English merchant.

Poor as Lazarus may be, let him not envy the position of Dives. Even in this world, riches cannot purchase happiness. Any pecuniary loss was enough to drive Rothschild to despair. His existence was further embittered by the dread of assassination—no uncommon symptom, when the mind is rarely at ease; and those who knew him best, said that he was often troubled with such thoughts, and that they haunted him at moments when he would willingly have forgotten them. "Happy!" he said, in reply to the compliment of a guest—"me happy! what! happy when, just as you are going to dine, you have a letter placed in your hands, saying, 'If you do not send me £500, I will blow your brains out?' Happy!—me happy!" We are not compassionate enough to wish that it had been otherwise. Such thoughts are the foreshadowing of the end of those who have prospered beyond their deserts, and have failed in making even that negative expiation, which conscience sometimes extorts from the apprehensions of unscrupulous men.

And here we shall close our remarks. There is still a fertile field before us, on which we might be tempted to enter; but that discussion would bring us too near our own days, and involve the resumption of topics which have already been handled in Maga.[29] The time doubtless will come, when, after the ces-

---

29. An abbreviated form of *Blackwood's Edinburgh Magazine*. [Ed.]

sation of some new fit of speculation, and when men are cursing their folly, and attempting by late industry to repair their shattered fortunes, some historian like Mr. Francis shall take up the pen, and chronicle our weakness, as that of our fathers is already chronicled. In the meantime, it would be well for all of us seriously to lay to heart the lesson which may be drawn from this interesting record. Speculation, carried beyond due bounds, is neither more nor less than a repetition of the old game of BEGGAR MY NEIGHBOUR[30] under another form. To fair and legitimate enterprise we owe much of our modern improvement; which has been further rendered necessary by the pressure which has increased, and is increasing upon us. To unfair and illegitimate enterprise, undertaken for the sole purpose of immediate gain, we owe nothing save periods of great misery and desolation. The game of BEGGAR MY NEIGHBOUR may be played privately or publicly. Some of us have taken a hand in it privately, with what results we shall keep to ourselves. For several years back, our statesmen have played the public game, and played it well. They have succeeded in inflicting successively a blow upon each great interest of the country, by dealing with each separately, and by alienating the sympathy of the others. The game is now pretty well played out; and when we come to reckon our counters, it is evident from the result, that not one of the parties so dealt with has been a winner? Who, then, are the gainers? We think the answer is plain. They are the Capitalist and the Foreigner.

---

30. A card game in which each player holds half the cards. When one player turns up an ace, king, queen, or jack, the other must give up, respectively, four, three, two, or one of his chards. The winner is the person who finally holds all of the cards. [Ed.]

CHAPTER FIVE

INVESTMENT AND SPECULATION

ANONYMOUS

STOCKBROKING AND THE STOCK EXCHANGE

The trade of a stockbroker is a modern one—hardly two hundred years old. It may be said to have begun in this country with the beginning of our funded debt, and with the incorporation of the Bank of England. Before that time the peculiar documents called stocks and shares did not exist in sufficient quantity, if at all, to make dealing in them a profitable business. But with the creation of this new form of representative wealth came a new occupation, which was early taken advantage of by the Jews, who have ever since been conspicuous as dealers on the Stock Exchanges of the world. There were, no doubt, loans and securities earlier than two hundred years ago, but until then they had been private or semi-private affairs; and invitations to the public to trust a nation or a small knot of traders with their savings had not become of that organised and customary kind which is implied in the free creation of bonds and shares. But, once started, the trade became a brisk one, and the disturbances, revolutions, and wars of the last century had a most stimulating effect on the production of new material of this kind for traders at home and abroad. Within little more than a century our national debt grew from 25,000,000*l*. or 30,000,000*l*. to nearly 900,000,000*l*., all told; and for the limited ways of doing business then possible that was itself capable of giving a most extensive field for speculation. Then, too, from the first the dealers in stocks and shares were fertile workers in the field of corporate enterprise. Every now and then

Anonymous, "Stockbroking and the Stock Exchange." *Fraser's Magazine* n.s. 14 (July 1876): 84–103.

their energetic pursuit of new fields of joint-stock speculation led to the per-
petration of some gigantic swindle or the committal of some perhaps more
disastrous folly, such as the famous and typical South Sea Bubble. It was not,
however, till almost the present generation that the Stock Exchange and the
trade of stockbroking took its grand position in the country, and became
nearly the most important business carried on in the City of London. With the
application of steam to locomotion on land the world entered on a new era—
the stockjobber on a field of enterprise which must have exceeded the most
fabulous of his dreams. As soon as the mania for developing the resources of
nations by means of railways fairly took hold on the world, the rapidity with
which money was borrowed for the purpose exceeded anything of the kind
that had ever occurred before, and was productive of a series of commercial
crises which, checking the onward rush for a time, did not hinder renewed
outbursts as soon as the speculators had got their breath again. As recently as
1845 the total capital sunk in railways throughout the world was only about
114,000,000*l.,* of which Great Britain had spent some 64,000,000*l.* and
America 18,000,000*l.* At the present time the railways of Great Britain alone
represent a nominal outlay of nearly 650,000,000*l.,* and those of the United
States 760,000,000*l.*

Besides these sums France has spent about 400,000,000*l.,* Germany about
220,000,000*l.,* and Russia about 250,000,000*l.* Many other foreign countries
have thus pledged the national credit for nominally at least the same kind of
"works of public utility" to an enormous extent; and hence the national debts
of Turkey, Austria and Hungary, Egypt, Italy, Spain, and of various petty
semi-barbarous South American republics, of the Empires of Brazil and of
Chili, have been swollen prodigiously. What the total pledges of credit in the
world may amount to, or what amount of savings may have been locked up in
corporate enterprises, it would be almost impossible to say, just as it is impossible to reckon how far the aggregate figures represent money spent
and how far mere paper; but the national debts of the world are now swollen
almost as much as the credit of separate enterprise and corporations. The
principal countries of Europe owe about 3,500,000,000*l.,* exclusive of the unsecured paper currencies and our home debt; and all other national debts
which come within the cognisance of civilisation may be valued at about
1,000,000,000*l.*

These huge and rapidly accumulated obligations are not, it is true, due, by
any means, exclusively to the spread of industrial enterprise—Austria, Spain,
Italy, France, the United States, and Russia having contracted large national
debts in the prosecution of wars and conquests; but for the purposes of the
stockbroker it is much the same whether the "securities" he deals in are based
on industrial undertakings or commerce, or are mere loans necessitated by a

national bankruptcy or an ambitious war. His business is to buy and sell and get gain out of these bits of paper; and it is of the essence of that business that quantity should have weight with him, not quality. And of quantity it cannot be denied that the modern stockbroker has enough. The nominal values of the stocks and shares quoted in the London Stock Exchange was computed by the compiler of *Fenn on the Funds* two years ago to be about 4,550,000,000*l.*, and at the present time rather exceeds that amount. There is also probably well on towards 50,000,000*l.* more, not on its list, comprising the capital of small joint-stock enterprises, mines of all kinds, country banks, &c., which London and provincial stockbrokers traffic in and make profit by.

What proportion of these huge totals represent really sound values we cannot now enquire: all we have to do is to point to the fact that the means of doing business has been thus swollen by the modern spirit of enterprise. Each unit of this total represents a pledge given by some nation of its credit and means, or a venture of some trader or traders on the spirit of the time; and each has its risks, its chances, its varying and infinitely varied gradations of stability or plausibility. The Limited Liability Acts of 1862 and 1867 helped to extend to trade enterprises generally the passion for corporate ventures which was here previously confined to certain channels, in some of which, such as joint-stock banking, it was showing signs of having spent itself. These Acts, by limiting the risks of individuals, helped to bring into being floods of new schemes. The Act of 1862 did much to bring on us the panic of 1866, and unquestionably stimulated to an exceedingly unhealthy degree the speculative tendencies of that time. Nor has the Act of 1867 done much to quench the evil. Companies have since 1862 and up to to-day started by the thousand, like mushrooms in the night, only to vanish as quickly as they came, leaving only a void in the pockets of the unsophisticated and gullible subscribers to the shares, till it may be almost said that the amount of capital which has run through the Stock Exchange in bubble companies as through a sieve has been as great as that which has found permanent rest in sound enterprises, whose stocks stand the test of the market. This state of things may have been an inevitable concomitant of "legitimate progress," but it has been a very painful one to many, and has brought "limited liability" into so great disrepute that what was sound and good in the principle promises to be now underrated.

Here, then, only briefly outlined, we have some idea of the materials out of which the modern stockbroker creates his trade. He is a buyer and seller of bits of paper which bear either that this or that company has so much of So-and-So's money, or that this or that Government or railway company has guaranteed for so long or for ever, in virtue of certain moneys paid down, so much per cent. per annum to the holder of this its certificate of indebtedness.

The varieties of bonds and shares are almost innumerable; but the classes into which they may all be divided are two—1st, The share or partnership certificate constituting the holder a partner entitled to a share in the profits; if any, of a joint-stock undertaking up to the extent of the capital which said share represents him to have paid; and 2nd, the "bond," which is in one form or other an acknowledgment for a loan, and a promise to pay fixed interest on that loan for a certain period or for ever, as the case may be, as well as in many cases to redeem it by a fixed date. Of the first class are all shares in banks, mines, industrial companies, and railways; and of the second national bonds of all kinds, railway bonds, debentures, and mortgage bonds generally. It would prove tedious to the reader to analyse the varieties of these securities in detail; but one or two of the distinctions amongst the numerous kinds of bonds may be given. Our own Consols are a perpetual form of bond, for instance. They do not specify dates of repayment, but only contain a promise to give so much per cent. to the holders. When cancelled they can only be so by the Government, through its brokers, buying them in at the market price of the day. Terminable Government or joint-stock companies' bonds are, on the other hand, quite another kind of document, though still an acknowledgment of indebtedness. They specify a date when they must be paid off, and generally make stipulations as to a sinking fund to be applied to annual or semi-annual drawings of bonds payable at par, no matter what the original or actual price of the bond may have been. These are in reality, therefore, usually annuity bonds, only that the annuity is split up into the interest at a fixed rate, and lottery payments at a cumulative rate; and this has been the favourite guise in which the chief speculative foreign loans have been dressed up for the investor's rather voracious appetite for "a little gambling." Then, again, there are the debentures of our English railways and the mortgage bonds of American and other railways—the one giving only a fixed interest with no mortgage powers over the line in event of the non-payment of that interest, and the other nominally enabling the mortgagees or bondholders to sell the property for their own benefit when default occurs. It is not found in practice that the latter form conveys, as a rule, any appreciable advantage, but rather the reverse; for when an American company of any size comes to grief, all that is produced by an attempt to enforce right of the kind is a wrangle among the various holders of bonds issued under, perhaps, two or three successive mortgage deeds, and under different States laws, and a very striking illustration of the extremely intangible character of the substance which the mortgages were taken to represent. It eludes the grasp as effectually as any Will-o'-the-Wisp. Another form of debt still is the Exchequer Bills of our own Government and the Treasury Bills of Foreign States; but these are neither more nor less than promissory notes.

It will not be necessary to enter further into details on these points. The reader will now have a general idea of the materials in which the stockbroker trades, and will therefore be able to follow the description which it is now proposed to give of the manner in which this trade is carried on in London. At the very threshold of this description it becomes visible that the Stock-market has to perform a double function. It deals in stocks and shares, buys and sells, and it is also the centre where the peculiar kinds of security there found can alone be successfully brought into being. Without the aid of the Stock Exchange it would never have been possible to bring the innumerable enterprises whose paper is dealt in, in that market to maturity; for the stock must not only be made but readily sold to those who will give money for it. As a medium for finding capital with which to start any corporate enterprise, the Stock Exchange stands in the same position as the banks do to the trades in want of discount accommodation—through the Stock Exchange agency the money is found in all cases of any importance.

We have, therefore, to contemplate the stockbroker in these two aspects. He may be a promoter of a scheme, or he may be the mere agent of clients who want to buy or sell this stock or that already "placed on the market." In his first capacity he has often a very arduous and peculiar work to do in order to persuade the public that the new security which he has to offer is a good one. Some recent trials in the criminal courts have made the general public familiar to a certain extent with these arts, and have conveyed a by no means favourable impression about them; and we are sorry to say that these arts have been but too prevalent in cases where one might have thought them not required. The only defence of the system of making false purchases and sales on the market in order to induce the public, who go by prices and not by facts as a rule, to come in and actually buy through belief that the price indicates a good thing, is that sometimes, but for a proceeding of this kind, a good enterprise would have been ruined. It is an insufficient defence, and cannot justify in any degree a practice which has led to incalculable evils. Before it is possible to understand this or any other part of the stockbroker's business, however, we must try to shape some sort of image of what the Stock Exchange is itself, of the leading rules under which it transacts business, of the divisions of that business, and of the nature of Stock Exchange speculation.

The modern Stock Exchange of London, to which it will be best to confine our observations, is in its most obvious aspect a large hall with a number of offices around it, built within the irregular quadrangle formed by Bartholomew Lane, Throgmorton Street, and Threadneedle Street and Old Broad Street. Primarily it is merely a convenient meeting-place where stockbrokers gather to transact their business, just as the Royal Exchange—now an almost deserted building—is a meeting-place for those who deal in foreign bills of exchange. Various circumstances have combined, however, to give the Stock

Exchange the character of an organised joint-stock undertaking of a quasi-public character, and to make it a sort of standard of worth as well as a market. In the first place the members of the "House" (as it is familiarly called) carry on their business under an elaborate code of rules, the practical aim of which is to make the body as much as possible a law to itself. The modes of making bargains, the responsibility of dealers, and the treatment of members who become bankrupt, with many minor matters, are all subject to this special code, the practical effect of which is, therefore, to make the Stock Exchange an *imperium in imperio* to a greater extent than any other mere market organisation in the country, except, perhaps, Tattersall's.[1] Members are forbidden to go to law with each other to enforce claims; all is to be settled by the governing body of the "House" itself—the Committee of the Stock Exchange. This body possesses ample powers for calling members who break the rules to account, and by a two-thirds majority vote in a meeting of not less than twelve the Committee-men can expel any offender. Members who fail in business, become by that failure unqualified to continue in membership; but they may be readmitted two years after they have got their creditors' discharge if they have paid 6s. 8d. in the pound, or sooner if they pay in full. The bankruptcy business of the "House" is managed by "Official Assignees," who examine into the bankrupt's affairs, and divide his assets.

This represents one side of the organisation, a side which has its uses and its defects. But before dwelling on this we must touch on another aspect of the Stock Exchange, which is not so habitually visible to those who look at it from the outside. Besides being an organisation for carrying on a special kind of business in a style suited to the ideas of its members, the Stock Exchange is a joint-stock company itself. The building belongs to the company and the members; both contribute to the profits of the company as subscribers to the institution, and partake of these profits as shareholders. Formerly, we believe, the shares were few, and for large amounts; but some years ago they were split up into 10ths, so that, if possible, every subscriber to the "House" might become also a shareholder, and interest himself in its affairs with a view to profit. The working of such an arrangement as this is visible in the extremely loose manner in which new members are admitted. In some of our provincial stock exchanges the rules of admission are very strict; and before a man can become a member he must not only find large securities for his well-doing, but must prove himself a man of substance by depositing a considerable sum

---

1. The celebrated sporting rendezvous and auction house for horses located from 1766 at Hyde Park Corner. In 1864, Tattersall's was moved to a more fashionable location at the junction of Brompton and Knightsbridge Roads. [Ed.]

of money in trust for the protection of fellow members with whom he deals. There can be no question that such a course tends to curb to some extent reckless speculation, and to keep stockdealing respectable; but this is not the manner of the London Stock Exchange. There, till quite lately, any man might be admitted who paid the 25*l.* or 50*l.* entry money, and 12*l.* 12*s.* per annum subscription, if he found three members to be security for him for a small amount—some 500*l.* each. Within the last three months the subscription was raised to 20*l.* per annum, and the entrance fee for principals to 100*l.*, and for their clerks to 60*l.*, while the three sureties have now to stand good for 750*l.* apiece; but otherwise the position is as before, with the result that the Stock Exchange has become the haunt of adventurers from all parts of the world, and is surrounded by a more repellent set of vagabonds, as the satellites of these, than can be found anywhere else in London. Betting-men, who have failed on the turf, take to stockbroking and jobbing, and either enter the "House," or gamble round the doors; and loafers, who have done no good at any legitimate trade, find their refuge here. Nondescripts from the Low Countries, Jews and Greeks from all parts of Europe and the Levant, gather to swell the total of those who are either members of the "House," or who "job" outside with kindred spirits within.

The Stock Exchange, in short, while almost in spite of itself performing great public functions, is conducted very much in the spirit of a private joint-stock company, with a particularly strong eye to profits; and on this principle it has thriven, until the dividends paid to the lucky shareholders are somewhere about 105 per cent. on the original value of the shares. This commercial policy has beyond question had something to do with the extreme disrepute into which stock-broking and the Stock Exchange have lately been brought, and therefore it would be well if the members could see their way to reform in time. It is already becoming an open question whether it would not be better to abolish the Stock Exchange altogether, and to make stockbroking no longer the privileged trade which it now is. If that reform takes place, the spirit which at present guides Stock-Exchange policy will be its cause. The members of the "House" are, in point of fact, trying to do two things of an opposite kind—to be guides of the public in the matter of investment, and at the same time to secure the profits of a prosperous gambling hell.

We must now, however, look more closely at the stockbroking trade itself, and the manner in which it is carried on, both in order to comprehend its nature, and to be able to grasp the defects of the present organisation in carrying it on. We shall also thus get at the whole *modus operandi* of Stock Exchange speculation, of company floating and loan manufacturing, and understand more clearly the position which the stockbroker holds in relation to these various branches of his trade.

The primary occupation of a stockbroker is, as we have seen, to buy and sell those securities which in a great variety of ways represent capital invested or spent; and in the pursuit of that business in its simplest form his work and duty would be to go and find a purchaser when he had stock of any sort to sell, or to seek a seller when he had stock to buy. Now, but for the Stock Exchange and its machinery, brokers would have to hunt for customers, and bargains would be less rapid, and more difficult to effect. The Stock Exchange simplifies the broker's labours to such an extent, however, that it is very much to be questioned whether he is of any real use at all. The pivot on which the business of the Stock Exchange, as now systematised, hinges is not the broker, but the dealer or jobber, whose functions are quite distinct from that of the broker, and must not be confounded with them. The stockjobber is a sort of wholesale merchant who buys and sells on his own account alone, and not, like the broker, at the bidding of another. In most cases a jobber attaches himself to one particular class of stock, and buys and sells in that with all comers. Thus there are jobbers who deal mostly in the debenture or preference stocks of one or other of the English railways; others who devote themselves to ordinary shares; others still whose staple or sole business is in foreign bonds; and by this arrangement, which has come about as it were by force of natural selection, the Stock Exchange is split up into a number of so-called "markets." The jobbers congregate in groups which are determined by the stocks in which they have elected to deal.

One very obvious advantage arising from this is the facility with which a broker can do his business. Instead of hunting about for a buyer or seller of stocks, which a client either has or wants to have, he goes into the "House" and direct to one of the jobbers who deals in the particular stock, and with him may at once strike a bargain. In order to make this mode of doing business still more easy, a rule prevails, the object of which is to prevent cheating on the part of the jobber, and to put all brokers on a level. When a broker goes to a jobber whether to buy or to sell, the jobber is compelled to what is called "make a price," i.e. he must tell both what he will sell and what he will buy a given quantity of a given stock at. Hence the invariable double quotations given in the newspapers. "Turks," we are there told, "closed $13\frac{1}{8}$ to $\frac{3}{8}$," or "Argentine 68 to 70;" by which the initiated understand that the lower figure is the one at which the jobbers in these stocks have agreed to buy, and the higher the price at which they have resolved to sell. Everyone who enters the market is therefore sure of fair play, because if a dealer names a false price the rules of the market force him to deal at that price should the broker so choose. This naming the double price has also the advantage of indicating to some extent the condition of the market in any particular stock. For example, in the above instances, the quotations for "Turks" would be called a close quotation—the dealer only taking a "turn" of $\frac{1}{4}$ per cent. as his profit; but in the case of the Argentine stock there is a difference of 2 per cent., indicating that the market is unsettled by speculation, and that the jobber feels that he must protect himself by a wider margin between what he buys at and what he sells at.

It will be at once seen that this power of the jobber to make prices and to deal freely is a very great one, and were it not tempered by competition it would be often mischievous. There is no doubt either that in the case of small adventures, loans, or joint-stock companies, in which, perhaps, only one jobber or two are really interested, along with a broker or two who manage the placing of the paper values, the power has been abused often to the injury of the public. These jobbers have been given the stock to place by the promoters or concocters of the swindle, and make what prices they like in collusion with brokers who buy and sell fictitiously in order to give a semblance of demand, and to get a false quotation marked on the official list. That list then and so far becomes a means of cheating the public instead of a means of telling them the truth. With great stocks, such as those of our leading home railways, or the funded debts of the two or three States in the world that have solid credit, this kind of roguery cannot of course be practised. With these, therefore, the prices depend purely upon the competition in the market. If there are many buyers, the jobbers can raise the price; if many sellers, they put it down just as the dealers in any other commodity have to do; but they are entirely at the mercy of the market in so doing. But where new securities are concerned the power of the jobber and his satellite the broker is almost without limit at times.

We must turn, then, to the most important function which this duality of position amongst the members of the Stock Exchange enables that institution to play—the function of aiding speculation. As at present constituted the London Stock Exchange is probably the most perfect organisation for the transaction of speculative bargains which exists, and it is so because of the peculiar relations in which jobber and broker stand to each other. In one sense, every purchase or sale that a jobber effects with a broker may be considered as a pure speculation in itself. The jobber may possibly have the stock to sell; but possession is in no sense requisite, and he may buy after he has sold. A jobber's work is to buy and sell to all comers (amongst members of the "House" of course) at the best prices he can get, and he may deal in hundreds of thousands of a security without ever handling any of it. Except so far as reputation may guide him, he has no knowledge even whether the purchases or sales effected with him by brokers are based on stock or merely fictions. He buys and sells, his sole care being to secure to himself the "turn of the market"—the difference between the price he bought at and the price at which he sells—and to guard himself from loss in a falling market. For example, a broker has an order from some client to go and sell 20,000*l.* of a given stock on speculation for the fall, and immediately goes to the dealer he knows best, or who has the largest business in that particular security, and asks him to make a price. If the price made be satisfactory the sale is effected, and this 20,000*l.* stock gets booked by the jobber as so much stock which he has bought, and which, in order to make his book "even," as it is called, he must try and sell again to some one else. Should he succeed in doing so at his own price to some other broker, or to a dozen brokers with orders to buy, he will have made a profit of $\frac{1}{8}$, or $\frac{1}{4}$, or $\frac{1}{2}$, or 1 per cent., as the case may be; but if the stock sinks rapidly, and he can find few purchasers at the price, he may have to submit to a loss on a part or the whole of the 20,000*l.* before he has balanced his book. On the other hand, of course, if the price rises he makes a larger profit. In either case where it is a big security that is dealt in, he has to submit to tendencies more or less beyond his control. And therefore, in times of financial panic, his position becomes a dangerous one, as indeed also in times of financial inflation; it is particularly dangerous also because the whole of the transactions involved in his buying and selling this 20,000*l.* stock or a hundred like sums may be based on a mere speculative opinion. The client of the broker who sold the stock originally may not have possessed a scrap of it, but sold merely because he was told, or had the opinion, that the stock was going to fall; and equally the ultimate buyer or buyers may have no wish to possess the stock, but merely buy because their speculative opinion is that the stock in question is going to rise.

It is within the mark to say that in recent years full five-sixths of the Stock Exchange business has been of this speculative character; and the jobber is the one who makes it so easy, because he is always—except when panic bursts out—ready to buy or sell, asking no questions. He and the brokers look to make their profits out of both classes of speculators—the "bulls," or speculators for the rise, and the "bears," or speculators for the fall, the one by commissions, the other by "turns" of the market and fluctuations up or down, contrive in the long run to let the speculators be the losers.

Still the game is a dangerous one, and, since the late bankruptcies of big foreign borrowers became the fashion, the jobbers and brokers amongst them must have lost prodigious sums of money. For, although the machinery of the Stock Exchange is all in favour of the members and against the outsiders, these members are very shortsighted persons as a rule. They seldom look much ahead, but are guided by the tendency of the day or even hour; and hence, when a current sets in in any particular direction with a particular class of stocks, they are seldom as a body able to see it till it is too late. In other words, for them the market value of a given stock is never gauged by its intrinsic worth so much as by the speculative furore of the moment. It is this that explains the marvellous effect of lies in the course of any one day's dealing. Almost every day readers of newspapers will find if they turn to the money columns that such and such stocks were raised or depressed by "rumours" of this and that; and to an unsophisticated mind it cannot but be a marvel how stories, usually false or only half true, should produce an effect on stocks often measured by gains or losses of millions. But it is easily explained when the character of the bulk of the business is taken into account. It is business founded on opinion and often on the chance of the moment. A thousand temporary influences are at work appealing to the passions of the hour with ten-fold the force of the permanent conditions or surroundings of the stock. The dealers may find a large preponderance of selling brokers coming to them, and want to raise the price of stock in order to tempt buyers, and straightway favourable rumours get bruited, or, when the reverse conditions obtain, unfavourable.

Now, were either the jobber or the broker done away with, this peculiarly unhealthy "gambling" condition of business could hardly obtain to the extent it does. The ordinary broker, for the sake of "commissions," tempts people, almost in spite of themselves, to speculate, and jobber renders such speculation easy by the facility which he gives for the transaction by buying and selling for the "turn."

It is urged, of course, that all these facilities are necessary to the transaction of business, and that the play of "bull" and "bear" tends to keep prices more equal in the long run than they would otherwise be. But is there any advantage in the system to constitute a sufficient compensation for the gambling fever which has in recent years more and more pervaded all classes of society, and without the aid of which the whole class of bubble companies, foreign loans, and frauds generally, that we are now suffering from the collapse of, could never have been perpetrated? The revelation which last year's parliamentary committee and late criminal trials have made of the modus operandi by which these frauds were "placed," makes the aid which this huge machinery for speculation gives them painfully evident. Take a foreign loan hoax for example, and observe how easily bonds, of which not one-fiftieth portion has been subscribed for by the public, can get quoted at a high premium. Buying goes on by the persons who are interested in seeing the swindle succeed and by their nominees. A little judicious outlay of capital in enabling these dummies to subscribe for bonds and to buy in the market, the skilful combination of brokers' and dealers' resources, in order to keep quotations up at a premium, are all so much baiting of the trap for the outside public. To the mass of these anything quoted at a premium offers an almost irresistible temptation; and, either with a view to investing in a good thing, or to make a snap profit by buying at the apparently rising prices to sell again at a higher level still, people are gradually sucked into the vortex. The public is pretty sure to come in the faster the higher the *premium* is run up, and, once well in, the price is allowed to drop gradually away. The "dummies" and the loan agents "get out" of as many of their bonds as they can, and the public are left to mourn their losses, for they nearly always object to sell out till it is too late, in the vain hope of another rise.

The facility which the intervention of the jobber gives for carrying on all the fictitious dealing which this involves is unquestionably at the root of half the mischief, his object being to buy and sell to all, regardless of the victims or of the worth of any security—the more bargains meaning for him of course usually the more profit. He takes care that in the case of a swindle which is being foisted on the public his gains shall be secure and his bargains real, and may easily, by working in collusion with one or two brokers, who also look after the solidarity of their commissions, behave so that when a member of the outside public wants to buy he can have any quantity of the rubbish at as high a price as he pleases, but that when one thus caught wants to sell again there shall be no market.

We know, at the moment of writing, not one stock but several where this is the situation. Let a man, for instance, go into that hottest of the hotbeds of speculation and fraud, the English mining market, and he can buy the shares of many most remarkable mines at a premium or even, perhaps, as a favour, at a slight discount; but supposing one tries to sell what he has got at the prices quoted in the list, he will be apt to depart with a clear conviction of the depth of his own folly. And quite lately there were some foreign bonds of obscure provinces in a bankrupt South American Republic which were quoted at a high figure in the Stock Exchange official list. At that price buyers were welcome to them; but a disposition to sell appeared, and the price fell suddenly 40 per cent. Instances of this kind might be multiplied infinitely; and, although the best class of jobbers and brokers would not be party to such roguery, there are too many who will. Nothing could show this more clearly than the conduct of certain Stock Exchange people over the Lisbon Tramways Company. After it had been made evident, even to Mr. Albert Grant, that the scheme was utterly impracticable, "a gentleman," Sir Henry James told the Court, "representing the company's broker, came before the board and declared that in the interests of the Stock Exchange the scheme must be allowed to go on." That is, jobbers had bought, and sold, and made profits which they did not want to forego, and brokers had acted in their buyings and sellings for clients from whom they wanted their commissions; therefore, swindle or not, the "scheme" must proceed. These brokers and jobbers were not considered disreputable either, but quite as good as their neighbours.

Working with such machinery and based upon such principles it is indeed purely impossible that the Stock Exchange can be other than an elaborately organised gambling hell, where all sorts of securities are dealt in merely as so many instruments for bringing profit and without regard to their intrinsic value. No doubt there are many members of the "House" who would scorn to stoop to such business, just as there are many securities which are as sound as such things can be in a world where all is changing; and no doubt also without the help of organised methods of bringing joint-stock enterprise before the public many good undertakings could not have prospered as they have done. But all this granted, it remains that the speculative facilities of the Stock Exchange outrun all necessities of legitimate business, and that the atmosphere of the "House" is so peculiar that those who frequent it are unable to see clearly what is right and honourable from what is wrong and despicable. The most upright men in it do things themselves, and are familiar with doings in others, such as anyone with sound moral vision would shrink from and shudder at.

In order to bring out more fully yet how thoroughly the speculative side of Stock Exchange business predominates, it will be necessary to proceed further and to describe the way in which transactions are effected by brokers and their clients with the jobbers in the "House." Those of the public who are among the uninitiated, but who have in recent months been drawn to read about the Stock Exchange in the disclosures made before the parliamentary committee and in our Courts of law, will, no doubt, have been puzzled by such phrases as "account day," "name day," "carrying over day," "contango," "backwardation," "differences," and the like, all of which are as much unintelligible jargon to ordinary persons as turf slang. These phrases have a strong meaning, nevertheless, and an intimate connection with the habits of business on the Stock Exchange.

It is, as we have said, a fundamental law of the "House" that no person is recognised in any business done within its walls except members, and no one is allowed to be a member unless he be a dealer or a broker, or the certified clerk of such. The outside public are consequently altogether shut out of reckoning, and when the client of a broker fails to pay him, that makes no difference whatever to the broker's liability as regards the jobbers with whom he dealt. The broker has to make good the deficiencies of his clients as long as he has anything left to do it with. For the convenience, then, of these two classes of men forming the Stock Exchange the settlement of all transactions between them is made once a fortnight:—Consols are settled for once a month; but they are more frequently dealt in for immediate cash than other stocks, and except when politics are unsettled are not favourite objects of speculation. The latter are indeed, as a rule, bought and sold "for the account," as it is called by the brokers, whether their clients pay for them at once or not; and it is round this credit system, as between broker and jobber, that the whole delicately adjusted machinery of speculation revolves. A fortnight is in these days a long time to come and go upon; and when a man can buy or sell stock which he need not attempt to pay for at the time, the temptation to try his chances of obtaining a snap profit is great. Nothing is easier in these days than for a man with credit enough to command a 10*l.* note to go to a broker and say, "'Buy me' or 'sell me' 1,000*l.,* or 2000*l.,* or 5,000*l.* of such and such a stock." Stocks bought or sold in this way will be indicated to the buyer in a statement sent to him by the broker, made up in the following way:

LONDON, *January* 3, *1876.*
A. Brown, Esq.

We have this day Bought and Sold for your account (subject to the rules of the London Stock Exchange):—

Stock or Shares	Price	£	s.	d.	Brokerage £ s. d.	Stamps & Fees	Total £	s.	d.
		Bought							
1,000*l.* Midland	145	1,450	0	0	¼ 3 12 6		1,453	12	6
		Sold							
1,000*l.* Chatham, prefce.	80	800	0	0	¼ 2 0 0		798	0	0

JONES & ROBINSON, Sworn Brokers.

For the January 13 account.

This transaction being entered upon, the fortnight, or part of a fortnight, runs away, and the speculator finds himself unable to pay for his stock; he, indeed, never intended to pay for it, but hoped to buy in or sell out at a profit. His ventures have gone against him, however, and if he closes his account at the settling day he will do so at a loss. The rule of the Stock Exchange is that every transaction must be so closed at the fortnightly settling day, and, *if that rule were adhered to* in spirit, speculation would be materially crippled. But it is not adhered to at all except pro formâ, and every speculator can in consequence leave his bargain unsettled for a year if he so chooses, or can afford it, should the stock he has dealt in be one that cannot be, as it is called, "cornered" against him. The form of closing the transaction is indeed kept up only as a means of making speculators pay the jobbers and dealers, as the following sample of carrying over accounts will show:

LONDON, *January* 11, 1876.
A. Brown, Esq.

We have this day Sold and Bought for your account (subject to the rules of the London Stock Exchange):—

Stock or Shares	Price	£	s.	d.	Brokerage			Stamps & Fees	Total		
					£	s.	d.		£	s.	d.
			Sold								
1,000*l*. Midland, for Jan. 13 account	142¼								1,422	10	0
1,000*l*. Chatham prefce. for Jan. 28 account	78½ – ¼	787	10	0	1/16	0	9 10		787	0	2
			Bought								
1,000*l*. Chatham prefce. for Jan. 13 account	78½								785	0	0
1,000*l*. Midland	142¼ – ⅜	1,426	5	0	1/16	0	17 10		1,427	2	10

JONES & ROBINSON, Sworn Brokers.

For the January 28 account.

There is a fractional brokerage charged in this example for carrying over and with the contango is added to the price. As between the speculator and the broker the account therefore stands as given below, showing a loss to the former so far of 18*l*. 2*s*. 6*d*.:

Account Mid January, 1876.
LONDON, *January* 11 account.

Dr., A. Brown, Esq., in account with Jones & Robinson, Cr.

1876.	£	s.	d.	1876.	£	s.	d.
Jan. 3. 1,000 Midland	1,453	12	6	Jan. 3. 1,000 Chatham prefce.	798	0	0
" 11. 1,000 Chatham prefce.	785	0	0	" 11. 1,000 Midland	1,422	10	0
				Balance	18	2	6
	£2,238	12	6		£2,238	12	6
Balance £18	2	6					

If the reader turns to the second sample of accounts which we have given above, he will see that the stock which was originally bought has been nominally sold and bought back again for the account a fortnight further on, and the stock originally sold has been bought in and resold at the "making up" price decided on by the jobbers according to the quotations of the day. In Stock Exchange parlance this is called carrying over, and the purchase and sale in each case is a mere fiction. The matter is arranged between the jobber and the broker, and the former charges interest at so much per cent., according to the state of the speculator's account, for carrying on the transaction for another fortnight, while the latter obtains a further small commission. This commission is in this example a sixteenth per cent., but it is sometimes foregone, and in other cases varies according to the position of the broker and his competition for trade, but the jobber seldom goes without interest one way or another on his part in the transaction. What the interest is depends upon whether a stock is scarce or plentiful in the market. If there is a great deal of stock on the market, a speculative buyer will be made to pay very heavily for not taking up what he has bought; but if stock is very scarce, it may happen that he can compel the jobber, or the sellers behind the jobber, to give him some consideration not to call for the delivery of the stock. In the one case the speculative buyer has to pay what is called "contango," a fine in the shape of interest for the fortnight, more or less high, for not taking away the stock he has bought; or, in the other, he receives "backwardation," or a fine paid by the other side for non-delivery of stock which he may not really want, but which the other side could not give him if he did. The possibility of making these charges depends more or less on the real state of the market or the stock; but in the case of securities whose amounts are small, a few speculators can often create a scarcity or an overabundance, and punish speculators for its rise or its fall at pleasure. Hence one reason for the clamours which speculators raise to have ordinary stocks of railways divided into preferred and deferred; the latter, or *A* stock, usually small, making a most admirable trap for the money of the ignorant outside speculator. At one time a stock of this kind will be driven up to an extravagantly high price for no reason in the world except that the hard speculators hope to tempt outsiders to try and snatch a profit; and when the outsider is so caught, he has to pay "contangos" in the meantime and to bear ultimate loss, for usually the stock is run down as fast as it was run up, and proves as mysteriously scarce in the running down as it was plentiful on the rise.

All that applies to the speculator for the rise applies, of course, equally to the speculator for the fall. If he has sold a stock that is very plentiful, and that the opposite side does not want him to deliver, he receives the "contango"; but if a stock that is scarce, he has to pay the "backwardation," and he is liable in the same way to suffer from plenty or scarcity fictitiously created. A hundred influences are in fact operating against the outside speculator in almost all cases, because he is gambling with an institution not only immeasurably richer than he is, but possessed of all sorts of special knowledge which the natural desire to make profits is sure to turn against him. At all events, by means of these skilful evasions of the rigid formulas of Stock Exchange dealings, and attention to the exigencies of the time, a man without much means can carry on his stock from account to account with little difficulty unless the "differences" go heavily against him; for of course the fiction of closing the transaction every fortnight is carried out so far as paying any difference in price that may have arisen against the speculator between the settling days. The following final samples of an account supposed to be closed by a speculator who has been losing, will make the working of the "difference" system clearer:

LONDON, *January* 18, 1876.
A. Brown, Esq.
    We have this day Sold and Bought for your account (subject to the rules of the London Stock Exchange):—

Stock or Shares	Price	£ s. d.	Brokerage £ s. d.	Stamps & Fees	Total £ s. d.
1,000*l*. Midland	141¾	Sold 1,417 10 0	*Nil*		1,417 10 0
1,000*l*. Chatham prefce.	80½	Bought 805 0 0	*Nil*		805 0 0

JONES & ROBINSON, Sworn Brokers.

For the January 28 account.

That is to say, the Midland stock, which had been originally bought and then at the settling day fictitiously sold and bought back again, is now disposed of outright, and the London, Chatham, and Dover preference stock, originally sold and afterwards manipulated in the reverse fashion, is now finally bought in. All these bargains have throughout been entered upon by a person who neither possessed nor wanted to possess a single 5*l*. worth of the stocks in question. The speculator has found the market price going against him too fast, and has not waited for the end of the month to come, but instead ordered his brokers to close the account at once. They have done so at the price of the day, and the result is that altogether the operation has cost the person who speculated 45*l*. 15*s*. 2*d.*, his broker's final statement standing thus:

Account end of January 1876.
LONDON, *January* 18, 1876.
    Dr., A. Brown, Esq., in account with Jones & Robinson, Cr.

1876.	£	s.	d.	1876.	£	s.	d.
Balance rendered	18	2	6	Jan. 11, 1,000 Chatham profce.	787	0	2
Jan. 11. 1,000 Midlands	1,427	2	10	" 18. 1,000 Midlands	1,417	10	0
" 18. 1,000 Chatham prefce.	805	0	0	Balance	45	15	2
	£2,250	5	4		£2,250	5	4
Balance	£45	15	2				

This is a mere illustration, but it will help to make the position of the broker and his client clear.

A man who speculates in 1,000l. stock stands to lose 100l. if that stock falls 10 per cent., besides the broker's commission and any other charges which "carrying over" may entail; and when the stock rises 10 per cent. he stands to win 100l., less brokerage, &c., so that whichever way matters go these latter are always against him; if it falls one fortnight and recovers the fall next, he does not get off clear, but minus two brokerages and probably a "contango." The speculator either pays or receives the difference between the price of the "carrying-over day" and the price he bought and sold at, plus or minus the charges of his broker; and if he is a winner, he is straightway tempted to double his stake on the chance of a further profit.

This kind of dealing forms the bulk of Stock Exchange business, and the simple investing of money is quite subordinated to it. Persons with very little money can speculate in this fashion, and may succeed once in a way in obtaining possession of some, but oftenest end by ruining themselves, and perhaps, but that is much less likely, those who deal for them. People with some money and more credit speculate in this style, and get loans from banks in order to take up huge quantities of stock that they may have bought for a rise, and thus stockbroking becomes a mere dealing in huge fictitious credits. A man deals in 100,000l. stock, meaning to make a thousand or two, and not to lose more than a thousand pounds, and another sells in the same way. At first "differences" are in his favour, and brokerage seems easy to pay, but the tide turns after he has been tempted deeper, and finally he collapses, and is found to be the "bull" and the "bear" of perhaps 600,000l. or 700,000l., or 1,000,000l. of stocks which he never possessed, or meant to possess, but which he contracted to take or deliver in order that he might make a profit on the contract. The recent collapse of foreign loan swindles has revealed not a few affairs of this magnitude.

It is indeed a dangerous game for all concerned, and unless a man plays it with loaded dice he generally loses in the end. The railway director, with special knowledge of the state of the company's accounts, with the power perhaps to adjust these accounts; the German Jew jobber, with his agents and colleagues all over the Continent, sharp as detectives, to pick up news and send it in advance—these, and such like people, may make huge fortunes, but not so the mere outsider who dabbles in Stock Exchange gambling, and knows nothing. Some people profess to make rules for themselves, and to follow them, but no rule will stand the test of the many influences that turn a market for wares so sensitive as all public securities are. It is, moreover, in the nature of these securities that they should often baffle the astutest and best informed, for they are affected by a thousand influences that no market can foresee. Take Consols for example. This great national security fluctuates little compared with most stocks, and yet it does move up and down. If all other influences are removed, "dear money" will make Consols fall, because people will sell them in order to lend the proceeds at high interest, and "cheap money" will, on the other hand, tend to raise their price, because credit establishments and the public will want to put the large balances they can get little for into Three per Cents. A political change; a small disturbance in the West Indies; a fall in foreign exchanges; the casual word of a king; a squabble about the extradition of a criminal even; every breath of change almost affects, more or less, this the most delicate barometer of credit that the world has ever seen. What applies to Consols has in some senses a more decided reference to other stocks. How, for example, could anyone foretell or foresee for a day the course of Turkish or Egyptian stocks all through the period since the Sultan denied the bankruptcy of Turkey? A new lie or a new fact was liable to fall on the market like a bombshell at any hour of any day. And so with securities of all kinds. Their values depend upon so many causes which are changing that they are almost all as restless as the compass needle. Of necessity this must be so, because all public "securities," of whatever class, are not wealth themselves, but merely the representative tickets, so to say, for so much wealth, which may be real one day and gone the next, or which may never have been anything save a shadow and a name. According to the reproductiveness of that wealth when it is wealth, is the value of the paper which testifies that so much capital has in this venture or that been sunk. Now the reproductiveness of all capital is something which constantly varies, and the opinion about it is as constantly fluctuating. It is easy, therefore, to get credence for any tale affecting credit so delicate as this kind of security implies, and hence it is that we find the stock market at the mercy of the rumour-monger. The jobber who has oversold himself and wants to lay in a quantity of stock cheap often scruples not about putting out some story calculated to depreciate the value of the security. The market hangs so together, besides, that what affects one class of stocks affects all more or less, and it is only now and then that one side of the market can be called "firm" while another is depressed. For some time back, for instance, the Eastern Question has affected the market for our home railways as much almost as that for Turkish or Russian stocks, and the same incubus depresses bank and joint-stock enterprise shares because, it is argued, there can be no revival of trade "while that nightmare hangs over Europe." A fine harvest in Russia would tend to depress American railway securities, and the fall in the Indian exchanges has seriously affected the value of all Indian Bank shares, as well as of such Government paper as may bear interest payable in rupees in India.

Enough has been said, perhaps, to indicate the extreme sensitiveness and variability in value of the peculiar credits and obligations which form the subject of the stockbroker's and jobber's trade; and it will be easily seen how great the temptations to speculate for the rise or the fall in their values must be. A man's nerve is put to the utmost tension; his mind is always on the stretch; not guiding the policy of a great commercial venture, but bearing up under and watching over the fluctuations of some stock which, in the opinion of the majority, or by virtue of what has been paid for it at the outset, is worth only so much, and which he has estimated at a different value. The trade is not a noble one, and there are few noble men engaged in it. It is in fact one of the lowest of human occupations.

Having seen the nature of the stockbroker's trade and the surroundings of it, as well as indicated the peculiar organisation of the Stock Exchange, we must now therefore go back to the question whether any remedy could be found for the gambling spirit which is more or less constant in that trade. It may be said that Stock Exchange speculation has ebbs and flows like the tide, and that every few years it culminates in a wave of ruin for tens of thousands. When trade generally prospers the Stock Exchange prospers, though not exactly at the same pace. Usually the gambles there get fiercest when ordinary trade is on the wane, and the crash of Stock Exchange speculation comes as the final stage in a period of depression. But at all times, by the very nature of its business, speculation is the chief occupation of the Stock Exchange. It goes on not only with every bargain of every dealer and broker, but exists in every issue of paper of any kind representing values which must fluctuate. And it appears to us that the reason why the Stock Exchange does real incalculable mischief lies in this fact not being fully enough recognised. The Stock Exchange proceeds on the assumption of a virtuous intention to control speculation—which, it is admitted, you cannot abolish. But where the Stock Exchange managers ought to be strict they are lax, in part because it pays the company that owns the House to be so, and where they ought to have no pretensions of any kind, it is all pretence together. If a rigid care were exercised in the admission of new members to the House, and substantial guarantees taken that those admitted risked considerable means, a material check could be put upon the wild gambling that now goes on. We heard lately of one new member who, after admission, wrote to the committee begging a month's delay in the payment of his subscription fee and entry money, and there have been hundreds admitted of late years nearly as poor. Yet irresponsible parties of that kind, with nothing to lose, will deal in hundreds of thousands of stock at a time, and will find jobbers in plenty, reckless enough to buy and sell with them for the sake of picking up any stray bit of money that may be to be had. The other day a firm of this kind failed for "differences" amounting to some 30,000*l.*, and had next to no assets; and quite recently a broker of this order came to grief for more than three times that amount with no assets at all; while it will have been seen from the papers that yet a third firm of brokers dealt in huge amounts of stock, over which a loss of 50,000*l.* was incurred, without even taking the trouble to inquire into the bona fides and responsibility of their client. These are but samples of what is constantly happening, and if the Stock Exchange is to retain the semblance of good repute, it will have to prevent this kind of utterly reckless gambling on the part of its members.

On the other hand, nothing can be more misplaced than the affectation of censorship which the Stock Exchange exercises over the loan schemes and adventures whose paper is brought before it. There is a quasi-official list where only those stocks that can command the favourable verdict of the committee are allowed to be quoted, and this committee must have certain evidence put before it, before it will recognise the dealings of members in any new venture. At the same time these dealings go on, sanctioned or not, as soon as the scheme is sufficiently out of embryo to have shares at a price or nominal value. Hence dilemmas like that of the Lisbon Steam Tramways Company—the thing must go on because the Stock Exchange is interested, and a special settling day is necessary, be "documents" good or no. All this sort of affectation of morality and censorship is utterly futile therefore, and most mischievous. The public is led by it to think that what the Stock Exchange allows to be quoted must be worth buying, and is therefore all the more readily drawn into the traps which are set for it on all sides. The most radical reform which the Stock Exchange wants is the abolition of all this mock moral censorship. Let the position, which its actual trade gives it, be the one actually assumed. The business of the Stock Exchange being to buy and sell securities which are themselves usually the mere emblems of a speculation, and to do this in a fashion which is purely speculative, it is absurd to set up a quasi-censorship, and to pretend to act as guide to the public. All rules tending to convey that impression ought to be withdrawn, and full freedom should be given to members to deal in whatever securities they please. There ought to be no such thing as an official list of quotations. Let such list be provided by private enterprise entirely, and let any or every thing be included in it for which there is a market. Changes of this kind would do a great deal to strip the Stock Exchange of its false pretences, and might therefore do not a little to restore to it some measure of respectability. And if greater care were exercised in admitting members, the tone might probably be raised. It would at least be saved from the abiding disgrace of not coming up to a self-imposed standard.

But here again the question rises—Why should the exclusive position of the Stock Exchange be kept up at all so far as regards the broker at least? At present jobbers and brokers have the whole trade to themselves, and no man can buy or sell any stock but through their means. But that is by no means necessary. While exercising very strict supervision over the admission of jobbers or dealers, who must always remain an essential to rapid business in stocks and shares, we should be disposed to advocate that the exclusive position of the broker ought to be entirely done away with. Instead of a closed market, in other words, the Stock Exchange ought to be made an open one, so that whoever had transactions to do could go in and deal direct with the jobbers. This sweeping reform would most likely do more to make business healthy than all the others put together. Brokers would no doubt still retain their place to some extent, but the pernicious secrecy of their craft would be gone, and so would be the disposition of the jobber to deal through the broker with all comers. A sufficient number of the public would avail themselves of the right to go and deal for themselves, to affect for the better the present system of really indiscriminate credit, and to make every transaction stand on its own merits. At present no jobber can tell what the status of the real customers he is selling to or buying from is, because he knows no one but the broker, and the broker never discloses names until the time comes for either taking up or delivering the stock. Nay, great sales may often be made by a broker which, for the sake of the interest he makes by lending the stock from fortnight to fortnight, he (or his client) does not complete for months, and all that time the jobber knows not whether the stock will be ultimately delivered or not. This is a close and unhealthy way of carrying on trade, and ought to be done away with. People cannot and ought not to be kept from speculation; but as at present constituted, and as business is now done, the Stock Exchange is not a place for speculation merely, but a scene of veiled and dangerous gambling. Therefore we think the House ought to belong to the jobbers so far as its maintenance goes, and that only jobbers should be allowed to have the control of it; while to brokers, trustees, insurance actuaries, and the public generally, the right of access, of buying and selling from these jobbers, ought to be perfectly free. We doubt not this would bring about a revision of the brokers' scale of charges as well, or lead to the extinction of many firms among them altogether; but nobody could regard either of these contingencies with much alarm or disfavour except the parties directly concerned.

A word may be said in conclusion on a collateral part of this wide subject. Few greater scandals have come to light in recent years than that connected with the systematic bribery of those connected with the press as "City editors,"[2] and several of them have had to depart from their positions under the

2. Editors of the City reports in newspapers, such as Thomas Massa Alsanger (*London Times*) or Charles Duguid (*Pall Mall Gazette, Westminster Gazette, Morning Post*). These editors

stigma of a tarnished reputation. We have no desire to defend these men; they were tempted and could not withstand the temptation, and now suffer a not unjust punishment. But in punishing them it is only fair to remember that they are not the chief sinners. The system of the Stock Exchange is at the root of the mischief. As has been already explained, the riggers of new loans or of new schemes are able, by its privileged mode of doing business, to carry on false buying and selling operations for the purpose of decoying the public into subscribing for rotten undertakings—undertakings got up usually merely that the public might be plundered on the Stock Exchange. Part of that rigging consists in quoting the particular security at a premium, before any of it has been allotted or issued on the market; and attached to this is the bribery system. So many shares are then allotted at a given price to the friends of the swindlers (as well as to the friends of men who believe themselves honest), which have been most probably sold beforehand at these fictitious premiums. This looks like a business transaction, and is a bribe. It has prevailed alike with good things and bad, and so much of the money required to "float" the stock is devoted to paying their "friends" and "supporters," the press amongst the number, the difference between the issue price and the fictitious premium at which the stock is sold being given away to these in the first instance, to be drawn from the public again in the end should the "rig" achieve its object. This being a regular branch of Stock Exchange business, and looked upon by the best and the worst of its habitués as a mere matter of course, is it greatly to be wondered at that ordinary men, who saw thus put before them a means of making money, merely perhaps at the cost of holding their tongues, should be unable year after year to resist the temptation? They met daily persons living in the highest luxury, whose minds did not recoil at all from these practices, who were to all appearance considered honourable members of society, were members of Parliament some of them, or otherwise distinguished in the eyes of the upper world. These persons took this kind of thieves' plunder as a matter of course, and naturally their example first lulled the writers for the press to sleep. The easy-going familiarity with rascality which these high and titled persons displayed disguised the reality of the evil, and the journalists were flattered and drawn on to imitate them to some degree in the habits of wealth so easily won. One way and another they fell victims to a system, and it is the system that ought to be condemned more than the men. It not only renders possible the frauds of bubble companies and of bad loans, but positively does its best to help them towards success; and the remedy for this also would, we imagine, be the extinction of the exclusive privileges of brokers and the raising the responsibilities of jobbers. Mere rules and regulations will do nothing; publicity and the risks and moral safeguards of open competition

---

were often accused of promoting the shares of particular companies that advertised with the paper.

are what is wanted to clear the air of this important centre of business from its moral miasma. Cogged dice are not usually considered emblems of fair dealing, yet the sham premium dealing and the mock allotment system are worse than any cogged dice, and while the public remain liable to be swindled by these means, bribery will also remain prevalent in one form or other, and the Stock Exchange be avoided by all high-minded men. Things are done there now which the most degraded bookmaker on the Turf would blush to be accused of, and by men, too, who associate with the highest in the land. Why should these go scatheless, and the "City editor" class get all the buffets and the scorn?

Besides the abolition of unfair privileges and the stoppage of all attempt at the assumption of moral and judicial airs and censorship where morality can have no chances of fair play and judgment very little, a great amount of good would be done by an end being put to the present system of paying up subscriptions to new issues of capital or new loans by long drawn-out instalments. At present the payment of "5 per cent. on application," or less, and often merely another 5 or 10 per cent. on "allotment," enables the riggers of the market and their friends to play any number of mischievous pranks such as these which came to light in the "Eupion Gas Company" case. After all, however, publicity is the great thing wanted, and, were it secured, the manner of doing business might be allowed to take care of itself. The law of the land might well interfere, however, to put an end to the system of secret allotments altogether. Were all company schemers and loan-mongers compelled to publish in the newspapers, or even in an open Stock Exchange, the names and addresses of the allottees of their paper, there would be no more secret rigging and no more playing with cogged dice, nor could bribery of the press or of agents then prevail very widely either.

A great deal more might be said on this subject, but the outlines of its main bearings have been given here and enough done, perhaps, to make the outside reader to some extent familiar with the machinery of the Stock Exchange. It will be seen that this is the one market in the country where, above all others, honour, probity, and fair open dealing should prevail, because it holds the weightiest monetary affairs, in its keeping, and yet it is equally visible that its system and the abuses thereof are a disgrace to any nation.

In seeking to mend this state of things, the truths ought to be boldly accepted that the Stock Exchange is primarily and properly the centre of the most important forms of pecuniary speculation; that speculation is a necessity of human nature and of all progress, and an essential of business; and, admitting these facts, let the reformers sweep away all that hinders this speculation from being done in the full light of day. Let nothing be done to overlay a lie with a gilding of truth, but leave lie and truth to at least find their level in an open market. Trickery and rascality, lying and theft, will not thereby be rendered impossible or uncommon, but they will, at all events, take place under more difficult conditions than now, when rules and modes of business are so framed that too often the more the rascality the greater the success.

ALEXANDER INNES SHAND

SPECULATIVE INVESTMENTS

We are safe in saying that speculative investors have seldom had more disastrous experiences than lately, and we should be sorry to hazard any reassuring predictions as to what may be awaiting them in the immediate future. We are aware that it is the habit to speak of them as a class who are entitled to little sympathy; as publicans who were born to point a moral for the satisfaction of moneyed Pharisees. Whenever they are caught in a squall on the stream as the tide of fortune sets against them—while they are tossing their damaged property overboard, or clinging to its dangerous dead-weight in imminent peril of swamping altogether—they are howled at by the onlookers who are standing safe on the shore or have been paddling ankle-deep in the shallows. That the old proverb of "Fools and their money" is perpetually finding fresh illustrations is a fact we are not concerned to deny; and we should be glad if the offenders who hastened to be unrighteously rich came more swiftly and invariably to well-merited retribution. But we have at least as little sympathy with the uncharitable denunciation of those who have been removed beyond reach of temptation, or who pride themselves virtuously on the unreasoning timidity that would be the bane of all action and enterprise. The parable of the talent in the napkin applies as forcibly to commercial and financial Europe in the nineteenth century as to agricultural Syria in the beginning of the first. The rayah of Hindustan who builds his rupees into the mud walls of his hovel; the French peasant who invests his five-franc pieces in the thatch of his cottage or among the roots of his cabbage-beds, may live on rice or maize, as the case may be, and go jogging along from the cradle to the grave as mildly useful members of society. But what would become of the movement of the world if everybody were to imitate their passive prudence? and we should remember in fairness that there are conditions of existence where bare necessities are only to be obtained by running a risk of falling back on charity.

Alexander Innes Shand, "Speculative Investments." *Blackwood's Edinburgh Magazine* 120 (September 1876): 293–316.

There are men who delight in excitement for its own sake, and who would never be content in the repose of the lotus-eater, for all the lusciousness of the insidious fruit or the soothing-languor of the drowsy atmosphere. But most people, if they might choose their lots, would undoubtedly elect to be landed to the lips or "consoled up to the eyes;" to be blessed with such a superabundance of riches, that they should be practically relieved of their accompanying cares. There are very few who are so fortunate, and perhaps the number is relatively diminishing. For although great fortunes are becoming far more common, and although they are rolled up with a rapidity which would have seemed fabulous to the plodding toilers of former generations, yet habits of profuse expenditure have been increasing even faster. Great noblemen, with half-a-dozen costly seats or as many domains, in as many counties, unless they are happy enough to be the possessors of deposits of coal or veins of metal, find themselves eclipsed in display by ostentatious *nouveaux riches.* They may despise these new men, and yet all the same they are goaded on to a race of competition in which the pace every year becomes more distressing. Mortgages of landowners are accumulating in unsuspected quarters, while industrial millionaires may be sinking their incomings in expenditure, instead of placing them away in an insurance fund against the vicissitudes of their business. As for the old-fashioned squires with their moderate rent-rolls, they find themselves nowhere nowadays, if they are once possessed by the demon of fashion. The railway tempts them up to town for the season, to cramp themselves in some third-class residence in Belgravia or Mayfair; to see themselves lost in the crowds that lock their carriage-wheels in crushes in the parks and throng the suites of modern reception rooms. Hereditary acres, descent, and high connections have their influence still; but apart from brilliant talents, money is becoming the essential requisite to achieving an average social success. If you are to hold your own, you must make a certain show, and do to others in the way of hospitality as you would that others should do unto you. The display and the hospitality cost more and more every year, while society grows more exacting in its demands on the habits and purses of its members. As fortunes are made faster and faster, as incomes are dissipated more and more furiously, an impulse is given to extravagance which reacts on the remotest parishes, and makes the quietest people conscious of the pressure, when it does not send them staggering to the wall. It is not only that if you strive to cut such a figure in the world as your father did before you, you must make up your mind to spend as much again. But if you are to have sound security for the sums that would have yielded you a decent competence in the last generation, it can only be at the cost of sacrifices and self-restraint, and very possibly of actual privation.

No doubt those moneyed Pharisees we have alluded to may object, with a stern show of justice, that the circumstance of your being straitened or poverty-stricken makes it the more incumbent upon you to be prudent: that if there is so little of a margin left between you and destitution, it is positively dishonest running any risks; and that in such cases, more than any other, the coat should be cut according to the cloth. But what if the cloth, when you have cut it, and patched it, and dragged at it, will barely serve the purposes of decency? while you see those who are nearest and dearest to you shivering in scanty raiment upon short commons. To drop metaphor, we can easily conceive of instances where some amount of calculated imprudence may appear a duty. Take a mother who has been left a widow with £5000 and a rising family. "Put your money safely away in the funds; it would be sheer insanity to do anything else with it," says one friend of the family whom she asks for advice as to its disposal; and he steps complacently into his carriage and is driven smilingly away. Another gentleman, a shade less scrupulous, is disposed to admit of first-class railway debentures, although he takes care to dwell on possible fluctuations to the extent of two or three per cent. Very good! The lady acts on the advice of one or the other. But she finds that with her £150 to £220, she is not only embarrassed as to providing food, clothing, and houseroom for her growing family, but that she is compromising their future beyond remedy, from better fortunes. She is falling out of the circle of family acquaintance where her boys would be likely to find helpful friends and her girls to make happy marriages. She is unable to give them the education indispensable to their taking advantage of future opportunities. If she is to persevere in pinching, she condemns them to sink to an inferior grade of life, unless something in the nature of a miracle come to save them. So, sorely against the grain, and at first in mortal apprehension, she has recourse to some of those more highly-priced stocks which are the refuge of the widow, the clergyman, and the reckless. Ten to one she acts thus with her eyes open; perhaps she may morbidly exaggerate the risks she runs, and it is not the fault of her family advisers if she does not. But the clouds that hang over the future begin to dissipate, as the shadows are lifted from her everyday life. Cheerfulness and serenity are restored to the little household, now that the heart of its mistress does not jump into her mouth at each rattle of the knocker or each peal of the bell. Now that she can afford them occasionally a fly, or a dress, or a bit of ribbon, the girls can be indulged in a little innocent gaiety; she sees them merry and light-hearted once more, instead of being insensibly embittered with the life that had scarcely begun for them. The boys are sent to a decent school, with a fair chance of gaining exhibitions, and getting on so as to be able to retrieve their position and lend a helping hand to their sisters. She may have been foolish in changing her investments. She may even feel bitter reproach and remorse when she is caught in some panic that suspends her interest and dissipates her principal. Yet she may be excused for having congratulated herself on her wisdom during those critical years of sunshine, when a doubled income brought her unspeakable relief, giving her family the advantages day after day that subsequent misfortunes can scarcely deprive them of.

That is no doubt an extreme case; but similar arguments apply with more or less force to innumerable other people, who, if they do come to trouble in the end, may at least plead extenuating circumstances. Then there is the great class who are thoughtless and somewhat greedy, and the predestined prey of promoters—victims who swim together in shoals like herrings, to be swooped down on by the cormorants of the Stock Exchange. Many of those who prove the greatest fools financially, are intelligent or even eminent in their own walks of life. Lawyers and doctors whose children have formed exaggerated ideas of their means, and whose wives will insist on setting up their carriages, go in for sleeping partnerships in banks and credit companies, although their utmost experience of the business they embark in has been the drawing of cheque or the paying in of fees. Young officers with a thousand or so besides their pay, sensible enough not to tamper with the principal of their little patrimonies, have been in the habit of lending it to the Sultan or the Khedive, and luxuriating in the rate of interest that indicated a remote danger. And we understand that Spanish stocks and second-rate South American loans have been exceedingly popular securities with retired butlers and superannuated ladies'-maids, whose savings have gone beyond the account at the savings bank. These worthy people see glimpses of Golcondas in stocks that are so low that they must certainly be cheap, since they promise their purchaser thirty per cent for his money.

And it must be remembered, after all, that in this seductive lottery of the Stock Exchange there are nearly as many prizes as blanks. Could men distinguish between what is sound and what is rotten by some light of supernatural revelation, they might stick to remunerative speculations, which are sufficiently legitimate, and will be carried out safely to the end. The averagely well-informed Englishman, had he seen anything to choose between Chili and Peru when they came first into our markets as borrowers, would probably have given the preference to the latter, in memory of the famous mines of Potosi. No doubt the original prospectuses in either case were equally enticing. As matter of fact at the present moment, Chilian 5 per cents stand steadily at something like 80; while Peruvians have had "the bottom knocked out of them" by the subsidence of the guano deposits, and have been bandied between bears and bulls till they have fallen to fluctuate between 10 and 15. Take our home joint-stock banks. Those in Scotland, and many of the leading provincial establishments in England, are quoted at steady and enormous premiums; while the moderate rate of interest on their shares at current prices, shows the serene confidence that is felt in their management. In London, original holders in the "London and Westminster," the "London and County," and the "London and Joint-Stock," in spite of such occasional indiscretions as have opened too liberal credits to the Collies and the Liardis, might plume themselves with reason on their foresight and judgment. Yet many similar associations, launched under almost equally promising auspices, came to the ground with a crash in the great collapse of 1866. There are numerous industrial undertakings in the English counties, working under limited liability, but never quoted on the metropolitan share-lists, which have regularly been paying their fortunate shareholders from 20 to 40 per cent, and which seem liable to nothing more serious than such vicissitudes in trade as may press upon the steadiest-going linen-draper or grocer. At the same time, it is impossible to surmise how many others, apparently as plausible, have turned out to be failures or swindles. People must invest, but they must form their own opinion on statements and statistics which may be as honest as they seem, or which may conceal or distort the most material facts. Damaging disclosures have made it evident enough that the names of those sponsors who promise and vow in prospectuses, and on boards of direction, offer no sort of reliable guarantee. Yet, without more or less venturesome speculations of the kind, what would become of the prosperity of the country? although it is true that we should not be troubled with the disposal of these floods of surplus economies which have long ago overflowed the surest channels of investment. Individuals may choose according to their necessities or their temperaments; but many of them must be forced into partnerships in concerns which they can only judge by appearances, and which they are practically powerless to influence. So far as the question of caution is concerned, it may come to much the same in the end, whether they lend their money to a dozen of respectable gentlemen who undertake the administration of some native enterprise, or whether they advance it on the guarantee of some foreign Government, that professes the intention of developing its resources, and which has every interest in paying its way. It is a question of deciding on the capacity of the administration or the solvency of the borrower. If investors act on an impulse or suffer themselves to be deceived, they must pay the penalty, like the tradesman who sets up in business and is unfortunate enough to make bad debts. But the sentiment of acquisition that makes so many victims, is a healthy and natural one all the same, when kept within proper limits.

We believe that in these observations, we have only done common justice to a class of people who are often unfairly judged and harshly condemned; while they suffer severely for indiscretions which are frequently rather their misfortune than their fault. But we should be sorry if we laid ourselves open to the imputation of indirectly encouraging reckless ventures, since it is our very object to point out that the choice of investments with elements of risk is yearly becoming more delicate and dangerous. It is certain that they will be sought after more eagerly than ever, so soon as we are in the swing of the next reaction from abject apprehension to sanguine assurance. But when the more reflecting of would-be investors survey their present position and their prospects, how sadly must the contrast strike them with the markets they were in the habit of dealing in! Who would have imagined that the sunny dreams of twenty or five-and-twenty years ago, which for a time seemed ripening into golden fruition, were really for the most part mere mocking illusions? As financial history is always repeating itself, it may be worth while glancing back in a hasty retrospect, even at the risk of repeating a too familiar tale. Twenty years ago the Crimean war[1] had cleared the political atmosphere, and the treaty which has been torn up during the Liberal tenure of the Foreign Office, seemed the pledge of a period of unruffled peace. The industries and the commerce that had been temporarily paralysed were everywhere reviving. "Limited liability" was the talisman that recommended joint-stock enterprise to the million, and henceforth everybody was to participate with safety and profit in these highly lucrative undertakings that had hitherto been monopolised by capitalists. Railways were being laid all over the world, and coal and iron companies were being multiplied to provide the rails that were being forged for foreign customers in English furnaces with English fuel. Whether those lines were to link together the populous Continental towns that had hitherto only communicated by the *vetturino* and the *eilwagen*—whether they were to open up the Russian steppes or the South American pampas—to traverse the frozen forests of Canada—to transcend the Balkan or tunnel the Andes—it was statistically demonstrated that their success was assured; and Englishmen were eagerly availing themselves of the privilege of supplying the lion's share of the capital. Everything was being carried out by co-operation. Contractors who had bid for concessions and obtained them, sold the goodwill of their connections for a handsome sum, and developed straightaway into full-blown corporations. Rival lines of shipping companies ran steam or sailing packets on unfamiliar routes across every ocean; and heaven-forsaken ports, lying in dangerous roadsteads, among fever-stricken lagoons, found themselves figuring suddenly, to their extreme surprise, as the salubrious outposts of tropical Paradises that awaited development under the coming immigration.

Though the outbreak of the American war[2] disturbed those dreams of the new millennium, to many of us in the beginning the war was an unmixed blessing. The closing of the Southern cotton ports, the ravages of the Alabama and her consorts among North American merchantmen, gave an enormous impulse to the English shipping trade. While we were fiercely abused at

---

1. A conflict that broke out in 1853 between the Ottoman Empire and Russia over the latter's access to Constantinople and its right to protect Greek Orthodox subjects. Britain, France, and Austria entered the war to keep Russian influence out of the Balkans and to maintain the neutrality of the Dardanelles. The war ended in 1856. [Ed.]
2. The American Civil War (1861–64), which had important implications for Britain because of the latter's reliance on the cotton supplied by the Southern states. [Ed.]

Washington as unfairly favouring the South, our coal-owners and metal-manufacturers were actively supplying the Northern belligerents with material of war, which was sent over to them in English bottoms. The shares of all these commercial and industrial undertakings ran up fast in spite of the rise in wages of workpeople and seamen, which employers could well afford to pay. Domestic trade was never brisker; and it would have been well for some of us had the impulse communicated to our prosperity been confined to England. But our great dependency of Hindustan was to profit even more. A rush of English capital was attracted thither, to flow back again almost as fast in handsome dividends; and for the first time it seemed as if the mythical wealth of the Indies was about to turn to a reality. Sea Island cotton was out of the market for the time—Surats and Dhollerah were to have it all their own way. With cheap native labour, the cultivation must infallibly pay enormously, and might be indefinitely increased. If the quality was scarcely all that could be desired, at least it was highly susceptible of improvement. Everybody believed as if there could not be a doubt that this blissful state of things must be permanent; that if the American combatants did not exterminate each other, at all events with the emancipation of the negro, the famous American cotton-fields must be given over to the alligators and mosquitoes.

Many sanguine speculators have reason to curse their passing connection with the financiers of Bombay. The city was to be the commercial Mecca of the new dispensation, and every one who had anything to do with the Indian trade, began to turn their eyes towards it. Parsees vied with English merchants in the vastness and audacity of their conceptions. The palaces they reared for their dwellings, the blocks they covered with their warehouses, were the visible symbols of the wealth they had at call. Everything they touched was turning to lacs of rupees; and as fast as they extended their credit, they discounted it by inviting fresh advances of capital. The state of society in moneyed circles there reminded one of the Paris of the faubourgs and boulevards under the Empire. Every one was buying, and selling and canvassing eagerly for good things, notwithstanding the height of the thermometer. Civilians of the highest standing, soldiers who had been laying by money while holding political appointments, judges, barristers, clerks, shopkeepers, residents in England with old Indian connections who had had stars set against their names in the books of the old Company—all made haste to realise that they might have their part in the new El Dorado. Men in the most exalted places set the example, giving substantial proofs of their boundless faith in grand harbour and reclamation schemes. Gas, water, building, burying, and body-burning companies, had only to ask and to have. Every applicant could not be made happy; so the mania of speculation, taking a Protean variety of forms, spread over the country districts into the other presidencies. The jungle was cleared from the slopes of the Himalaya and Nilgherries, to be replaced with blooming tea-gardens; and companies sent managers to administer great estates among their newly-acquired coffee plantations of Ceylon and Mysore. Above all, there came the schemes of irrigation and canalisation that were to combine philanthropy with marvellous returns, and bring cheap water carriage to the door of each peasant in provinces that had been saved from famine and inundation.

This sudden excitement in the East naturally reacted on England. People were in a way to become capitalists who had seldom owned a score of rupees, and there was an obvious demand for fresh banking facilities. The many new Anglo-Indian banking companies saw their shares on the rise with rapidly advancing premiums simultaneously with the appearance of the prospectuses. Allotments were as good as enclosures of bank-notes if you chose to send them into the markets. But few were imprudent enough to eat their wheat in the ear and anticipate the future of a valuable property. Nothing then paid better than those Indian banks. There seemed no limit to the expansion of their principal and dividends, and the most cautious shareholders were reassured by regular additions to their reserve funds. The shares of some of the older of them had gone to three or four times the original value; but there still seemed room for all, and the young competitors assured themselves a profitable start by the names they paraded on their bonds. Their directors were men who had made themselves a notoriety for riches—thanks to the extent of their miscellaneous engagements and the number of variously-shaped irons they had thrust into the hottest of the fire. It would have been heresy to hint in a community so universally interested in inflating prices, that all this marvellous prosperity might be as ephemeral as the circumstances that had originated it were unexpected—that reckless competition offering a premium on rotten business was making a trying ordeal inevitable in any case. Confidence was contagious, and the unwonted energy and the success of these lucky Indians stimulated the emulation of the English public in a variety of shapes. Many cities out of London, at home and in the colonies, were imitating the example of Bombay, although they might be following it at a modest distance. Every society of any pretensions was becoming more or less deeply interested in trade, and for the first time in their industrial history it really appeared as if the English were turning into a nation of shopkeepers.

These were merry and most lucrative times, when, dispose as you might of your money, it must almost infallibly multiply; and many a man who is now ruined, disgraced, or impoverished, or sorely embarrassed over the disposition of the wrecks of his property, may well recall them with a sigh. But it is a common phase of financial experience, though so few seem to lay it to heart, that every mania is breeding a panic, and that each period of undiscriminating confidence is the invariable precursor of a collapse. The worst of it is, that investors suffer not only directly but indirectly, since in the general disappointment and alarm the soundest ideas are unjustly discredited; while institutions that should be stable must pay for the follies of the reckless rivals that have been running them hard. It is only comparatively lately that the most flourishing of our English railways have begun to overcome the prejudices created against railway property by the lavishness, carelessness, and corruption of so many of the original promoters. And the sharp panic of the spring of 1866, awakening many people to the perception of facts which should have been perfectly plain to them all along, sent them from one extreme to another. It was discovered of a sudden that the principle of joint-stock liability had been extravagantly abused; and the complicated system of credit that had been reared upon it has been tottering at the foundations ever since. The very wariness of certain investors turned against them, tending at the same time to depress the markets. They acted on the time-honoured maxim of distributing their eggs in a number of baskets. In the general crash, it was of course inevitable that more than one of the eggs should be broken, and it was then they learned the real meaning of a £50 share with £10 paid. They found that, so far as they were personally concerned, limited and unlimited liability were identical. The general rush to sell that calls might be met, sent all stocks down in the market in an immense preponderance of sales. Liquidators and lawyers became so many sworn tormentors, set to screw the last available shilling out of their victims. The process is so exquisitely painful, that it is likely to impress itself indelibly on the recollections of those who have once experienced it; while such sufferers as appeal for help and sympathy are sure to make themselves heard, and their misfortunes remembered, in the circle of their friends and intimates.

The consequence is, that joint-stock companies, and specially joint-stock credit companies, have been regarded since 1866 with extreme suspicion. Luckily for their shareholders, Mr. Leeman's Act has secured them against the unscrupulous bearing which used to be the fashion; but their morbid sensibility to the agitating influences of panic-time is a decided objection to holding their shares. There were men who bought in the evil days of 1866, choosing establishments they thought to be intrinsically safe, and fondly believing that with the restoration of calm their calculated daring would be rewarded. They have found that they miscalculated the weight of the shock which had shaken the most solid foundations. Since then a few exceptional establishments have paid good dividends, and seen their shares at fair figures. But by far the greater number, although they have lived, and are likely to live, have never recovered the elasticity of their younger days. Banks, and especially those connected with India, the colonies, and the Continent, have seen deposits withdrawn, their proprietary changing for the weaker, and their resources enfeebled, if not crippled. They may be solvent enough, but their shares are always inclining to droop, and show no signs of coming into favour again. As for those newfangled credit associations that made a business of company-floating on easy terms, and so became responsible for so much of the subsequent mischief, such of them as are still surviving have been suffering from the partial suspension of their faculties, like the paralytic who has lost the use of his limbs. Calls or retrenchment may have kept them going in a very different way of business from the ambition of their former enterprises; but the bulk of their original capital has been lost, or else it is locked away so securely that there is no possibility of getting at any portion of it. There seems to be no reason why joint-stock banking and credit companies should not conduct their business as safely and profitably as the old private firms in Fleet Street and Lombard Street, whose names have long been synonymous with stability; and the public banks have decided advantages from their superior facilities for extending their connection. They may guarantee themselves absolutely against all reasonable risks, by picking their business, by being less emulously liberal of interest on deposits, and by strengthening their reserves. But then, if they necessarily moderate their dividends, while the rising price of their shares keeps pace with their growing reputation for prudence, they no longer tempt those needy buyers with whom the primary consideration is high interest. While the banks that have been falling back on the old reckless touting for business, extending excessive credit to doubtful customers on usurious terms, have seen their shares trembling at quotations which foretell their probable fate in the next mercantile convulsion. The least considerate people have learned more or less consciously to estimate a variety of contingencies which formerly would never have occurred to them. Caught once, they are determined not to be caught again in the same way; so that nowadays the dealers may tempt them in vain with securities that once were universal favourites.

In 1866 and before it, many investors strongly fancied foreign stocks, though these scarcely satisfied the desires of the more covetous. The interest was but moderate!—say from 8 to 12 per cent; and though, to be sure, there was the chance of the periodical drawings, still there was little capacity of expansion in the capital, compared to that of a promising credit company or a contract corporation. They were considered excellent things, known as a safe *pis aller*—securities to be recommended by their admirers to the widow or the elderly, who had no heads for business, and sought permanent investment for their money. Effete countries like Spain might have been guilty of default; the sturdy republicans of Pennsylvania had pushed their independence to the extreme length of repudiating their state obligations; but there were young and vigorous countries with magnificent expectations, which it would be a privilege to be admitted to participate in even by way of debentures or mortgages. Geography and statistics are not the strong points of the average British investor; and when he is dazzled by fascinating lights brought out in strong relief, he is apt to ignore the facts that are left in the shadows of the background. We know how freely he honoured the drafts that Honduras, Costa Rica,

Nicaragua, and St. Domingo drew on his credulity. He lent as if he believed that swamps were solid land, studded with populous towns, and opened up by excellent highroads—as if countless cords of mahoganies and dyewoods could be cut, and hauled, and stacked just as if they had been grown in the New Forest or the Home Park at Windsor—as if pontoon railways, that cost a life a yard, were to carry the traffic of one of our metropolitan extensions. Judging foreigners by his experiences of our own honourable Stock Exchange, it no more struck him that there might be an easier standard of financial morality among Indians, and half-breeds, and curly-headed negroes, than that there might be a bottom to the deposits even of those innumerable seafowl that whiten the islands of the Peruvian seaboard.

After the recent disclosures elicited before the Royal Commission, contributors towards the development of Costa Rica or Nicaragua must have felt on consideration that they had been somewhat hasty and indiscreet; that a little research into no more recondite authorities than geographical schoolbooks might have saved them much money and worry. But the original creditors of such countries as Turkey or Egypt came under a very different category. We maintain that they had every reason to believe that they were making a wise and reasonable bargain. We have already made reference to the position of Turkey after the Crimean war. She had taken out a fresh lease of life, and her rulers had been brought into intimate contact with civilised ideas. Had she relapsed into her former barbarous stolidity, she might have indefinitely deferred a second political crisis, as she certainly would have missed the opportunity of repudiating an enormous debt. But her revenue, in place of having nearly doubled in spite of everything, would have remained stationary under her time—discredited system of waste, oppression, and abominable corruption. In short, she would have acted like the landowner who, with every facility for borrowing, declines to risk a few thousands in improvements that would pay him 20 or 30 per cent. Turkey has let slip a magnificent chance, and abused opportunities that can never recur for her. But if we glance back at her position as it was, and as it appeared then to dispassionate onlookers, we must confess that we cannot blame the politicians and capitalists who were ready to come to her assistance. A risk there was—the risk that has proved a reality—that of her squandering the large sums she borrowed on false promises. But the chance of that risk was amply covered by the rate of interest she has paid so long, although that rate was by no means unduly onerous to a Government where farmers have to pay 20 to 40 per cent for short advances in seed-time, secured upon sown crops. The first mortgagees had their security upon an empire that abounded in resources which had never been turned to profitable purpose. These resources are now just as they were then, for literally nothing has been done in the meantime. There were boundless plains of extraordinary fertility that only needed to be drained or irrigated. There were forests almost as fine as those of Honduras, and far more healthy and accessible. There were coal beds cropping out on the surface of the soil, and mines that had been left abandoned for centuries after their riches had been carefully tested by a most primitive system of working. The people are industrious, and would have helped themselves, had the State done ever so little towards helping them. There was a plethora of Western capital waiting to be poured into the country. Next to security and a beginning of reform in the administration, all that was needed to make much of those untold riches available were some cheap and simple public works. Some roadmaking or laying of rude tramways; some embanking and clearing the beds of the river; some dredging of the silted-up harbours; some weather-tight warehouses, and some wharves at the principal ports, for even at such centres of activity as Smyrna and Salonica, vessels had to load from lighters in an open roadstead. It all depended on the absolute Padishah; but the reigning Sultan was supposed to be an intelligent man; and there was the widest margin for waste. Provided that half the loans had been judiciously expended, the other half might have been lavished on Court follies and official corruption. Even in that case the Porte might still have fulfilled its obligations, while the Sultan enriched his Sultanas and Pachas, and abandoned himself to a life of luxurious debauchery, without having to listen to the curses of his subjects.

Had the Ottomans had a man at their head at that turning-point of their fortunes, they and their foreign creditors might now have been well to do and comfortable. What happened we all know, and we have nothing to say of the careers of Abdul Medjid and his brother, except in so far as they concern the bondholders. But the decline of Turkish credit supplies a striking illustration of a habitual failing of the speculative investor. He never knows when to close a current account, when to be satisfied with a run of profits, or to cut clear from a threatened loss. He might have seen that in this case the character of his property was changing, that the pledges had been consistently falsified which originally induced him to lend. He was being made a tool to undermine his own security. Even when those Turkish bonds were fetching their highest prices, the inevitable end was full in view. Interest was being defrayed out of temporary accommodation, while the fast accumulating floating debt was being consolidated at intervals, which were made the occasion for fresh loans. It was the fashion to say that the Turk was honourable; and, in his individual capacity, it must be admitted that he compares advantageously with his Christian fellow-subjects. But the most honourable man cannot be held to impossibilities; and though the Turkish taxpayer had reason to deplore more than any one the wild expenditure of his lord and master, he was powerless to help himself or any one else. And if the bondholders had taken the trouble to inquire, they would have found that it was they alone who were being punctually paid. Nothing could possibly be more overbearing or dishonest than the dealings of the Government with its smaller creditors. Furnishers or private contractors had to make exorbitant charges in consideration of the chances against getting their money. If they looked to have their accounts settled in the end, and to clear a satisfactory profit, it was only because they had allowed so much for indispensable bribery. Moreover, the outbreak of a war, or the fomenting of these internal troubles which have come at last on the mainland after the premonitory warnings in Crete, might at any time have precipitated bankruptcy. But so long as stocks kept up, bondholders were loath to transfer the money which it would have been difficult to employ to equal advantage elsewhere, now that so many things had been discredited by the panics. And when stocks began to fall, as there was a difficulty in placing the periodical loans, they were still more unwilling to accept their first loss, although all the odds were against a recovery. Hoping for yet another year or so of high dividends, they held on term after term, while each payment was preluded by rumours of default; and however they may have been pained by the firman of repudiation they read on that fine autumn morning, we suspect there were few who were astonished by the blow.

The history of Egyptian finance is another example of the perils of the speculative investor, under entirely different circumstances. Last October no sane man could have been greatly disposed to fall in love with "Egypts." It was known that the immediate straits of the Khedive were nearly as great as those of his suzerain: his paper was being hawked about Alexandria and Paris, to be discounted by the usurers on the most exorbitant terms. Like his co-religionists in Constantinople, he had never as yet made public default; but it was notorious that he was moving heaven and earth to meet a payment that was falling due in a few days. The loan of 1873 was selling at about £50, and by no means much of a bargain at the money. Suddenly everything changed, and the financial world had a second surprise, decidedly more sensational than the Turkish repudiation. When it was published that our Government had given the Khedive four millions sterling for his Suez Canal shares, a section of the investing public jumped, not altogether unreasonably, to certain conclusions. The rapid rise in a day or two from £50 to £74 may not have been altogether justified; but a speculator might argue fairly enough that what had been selling for £50 before must be worth 50 per cent more under the altered circumstances. The question seemed fully as much political as financial. The Turkish empire seemed breaking up under pressure from St. Petersburg, and this interference of England in Egyptian affairs was a significant answer to the northern challenge. The Khedive was by no means past helping, and it might well be that it had been determined to help him in spite of himself. We had brilliant Indian precedents for the successful administration of an oriental State through the agency of a political resident who made the finances his first concern. Even without going so far as that, indirect English assistance through such a house as that of the Rothschilds might have set the Khedive on his legs again. He appeared to be willing to be docile, and to give substantial guarantees for amendment. His debt was doubtless large, but it was not supposed to be unmanageable; and there was always the resource of lightening the burden by diminishing the interest in consideration of better-assured principal. When the Ministry sent out a member of their own body to look into the Egyptian accounts, it might be taken as confirmation of their being really in earnest. If we suppose the case of a speculative investor buying £5000 of Egyptian bonds—say of the 1873 loan, at £73—with the idea of holding them, we may easily see how an intelligent man may be induced to cling to a sinking security, by considerations and arguments that were always apparently reasonable, although they kept being modified by changing circumstances. But if our imaginary friend has burned his fingers seriously, in spite of making good use of his judgment, and possibly of some special information to boot, what is likely to be the fate of the happy-go-lucky investor who buys blindly on a caprice or the advice of a broker, and resigns himself to abide the event like a fatalist?

It might have been thought that the appointment of the Paymaster of the Forces to this financial mission would have been favourably received by gentlemen in the Stock Exchange. But the City has its own manner of looking at things; it had set its heart on the employment of Mr. Lowe, and marked its disappointment by depressing the stocks. Then came the resignation of Nubar Pacha, the Egyptian statesman in whom Europe had most confidence, and the 1873 loan fell sharply to 60, to rally considerably, however, the following day. As it happened, it was the new tribunals and not the financial arrangement that was at the bottom of Nubar Pacha's disgrace; but from that event may be dated the beginning of the real struggle between bulls and bears, in which the bears have had so much the best of it. Rumours were freely floated and circulated to interpret facts that might be more or less significant. Mr. Cave having landed at Alexandria, the eyes of jobbers and dealers began to be riveted on his movements. The Khedive received him courteously—that was a matter of course. But then came stories of an interruption of these agreeable relations, when the host and the envoy passed to the discussion of business from receptions of ceremony. The Khedive resented the demand for an unreserved disclosure of his treasury secrets, with an absolute surrender of the corresponding vouchers. It was evident that the most he had desired was the assistance of a financial expert to advise upon such information as it pleased the treasury to furnish—he had been saddled with a financial father confessor, who insisted on his making a clean breast of it. Perhaps when this intelligence leaked out, it might have been more prudent if our investor had sold, on the probability of being able to buy in again at a lower price. But the very fact of this member of the British Ministry going about his business with such thoroughgoing zeal, seemed to argue that his colleagues had come to the resolution of forcing the Khedive through his difficulties. It was clearly their policy to make a friend of the master of Egypt; and if they pressed him to disclosures which would certainly be disagreeable and humiliating, it was to be supposed that they had come to the resolution of making it all up to him in the end.

It was to be presumed, too, that that was the expectation of the Khedive. At all events it was said that upon second thoughts he had decided to have no reservation, and had given orders to that effect to his treasury officials. Mr. Cave drew up his report, and the contents of the mysterious document were discounted in different senses by speculators in France and England. The moment when it should be laid before the House of Commons was awaited with feverish anxiety. But in the meantime the stocks were tending upwards, on the declaration of the Chancellor of the Exchequer, that Mr. Cave had come to the conclusion that Egypt could meet her onerous engagements and continue to pay her way. A serious shock was given to them by the Premier's discouraging answer as to the publication of the report. Whether the objection to publication came from Cairo or Whitehall, it was argued that if concealment could be advisable in any case, the disclosures must be damaging indeed. But the Parisian was slow to be persuaded of this, and French buying sustained the markets. Then, again, our friend might have done well to sell. But, on the other hand, he might fairly pin his faith on the declarations of the cautious Chancellor of the Exchequer, who must have had cognisance of all that was known to Mr. Cave, who had taken an opportunity of explaining and toning down the damaging suggestions of Mr. Disraeli. Meantime, however, with the exception of one or two thorough-going partisans, the journals had taken to bearing Egyptians, thus upsetting all probable calculations as to the line they might have been trusted to follow. They might have been justified patriotically in striving to prevent the Government from involving itself with the finances of an embarrassed State; but, considering the interest we have in keeping on cordial terms with Egypt, it might have been imagined that they would have sought to soften the blow to the Khedive, by doing every justice to his better intentions. On the contrary, they had little for him but sneers and abuse just when he was showing a tendency towards reformation; they gave him no credit for the proportion of really remunerative outlay on the public works which had been prematurely undertaken and extravagantly carried out; and they assumed a state of insolvency which Sir Stafford Northcote had denied. The report, when it did appear at last—containing nothing to justify the delays that had been so injurious to Egyptian credit—was judged in the same hypercritical spirit. In the words of M. Beaulieu Leroy in the *Débats,* it really showed that, though everything was imperilled, nothing was lost; yet the majority of English journalists spoke of it as if everything was lost already.

The time was a crisis in the affairs of the bondholders. The tone of the journals indicated the probable turn of public opinion; it might have its influence on the action of the Government, and was necessarily most damaging to the credit it impeached. Mr. Disraeli had intimated his refusal to appoint an official director to the board of a new State bank; but there were obvious objections to such a proposal on the face of it, and the most ardent partisans of the Khedive were ready to admit them. But Mr. Disraeli had gone on to state, that had a proposal been made to appoint a commissioner for the receiving of revenues, it might very possibly have been favourably entertained; and that seemed tantamount to an invitation, and to imply a good deal more. Of course, circumstances and the conditions attached to such a request, might render it unacceptable; but the effect of that language was to prolong the impression that our Government might still interpose. Already it had taken a second step officially, in sending out Mr. Rivers Wilson on a temporary engagement to Cairo, that might be changed into a permanent one. Even when English interest in Egyptian affairs had visibly cooled, as opinion expressed itself more and more decidedly against any further commitments there, the bondholders found consolation in the agitation that was going on in France. French patriotism, disgusted by the Suez Canal purchase, was to take its revenge by financing the Khedive. It was notorious that the leading French financial establishments had an enormous interest in preserving his credit—that small French investors had lent to him largely; and it was believed that political as well as pecuniary considerations were weighing on the anxious deliberations of a Government that had everything to fear from a financial crisis. The finance minister had actually persuaded the Parisian bankers to help the Khedive over a pressing embarrassment; and a step that would have been impossible in London, seemed proper and natural in Paris. The drafts of various projected schemes were published authoritatively, and any one of these would have probably proved satisfactory even to the bondholders who had bought at the highest prices. And in the meantime, one of the Rothschilds had gone on a tardy mission to France, by the wish or with the assent of our Government, to see what might be done. Had he said "yes" instead of "no" to the proposals submitted to him, our investor might have seen such a rebound in his stock as had taken place on the announcement of the purchase of the Canal shares.

Things had undoubtedly been going from bad to worse; disappointments and disillusioning had been following each other fast; but it must be remembered that the steady subsidence in the stocks had been more than keeping pace with the sinking of the investor's hopes. When anything occurred to disturb the stock markets in any corner of the wrold, Egyptians were sold as a matter of course; and anything approaching a satisfactory and definite settlement must catch the speculators heavily, and be the beginning of a rapid rally. The Khedive was left face to face with the representatives of the embarrassed French financiers; but he had such independent counsellors as Mr. Rivers Wilson and Senor Scialoja, and after all he was master of the situation. He had a reputation for shrewdness, statesmanship, and patriotism; and he knew that the future of his kingdom and dynasty depended greatly on the scheme he might promulgate. If England had been holding aloof in the meantime, France, Italy, and Austria had consented to appoint semi-official trustees to see to the liquidation of his affairs. His creditors had been so scared by Bourse rumours and operations, they had seen their property so steadily depreciated, that they would gladly have assented to any reasonable sacrifice that seemed likely to improve the stability of the stocks. If he acted rationally his course seemed clear. He would consolidate on equitable terms the stocks held by his secured creditors, obtaining their consent to a diminution of the interest and a postponement of the sinking fund operations; and few people would have objected to his dictating terms of compromise to those holders of treasury bills who had been making their fortunes out of him for years, and whose doubts as to ultimate payment in full were indicated by their extravagantly usurious charges. Had he done this he might have placed them in a better position than that in which they have been landed by their short-sighted grasping. An ample margin would have been left for the expenses of administration, as well as for any reasonable amount of that waste and extravagance which is almost entailed upon oriental potentates. It is not unreasonable to suppose that a five and a half per cent stock, whose payment was assured by a somewhat more satisfactory arrangement of the new financial machinery, would soon have gone up to £75 or £80: and our investing friend would have done well in the end, although he would certainly have passed through some worry and anxiety. So that, up to the promulgation of the Khedive's unjust and disastrous decree, we maintain there was no point of this strange and eventful history at which it would have been clearly wise for the investor to sell at current prices, except, perhaps, as we said, when there was an inexplicable rise on the announcement that Mr. Cave's report was to be published at last. And if our résumé of the recent phases of Egyptian finance has been somewhat desultory and imperfect as we have necessarily left it, it must be admitted, at least, that it is a striking illustration of the difficulties that may embarrass the judgment of the speculative investor.

It scarcely falls within the scope of our article to survey the present prospects of "Egyptians." Now they are speculative indeed, should Mr. Goschen's mediation lead to nothing in particular, if holders were counting upon being paid in full after the present year. *If* the figures that bring out such extremely delicate balances have been accurately estimated; *if* the country has fortitude and patience to endure the oppressive burden of arbitrary taxation, when the example of their Turkish neighbours has shown them a summary means of relief; *if* the Khedive and his successors resign themselves to be miracles of self-sacrifice, abandoning those habits of reckless generosity and spend-thrift profusion which have become their second nature; *if* Pharaoh renounces the too advanced ambitions which have gone so far to ruin him in unremunerative public works; *if* he can keep out of wars in Abyssinia and Central Africa; *if* he can avoid troubles with the powers at Constantinople; *if* he need send no bribes to his new superiors, and if he is not cruelly squeezed for the furnishing of military contingents;—if all these things can be managed somehow, then it is possible that foreign bondholders may get the seven per cent that is promised them. But the occurrence of any one of the contingencies we have suggested may endanger any possible scheme by compelling a default, which will lead to considerable oscillations in the stocks, preliminary to fresh compromises with the creditors.

In consequence of the collapse of the South American bubbles, the default of Turkey, and the short-sighted injustice of the Khedive, a long list of popular foreign stocks has been erased from the list of legitimate investments, while others of higher standing have suffered either in sympathy or from extraneous causes. Now that the Eastern question has been re-opened, it must for some time to come remain a matter of uncertainty whether Europe may not be plunged into war. No wonder that distrust is so general. The credit that used to be taken for granted is now exposed to prejudiced scrutiny; and contingencies that would never have suggested themselves some years ago, are brought conspicuously forward in present calculations. Germany having expended the milliards of the war indemnity, has been trying to obtain accommodation with imperfect success, and begins to groan under the double burden of her military system, and the emigration of able-bodied men that it stimulates. France has given proof of marvellous elasticity of resources: and it is an excellent omen for her that her funds are so high in favour with the small home investors, who give guarantees for their loyalty and good behaviour by having a material stake in their country's prosperity. But the French funds are scarcely cheap in the eyes of foreigners, who are scandalised by the violence of French parties, and are alive to the probable consequences of a possible war of revenge. Italy avers that she has succeeded in establishing an equilibrium, and at all events she is approaching that desirable consummation. Italian stocks have been steadily advancing, and might be considered by no means dear, were we satisfied she would be content with a state of modest neutrality like that of Belgium. But although prudence and parsimony are Italian virtues, the people are ambitious and vainglorious, and have still an eye on some of the Austrian possessions. There is always the chance of their putting themselves forward as Sardinia did in the Crimea, involving themselves in a war with which they had no direct concern, and so contracting fresh obligations that would upset their plans of reform.

This reopening of the Eastern question, however, bears chiefly on the finances of Russia and Austria-Hungary. The late heavy fall in Hungarians, a stock held deservedly in considerable favour, shows the danger to which it is exposed. It threatened to supersede Egyptians in rivalry with Russians, as the fashionable stock to be beared, when the deposition of Abdul-Aziz happily reprieved its holders. But it is in the condition of the Russian funds that Englishmen are more nearly concerned, politically as well as financially. So far as we can judge, the Russian fomenting of troubles in the East has been simply suicidal. The game might have been worth the candle, had the ripe or rotten fruit of the Bosphorus been likely to drop into the Czar's hand for the shaking. As it is, however, the peaceful instincts of Alexander were in reality patriotic presentiments. For, until comparatively the other day, the solidity of Russian credit was a primary article of faith in the creed of the English investor. The honest policy that had been pursued through the Crimean war had proved extraordinarily profitable by way of advertisement. The growing empire obtained any amount of accommodation on easy terms. The first financial houses in London stood sponsors to successive loans. It was said that the bulk of the borrowed money was laid out on works of public utility which would indefinitely develop magnificent internal resources. What the real truth about Russian credit is, we do not pretend to affirm. It is certain that on the proposal for a loan that might be intended for war purposes, Russian credit has been assailed with rude and frank plausibility. It is asserted that the financial proceedings of the Czar have closely resembled those of the Sultan: that half the money borrowed for railways, &c., has been diverted for the barren purposes of war preparation, while the bulk of the lines that have been laid down are primarily strategic, only communicating incidentally between centres of industry and commerce; in short, that Russia has been paying her way by borrowing, and can only go on paying by borrowing more. It is sure that American discoveries have diminished the value of her silver-mines; and what is of much more consequence, the grain-producers of her southern provinces are being steadily undersold by American growers. Her embarrassments may be exaggerated; but the credit of such a country is like a woman's reputation; and when false accusations are believed, they may be quite as fatal as true ones. Besides, our cautious Foreign Minister has admitted that she is actually in financial straits; and when she came to the money-dealers the other day, as has been her regular practice of late, she found their doors shut in her face. Had she gone to war and seen her commerce crippled, if not destroyed, it is simply incredible that, with the best intentions, she could have gone on meeting the numerous claims upon her. Thus, in spite of their former high reputation, there is some reason for people holding aloof from "Russians." Of late the securities that have hitherto been so popular with us have only been finding support from foreign buyers; and the loss of confidence among their English friends would have been indicated by a far heavier fall, had not France and Germany come to the rescue.

But we need not go on passing whole lists of securities under review, and multiplying special illustrations, to show how severe and general has been the discrediting. The sinister course of events, the coincidence of flagrant scandals with heavy misfortunes, has been forcing the speculative investor into a position that has become more and more embarrassing. He is in painful perplexity as to what he had best do next, or how he may bestow what remains of his means. Committed as he involuntarily is to a course of retrenchment, what he would have considered reasonable interest becomes of more consequence than ever. Yet his financial nerve is shattered altogether; and when in fear and trembling he decides where to reinvest, he will be more fatally predisposed to panic than he has been, which is anything but an encouraging outlook for his brother stockholders. As to his combining these two incongruous objects of his desire—high returns and reasonable safety—we believe it to be quite within the range of possibility; just as there are fortunes to be made on the Derby, should you chance to "spot" the winner beforehand. But getting upon the right horse in the great race is decidedly the less speculative affair of the two; for on the turf you may be guided by public form, while among the outside ventures on the Stock Exchange you can only go upon chances depending on circumstances it is quite impossible to foresee. And this we may repeat for the encouragement of the class we are addressing, that while the dangers they have suffered from so severely tend to become more serious than ever, new sources of insecurity are springing up all about them.

It is clear that, in the first place, the accumulation of money seeking for outlets, coupled with the extinction or neglect of comprehensive classes of investments, must make those that have kept any kind of character more expensive luxuries than they have been: what used to yield $4\frac{1}{2}$ per cent will now be paying 4; what returned 6 may have gone down to 5. Already we see the effect of the process in the set towards the choicer American railway bonds, as well as in those preference stocks of our own lines, which the companies find themselves able to renew on more favourable terms. The consequence is, that if a man is determined to have 7 per cent, he must hazard himself in something that has more elements of doubt about it than the stocks that paid him 7 per cent formerly: while if he has set his heart upon 10, heaven knows where he is to look for it, without scrambling about the galleries of an American mine, or having the sense of seating himself in the crater of a volcano. Last year, for example, you might buy into such an institution as the Imperial Ottoman Bank—really admirably managed in its way, by Englishmen of high position and some of the most prominent Paris financiers—and make merry on excellent dividends and bonuses with no disagreeable idea that you were living in a fool's paradise. But now, anything that is unquestionably of the first class, seems to the needy altogether beyond the reach of any one but a trustee or a millionaire; what was ranked in the third class begins to be promoted to the second, and so on. The result must be a greater predisposition to uneasiness even in circles whose serenity used to be comparatively little disturbed in times of crisis, and whose example had a tranquillising effect on their more excitable neighbours. And all such tendencies to uneasiness are far more adroitly manipulated than they used to be, to the injury of the uninitiated in Stock Exchange intrigue, and the advantage of unscrupulous cliques. Without taking a specially gloomy view of the world in general, we see that at least in its financial department and on the Stock Exchange, the powers of evil for the time are decidedly in the ascendant. Bulling and bearing are carried on as recklessly as "plunging" on the race-courses was a dozen of years ago, although with far greater astuteness. The system of syndicates has created a disturbing force which individuals can neither control nor contend with. How far it may be carried is shown by that history of the Egyptian finances. The Khedive, in a dozen of years, has found credit to the amount of some ninety millions; but so much of his debt is held by a knot of Frenchmen, acting in concert, that he has ceased to be a free agent. He seems to have been sincerely desirous to amend his ways and escape insolvency, while escape was possible; but, failing the official assistance of friendly powers, which might have been extended to him for political reasons, he had no alternative but to make fresh terms with the Credit Foncier, its affiliated establishments, and the Alexandria banks, although, by doing so, so far as appearances go, he may have put the finishing touch to his discredit. Low as Egyptians had fallen, it is only the interested operation of the French syndicate that has kept them at their present level; it might have been their policy to depress the stocks in place of sustaining them; and they are themselves liable to be paralysed at any moment by a financial crisis in Paris, which must necessarily involve their Egyptian protégé and the private individuals who have lent to him. So at this moment the holder of Egyptian debt is not speculating only on the honesty of the Khedive, on his good intentions, and on the peace and prosperity of his dominions, but on the dispositions, motives, and solvency of a set of foreign gentlemen who get their living by launching themselves on venturesome undertakings. Nor is that by any means an extreme instance of the power of combination, and we have only singled it out as a patent one. In this case the French syndicate, though it is made so formidable by its concert, holds, after all, but a relatively small proportion of the total Egyptian stocks. The "Autobiography of a Joint-Stock Company,"[3] which appeared in the Magazine for July, shows, with scarcely a shade of exaggeration, although under the form of fiction, how absolutely shares may be manipulated by the wire-pullers,

---

3. Thinly fictionalized exposé of Albert Grant, written by Laurence Oliphant and published in *Blackwood's Edinburgh Magazine* in 1876 (included in this volume). Grant created the Credit Foncier and Mobilier of England in 1864, which specialized in loans to foreign railways, mines, and public utilities. By 1877, Grant was bankrupt and disgraced. [Ed.]

who alone have access to the official records. The innocent outsider may have no clue to the causes or the courses of the market movements, for plausible reports may be cooked with the special purpose of misleading him. The rise on false intelligence which encouraged him to increase his holding, may be merely a preliminary to the collapse for which directors and promoters have been unloading; while the sudden drop which sent him to sell in a fright, may portend the arrangement of some satisfactory amalgamation which would speedily have doubled the value of his shares.

What aids these syndicates in the magnitude and rapidity of their operations, is the extraordinary increase in the sheer unadulterated gambling which now goes on in the Stock Exchange. There are at present, we believe, between 1700 and 1800 brokers on the London lists; and, had they to confine themselves strictly to legitimate business, instead of being a tolerably thriving body on the average, it is certain that the better half of the fraternity would be starving. But the chances of legitimate business enter scarcely at all into the calculations of many of them when making choice of their profession. They know, in so far as it is possible to estimate what must after all be matter of guesswork, that some five-sixths of the business of the House is in time bargains, involving no actual delivery of scrip, but a mere settlement of differences. In old times, substantial City men were in the habit of occasionally making heavy speculations in consols, but it was generally with a definite purpose, and as an insurance against some contingency. Now, the practice of buying quantities of securities you cannot possibly pay for, is become especially popular among the penniless. Perhaps the mania assumes its most virulent form among those whose congenial pursuits are carried on in the precincts of Threadneedle and Throgmorton Streets. Periodical disclosures in the police courts show some manager or clerk abusing the confidence of his employers; obtaining credit to an extent that appears incredible, from some firm of covetous and confiding brokers, on a running account which has been kept open by the aid of contangos and backwardations. City *employés* who have the ingenuity to trade upon feloniously-obtained credit, are the most dangerous customers of the more speculative brokers, because they have learned how to let them in most heavily. But there are men about town, both in the City and at the West End, who are always on the look-out for "good things;" and failing these, who fall back on gambling in indifferent things in the blackest ignorance. To all except very exceptional natures, the first loss is as fatal as the first gain, especially when the gambler is under difficulties to begin with. He had urgent occasion for the money he hoped to win; and now that he is out of pocket instead, he positively burns to recoup himself. He follows with feverish pulse the fluctuations of the stock that scorched his fingers. He opens with trembling fingers each successive edition of the evening papers. He may have been betrayed into dealing at first by some friendly "tip" that proved false, given perhaps in the genial *abandon* of an after-dinner conversation. His taking action on that unlucky piece of information seems wisdom to him still, even in the bitter retrospect. Now he has nothing more to guide him than a matter of public notoriety; and there are scores of jobbers and dealers who are far better posted than he. No matter—he must cut in again; and so he does, and he loses, and carries over, and pays for doing it, and gets involved deeper and deeper, till the brokers become pressing for settlement, or some unexpected political incident makes his open bargains disastrous. With stockbrokers it is a point of honour as of self-interest to keep the secrets of their chambers as punctiliously as consulting physicians. But it is no secret that the fair sex, and ladies of the highest station too, are in the habit of throwing themselves into the national game with characteristic feminine impetuosity. The stolen joys and griefs of the Stock Exchange are more exciting than the faro and spadillo of our grandmothers, and infinitely more ruinous. The stakes are practically unlimited, while to a certain point you may play on credit. Of course we need not speak of those professional speculators with more or less money at their disposal, who are always busying themselves in the markets that chance to be most the rage for the moment.

But it is that promiscuous gambling by people of straw, with the fashion in stocks that is its natural consequence, which plays into the hands of the syndicates. It may be an object with a group of schemers to get rid of stock to the value of a million or so. Did they wait for bona fide investors to relieve them, the operation must necessarily be tedious; and possibly if they pressed sales they might have to sacrifice the property in a panic of their own creation. But by creating a gambling run upon the stock by means of fictitious bargains and fluctuations, they may unload quietly among the clouds of transfer notes that are flying about, by the aid of the favourable rumours with which they have judiciously fed the speculators. Necessarily such periods of excitement, with the extreme sensitiveness which is caused by these time bargains, and the swarms of canards which invariably precede and accompany them, are all against the investor who means to hold. Reaction follows inflation, disappointment subsides into depression, and the sense of instability is a lurking danger which may lead to serious mischief at any moment.

That propagation of rumours is another fruit of the new state of things, for which we are greatly indebted to the progress of science and enterprise. Formerly, it might be worth the while of leviathan capitalists operating on an extensive scale, to elaborate some deep-laid plot; and one or two famous instances of the kind during the war agitations early in the century will naturally occur to everybody. But most men then, as a rule, could only act on the regular mail deliveries, when the foreign letters necessarily corrected each other. The correspondent of a City house communicated to it all he knew; but his knowledge was probably public property, and amounted to very little. If a piece of really useful information reached an individual, he naturally kept it for his private use, so that his small sales or purchases produced no appreciable effect. Now, the journals have their correspondents everywhere—correspondents who are always rushing about among telegraph offices, when they have not a wire of their own at their elbows for which they are bound to find constant occupation. Competition among them is as keen as the public cravings they have to satisfy. It may be safely said that they best discharge their duties to their employers as to the public, by despatching doubtful news rather than none at all; and very often the shrewdest of them may be the victims of mystifications that have been carefully planned in secret conspiracy. For some years past, the Bourses of London and Paris have ceased to have a practical monopoly of the speculative dealings of Europe. There is gambling going forward in international stocks, and as much excitement, although on a smaller scale, in Vienna or Berlin, or even at Alexandria or Galata. Men on the spot, with money and means of information at command, give the reports they desire to be believed, the consistency or the colour that suits them; and prepare a story for foreign circulation whose plausibility might impose on the most distrustful of mortals. So the fever flame of an agitation in Egyptians or Peruvians is always being fanned by fresh announcements, each of them apparently authenticated by pieces of circumstantial evidence. Half-a-dozen times in a day, a bellow and a roar in the Stock Exchange may greet the arrival of some new sensation, to be followed by a rush of sales or purchases; and the property that is liable to be blown about with each breath, naturally comes to be more doubtfully regarded.

Nor can we say that we consider the daily lucubrations of the City editors to be much of a safeguard for the ignorant or unwary. It is true that in point of independence and honesty, most of our papers compare most advantageously with the French press, the greater part of which is regularly in the pay of capitalists, and makes little secret of it. Nor are we inclined to lay much stress on the cases of corruption that have recently been brought to light in certain causes célèbres. It has been proved that these things do occur, and a chance that your seemingly impartial adviser has been bought over by scheming knaves, is not a pleasant thing to contemplate. But we are willing to believe that they are exceptional; and what seems to us more serious as a habitual danger, is the increasing tendency to sensational writing, since it seems to be desired that "our City columns" should be made a sensational feature in the journal. The stocks that are most frequently dealt in by speculators, and which are consequently for the time the most sensitive, are made the themes of daily animadversion. The modern City editor feels himself bound to account for each passing fluctuation in his own ingenious fashion. He selects his particular rumour or telegram on which to construct a theory, which the event of the day or the morrow may demolish. Instead of waiting to state ascertained facts, or giving a word of sound advice in season when he has cogent grounds to go upon, he projects his lively mind into the future, and almost unconsciously makes himself an ardent partisan of promiscuous conclusions of his own. Before the light of research has been thrown on the subject, he takes the credit of the Argentine Republic or the depth of the Peruvian guano deposits under his special protection. Then when an agitation that may be more or less reasonable sets in, in the stocks of these countries, he makes it his mission to explain away each fresh fall, as due to interested intrigues or causes that are entirely adventitious. Certain readers regard him as an inspired prophet, nor do they correct his assertions by those of his colleagues, who are asserting South America to be a howling wilderness peopled by jaguars and half-savage repudiators. Holders are persistently warned, "not to be tempted into realising their property," until possibly all they may have to realise in the end is the fact that there is no property to part with. It is clear that caution and judicious reticence should be the guiding principles of a man who undertakes to offer most delicate advice in matters that may affect the happiness and fortunes of thousands: and the gentlemen who let their imagination run daily riot in their articles, as if they were dashing off the *feuilleton* of a French journal, can scarcely expect to be listened to with respect, should they really have something important to say.

It is not so many years ago, as we said, that enterprise or speculation, call it which you will, was very much limited to France and England. Italy, broken up among the Pope, the Bourbons, and the Austrian Archdukes, had been stagnating for long; the little kingdom of Sardinia was beginning cautiously to feel its way. The great German race kept moving along very placidly in the old grooves, just as they lived contentedly in their uncomfortable, old-fashioned capitals. But now the diffusion of speculation and financing may multiply graver perils than ever can be brought about by the propagation of disquieting rumours. There came a great and general movement, with a passing of the people north and south of the Alps from one extreme to the other. United Italy,[4] among other blessings that came to her with her regeneration, had to be grateful for a most creditable national debt; and the embarrassments of her finances and the clouds that were hanging over her prospects gave room for some very pretty gambling in it. Syndicates, companies, and individuals had followed the example of the State, and betaken themselves to borrowing likewise; the moneyed classes struck out forms of excitement that promised to become as popular as the lotteries; banking accounts were opened and consequently banks, by people who seldom before had had more money than they could comfortably spend; railways, harbour works, irrigation works, &c.,

4. England supported the unification of Italy in the 1860s. The movement was led by Guiseppe Garibaldi and opposed by Napoleon III. [Ed.]

were pushed briskly forward with foreign capital; and the development of the stock markets gave an unwonted animation to dealings in Turin, Florence, and Milan. But the financial renaissance of Italy was nothing to what was witnessed in Austria and Prussia. Of a sudden the North and South Germans aroused themselves simultaneously from their lethargy. Banks and great credit associations started into existence to accommodate the shareholders in hundreds of companies with the means of carrying out their patriotic ideas. The long-neglected harvest had been ripening for the reapers; and the returns were to be so certain and so immediate that the risks might be counted as nil. So it seemed at first, and the German credit establishments in the beginning paid nearly as handsome dividends as those financial societies of our own that have since failed so signally. The primary objects of the new Teutonic joint-stock enterprise, as a rule, were patriotic as much as personal. Concessions were granted to reclaim the naturally rich country that had been forest, fallow, or swamp from time immemorial. New railways were constructed cheaply between flourishing cities whose inhabitants had seldom stirred from home; canals were cut to facilitate heavy traffic; timbered hills that had hitherto been inaccessible began to be *exploité;* forges and smelting works were opened in remote valleys. But above all, the new excitement broke out in the cities in the shape of house-building. Hitherto it had been the habit and the fashion to live in the most homely guise; the Viennese burghers for instance huddled together over their shops in crooked alleys, while the palaces of the proudest nobility in Europe were crowded up in the gloomiest thoroughfares. Now, all was to be changed. New-made millionaires advertised the credit they were trading on, by the imposing exteriors of their gaudily-furnished mansions. People who were slow to learn that art of everyday spending which neither they nor their fathers had ever practised, could at least make a grand show once for all, by housing themselves sumptuously behind columns, and caryatides, and sculptured stone-work. The nobles who could afford it consented to abandon their hereditary halls, and exchange darkness and unsavoury stenches for sweetness and light. The result was, that along the Danube and the Wien, and on the banks of the Spree as well, there was a general rising of Rings, Boulevards, Faubourgs, Squares, and Places. The odd thing was, that notwithstanding the increase of accommodation, the rents were rising with the houses; the various building companies paid fabulous dividends—shrewd capitalists kept securing promising building sites at fancy prices; then borrowing on them and then building again. There was no perceptible check to the movement until it was pulled up so sharply in South Germany by the commercial crisis of Vienna in the Exhibition year.

That crisis furnished a significant illustration of the new danger to which we are inviting attention. A panic in London is disastrous enough, but it may almost be said to be calculation and calm compared to possible panics on the

Continent. In London the property most freely flung about is that which, depending chiefly on credit, may not improbably disappear if it once fall into disrepute. But the Viennese parted just as wildly with shares that, being based mainly upon the real security of houses and land, were almost certain to recover materially when the worst of the fever was past. We cannot easily forget the spectacles that were to be witnessed at the temporary Bourse when the alarm had culminated, in a couple of days or so; and all through the city the adventurers appeared to have but one idea—to get rid of everything they held, and realise what remained of it in specie. When companies and private firms were shaking and falling, the most extravagant reports find ready credence; it was even gravely asserted, in journals of some position, that the Rothschilds were tottering on the verge of insolvency. Yet that state of mind was so far from being unnatural that it is certain to repeat itself for many years to come in any similar circumstances, for risky enterprise of any kind is an entire novelty to the German. The mass of investors, when they had money to lay by, have been in the habit of putting it away so very safely, that there was little chance of seeing it diminished. But they take as kindly as their neighbours to possibilities of gain; and when they saw their Hebrew fellow-citizens and the foreign capitalists turning everything that they touched into gold, they could not resist following the example. As yet, however, they have scarcely made a beginning of studying that difficult art of keeping their heads through reverses and fluctuations in which our own countrymen have made so little progress. Panic masters them more absolutely, and its contagion spreads among them with most demoralising rapidity. Overdone enterprise and unnatural inflation have sown broadcast the seeds of mistrust, which may be forced to maturity at any moment; and, thanks to the intimacy of international financial relations now-a-days, should there be a crisis on the Exchanges of Vienna or Berlin, the shock will be communicated to London or Paris. So that henceforward the speculative investor ought to watch carefully the course of events in a plurality of highly sensitive centres, and that is, of course, practically impossible. All may be apparently quiet in London, even when there may be some tendency towards activity in certain threatened markets, owing to the operations of the few farsighted ones who are behind the scenes. Yet he may awaken some fine morning to hear of an acute crisis abroad, which is to throw everybody into alarm, and precipitate a convulsion here which might otherwise have been staved off indefinitely. The rapidly downward course of his favourite securities may give him disagreeable proof of the solidarity of English interests with those of our foreign friends, and may remind him that it would only have been commonly prudent to examine into their circumstances and their finances as well.

How it may all end, it is worse than idle to surmise. We presume that Time may be trusted to open up new fields of investment, and it is certain that he will not want any assistance that can be given him by the interested ingenuity of professional financiers. In the meantime the moral of the situation seems to be that wary investors should hold more closely than ever by the good old-fashioned maxim that great interest means bad security. If they are hesitating between low and high dividends, they will do well to remember that although in the one case they may have to put up with disagreeable privations, in the other they may be inviting irremediable ruin.

CHAPTER SIX

INTERNATIONAL IMPLICATIONS

WALTER BAGEHOT
✠✠✠

THE SINGULARITY OF INDIAN FINANCE

THE details of the annual budget—the amusing strife between Mr. Grant Duff[1] and Mr. Fawcett,[2] the various side suggestions offered from various quarters—must not blind us to the essential strangeness of what we are doing in India. We are, to speak broadly, applying civilised finance to a semi-civilised country. We inevitably take with us the financial habits and maxims of Englishmen, and we have to apply them to a world of Asiatics; we take with us modern financial ideas which, even in Europe, are of yesterday, and we apply them to an ancient world of arrested civilisation, which was pretty much what it is now before history began. We are not blaming, but explaining, and let us examine the particulars.

First, we have applied the English "budget" idea—almost the most recent development of our parliamentary system, and one of the boldest. It is only our familiarity with it which blinds us to its audacity. In England, at the beginning of each year the Chancellor of the Exchequer makes up an imaginary account: he sets on the one side the taxes he expects to receive, and on the other the charges he expects to incur. If he finds he has more money than he

Walter Bagehot, "The Singularity of Indian Finance." *Economist* 30 (August 10, 1872): 985–86.
1. Sir Mountstuart Grant Duff (1829–1906). Under-secretary for India 1868–74. Became governor of Madras in 1881.
2. Henry Fawcett (1833–84). Friend of John Stuart Mill and author of *Manual of Political Economy* (1863). As a member of Parliament, he opposed Indian revenues. As member of the committee upon Indian finance (1871–73 and 1874), he became known as the "member for India."

wants for that particular year, he takes off taxes; if he has less than he wants, he imposes taxes. He makes an hypothesis as to one year which is still future, and according to the issue of that hypothesis he augments or pares the revenue of the country. But this is entirely a modern idea. Even in England it is much newer than is generally known. And most statesmen in most nations would have thought it most dangerous. They would have said;

> You cannot safely "pull about" and alter your "plans" of taxation in that way. It is madness to take off good taxes because you do not want them in one year; still worse madness is it to take them off at the beginning of the year because by an imaginary account it seems that you *may* not want them. And if you have not enough money for a particular year, or may not have, probably it will be better for you (unless the emergency is great) not to impose new taxes. Nations do not easily bear new taxes; you ought to have a treasure in hand to meet minor deficits.

In a word, our English system proceeds on the notion that the public revenue consists of taxes easy to increase and easy to recover. But exactly the reverse is true, taking the world at large and history as a whole. In most states it is extremely difficult to find new taxes; their revenue consists of the produce of fixed property and of customary charges, which have been placed as high as permanently as they can be. At a crisis, as in a war, something more may be wrung from the people; but even then it is difficult, and for a series of years it is impossible. National finance in most countries resembles domestic finance: there is a certain fixed income, which it is not easy to augment; you must not spend it all in good years, for in bad years you may have to meet extra expenses. Only England and a few civilised countries have a revenue such as our English budgets presume—a revenue which the taxpayers are ready and able greatly to augment, and which may be diminished without apprehension, because it can be recovered without risk.

The application to India of this budget system might be expected to occasion grave mistakes. If it has not been so fatal as might seem, it is mainly owing to the English caution, which shrinks from a full development of its own principles, and so often escapes bad results. But one great error has plainly been committed. Either the income tax ought not to have been taken off in 1865, or it ought not to have been re-imposed in 1869. If it was good enough to be permanent, it should not have been relinquished; if it was not good enough, it should not have been reimposed. Still worse was Lord Mayo's[3] error in 1869, in augmenting the rate of the income tax in the middle of a year, and on a sudden. These abandonments and re-impositions belong to western finance and not to eastern; they belong to a progressive world, of

---

3. Richard Southwell Bourke (1822–72). Appointed viceroy of India in 1869.

which change is the essence, not to an arrested world whose essence is no change.

Secondly, we have introduced into India a still greater and more marvellous western invention. We have created a large and permanent public debt. All decent governments have been able to contract temporary debts; almost all of them have done so; but permanent national debts, which the borrower does not mean to repay, and which the lender does not want repaid, are a European creation of the last two centuries. No classical statesman, no English statesman even of the 16th century, would have believed in the possibility of them. Yet such is the credit of English rule, that the Indian Treasury—without recourse to the English Exchequer, and without any idea of such recourse—can borrow what it likes. And in so doing, the English government employs one of the greatest engines of civilisation, but also one which entails the gravest responsibilities. Most of the half-civilised communities to which Europe lends Europe demoralises. It gives them more money than they can bear. It is a discouragement to thrift, and an incentive to expense and waste. It has been justly said that imperfect governments have a "violent propensity" to expense; that propensity is commonly counteracted by the want of money, but that check is now removed by the help of Europe, and the incessant loans which she is ready to make even to very imperfect governments.

The English government of India is not to be classed with these governments; its defects are not those of Egypt or Turkey. But it is impossible not to see that the most universally dangerous thing in the world—the unbounded command of money—has dangers even in its case. It is wholly free from the waste of tyranny, but it is not free (and cannot be) from the waste of beneficence. Mr. Fawcett says that it is wasteful throughout; that its public works are excessive; that it almost never gets money's worth. No doubt this judgment is far too sweeping; calmer and more judicial minds than Mr. Fawcett's must be applied to the subject before we can know the truth about it. But still the rational probability is that in some cases Mr. Fawcett is right, and that the Indian government, being able to borrow as much money as it liked, has, like all other persons in that misleading position, sometimes spent when it should not, and borrowed when it ought not.

Thirdly, the English government have given up all the bad resources of taxation employed by the rude native governments. Adam Smith laid down as a cardinal maxim that taxes should be paid at the time when and in the manner in which it was most convenient to the taxpayers to pay them. But the exact reverse has been the natural maxim. Till very recently taxes have always been levied at the time when and in the mode in which it was most convenient to the tax receiver to receive it. When governments saw a man with property they took some of it: if he attempted to earn money they made him pay for attempting it. In consequence, the finance of half-civilised nations is complex, and that complexity has made them poorer. Oriental communities abound in bad taxes. Our history in India, as Mr. Grant Duff says, has been the history of the remission of specially burdensome taxes.

And lastly, instead of these old oriental taxes we have imposed a tax which is the last refinement of western finance—which is so peculiar that even the French do not think themselves fit for it: we have imposed the income tax. Nothing is so contrary to the ideas of primitive finance as this. Primitive finance always deals with *gross* produce. It takes a certain share of the gross yield of each field; it puts on a transit duty of so much a package; it deals with visible things and visible privileges. But the income tax deals with *net* profits; its subject is an impalpable balance which only the trader knows, and which the bystander in most cases can only vaguely conjecture, and which in many cases he cannot estimate at all. In some cases oriental communities have attempted to use a kind of income tax, but only in a few, and then it was generally used as an instrument of extortion. The subject of the tax being vague, the native ruler made the taxpayer pay as much as ever he could be made to pay. But even these cases are only rare exceptions and, speaking broadly, it is a modern and European idea to think of really assessing an invisible net profit; the primitive oriental idea is to take some part of some tangible gross product.

As we have said before, we are not blaming, but explaining. No doubt in particular cases western ideas of finance were likely to guide, and (as we think) have guided, Englishmen too far in Indian finance. But in the main the choice was not left them. They could not tax as the native Indian governments; their ends were utterly different, and in consequence their means could not be the same. Even the best oriental [ruler] is satisfied if he can make his people fairly comfortable in their own hereditary way. A common oriental ruler does not even care for their comfort; he only wants to keep them quiet and enjoy his pleasure. But we are endeavouring, as rapidly as possible, to improve the people; we want to lift them out of their inherited way; if we can, we want to teach them a better way. If we are not in India for that purpose, we are there for no purpose. Mr. Grant Duff says we have spent since 1861:

In railways	£2,750,000
Other roads, etc.	7,500,000
Canals and irrigation works	8,000,000
Harbours and reclamation from the sea	1,750,000
Buildings of Civil Government	6,500,000
Total	26,500,000

Now no native government ever dreamed of such expenditure, and therefore as we do, we must have financial resources which the native governments had not. But that only shows our difficulty to be inevitable; it does not lessen the

difficulty; we are obliged to use the new finance of the West upon the old nations of the East, and so great is the contrast that long after the present generation is forgotten, ingenious officials and dissatisfied committees will be
labouring, and labouring heavily, to make the best of it.

HENRY FAWCETT

THE FINANCIAL CONDITION OF INDIA

As there seems to be every probability that during the next few months an unusual amount of public attention will be directed to Indian affairs, I think the
present may be regarded as a suitable time to consider the financial condition
of that country. With the view of treating the subject with as much clearness as
possible, it will be desirable in the first instance to ascertain what is the real
revenue of India. Much of the complexity which so often confuses discussions
on Indian finance arises from the want of any definite understanding as to the
sense in which certain terms are employed. From the last financial statement
of the Indian Finance Minister, it appears that he estimates the real revenue of
India at between 37,000,000*l.* and 39,000,000*l.;* whereas a short time afterwards the revenue was officially stated at more than 63,000,000*l.* This great
disparity of course arises from the gross revenue being referred to in the one
case and the net revenue in the other. It has not unfrequently been said, in discussions on Indian finance, that it cannot be of any moment whether the revenue is estimated at its gross or its net amount; it is, after all, simply a matter
of account. In one sense this, no doubt, is true; but I believe there will be no
difficulty in showing that it is of the first importance to give as much prominence as possible to the net, as distinguished from the gross, revenue of India.

Few things have done so much harm to Indian finance in the past, or may
cause greater embarrassment in the future, than an exaggerated idea as to the
revenue which the Indian Government has to spend. Although there is much
in the present financial condition of India to cause most serious apprehension,
yet there is one circumstance connected with it which may fairly be regarded
as a most hopeful omen for the future. Until quite lately, India was looked
upon as an extremely wealthy country, and there was no project, however
costly, that India was not supposed to be rich enough to pay for. Now, however, juster ideas of the resources of the country and of the condition of the

Henry Fawcett, "The Financial Condition of India." *Nineteenth Century* 5 (February 1878):
193–218.

people prevail. The recurrence of famines, and other circumstances which have caused more attention to be directed to Indian questions, have at length led the English public to take firm hold of the fact that India is an extremely poor country, and that the great mass of her people are in such a state of impoverishment that the Government will have to contend with exceptional difficulties if it becomes necessary to procure increased revenue by additional taxation. It is not more true of an individual than it is of a nation that, if it is desirable to check all extravagance and secure rigid economy, the amount of the income which is available for expenditure should not be over-estimated. It is often said that if a man comes into possession of an encumbered estate, the mere amount of the mortgages and other debts upon the property does not form an accurate measure of the real extent of his embarrassments, for he has constantly to contend with the difficulty of possessing an income so much less than its nominal amount. Having perhaps ten thousand a year to spend, he is regarded by the world as the possessor of twice as much, and is expected every hour of his life to live accordingly. The position of India is, I believe, not dissimilar to this. Year after year the Government of India has been living beyond its means. Deficits have been repeatedly recurring, and debt has been steadily and surely accumulated. Nothing, therefore, can be of greater importance, and nothing can be more likely to bring about a better state of things, than to ascertain what is the real amount of the revenue which the Indian Government has at the present time to spend. [. . .]

This brief review of the general prospect of the Indian revenue is, I think, sufficient to show not only that this revenue is comparatively stationary in amount, but that as the revenue is received in silver, and a large part of it has to be devoted to making payments in gold, the real value of this revenue has been, and may continue to be, most seriously diminished by the depreciation of silver. This conclusion as to the inelasticity of the Indian revenue is strongly confirmed by the extremely slow growth of the revenue during the past ten years, from 1868 to 1877. This particular period is selected for comparison because the figures are to be found in the latest number which has been published of the *Statistical Abstract of British India.* It appears . . . that four-fifths of the entire net revenue of India is derived from land, opium, and salt; and the inelastic character of the Indian revenue is at once shown if the average yield of these three sources of revenue, from 1868 to 1872, is compared with their average yield from 1873 to 1877.

	Average during five years, from 1868 to 1872 £	Average during five years, from 1873 to 1877
Net land revenue	17,991,951	18,526,451
Net opium "	6,720,672	6,388,555

Net salt " 5,466,370	5,735,936
Totals 30,178,993	30,650,942

It will be extremely important to keep these conclusions as to the inelasticity of the Indian revenue steadily in mind when considering, as I now propose to do, the prospects of Indian expenditure. It will not be necessary to examine all the detailed items of this expenditure, for I believe it will be perfectly possible to obtain data from which a correct opinion on the subject can be formed, by directing attention to the four chief branches of expenditure—namely, military expenditure, cost of administration, loss by exchange, and interest on loans for the general purposes of government, as well as for public works.

No subject connected with Indian finance demands such prompt and anxious attention as the enormous and increasing burden which is thrown upon India by her military expenditure. I have already referred to the fact that, even in a time of peace, the cost of the army to India is upwards of 17,000,000*l.* a year, 45 per cent. of her entire net revenue of 37,500,000*l.* being thus absorbed. It seems moreover that no limit can be placed to the extent to which India may not be exhausted by this drain on her resources. In his financial statement last year, Sir John Strachey made a pointed allusion to the significant fact that the cost of the army, being, as he said, at the time he spoke, more than 17,000,000*l.*, had increased by "upwards of 1,000,000*l.* since 1875–76, and that a large part of this increase was in the expenditure recorded in the home accounts." But serious as seemed to be the danger, at the time when these words were spoken, that India was gradually having thrown upon her a military expenditure which with her stationary revenue she would be absolutely powerless to bear, yet how indefinitely has this danger been increased by the events of the last three months. I shall carefully abstain from saying a single word on the Afghan war[1] which is not most strictly relevant to the subject now under discussion. It is, however, of the utmost importance to the future of India that the consequences involved in carrying out what is known as a "forward" frontier policy should be considered in their financial as well as in their military aspects. It would not be more unreasonable to decide what is the best house for a particular individual to live in, without having any regard to his income, than it is, on a mere consideration of military tactics, to determine to advance the frontier of India, without first ascertaining the expenditure which such an advance would necessitate. It is particularly worthy of remark that those who have been foremost in advocating a "forward" frontier policy in India have apparently ignored any consideration of its cost. The long

---

1. Britain twice invaded Afghanistan in the nineteenth century in order to gain military control over the Afghan passes and Afghan foreign policy. England forced India to pay for these wars out of its revenue, thus further undermining the financial health of India. [Ed.]

and able statements of Sir Henry Rawlinson, Sir Bartle Frere, and Lord Napier of Magdala contain scarcely a single reference to the financial aspects of the policy which they advocate. On the other hand, nothing can be more precise than the declarations of many of those most competent to express an opinion on the question, that the frontier could not be advanced without causing a most serious permanent addition to the military expenditure of India. Lord Lawrence, speaking of such an advance as is now contemplated, declared that it would "paralyse the finances of India." This was not simply his individual opinion. It has been often said that no Governor-General was ever surrounded by abler men than those who constituted the council of the Viceroy in 1867, and the despatch which contains this remarkable declaration was signed not only by Lord Lawrence, but by the Commander-in-Chief, Sir W. H. Mansfield (afterwards Lord Sandhurst), Sir H. S. Maine, Mr. G. N. Taylor, Mr. W. N. Massey, Sir Henry Durand, and Mr. G. U. Yule. This despatch, moreover, was addressed to Sir Stafford Northcote, who was then Secretary of State for India, and its conclusions were accepted by him and the Government of which he was a member. In view of these facts I think it may be fairly asked, if the expenditure necessary to carry out a particular policy would have paralysed the finances of India in 1867, what single circumstance can be pointed to which would show that such an expenditure would produce less serious consequences at the present time? No one can pretend to say that India's financial condition is more flourishing now than it was then. Since 1867 she has had to bear the severe strain of successive famines; and in 1867 there seemed to be no probability that her finances would be crippled by that depreciation of silver which has been said by one who spoke with the authority of a Finance Minister "to cast a grave shadow on the future of Indian finance." In case it may be objected that these opinions of Lord Lawrence and his council were expressed before the publication of the memorandum of Sir Henry Rawlinson, who throughout has been the most influential advocate of a "forward" policy, it may be well to point out that after this memorandum had been submitted to all the highest authorities in India, there is not a single word to be found in any of the minutes which they wrote upon it, which can be interpreted as the expression of a more favourable opinion of the financial results which would be produced by advancing the frontier into Afghanistan. Thus Sir R. H. Davies, the Lieutenant-Governor of the Punjaub, says: "Sir H. Rawlinson's proposals would again plunge us into the ever-shifting sands of Central Asian intrigue at a cost which we cannot afford." Sir Richard Temple, who has filled many influential positions in India, says: "Under Providence we are trustees for the public funds of India, and we are responsible for the careful application of them. When there are so many objects of certain usefulness and necessity within India itself on which to spend this money, it is a grave thing to expend such money in foreign regions on objects of doubtful expediency."

The very evil which Sir R. Temple thus anticipated has actually come to pass; for as Governor of Bombay he has himself been obliged, under the financial pressure caused by the military expenditure in Afghanistan, to peremptorily order that all public works, nay, even all repairs except those which are absolutely necessary, should be stopped in that Presidency.

In order to obtain as distinct an idea as possible of the consequences which may be produced on the financial condition of India by carrying out this "forward" frontier policy, it will be desirable to refer to some estimates which have been made of its cost by those most competent to form an opinion. The late Lord Sandhurst, who was scarcely less distinguished as a financier than as a soldier, writing in 1875, declared that the occupation of the advanced positions which it is proposed should be held beyond our present frontier, would require an addition to the strength both of the European and native army in India which would permanently increase her military expenditure by more than 3,000,000*l.* a year. Within the last month one of the very highest of Indian military authorities, Sir Henry Norman, has declared that if the advance were confined simply to the occupation of Koorrum, Jellalabad or Daka, and Candahar, at least thirteen or fourteen thousand additional troops would be required, one-third of whom would have to be British, and that their cost would be 1,000,000*l.* per annum; this sum, moreover, is independent of the large amount that would have to be expended on fortifications and other military works, and also in subsidising the hill tribes. It is, however, scarcely necessary to refer even to such high authorities as those just quoted. It can no longer be regarded as a matter of surmise that the frontier policy, which is now being pursued in India, will make a most serious permanent addition to her military expenditure. Less than a month had elapsed from the time our troops had crossed the frontier when it was announced that it had been decided to increase the native army by 15,000 men, or about 12 per cent. There is no point connected with the government of India on which there is greater unanimity of opinion than that it would not be prudent to add to the number of the native army without proportionately increasing the strength of the European army. An increase of 12 per cent. in the European and native army will certainly involve a cost of not less than 1,500,000*l.* a year. It would therefore appear that two powerful agencies will be brought simultaneously into operation most seriously to augment the military expenditure of India. In the first place, as Sir John Strachey has pointed out, the army, from administrative causes, is becoming more costly in proportion to its numbers; and, in the second place, the policy which is now being pursued is necessitating a very material addition to the strength of the army. The extremely grave consequences involved in such an increase of military expenditure will be shown when considering whether, in the present financial condition of India, there is any probability that such new charges can be met, without imposing taxes intolerably burdensome to the people, or accumulating an indebtedness which will augment the taxation that will ultimately have to be imposed.

Passing on to consider the second of the four chief branches of expenditure—namely, the general cost of administration—the evidence which was given before the Parliamentary Committee on Indian Finance affords almost innumerable examples of the striking manner in which the various items which compose this general cost of administration have increased during the last twenty years. A most valuable table was furnished to the committee by Mr. Gay, the Deputy Comptroller-General of the Finances, in which a comparison is made between the cost of administration in 1871 and 1856, two years before the abolition of the East India Company. From this table it appears that the cost of the government of India, excluding expenditure on the army and public works, has increased during the period referred to from 14,964,867l. to 23,271,082l. There is scarcely a single item in which there has not been a marked augmentation, and this growth has continued up to the present time. Thus, taking a few instances:—

	1856–57.£	1870–71.£
Superannuation, retired, and compassionate allowances	424,930	655,969
Stationery and printing	128,197	233,675
Medical services	175,714	523,486

I believe it can be shown that a part at least of the large increase in the general cost of administration is undoubtedly due to a want of adequate economy; but without, for the moment, inquiring what portion of this increase of expenditure could have been prevented if India, since the abolition of the East India Company, had been governed with less extravagance, it is obvious that the greater the extent to which this additional outlay has arisen from causes the operation of which cannot be controlled, the more serious is the prospect for the future. If money has been wasted in the past, the continuance of this waste can be prevented; but a remedy cannot be so easily applied if the cost of a particular department becomes greater in consequence, for instance, of a rise in prices. The very detailed evidence which was given before the Indian Finance Committee by Mr. Harrison, Comptroller-General of India, leaves no room for doubt that a not inconsiderable portion of the increase in the cost of administration between 1856 and 1871 was due to a rise in general prices. There was during this period, and especially at the time of the American Civil War, a very large influx of silver into India. A portion of this silver was sent to purchase cotton at extremely high prices; and another portion represented capital which was raised in England and sent to India for the construction of railways and other works. At the present time there seem to be indications that the financial position of India may be prejudicially affected by a rise in general prices consequent on a depreciation in the value of silver. Allusion has already been made to the fact that as recently as December last an official paper was published from which it appears that the military expenditure of the present year will be greater than its estimated amount by 330,000*l.,* which is described as "compensation for high price of food." It is evident that if there is a rise in general prices there is scarcely a single department, the cost of which may not, sooner or later, very materially increase. It is not, however, necessary here to pursue the subject further, because the extent to which general prices in India may be affected by the depreciation of silver can be more appropriately considered when discussing the third of the four branches of expenditure—namely, that which arises from loss by exchange.

In the current financial year the loss by exchange was estimated, when the Budget was brought forward, at no less than 3,000,000*l.;* but, large as this sum is, the Government, in a revised estimate issued within the last few weeks, calculate that it will be exceeded by 500,000*l.* In 1876–77 the loss by exchange, as appears from the table already given, was 1,676,482*l.* In 1874–75 the loss by exchange was only about 500,000*l.* A few years previous to this the loss was so trifling as scarcely to be worth notice; and in 1870 the amount which was gained by exchange exceeded, by a few thousand pounds, the amount lost. These figures show, with striking distinctness, with what remarkable rapidity this item in Indian expenditure has assumed its present serious proportions. Whether it is more likely that this charge on the Indian revenues will in future years diminish or increase, depends upon so many uncertain conditions that it would not be prudent to make a confident prediction on the subject. The loss by exchange, as previously explained, is primarily due to a depreciation in the value of silver, and one of the chief causes of this depreciation is the large additional supply of silver yielded by the Nevada mines in recent years. In 1875 the aggregate production of silver throughout the world is estimated to have been about 15,000,000*l.,* more than half of this amount, 8,000,000*l.,* being obtained from the American mines. Twenty years previously—namely, between 1852 and 1862—the average annual production was only from 8,000,000*l.* to 9,000,000*l.,* and at that time no appreciable quantity came from the United States. Simultaneously with this large increase in the supply of silver many circumstances occurred which greatly diminished the demand for silver. Silver was demonetised in Germany; and Germany consequently not only ceased to require the large amount of silver which she had previously used for coinage, but a great portion of the silver in circulation was withdrawn and sold by the German Government. Another circumstance which has produced a very important effect in diminishing the demand for silver is the great increase in recent years in the Indian home charges. The value of the products exported from India has always been much in excess of the value of those imported. Until quite lately the balance was liquidated by transmitting silver to India. In some years the silver thus sent amounted to more than 10,000,000*l.* Such a transmission of silver constituted one of the chief sources of the demand for silver, and was indeed one of the most important factors in maintaining its value. Each addition, however, that is made to the home charges diminishes *pro tanto* this demand for silver. An English merchant, for instance, who has purchased a hundred thousand pounds' worth of Indian produce, instead of sending silver to India to pay for it, purchases bills from the Indian Government in England, drawn upon the Indian Government in Calcutta, and the amount of bills which the Government has to sell in England increases, of course, with each increase in the home charges. It is, I think, made sufficiently clear from this brief review of the various circumstances which have produced a depreciation in the value of silver, and a consequent loss by exchange to the Indian Government, that the value of silver depends upon various causes, some of which may be regarded as entirely beyond the power of any Government to control. Thus the value of silver will be to a very considerable extent determined by the future yield of the American mines. It is impossible to foresee whether the future productiveness of these mines will increase or diminish, and it may of course happen that silver mines may be discovered in other parts of the world. It has, however, been shown that a powerful effect is being exerted at the present time in depreciating the value of silver by the large amount of bills which have to be sold by the Indian Government in England to provide for the home charges. The amount of the home charges has increased to a most serious extent in recent years. Nothing, moreover, can avert a still further increase, if the expenditure is permitted so habitually to exceed the revenue that money has to be borrowed to make good the deficit. The loans being chiefly raised in England, it is obvious that the interest on these loans represents so much more which has to be transmitted from India to England, or, in other words, so much added to the home charges.

I have thought it important to direct particular attention to the influence exerted by each increase in the home charges in adding to the loss by exchange which India has to bear, because under any circumstances it would be a cause for apprehension to see a constantly augmenting proportion of the revenue of a country not spent in the country itself; but this circumstance becomes more serious when it can be shown that this expenditure of the revenues of India out of India exerts a direct influence in depreciating the value of silver, and in thus lessening the value of all that large part of the Indian revenue which, either permanently or temporarily, is received in the form of a fixed payment made in silver.

With regard to the fourth and last branch of expenditure to which I have called attention—namely, the interest on loans—it is manifest that this subject is closely connected in many of its aspects with the question which has just been considered. The largest portion of the money which has been borrowed in recent years by the Indian Government has been obtained by loans raised in England; and the additional amount which has to be provided to meet the interest on these loans represents, of course, so much added to the home charges. In 1856 the sum annually required to pay the interest on the Indian Debt was 2,190,000*l.,* in 1870–71 it was 3,200,000*l.,* and in 1876–77 it was 4,350,000*l.* From these figures it appears that in twenty years the indebtedness of India increased by about 100 per cent. Nothing can be more certain than that, in the present financial condition of India, this indebtedness must continue steadily to increase. The figures which have already been quoted, conclusively show that the ordinary revenue of India is only barely sufficient to meet the ordinary expenditure, and that consequently, in the words of one who speaks with official authority, every fresh contingency and every new charge involves some addition to the debt of India. Thus, within the last few years, 16,000,000*l.* has been spent in famine relief, and nearly the whole of this amount has been obtained by loans, the interest on which involves an annual charge of about 700,000*l.* Money, however, is not borrowed by the Indian Government simply to meet such charges as these; it has for some time been their settled policy to borrow each year not less than 4,000,000*l.* for the construction of railways and works of irrigation. The public works, which are thus constructed out of borrowed money, are no doubt undertaken by the Indian Government with the idea that they will be reproductive, or, in other words, that they will yield a net revenue which will be sufficient to pay the interest on the capital expended. The experience of the past, however, proves that, although it is intended that these public works should be reproductive in the sense just described, yet, regarding the transaction simply as a financial one, the money thus spent is really embarked in a most speculative and uncertain investment. Lord Salisbury, speaking at Manchester in January 1875, when he was Secretary of State for India, said:—

> The difficulties which surround the question of irrigation are very great. We can scarcely yet be said to have had one genuine instance of financial success. The irrigating projects that have been carried out, if they have had for their basis the former works of native rulers, have in many instances been a financial success; but then of course that favourable appearance of the account has been obtained by not charging the former expenditure of the native ruler. In those cases where we have begun the projects of irrigation for ourselves we have not reached, I believe, in any one instance, the desired result of a clean balance sheet.

Although I think that Lord Salisbury, in making this sweeping assertion about the unsatisfactory financial results of these irrigation works, somewhat overstated the case, yet it is impossible for any one to deny the absolute correctness of the conclusion which has been officially arrived at, that on the 9,000,000*l.* which has been spent in recent years on schemes of irrigation in Bengal, the return which is yielded is only $\frac{1}{2}$ per cent. When it is remembered that every one of these particular works, at the time it was undertaken, was regarded as reproductive, nothing more need be said to show that, however useful or desirable public works may be in India, it is more than probable that if they are constructed out of borrowed money, they will not yield a return sufficient to meet the interest on the capital expended; and consequently there will be a deficit which will represent another item of expenditure, another charge upon the revenues of India. It therefore appears that at the present time the indebtedness of India must almost inevitably continue to be augmented by two distinct causes. In the first place, as there is no surplus of ordinary revenue beyond ordinary expenditure, every such contingency as war or famine is certain to lead to the debt being increased; and, secondly, so long as the present policy is continued of constructing public works out of borrowed money, the loans which are raised for these works represent constant additions to the debt of India.

Many other branches of Indian expenditure might be referred to besides those to which attention has been here directed. I think, however, enough has been said on the subject of revenue and expenditure to establish the following conclusions with regard to the financial position of India:—

1. The revenue is characterised by great inelasticity.
2. The expenditure has increased in a marked manner in recent years, partly from the general increase in the cost of administration, and partly from a depreciation in the value of silver.
3. The military expenditure is excessive, absorbing 45 per cent. of the entire net revenue of the country; and this expenditure is likely to be greatly augmented if the frontier of India is advanced, as now seems to be contemplated.
4. A comparatively stationary revenue having to meet an increasing expenditure, it will be necessary sooner or later to add to the taxation of India. If a deficit is temporarily met by borrowing, the money which will have to be provided to pay the interest on the loan must ultimately increase the deficit, which will have to be met by increased taxation.
5. There has already been a most serious increase in the indebtedness of India, amounting in twenty years to 100 per cent.

Such being the present condition of Indian finance, I think scarcely another word need be said to show that if some fundamental change is not promptly introduced, if expenditure is not rigorously curtailed, it will be absolutely impossible to avoid the necessity of imposing on the people of India a large amount of additional taxation. In order adequately to appreciate the grave consequences which may be produced by an increase of taxation in India, it is essential to bear in mind that the question cannot be regarded as if it were simply a financial one. Between England and India, in matters of taxation, there is a most fundamental difference. If some contingency should occur in England which would render it necessary to obtain 5,000,000*l.* by additional taxation, it is perfectly well known how easily the money could be provided. More than 5,000,000*l.* could be raised by adding twopence in the pound to the income-tax, and by slightly increasing the duty on some article of general consumption, such as tea or spirits. But in India, if it became necessary to raise not 5,000,000*l.*, but even a smaller sum, say 3,000,000*l.*, by additional taxation, it will scarcely be denied that taxes might have to be imposed which would be regarded by the people as so burdensome as to create a most serious amount of discontent. When examining in detail the present sources of revenue, I believe it was clearly proved that they present so little prospect of increase that, if additional revenue has to be obtained, it will be absolutely necessary to have recourse to some new forms of taxation. The truth of this conclusion is corroborated in a most striking manner by the recent action of the Indian Government. In order to obtain the comparatively trifling sum of 750,000*l.*, the Government came to the conclusion, as already stated, that no better course was open to them than to impose a trades license tax of fivepence in the pound upon all trade incomes, even on those as small as 4*s.* a week. As the Government of India must have been fully aware of the discontent which such a tax would inevitably cause, it may be fairly concluded that they would never have sanctioned it, if they could have discovered any less unsatisfactory way of obtaining the money required. But if the trades license tax was regarded, a twelvemonth since, as the best mode of obtaining additional revenue, one of two things must occur if it becomes necessary still further to add to taxation in order to provide for the increasing expenditure which is now taking place—either the rate of the license tax must be advanced, or some tax which the Government considered, a twelvemonth since, still more objectionable must be resorted to. It is already rumoured that the income-tax will again be imposed; and although this tax has often been supported on the ground that it will reach a wealthy class who are least heavily taxed, yet nothing can be more unwise than to ignore the very serious disadvantages associated with the levying of such a tax in India. It was unequivocally condemned by three successive Indian Finance Ministers. The practical objections to the tax, as distinguished from the theoretical arguments that may be adduced in its favour, have been stated with remarkable clearness by Mr. Laing, who for many years served in India as Finance Minister. He has said that he regarded the income-tax as "about as bad and obnoxious a mode of raising revenue as it is possible to imagine in a country like India. . . . I think that for an Oriental country, and with the Eastern habit of mind, any tax which imposes inquisition into individual means is attended with innumerable evils which are little felt in a country like England." And he further expressed an opinion that, in consequence of the impossibility of preventing abuses connected with the assessment of the tax in a country like India, "for every rupee that comes into the Treasury, two rupees are extorted from the population that have to pay the tax."

Probably, however, one of the most weighty objections that can be urged against the imposition of an income-tax in India is that a great machinery of assessment, which it has been shown is liable to the gravest abuse, is brought into active operation over the length and breadth of the country, in order to realise a very trifling financial result. When this tax was last levied in India, it was at the rate of twopence-halfpenny in the pound, and the net revenue realised was little more than 500,000*l*. From an income-tax of twopence-halfpenny in the pound in England about 5,000,000*l*. would be obtained, and many small incomes which would be exempted in England would certainly be assessed in India. No fact can bring out with more striking distinctness the remarkable contrast between the wealth of England and the poverty of India. India contains a population more than seven times as great as that of England, and yet a tax which in England produces 5,000,000*l*. yields little more than 500,000*l*. in India. The amount, therefore, which can be raised by any form of direct taxation in India is, in consequence of the general poverty of the country, extremely small; and the amount which can be raised by indirect taxation may be regarded as having already nearly reached its utmost possible limits. Nothing more than a very trifling amount can ever be raised by imposing taxes on luxuries which are consumed by the few. The indirect taxes which are really productive are those which are imposed on articles of general consumption. In India the mass of the people are so poor that they use no article which can be taxed except salt, and the taxation on salt has already reached that extreme point when any increase of duty would most seriously diminish consumption. It has been sometimes said that a duty might be imposed on tobacco, but by the evidence given before the Indian Finance Committee it is shown that the proposal has often been considered by the Indian Government, who have always concluded that the objections to this tax are so strong that it ought not to be imposed. The late Sir Donald McLeod, who was for many years Lieutenant-Governor of the Punjaub, and who was admitted to be one of the ablest financial administrators India ever produced, when examined before the Parliamentary Committee on Indian Finance, directed the attention of the committee to an elaborate minute that had been prepared by Mr. (now Sir John) Strachey condemnatory of a duty on tobacco. Before the same committee Lord Lawrence, in a most comprehensive review of the financial position of India, pointed out grave objections to the imposition of such a duty. He showed that, in order to levy it, it would be necessary either to increase the assessment on the land on which it was grown—and this would be interpreted as an augmentation of the land revenue—or to levy an excise duty on tobacco. As tobacco is freely grown in all the native states whose boundaries are conterminous with our own territories, it would become requisite, in order to prevent the importation of tobacco from these states, to establish customs lines extending over thousands of miles. As, moreover, tobacco is often grown by the Indian people for their own use, it would in all probability be found essential, in order to prevent the evasion of the duty, to make the growth of tobacco a Government monopoly. Scarcely any arrangement that could be adopted would be regarded as more harassing by the people of India.

Unless it can be shown that the description which has been here given of the financial condition of India is inaccurate, I think it must be admitted that the subject is one which should cause the gravest anxiety. But it will probably be said: If the finances of India are in so critical a condition, can nothing be done? Can no effort be made to avert impending embarrassment? Of all the things connected with the financial administration of India that require to be done, nothing is so essential as the immediate recognition of the fact that India has hitherto been governed on far too costly a scale. Her position is like that of a landowner who has been living beyond his income. Each year some new mortgage has to be raised to make good the deficiency; and as the interest on these successive mortgages accumulates, and as there is no reduction but rather an increase in the scale of his expenditure, his estate steadily becomes more burdened with debt. To add to his difficulties, he has borrowed large sums of money to carry out various improvements; and, however desirable these improvements may be, many of them do not pay the interest on the capital expended. If, under such circumstances as these, a practical man of business were called in to advise what ought to be done, it is obvious that he would insist above all things that expenditure should be reduced. He would probably soon discover that which is usually the case when a man lives beyond his means, that in all directions too much money had been spent. There would be no chance of placing the estate in a secure position, unless its owner were prepared by rigorous retrenchment to bring his expenditure well within his income. Mortgages might then be gradually reduced, and when a surplus had been secured many improvements might be carried out which could not prudently be undertaken when there was a risk that they would burden the property with a still heavier load of debt. The remedy which would have to be applied under the circumstances just described, not inaccurately represents what is necessary to be done in order to place the finances of India in a sound position. For some years the Indian Government has been living beyond its means. In almost every direction too much money has been spent; and those who have been responsible for this expenditure seem too often to have forgotten that India, instead of being one of the wealthiest, is one of the poorest countries in the world. Page after page might be filled with instances of reckless extravagance. At one time a private irrigation company with a capital of a million, the 100*l.* shares of which are unsaleable at the nominal quotation of 60*l.*, is bought by the Indian Government at par, and in addition a large bonus is given to be distributed among the officials of the company. At another time 175,000*l*. is expended in building and furnishing a country house for the Governor of Bombay. It is no exaggeration to say that it would not be one half so mischievous to permit a million of English money to be spent in building a mansion for an English minister. It is quite within recent years that the Public Works Department has assumed its present large proportions. No care apparently has been taken to adjust the supply of highly paid European officers in this department to the demand, and it is now admitted that there is a complete block in the higher grades of the service. Employment cannot be found for many who are drawing large salaries from Indian revenues, and it is acknowledged that many are simply holding on to become eligible for pensions. But it is not simply that money has been thus recklessly squandered. It is just the same with a nation as it is with an individual. Whether or not a particular outlay can be justified depends upon the amount of income out of which it has to be made. Nothing, for instance, may be more appropriate than for a man with 4,000*l*. a year to live in a house the rent of which is 400*l*. But if his income is only 1,000*l*., to live in such a house would be an act of reckless folly. It is no use to dilate upon the advantages which a man would derive from keeping a carriage. If he cannot afford a carriage, he must submit to the discomfort of a cab. Without an hour's delay the fact should be recognised that India is not in a position to pay for various services which she receives at their present rate of remuneration. A most important saving might be effected by more largely employing natives in positions which are now filled by highly paid Europeans, and from such a change political as well as financial advantages would result. A single example will show the great economy which might thus be effected. Mr. Rendel, Consulting Engineer of the East Indian Railway Company and of the Government Railways, stated in his evidence before the Public Works Committee last session that three years ago not a single native engine-driver was employed in India; that on one railway, the East Indian, 150 are now employed, and that the saving thus effected is 15,000*l*. a year. Mr. Rendel added that the European is paid at least ten times as much as the native driver, and "the native does a lot more work—he works longer hours and gives less trouble. We are entirely satisfied with the native drivers."

It is, however, scarcely necessary to remark, after what has been said about the present and prospective cost of the Indian army, that excessive military expenditure has done more than anything else to create the present financial embarrassment. It is particularly to be borne in mind that the great increase in this branch of expenditure has not been brought about by its being necessary for India to maintain a larger army. A few years after the abolition of the East India Company, what is known as the army amalgamation scheme was carried out in direct opposition to the advice of the most experienced Indian statesmen. India was thus, as it were, bound hand and foot to our own costly system of army administration, without any regard apparently being had to the fact that various schemes of military organisation, which may be perfectly suited to a country so wealthy as England, may be altogether unsuited to a country so poor as India. A single example will show to what an extent the pecuniary interests of India may, under the present system, be sacrificed. When, a few years since, the plan of short service was introduced, it was solely considered as an English question, and not a thought was apparently given to the effect it would have upon India. It need scarcely be said that a more costly scheme for India could hardly have been devised. The shorter the term of service the greater must be the charge for transport; and the men, after they have completed a short term of service, are a reserve ready at hand for England, but many thousands of miles away from India. I cannot do more on this occasion than thus incidentally allude to the question of army organisation, with the view of showing that, in order to reduce the military expenditure of India, it is not necessary to diminish the numerical strength of the Indian army. It is, however, not to be forgotten that most distinguished Indian statesmen have declared that it would be far better to incur whatever risks may be involved in the reduction of the Indian army than to face the danger which is certain to arise from an increase of taxation in India. No man could be less likely than Lord Canning inconsiderately to recommend a reduction in the Indian army, for he was Viceroy during the troublous days of the Mutiny;[2] and yet Lord Canning unhesitatingly affirmed, and the opinion has subsequently been endorsed by Lord Northbrook, that if it were a question between imposing new and irritating taxes in India, such as the income-tax, "danger for danger, he (Lord Canning) would prefer to reduce the army." It is well known that an equally strong opinion as to the peril of adding to the taxation of India was expressed by Lord Mayo, a Viceroy who was alike distinguished for prudence, courage, and common sense. He had the sagacity to see that taxation in India could not be regarded as simply a financial question, but that it involved political consequences of the gravest moment. In a passage which has been often quoted, he said that it was almost impossible to exaggerate the discontent which was produced among all classes in India, both European and native, by the "constant increase of taxation which had for years been going on." Deaf to these warnings, instead of anything effectual having been done to arrest the growth of taxation, the financial position of India now is far more unsatisfactory than it was in Lord Mayo's time. Not only has there been an increase of Imperial taxation—new and irritating taxes, such as the license tax, have been

---

2. Reference to the uprising that began in north India against the East India Company. The uprising was sparked by opposition to Christian missionary activity, social and economic changes brought on by British rule, and the company's annexation of numerous princely states in the 1850s. [Ed.]

imposed—but in recent years the country has been enveloped in a network of local taxation. Lord Northbrook last August, in presenting an important petition from India in the House of Lords, endorsed the statement that "within the last seven years, in Bengal alone, there has been an increase of about a million, and for the whole of India more than three millions, per annum by provincial taxation."

When such opinions as these have been expressed by those who must be regarded as the very highest authorities on all questions affecting the government of India, it is not too much to say that the very existence of our rule in India may be gravely imperilled unless the finances of that country are placed in a more satisfactory position. The English people should awaken to the fact that the question is one which vitally concerns themselves as well as the people of India. There is scarcely any event which would bring greater discredit and greater misfortune on England than for the Indian Government to be forced to say: "Our financial exigencies are such that it is impossible to pay our way without coming to England for pecuniary aid." A burden might thus be cast upon English taxpayers which they would find hard to bear, and the consequences to India would be still more disastrous; for from the hour in which she was obliged to seek subventions from England, her virtual insolvency would be proclaimed. Before it is too late, England should resolve that such a contingency should be averted. Hitherto, it has unfortunately too frequently happened that the influence of England has been exerted not to save, but to spend, the money of the Indian people. The well-known saying of one who held a high official position is only too true, that "Indian finance has again and again been sacrificed to the exigencies of English estimates." No one can reasonably desire that the English Parliament should perpetually meddle in the details of Indian administration. It should, however, never be forgotten that when the East India Company was abolished, the English people became directly responsible for the government of India. It cannot, I think, be denied that this responsibility has been so imperfectly discharged, that in many respects the new system of government compares unfavourably with the old. Figures have already been quoted to show to what a remarkable extent the cost of administration has increased since the East India Company was abolished. There was at that time an independent control of expenditure which now seems to be almost entirely wanting. It was, no doubt, intended, when the government of India by the Act of 1858 was transferred from the Company to the Crown,[3] that the Council of the Secretary of State should exercise the same control over Indian expenditure, as had formerly been exercised by the directors of the Company and by the Court of Proprietors. But

---

3. In 1858, an Act of Parliament transferred administrative control over India from the East India Company to the British Crown. [Ed.]

gradually the influence and control of the Council have been so completely whittled away that it is now openly declared by a Secretary of State that he can spend the revenues of India, beyond her frontiers, without obtaining the consent, or even bringing the subject under the notice, of his Council. Whether or not the power thus claimed is really conferred upon him by the Act of 1858, and by Acts which have subsequently been passed, raises questions which I cannot attempt to enter upon here. The whole subject, however, of the inadequacy of the control now exercised on the expenditure of the revenues of India, is one that urgently demands the most careful investigation. Nothing can be more unsatisfactory than the present state of things. When the Secretary of State desires to avoid responsibility, he can shelter himself behind his Council; when he desires to act, untrammelled by their control and unhampered by their advice, he can ignore them as completely as if they did not exist.

In attempting to direct attention to the present financial condition of India, I have been chiefly desirous to show how important are the issues involved, and how urgently the subject demands prompt consideration. Englishmen of all political parties are, I believe, alike anxious that no misfortune should befall our Indian Empire. Opinions may differ as to the importance to be attributed to certain dangers with which she is sometimes said to be threatened; but no one can deny the reality of the peril which will be brought upon her by financial embarrassment; and the day, I believe, is not far distant when, with common consent, it will be said that those are the wisest governors of India who act steadily upon the maxim of a great statesman, that "finance is the key of England's position in India."

KARL MARX

THE GENESIS OF THE INDUSTRIAL CAPITALIST

The system of public credit, i.e. of national debts, whose origin we discover in Genoa and Venice as early as the middle ages, took possession of Europe generally during the manufacturing period. The colonial system with its maritime trade and commercial wars served as a forcing-house for it. Thus it first took root in Holland. National debts, i.e., the alienation of the state—whether

---

Karl Marx, "The Genesis of the Industrial Capitalist." *Capital,* vol. I: chapter 31 (1867; London, 1887; trans. Samuel Moore and Edward Aveling). Pp. 827–34.

despotic, constitutional or republican—marked with its stamp the capitalistic era. The only part of the so-called national wealth that actually enters into the collective possessions of modern peoples is—their national debt. Hence, as a necessary consequence, the modern doctrine that a nation becomes the richer the more deeply it is in debt. Public credit becomes the credo of capital. And with the rise of national debt-making, want of faith in the national debt takes the place of the blasphemy against the Holy Ghost, which may not be forgiven.

The public debt becomes one of the most powerful levers of primitive accumulation.[1] As with the stroke of an enchanter's wand, it endows barren money with the power of breeding and thus turns it into capital, without the necessity of its exposing itself to the troubles and risks inseparable from its employment in industry or even in usury. The state-creditors actually give nothing away, for the sum lent is transformed into public bonds, easily negotiable, which go on functioning in their hands just as so much hard cash would. But further, apart from the class of lazy annuitants thus created, and from the improvised wealth of the financiers, middlemen between the government and the nation—as also apart from the tax-farmers, merchants, private manufacturers, to whom a good part of every national loan renders the service of a capital fallen from heaven—the national debt has given rise to joint-stock companies, to dealings in negotiable effects of all kinds, and to agiotage, in a word to stock-exchange gambling and the modern bankocracy.

At their birth the great banks, decorated with national titles, were only associations of private speculators, who placed themselves by the side of governments, and, thanks to the privileges they received, were in a position to advance money to the state. Hence the accumulation of the national debt has no more infallible measure than the successive rise in the stock of these banks, whose full development dates from the founding of the Bank of England in 1694. The Bank of England began with lending its money to the Government at 8%; at the same time it was empowered by Parliament to coin money out of the same capital, by lending it again to the public in the form of bank-notes. It was allowed to use these notes for discounting bills, making advances on commodities, and for buying the precious metals. It was not long ere this credit-money, made by the bank itself, became the coin in which the Bank of England made its loans to the state, and paid, on account of the state, the interest on the public debt. It was not enough that the bank gave with one hand

---

1. In his theory of primitive accumulation (*Capital*, I, part vii), Marx argues that the initial capital that fuels the rise of capitalism comes not from the abstinence of the well-to-do but from their driving the peasants from the land. Marx argued that this change in the relations of production created a force of wage laborers for agriculture and industry. [Ed.]

and took back more with the other; it remained, even whilst receiving, the eternal creditor of the nation down to the last shilling advanced. Gradually it became inevitably the receptacle of the metallic hoard of the country, and the centre of gravity of all commercial credit. What effect was produced on their contemporaries by the sudden uprising of this brood of bankocrats, financiers, rentiers, brokers, stock-jobbers, &c., is proved by the writings of that time, e.g., by Bolingbroke's.

With the national debt arose an international credit system, which often conceals one of the sources of primitive accumulation in this or that people. Thus the villanies of the Venetian thieving system formed one of the secret bases of the capital-wealth of Holland to whom Venice in her decadence lent large sums of money. So also was it with Holland and England. By the beginning of the 18th century the Dutch manufactures were far outstripped. Holland had ceased to be the nation preponderant in commerce and industry. One of its main lines of business, therefore, from 1701–1776, is the lending out of enormous amounts of capital, especially to its great rival England. The same thing is going on to-day between England and the United States. A great deal of capital, which appears to-day in the United States without any certificate of birth, was yesterday, in England, the capitalised blood of children.[2]

As the national debt finds its support in the public revenue, which must cover the yearly payments for interest, &c., the modern system of taxation was the necessary complement of the system of national loans. The loans enable the government to meet extraordinary expenses, without the tax-payers feeling it immediately, but they necessitate, as a consequence, increased taxes. On the other hand, the raising of taxation caused by the accumulation of debts contracted one after another, compels the government always to have recourse to new loans for new extraordinary expenses. Modern fiscality, whose pivot is formed by taxes on the most necessary means of subsistence (thereby increasing their price), thus contains within itself the germ of automatic progression. Over-taxation is not an incident, but rather a principle. In Holland, therefore, where this system was first inaugurated, the great patriot, De Witt, has in his "Maxims" extolled it as the best system for making the wage-labourer submissive, frugal, industrious, and overburdened with labour. The destructive influence that it exercises on the condition of the wage-labourer concerns us less however, here, than the forcible expropriation, resulting from it, of peasants, artisans, and in a word, all elements of the lower middle-class. On this there are not two opinions, even among the bourgeois

---

2. Reference to the use of children as waged laborers in factories. See also the reference to "the necessity of child-stealing." [Ed.]

economists. Its expropriating efficacy is still further heightened by the system of protection,[3] which forms one of its integral parts.

The great part that the public debt, and the fiscal system corresponding with it, has played in the capitalisation of wealth and the expropriation of the masses, has led many writers, like Cobbett,[4] Doubleday and others, to seek in this, incorrectly, the fundamental cause of the misery of the modern peoples.

The system of protection was an artificial means of manufacturing manufacturers, of expropriating independent labourers, of capitalising the national means of production and subsistence, of forcibly abbreviating the transition from the mediæval to the modern mode of production. The European states tore one another to pieces about the patent of this invention, and, once entered into the service of the surplus-value makers, did not merely lay under contribution in the pursuit of this purpose their own people, indirectly through protective duties, directly through export premiums. They also forcibly rooted out, in their dependent countries, all industry, as e.g., England did with the Irish woollen manufacture. On the continent of Europe, after Colbert's[5] example, the process was much simplified. The primitive industrial capital, here, came in part directly out of the state treasury. "Why," cries Mirabeau,[6] "why go so far to seek the cause of the manufacturing glory of Saxony before the war? 180,000,000 of debts contracted by the sovereigns!"

Colonial system, public debts, heavy taxes, protection, commercial wars, &c., these children of the true manufacturing period, increase gigantically during the infancy of Modern Industry. The birth of the latter is heralded by a great slaughter of the innocents. Like the royal navy, the factories were recruited by means of the press-gang. Blasé as Sir F. M. Eden[7] is as to the horrors of the expropriation of the agricultural population from the soil, from the last third of the 15th century to his own time; with all the self-satisfaction with which he rejoices in this process, "essential" for establishing capitalistic agriculture and "the due proportion between arable and pasture land"—he does

---

3. Laws that protect domestic industries and agricultural producers through taxes on imports. An example of this system of protection is the English Corn Laws, which kept grain prices high for English landowners by taxing imported grain. [Ed.]
4. William Cobbett (1762–1835). Radical founder of *Cobbett's Weekly Political Register* (1802) and author of *Rural Rides* (1830). Cobbett was a fierce defender of the working class and an advocate for the reform of voting laws. [Ed.]
5. Jean-Baptiste Colbert (1619–83). Controller General of France and mercantilist who supported a strong economic role for the central government and establishing a favorable balance of trade through limiting imports. [Ed.]
6. Marquis de Mirabeau. French author who created a systematic social theory from the physiocratic ideas of François Quesnay. Physiocracy, which emphasized the importance of agricultural production as a source of state revenue, was at its height of popularity from 1764 through 1766. [Ed.]
7. Sir Frederick Eden (1766–1809). Author of *The State of the Poor, or an History of the Labouring Classes* (1797). [Ed.]

not show, however, the same economic insight in respect to the necessity of child-stealing and child-slavery for the transformation of manufacturing exploitation into factory exploitation, and the establishment of the "true relation" between capital and labour-power. He says: "It may, perhaps, be worthy the attention of the public to consider, whether any manufacture, which, in order to be carried on successfully, requires that cottages and workhouses should be ransacked for poor children; that they should be employed by turns during the greater part of the night and robbed of that rest which, though indispensable to all, is most required by the young; and that numbers of both sexes, of different ages and dispositions, should be collected together in such a manner that the contagion of example cannot but lead to profligacy and debauchery; will add to the sum of individual or national felicity?"

In the counties of Derbyshire, Nottinghamshire, and more particularly in Lancashire, says Fielden,[8] the newly-invented machinery was used in large factories built on the sides of streams capable of turning the water-wheel. Thousands of hands were suddenly required in these places, remote from towns; and Lancashire, in particular, being, till then, comparatively thinly populated and barren, a population was all that she now wanted. The small and nimble fingers of little children being by very far the most in request, the custom instantly sprang up of procuring *apprentices* from the different parish workhouses of London, Birmingham, and elsewhere. Many, many thousands of these little, hapless creatures were sent down into the north, being from the age of 7 to the age of 13 or 14 years old. The custom was for the master to clothe his apprentices and to feed and lodge them in an "apprentice house" near the factory; overseers were appointed to see to the works, whose interest it was to work the children to the utmost, because their pay was in proportion to the quantity of work that they could exact. Cruelty was, of course, the consequence . . . In many of the manufacturing districts, but particularly, I am afraid, in the guilty county to which I belong [Lancashire], cruelties the most heart-rending were practised upon the unoffending and friendless creatures who were thus consigned to the charge of master manufacturers; they were harassed to the brink of death by excess of labour . . . were flogged, fettered and tortured in the most exquisite refinement of cruelty; . . . they were in many cases starved to the bone while flogged to their work and. . . . even in some instances . . . were driven to commit suicède . . . The beautiful and romantic valleys of Derbyshire, Nottinghamshire and Lancashire, secluded from the public eye, became the dismal solitudes of torture, and of many a murder. The profits of manufactures were enormous; but this only whetted the appetite that it should have satisfied, and therefore the manufacturers had re-

---

8. John Fielden (1784–1849). Member of Parliament for Oldham and author of "The Curse of the Factory System" (1836). [Ed.]

course to an expedient that seemed to secure to them those profits without any possibility of limit; they began the practice of what is termed "night-working," that is, having tired one set of hands, by working them throughout the day, they had another set ready to go on working throughout the night; the day-set getting into the beds that the night-set had just quitted, and in their turn again, the night-set getting into the beds that the day-set quitted in the morning. It is a common tradition in Lancashire, that the beds *never get cold.*

With the development of capitalist production during the manufacturing period, the public opinion of Europe had lost the last remnant of shame and conscience. The nations bragged cynically of every infamy that served them as a means to capitalistic accumulation. Read, e.g., the naïve Annals of Commerce of the worthy A. Anderson.[9] Here it is trumpetted forth as a triumph of English statecraft that at the Peace of Utrecht, England extorted from the Spaniards by the Asiento Treaty the privilege of being allowed to ply the negro-trade, until then only carried on between Africa and the English West Indies, between Africa and Spanish America as well. England thereby acquired the right of supplying Spanish America until 1743 with 4800 negroes yearly. This threw, at the same time, an official cloak over British smuggling. Liverpool waxed fat on the slave-trade. This was its method of primitive accumulation. And, even to the present day, Liverpool "respectability" is the Pindar of the slave-trade which—compare the work of Aikin [1795] already quoted—"has coincided with that spirit of bold adventure which has characterised the trade of Liverpool and rapidly carried it to its present state of prosperity; has occasioned vast employment for shipping and sailors, and greatly augmented the demand for the manufactures of the country." Liverpool employed in the slave trade, in 1730, 15 ships; in 1751, 53; in 1760, 74; in 1770, 96; and in 1792, 132.

Whilst the cotton industry introduced child-slavery in England, it gave in the United States a stimulus to the transformation of the earlier, more or less patriarchal slavery, into a system of commercial exploitation. In fact, the veiled slavery of the wage-earners in Europe needed, for its pedestal, slavery pure and simple in the new world.

Tantæ molis erat, to establish the "eternal laws of Nature" of the capitalist mode of production, to complete the process of separation between labourers and conditions of labour, to transform, at one pole, the social means of production and subsistence into capital, at the opposite pole, the mass of the population into wage-labourers, into "free labouring poor," that artificial product

---

9. Adam Anderson (1692–1765). In 1805, David Macpherson (1746–1816) published *Annals of Commerce . . . Comprehending the Most Valuable Parts of the Late Mr. Anderson's "History of Commerce".* [Ed.]

of modern society. If money, according to Augier,[10] "comes into the world with a congenital blood-stain on one cheek," capital comes dripping from head to foot, from every pore, with blood and dirt.

---

10. Marie Augier. French economist and author of *Du credit public* (Paris 1842). [Ed.]

THREE

BANKS AND BANKING

Published in 1839, six years after joint-stock banks were allowed to form in London, James William Gilbart's "Ten Minutes' Advice" reveals the kind of concerns that early bankers had to overcome to persuade ordinary citizens to entrust their money to banks. Especially noteworthy is Gilbart's final reassurance that the "desire of lodging money in a bank will grow" in the trusting client: "the more money you lodge in the bank, the more you will desire to lodge." This habitual consignment of money to a banker is precisely what R. J. Richardson wants to disrupt in his "Exposure of the Banking and Funding System." Published during the Chartist campaign for working-men's rights, Richardson's attack on "the GREAT SWINDLE" (the banking system) and "the great Moloch" (the Bank of England) is part of a more sweeping exposé of the political control indirectly exercised over the English government by the banking system. Richardson's series, like the "Black and Red books" with which he credits himself, was printed for the working and unemployed poor. Gilbart's essay, by contrast, which was initially published for the middle classes, was reprinted repeatedly in the numerous editions of Gilbart's *A Practical Treatise on Banking* that appeared throughout the century.

Like Gilbart's essay, George Rae's "Personal Credit" was written by a practicing banker. Rae's selection is actually addressed to other bankers, however, not to the clients whom, by 1885, bankers could count on attracting in numbers so great that the problem had become one of distinguishing good creditors from bad. As in the selection from Rae's *The Country Banker* included in Chapter 1, this essay uses fictional examples to make his points vivid. We might note that one of these examples, Mr. Bounderby, also appears in Dickens's *Hard Times.* The anonymous review of Henry Ayers's two reports for bankers is an example of the relatively technical discourse on the monetary system being published by the late 1850s. This essay is useful because it reveals that a picture of the entire international monetary system had begun to be visible by this date. The reviewer is fully aware that events in other countries dramatically affect the British financial system, even if the preventive he recommends—repeal the 1844 Bank Act's ban on the issue of country bank paper—falls far short of an adequate solution. This essay was published in the *London Review,* which was edited by John Stuart Mill. A. J. Wilson's 1878 essay on "The Position of English Joint-Stock Banks" is another relatively technical article, intended for a well-informed middle-class and professional audience. This article is noteworthy for three reasons: its sophisticated survey of the various parts of the English banking system; its plea for the more frequent publication of more accurate bank records; and its explanation of the importance of the concept of "bank money," which is also the subject of Henry Sidgwick's essay in Chapter 3.

The two newspaper articles and the chapter from Gilbart's *History, Principles, and Practice of Banking* help us understand how nineteenth-century Britons experienced a bank pressure. The articles from the *Times* provide a sense of the panic that escalated in 1825, during the century's first monetary crisis. The mixture we see here of matter-of-fact reporting, share price quotations, and atmospheric coloring ("a dense fog pervaded the city during the whole of the day") reveals early newsmen struggling to find a style appropriate to what they witnessed. Gilbart's more matter-of-fact survey of the pressures that had erupted before 1882, along with his account of the phases that precede and follow a pressure, suggest that by that date economic writers had attained sufficient experience of these events to place them in a coherent narrative. By that date, and writing for other professional bankers, Gilbart could see that fear and rumors could actively contribute to a monetary pressure, and he seems as intent upon conveying a psychological lesson to bankers as in analyzing the distinctions among the century's panics.

CHAPTER SEVEN

PRINICIPLES OF BANKING

JAMES WILLIAM GILBART
⚜

TEN MINUTES' ADVICE ABOUT KEEPING A BANKER

"He that hearkeneth unto counsel is wise."

—Proverbs.

1. A banker is a man who has an open shop with proper counters, clerks, and books, for receiving other people's money in order to keep it safe, and return it upon demand.

2. The building or shop in which this business is carried on, is usually called in London a "Banking-house," but in Scotland, and in the country parts of England, it is called a "Bank." The word "bank" is also employed to denote the partnership or company who carry on the business of banking. Thus we say, the Bank of Scotland, the London and Westminster Bank, the Bank of Messrs. Coutts & Co.

3. When a company of this kind does not consist of more than six partners, it is called a "Private Bank"; but when the company consists of several hundred partners, it is called in Scotland a "Public Bank," and in England a "Joint-stock Bank."

4. A private bank is usually managed by one or more of the partners, and all the partners are styled bankers. A public bank is managed by a principal officer, who is usually styled a manager. In England a bank manager is not

---

James William Gilbart, "Ten Minutes' Advice about Keeping a Banker." *A Practical Treatise on Banking.* 1839; rpt. 1849; rev. ed. Philadelphia: G. D. Miller, 1855 (3rd American ed. From the 5th London ed.). Pp. 424–30.

commonly called a banker; but in Scotland all managers of banks, and managers of branch banks, are called bankers. So mind, when I use the word "banker," you may apply it to either a private banker, or to a bank manager, whichever you please, as my observations will be as applicable to one as to the other. A banker is a man who carries on the business of banking; and whether he carries it on upon his own account, or as the agent of a public company, it appears to me to make no difference as to his claims to be called a banker.

5. It is the business of all these banks to receive other people's money, and to return it upon demand. And when any person puts money into one of these banks he is said to open an account with the bank; and when he has thus opened an account, and continues to put in and draw out money, he is said to have a current account, or, in London phraseology, "to keep a banker."

6. In Scotland almost every man has an account of some sort with a bank. The rich man in trade has an account because of the facility of conducting his operations; the rich man out of trade has an account because he gets interest upon his lodgments, and he keeps his money in the bank until he has an opportunity of investing it elsewhere at a better rate of interest. The middle class of people have an account because of the convenience of it, and because they obtain the discount of their bills, and perhaps loans, on giving two sureties, which are called cash credits. The poorer classes lodge their small savings in the bank, because of the security, and because they get interest on the sums which are lodged.

7. But in London the practice of keeping an account with a bank is by no means so common as in Scotland. The London banks are banks only for the rich. The bankers require that every person opening an account shall always have a sum to his credit; and if the sum thus kept is not what they deem sufficient, they will close the account. Hence the middle class of people in London have no banker at all, and the poorer class lodge their money in the savings banks, where they get interest, which they would not get from the London banker. It should also be stated, that besides keeping a sufficient balance, a party opening an account with a London banker is expected to give a certain sum every year to the clerks. This is called Christmas money, and the object is merely to enable the banker to pay a less salary to his clerks, at the expense of his customers.

8. But, within a few years, public or joint-stock banks have been established in London. These banks, or at least some of them, will allow you to open an account without promising to keep a large balance, or even any balance at all, provided you pay a small sum annually as a commission. This sum is fixed when you open the account, and it is about the same that you would be expected to give as Christmas-money to the clerks of a private bank. Hence people of moderate incomes, and those who can employ the whole of their

capital in their business, are now able to keep a banker. These banks, too, give interest on deposits, whether the sums be large or small, as I shall hereafter explain.

9. The first public or joint-stock bank established in London was the London and Westminster Bank. This bank is in Lothbury, and it has branch establishments at No. 1 St. James's Square; No. 214 High Holborn; No. 3 Wellington Street, Borough; No. 87 High Street, White-chapel; and No. 4 Stratford Place, Oxford Street. The success of this bank has led to the formation of several others. You will observe, that all banks which have branches conduct their business on the same terms at the branches as they do at the central office.

10. Since, then, the Scotch system of banking[1] is established in London, why should not the keeping of a banker be as general in London as in Scotland? I have stated, that, under the old system, those chiefly who were denied banking facilities were the middle class of people. Now, these people may be subdivided into two classes,—those who are engaged in trade, and those who are not. I shall address myself, in the first place, to the former class.

11. Now, I ask you, why don't you keep a banker? You say you have been in business several years, and have never kept one. Of course, if no banker would take your account, you could not do otherwise; but now there are bankers willing to take your account. But you say, you can do without a banker. Of course you can. The question is, not whether by possibility you can do without a banker, but whether you cannot do better with one. But you reply, it would not be worth any banker's while to take your account. That is for his consideration, not for yours. The question for you to decide is, not whether your keeping a banker would be of use to him, but whether it would be of use to yourself. I shall point out to you some of the advantages.

12. In the first place, by keeping a banker your money will be lodged in a place of security. You have now £50 or £100, or perhaps sometimes £200, that you keep in your own house; you take it up into your bedroom at night, and when you go out on Sunday you carry it in your pocket. Now, you may lose this money out of your pocket, the till may be robbed by your servants, or your house may be broken open by thieves, or your premises may take fire and the money may be burnt. But even should you escape LOSS, you cannot escape ANXIETY. When you have a little more money than usual, you have fears and apprehensions lest some accident should occur. Now, you will avoid all this trouble by keeping a banker.

13. The banker will not only take care of your money, but also of any thing else you commit to his charge. You can get a small tin box with your name

---

1. The combination of joint-stock banks, trunk and branch banks, and a weak central bank that characterized the Scottish banking system from the eighteenth century. [Ed.]

painted on it, and into this box you can put your will, the lease of your house, policies of insurances, and any deeds or other documents that require particular care. You can send this box to your banker, who will take care of it for you; and you can have it back whenever you like, and as often as you like. If your premises are insured, it is clearly improper to keep the policy on the premises: for if the house be burnt, the policy will be burnt too; and where then is your evidence of claim upon the insurance office?

14. Another advantage is the saving of time. When you receive money you will send it in a lump to the bank; and when you pay away money you will draw cheques upon the bank. Now to draw a cheque takes up much less time than counting out the money that you have to pay, and perhaps sending out for change because you have not the exact sum. Besides, you sometimes hold bills which, when due, you have to send for payment; now you can lodge these with your banker, who will present them for you. And when you accept bills, you will make them payable at your banker's, instead of making them payable at your own house. Now in all these cases there is a great saving of time; and, besides, your bills, from being made payable at a bank, will be considered more respectable.

15. Another advantage of keeping a banker, is, that it will be a check upon your accounts. I need not speak to you, as a trader, of the importance of correct accounts. Your banker's book will be an authentic record of your cash transactions. If you make a mistake in your trade books, the banker's book will often lead to a detection of the error. If you have paid a sum of money, and the party denies having received it, you can refer to your banker's account, and produce your cheque, which is as good as a receipt. By means of a banker's account, you could trace your receipts and payments, even after a number of years had elapsed; and hence disputed accounts could be readily adjusted, and error, arising from forgetfulness or oversight, be speedily rectified.

16. I could mention several other reasons why you should keep a banker. But what I have said will be enough to induce you to make a trial; and when you have once opened an account, you will find so much convenience from it, that you will require no further reasons to induce you to continue it. If it should not answer your expectations, you can, whenever you please, close it again.

17. Now, then, as you have made up your mind to keep a banker, the next thing is to determine at what bank you will open your account. On this point I must leave you to make your own choice. All the PUBLIC BANKS issue prospectuses, containing a list of their directors, the amount of their paid-up capital, the names of the bankers who superintend their respective establishments, and their rules for transacting business. You can get a prospectus from each bank, compare them together, and please your own fancy. But if you

have no other grounds for preference, I advise you to open your account with the BANK or BRANCH BANK that is NEAREST TO YOUR OWN PLACE OF BUSINESS. You will often have to go or send to the bank; and if it be a great way off, much time will be lost, and you will at times be induced to forego some of the advantages of keeping a banker rather than send to so great a distance. On this account, let your banker be your neighbour. Recollect, time is money.

18. There is no difficulty in opening an account. You will enter the bank, and ask for the manager. Explain to him what you want to do. He will give you every information you may require, and you will receive, without charge, a small account book called a Pass-book, and a book of cheques. I advise you to keep these two books, when not in use, under your own lock and key.

19. You now require no further advice from me, as your banker will give you the most ample information respecting the way of conducting your account. Nevertheless, I may mention a point or two for your own government:—Do not depend entirely upon your banker's Pass-book, but keep also an account in a book of your own. Debit your banker with all cash you may pay into the bank, and credit him for all the cheques you may draw at the time you draw them. Send your Pass-book frequently to be made up at the bank; and when it returns, always compare it with your account-book. This will correct any mistake in the Pass-book. Besides some of your cheques may not be presented for payment until several days after they are drawn; and if, in the mean time, you take the balance of the banker's Pass-book, you will seem to have more ready cash than you actually possess, and this may lead you into unpleasant mistakes.

20. When you lodge any money at the bank, always place the total amount of the cash and your name, at full length, upon the outside of the parcel, or on a slip of paper. The cashier will then see at once if he agrees with your amount. This will save time, and prevent mistakes.

21. Be always open and straightforward with your banker. Do not represent yourself to be a richer man than you are; do not discount with your banker any bills that are not likely to be PUNCTUALLY paid when due; and should any be unpaid and returned to you, pay them yourself IMMEDIATELY. Do not attempt to OVERDRAW your account; that is, do not draw cheques upon your banker for more money than you have in his hands, without first asking his consent; and if you make him any promises, be sure that they be strictly performed. If you fail ONCE, the banker will hesitate before he trusts you again.

22. Should you be dissatisfied with any thing connected with your account, make your complaint to the BANKER himself, and not to the clerks. Let all your communications be made in PERSON, rather than by LETTER. But do not stay long at one interview. Make no observations about the weather or the news of the day. Proceed at once to the business you are come about, and when it is

settled, retire. This will save your banker's time, and give him a favorable impression of your character as a man of business.

23. If you are in partnership, besides opening an account with your banker in the names of the firm, you should open a private account for yourself, that your personal affairs may be kept separate from those of the partnership. Or if you are in an extensive way of business, and have a large family, it is advisable that you open a separate account with your banker in the name of your wife, that your trade payments and your household expenses may not be mixed up together in the same account. This is a good way of ascertaining the exact amount of your family expenditure.

24. If you are appointed executor or assignee to an estate, or become treasurer to a public institution or charitable society, open a separate account with your banker for this office, and do not mix other people's moneys with your own. This will prevent mistakes and confusion in your accounts. These separate accounts may be kept still more distinct by being opened with another banker, or at another branch of the same bank.

25. There are a good many of the middle class of people who are not in trade, and I must now address them. Perhaps you are a clergyman, or a medical man, or you are in a public office, or are living on your rents or dividends. At all events, whatever you may be, I conclude you are not living beyond your means. If you are, I have not a word to say to you about keeping a banker; you will soon, most likely, be within the keeping of a gaoler.

26. Several of the reasons I have given to the trader will also apply to you; but there is one that applies with much greater force,—the tendency to insure accurate accounts. As you are not a man of business, I shall not advise you to keep an account of your receipts and your expenditure. I know you will do no such thing. Should you ever commence to do so, you will get tired before the end of the year, and throw the book aside. Now, if you keep a banker, he will keep your accounts for you; his Pass-book will show you the state of your accounts. All the money you receive you must send to the bank, and all your payments must be made by cheques upon the bank. If you want pocket-money, draw a cheque for £5 or £10, payable to cash, but by no means disburse any money but through your banker. Your book will be balanced every half-year. You will then see the total amount of your receipts during the half year, and your various payments to the butcher, the baker, the tailor, &c. The names to which the cheques are made payable will show you for what purpose they were given; and you should write these names in a plain hand, that the clerks may copy them correctly in the Pass-book. Now, if you look through your book once every half year in this way, you will probably see occasion to introduce some useful reforms into your domestic expenditure. But if you are too lazy to do this, hand the book to your wife, and she will do it for you.

27. I shall now address another class of people. Perhaps you are a clerk, or a warehouseman, or a shopman, or a domestic servant. Well, you have no occasion to keep a banker; that is, you have no occasion to open a current account. But you have got a little money which you would like to put into a safe place, and upon which you would like to receive interest. Well, now, listen to me.

28. If the sum be under £10, or if the sum be above £10, and you are not likely to want it soon, put it into the savings banks; you will receive interest for it at the rate of about £3 for every £100 for a year. But mind, you can only put money into the savings bank at certain hours in the week, when the bank is open; and you cannot put in more than £30 in any one year, nor more than £150 altogether, and you will receive no interest for the fractional parts of a month, and you cannot draw out any money without giving notice beforehand.

29. If, then, your money is more than £10, and you have already lodged £30 this year in the savings bank, or £150 altogether, or if you will have occasion to draw out your money without giving notice, then lodge it in one of the public banks. These banks are open every week day from nine o'clock in the morning till four in the evening; they will take lodgments of money to any amount, and interest will be allowed from the day it is lodged until the day it is drawn out; and if the sum is under £1,000, no notice is required. For all sums lodged on interest the bankers give receipts called deposit receipts.

30. When you go to the bank to lodge upon interest any sum under £1,000, you need not inquire for the manager. Hand your money to any clerk you may see standing inside the counter, and ask for a deposit receipt. You will be requested (the first time you go) to write your name and address in a book which is kept for that purpose, and then the deposit receipt will be given to you without any delay.

31. Mind, this deposit receipt is not transferable; that is, you cannot lend it or give it to any body else. When you want the money, you must take it yourself to the bank, and ask the cashier to pay you the amount. You will then be requested to write your name on the back of the deposit receipt; the cashier will see that the signature corresponds with the signature you wrote in the book when you lodged the money, and will then pay you the amount, and keep the receipt.

32. Although you cannot lodge upon a deposit receipt a less sum in the first instance than £10, yet, having lodged that sum, you can make any additions to it you please. Thus, if you wish to lodge £5 more, you can take your £5 note and your deposit receipt for £10 to the bank, and get a new receipt for £15. If, after having lodged £10, you wish to lodge £10 more, you can get a separate receipt for the second £10, or have a new receipt for £20, whichever you please; and, observe, whenever any addition is made to a former receipt, the old receipt is cancelled, and the interest due upon it is either paid, to you in

money, or added to the amount of the new receipt, as may be most agreeable to yourself.

33. The interest allowed you by the bank will at present be at the rate of 2 per cent; that is to say, after the rate of £2 upon every £100 for a year.

34. Upon sums above £1,000 the interest allowed is sometimes more and sometimes less than 2 per cent., according to the value of money, that is, according to the rate at which the bankers can employ it again; and a few days' notice is usually required before the money is withdrawn; but upon sums under £1,000 the rate of interest varies less frequently, and they are always repayable upon demand.

35. You will be surprised to find how the desire of lodging money in a bank will grow upon you. When you had the money in your pocket, you were anxious to find reasons for spending it. When you have placed it in the bank, you will be anxious to find reasons for not spending it. All habits are formed or strengthened by repeated acts. The more money you lodge in the bank, the more you will desire to lodge. You will go on making additions, until, at last, you will probably have acquired a sum that shall lay the foundation of your advance to a higher station in society.

R. J. RICHARDSON

EXPOSURE OF THE BANKING AND FUNDING SYSTEM

Paper money is strength in the beginning, but weakness in the end.

—*Translation from the French.*

A celebrated Frenchman, the inventor of the present system of banking, once made use of the above sentence when interrogated by the king as to the effect likely to be produced by the establishment of a National Bank. The king in answer asked him "How it was that he, the banker, had become so rich?" "Why," he replied, "I have found the people foolish enough to bring me their gold and take back my paper." "Then," said the king, "we will have a bank!" "But to be warned, Sire, I am insolvent if I attempt to pay back the gold lent, and my insolvency will ruin a few others; if you turn banker your insolvency will ruin the nation."

How fearfully has this doctrine operated in England. The curse of paper

R. J. Richardson, "Exposure of the Banking and Funding System," chapter 4. *English Chartist Circular: The Temperance Record for England and Wales* 1: 23 (1841): 90.

money and banking new blasts the constitution of society, and its attendant curse, the practice of usury, has not only been productive of an incalculable deal of mischief, but it still fosters the evils it has engendered, and holds the whole nation in a state of subjugation. We have now no less than 400 banks in this kingdom, with the great Moloch of Mammon, the Bank of England, at their head.

The Bank of England owes its origin to the poverty of the English nation in 1694, when "the good King William, of pious and immortal memory," had spent the nation's resources in endeavouring to put down the Jacobites, and wanted money to carry on the war with France. He consented to incorporate a set of fellows, under the name of "The Governor and Company of the Bank of England," on condition that they, the Company, would lend him £1,500,000; for which sum £100,000 of interest at eight per cent., had to be paid by the nation every year so long as the debt existed.

This may be said to be the origin of the National Debt. So far, the National Debt and the Bank of England are twins of mischief; or to complete the *Tria junota in uno,* the Customs and Excise Laws may be added, for they were made in the 5th and 6th William and Mary, to pay the interest of the £1,500,000 borrowed by the Government, and other exigencies of the state.

The object of the Company is defined by the 28th section of the 5th William and Mary, cap. 20, July 27th, 1694, which recites, "That the Company may not trade in anything except Bills of Exchange and bullion; but it *may lend money out at interest,* on goods, wares, or merchandise, and sell the same if not redeemed by the time agreed upon, or within three months of the date of the deposit." So, henceforth, we may imagine a huge sign the whole length of Threadneedle-street, stuck up against the bank, on which is inscribed "Money lent on goods (honestly come by) by Abram Newland, Licensed to take in plate," and believe me, Sir, the vaults of this great PAWNSHOP contain more than one strong oak chest, in which is deposited the family plate and jewels, and title deeds, too, of some of England's proudest nobles. The bank has ever been the main prop of the Government; the exclusive privilege enjoyed by the company have been the means of making them immensely wealthy, and the Government, in times of embarrassment, have been necessitated to borrow at different times large sums of money; these obligations have secured to the company a perpetual enjoyment of their monopoly, in fact, hath bound the Government hand and foot to the bank; so far is the Government of England dependent upon the bank, that upon several occasions when the bank has been hard run, and on the point of stopping payment, orders in council have set aside the law of debtor and creditor, and allowed the bank to suspend cash payments during the embarrassments. Upon all occasions of a renewal of the Bank Charter, the Government have been obliged to yield additional powers to the company. In consequence of the loans advanced to the government by the Company in 1838, when the Charter was last renewed, the Government owed them £14,553,000, the price of such obligations was a clause in the act, making bank notes a LEGAL TENDER everywhere except at the bank in London, and its branches; also a clause prohibiting any company of more than six persons, within sixty-five miles of London, from issuing any bill of exchange, or promissory note, payable on demand; these, and other monopolies formerly enjoyed by the Company, yield immense profits, the amount of which is shewn in evidence before a committee of the House of Lords, 1819. Mr. Ricardo[1] says, "The average amount of capital employed for a period of nineteen years by the Bank, has been £11,642,000, on which sum a profit of £29,280,636 has been realised in the same period." It may be asked, how are such enormous profits raised? The answer of the French banker tells you, that fools deposit their hard cash, and take back promises to pay: this brings us at once within the arcana of banking. The bank is privileged; to issue promissory notes, or bank notes, for all sums above five pounds. The average amount of notes in circulation will be about £18,000,000; not one farthing of interest is paid by the bank to any holder of their notes. Now, as these notes are made a legal tender, they bear the value of money in all mercantile transactions, and are as a efficient, for the time, as gold is in making purchases; consequently, the notes issued by the bank are worth to them £900,000, being five per cent. upon the amount of bank notes in circulation. Here is so much profit to the company, not taking into account the profits of notes destroyed by accident, or otherwise, whilst in circulation. Every £5 note, including duty, and labour, and materials, does not cost the company more than 1s. 6d., consequently, every note so lost, or destroyed, would yield a clear profit of £4 18s. 6d. to the company. Another great source of profit is in the PAWN SHOP, where they lend bank notes on "Goods honestly come by" at five per cent., and which they sell if not redeemed. Another very extensive source of profit is in discounting bills for their customers, the rates of discount varying according to the pressure of the times, sometimes it runs as high as six per cent., and it has been much higher when money was scarce. It is here where the grand junction betwixt the country bankers, money-mongers, stock-jobbers, and loan-mongers is effected, and the slightest movement on the part of the banker in raising or lowering the rate of discount, creates an unsettled fluctuation amongst them; for as the demand for money is created, all kinds of stock is thrown into the market, trade becomes sacrificed, distrust and panics succeed, and the whole of the paper credit becomes shaken. Another source of profit is in effecting exchanges between one nation and another; another in receiving deposits for gold, paying two, or two-and-a-half per cent. for the use of it, turning it over in the pawn-shop, and other departments of the bank at an increased rate of

---

1. David Ricardo (1772–1823). Stockbroker and economist who developed the political economic ideas initially set out by Adam Smith. Author of *Principles of Political Economy and Taxation* (1817) and radical member of Parliament from 1819. [Ed.]

interest, and paying the depositor back in "promises to pay," bearing no interest at all; another source of profit is in receiving Exchequer Bills on account of the Government, who is too poor to pay them off, paying the holder in "promises to pay," and receiving the interest upon them at two-and-a-half per cent. per diem, until the Government get leave from Parliament to fund them; this is the way they help the lame dog over the stile. Another source of profit is in receiving the gold and silver from the Savings' Banks, deposited there by silly working men, and turning it over in the way of trade. Another source is the receipt of £158,141 19s. 3½d. from the taxes for managing the GRAND SWINDLE, which it affects to do for nothing; another infamous source of profit is in Stock Jobbing, both on their own account, and on the account of Government. In every way is the English Government trammelled by its connection with the Bank. When the present Charter was granted in 1833, our Government owed to the bank £14,553,000. This was to have been reduced to £10,914,750. This reduced sum is termed Bank Stock, which bears interest at three per cent, as long as it exists, and that interest is paid out of the taxes; this is National Debt too. I find we are now charged with interest upon £11,015,100 debt due to the Bank, besides interest at three per cent upon £826,636 of Bank Annuities, created in 1726; this too is part of the "GRAND SWINDLE." With all their apparent wealth, they have been compelled to STOP PAYMENT THIRTEEN TIMES since 1797; or in plain English, the Company have been obliged not only to shut up the pawn-shop, but to refuse to pay their *just debts*. The following statement will shew how rotten is the great depot of paper money, and how poor a crutch the paper system is to prop up a falling Government, and an insolvent nation. The following Bank restriction acts have been passed to prevent the Bank from doing that which it never can do, settle its "promises to pay" in gold, and pay back the deposits in hard cash, when it never had half the amount of bullion in its possession for such purposes.—

 1. 26 Feby. 1797.
 2. 3 May, 1797.
 3. 22 June, 1797.
 4. 30 Nov. 1797.
 5. 30 April, 1802.
 6. 28 Feb. 1803.
 7. 15 Dec., 1803.
 8. 18 July, 1814.
 9. 23 Mar., 1815.   Waterloo year.
10. 21 May, 1816.
11. 28 May, 1818.
12. 26 April, 1819.   Peterloo year.
13. 2 July, 1819.   Continued to 1 May, 1823.

Would any ordinary tradesman go on trusting another tradesman who had *broken* thirteen times in twenty-six years? Then how can we rationally go on trusting a set of fellows to manage our affairs, who are perpetually insolvent, and dragging down our industrious nation along with them. These fellows are supported by the Government and the Legislature when they are in difficulties, and acts are passed to restrict them from paying *their just debts.* But the Government and the Legislature never pass acts to save the people from paying the interest in full, even to the farthing, of the accursed debt. No; the GRAND SWINDLE must be supported though the nation perish; the Bank Monopolists and the debt are inseparable; the Government and the Company are linked together, and nothing short of a Radical Reform can, by sap and mine, blow them up into the air.

R. J. R.

ANONYMOUS

THE BANK CHARTER AND COMMERCIAL CREDIT

ART. III.—*Ayres' Financial Register of British and Foreign Funds, Banks, &c., &c., for 1857, containing an Account of the principal Matters relating to the Finances of the United Kingdom; with a Sketch of the Revenues, Expenditure, and Commerce of Foreign Nations: also an Account of Foreign Banks and Banking, &c.* By HENRY AYRES, Editor of the Bankers' Circular and Finance Gazette, &c. London: Richardson, Brothers.

The late Mr. Butler, in his *Reminiscences,* relates, that in a conversation with Charles James Fox, he happened to say, that he had never read Smith's *Wealth of Nations.* "To tell you the truth," replied Fox,[1] "nor I either. There is something in all these subjects which passes my comprehension,—something so wide, that I could never embrace them myself, or find any one who did."

    What Fox here states of the science of political economy, is equally appli-

Anonymous, "The Bank Charter and Commercial Credit." *London Review* 10 (April 1858): 59–76.
1. Charles James Fox (1749–1806). Whig politician and leader of the opposition in Parliament. Fox was a rival of William Pitt and a critic of royal authority under George III. He promoted the reform of Parliament and the end of the slave trade. [Ed.]

cable to that branch of it called "the currency question," or, in other words, the monetary operations of the Bank of England in connexion with the government. We much question whether one intelligent and well-educated person in a hundred could give any tolerably clear account of those operations, or of their bearing upon the trade and commerce of the kingdom. It may be some consolation to ordinary folks, to hear a great statesman declare his inability to fathom a subject of such national importance; but most assuredly it is precisely these, constituting *the middle classes,* who are the most deeply concerned in those questions, who feel most acutely their effects, and have therefore the most reason to study those operations which at times involve the commerce of the country in a climax of distress and embarrassment, that shakes its prosperity to the very foundation.

But the English are a very forgiving people, and are soon pacified. Possessing a degree of energy that overrides all difficulties, they conquer in the field against all odds, in spite of the imbecility of their leaders, or the blundering mismanagement of their government; and they impart to their commerce a reactionary power and spirit, which enables it, when apparently crushed to the very earth, to rise unscathed and vigorous as ever.

The monetary crisis through which the country has lately passed, is one of a series of financial epidemics which during the last sixty years have, at intervals, caused so much distress in the commercial world, and which have been aggravated, if not originated, by the way in which the currency has been managed between the Bank of England and the government. Any of our readers who wish to understand more of these matters, will do well to read Mr. Ayres's work, which contains a clear and full statement of everything relating to finance, both British and foreign; and in the meantime we propose to draw up from these and other data a short account of the causes that produced the 'panic,' and especially of the Bank Charter of 1844–5, which is considered by many the *primum mobile* of the evil.

It is unnecessary for us to go into the history of the by-gone connexion between the Bank of England and the government. Suffice it to observe, that the Bank was instituted by William III. in 1694, and arose out of a *political necessity;* and that such is the interwoven texture of the interests and monetary operations of the Bank and the government, that they are still as necessary to each other as ever. Yet they may be compared to hounds running in couples, one of which keeps steadily on the scent, whilst the other (a hungry dog) spies or smells a bone near his path, and attempts to start aside to ascertain whether it is worth picking. In other, and perhaps more courteous, words: whilst the government has, or ought to have, only *one* object in view,—the public good,—the Bank has, in addition, not only its own general interest, as a monster commercial establishment, but also the private interests of the proprietors, including, of course, those of the governor and directors, who are all also private merchants or bankers. We give the Bank directors full credit for always consulting the interests of the public, when they do not interfere with those of the proprietary, general or special; but it is contrary to human nature to expect that anything short of an Act of Parliament should prevent them from throwing overboard the public interests, when these would clash with their own, or those of the Bank. We shall see, as we proceed, how far the existing condition of things has been instrumental in producing those financial convulsions or crises that have so frequently occurred of late years, and especially under the Bank Charter of 1844–5.

Previous to the above period, there was no restriction upon the issue of notes by the Bank of England; and when contemplating the new arrangement, Sir Robert Peel, as the head of the government, and the concocter of the measure, appears to have had in view the establishment of an office of its own for the issue of promissory notes, and thus to have taken the paper as well as the metallic currency entirely into its own hands. This we learn from Mr. Goulburn's letter to the governor; but before adopting this scheme, which would have been equal to cutting off one of the wings of the Bank, the governor was asked whether the directors would consent to certain conditions, the principal of which were as follow:—

1. That the two departments,—the bank of issue, and the bank of deposit,—should be entirely separated, so that in no respect should the one interfere with, or be dependent upon, the other.
2. That a certain amount of notes should be issued on securities, public and private; and that all other notes issued by them should be only in exchange for bullion or coin.
3. That the securities should, to a certain extent, be of such a nature as to admit of ready convertibility, and should not be increased beyond the amount originally fixed, excepting under circumstances to be stated by the Bank to the government; and after the consent of certain members of the government, namely, the first lord of the treasury, the chancellor of the exchequer, and the master of the mint, shall have been signified.
4. That no new banks of issue should be established; the issue of notes of those banks exercising that privilege to be confined to amounts originally fixed, and their issues to be limited to the average amount of a given period preceding: and in the event of a failure or liquidation, a resumption to be prohibited of their own circulation; the deficiency in the circulation thereby created, to be supplied, if necessary, by the substitution of notes of the Bank of England; an increase of the securities to the amount thereof being authorized by the government, as the foundation of the paper; the net profit of the measure to be carried to the account of the government.
5. A weekly, instead of the usual quarterly, statement of the affairs of the Bank to be published in both departments; and the private joint-stock banks to do the same, if their notes are in circulation. Charter to be granted for ten years, from August 1st, 1845; and at the termination of that period, the Charter to be

terminable on twelve months' notice, but continuing in force until such notice be given.

Such were the conditions on which the government proposed to grant a new Charter to the Bank of England, and which were, with slight alterations, accepted by that establishment. In 1844, the Act of Parliament gave its final sanction; and from that period the two departments of the Bank,—that of issue, and that of deposit, or ordinary banking business,—became as separate and distinct as if they belonged to separate firms.

The Bill which enacted this state of things had not passed more than three years, before the inconvenience to the public became manifest. In 1847, in consequence of the railway speculations, the large imports of corn, and the extension of our foreign commerce, all which demanded an extended capital, the pressure on the money market became seriously heavy; and such was the critical situation of the Bank of England, that it was compelled to appeal to the government, to be allowed to extend its issue of notes beyond the legal limit; the bank of deposit being so close run as to be on the eve of stopping payment, whilst the other department held a large amount of specie, for which it had no use. For any private mercantile house of business, or a private bank, to be placed in such a position, (if it were *possible,*) would render it the laughing-stock of every sensible merchant in the country.

It is here proper to state what are the securities referred to in the second and third clauses of the government proposition.

First, there is the debt due to the Bank from the government, which amounts to the sum of £14,015,100, to which other sums have been added, amounting in all, in round numbers, to £16,500,000. For this, adequate securities are undoubtedly held by the Bank, the whole nation standing pledged, by its representatives in Parliament, for the payment; but so far from the securities being of such a nature as to be convertible, it would be impossible to negotiate them in any market, and the debt itself is strictly in the nature of a book debt for which a simple bond is given.

Secondly, there are private securities, upon which the Bank is allowed to issue notes to the amount of £14,000,000.

Thirdly, the amount of gold and silver coin and bullion held by the Bank.

With regard to the first two items, it is evident that, in case of extreme pressure, these would be of no avail, the very circumstances that occasion such pressure rendering it doubly impossible to realize the securities, except at the most ruinous sacrifices; so that if the pressure continued, the government would have no alternative but to imitate the example of Pitt[2] in 1797, when, upon the Bank of England *stopping payment,* an order in council was issued

---

2. William Pitt (1759–1806). Founder of the Conservative Party and government official who ordered the Bank of England to stop cash payments during the war with France in 1797. [Ed.]

to suspend cash payments; which order was confirmed by Parliament, and continued until 1819, when by "Peel's Act," as it is called, the resumption of cash payments was provided for. And in respect to the amount of coin and bullion held by the Bank in the issue department, and which is the regulator of the issue of notes, it fluctuates day by day, and is in the nature of things the smallest, and consequently contracts most the issue of notes, at the time when an extension of the latter is most needed.

Nor has the Bank the smallest power to check the efflux of the precious metals under the Charter. In five years it has raised its interest from one and a half to ten per cent., for that purpose; but still the amount continued to decrease, until, alarmed at the ruin which stared the whole trading community in the face, the Charter was for the second time suspended, and the Bank allowed to extend its issues.

It is evident, too, that with such large liabilities as those of the Bank of England, the amount of the specie held by it can hardly warrant the assumption that the currency rests upon a metallic basis. It may or may not be true, that there is coin enough in the country to meet the wants of the internal trade under ordinary circumstances; but this alone cannot constitute a metallic basis, when the Bank, which is the representative or fountain of the currency, holds not enough to meet its liabilities by one half, one fourth, or one eighth, as the case may be. Under such circumstances, it would be far more correct to say that the basis of the currency is *public credit,* which alone sustains the solvency of the national Bank.

Perhaps the separation of the two departments of the Bank,—the issue, and the deposit,—is the greatest commercial anomaly this country has ever seen. Let us suppose, by way of illustration, a merchant having a business establishment in one part of his house for selling tea, and another in a separate portion for selling sugar. One of these—say the tea warehouse—finds itself without funds, having made heavy purchases; whilst the sugar department has amply sufficient to meet the requirements of both. What would be thought of the wisdom or prudence of the party, if he had bound himself by an irrevocable deed to keep the two establishments so distinct, that under no circumstances of pressure could he allow the funds of the one to be appropriated to the relief of the other; and he must risk a bankruptcy rather than violate his engagement? Yet such is the actual *legal* position of the Bank of England, by virtue of its Charter, as we shall presently show.

At the time (1844) when the new Charter was granted to the Bank, the amount of bullion and specie in its coffers was about £16,000,000, the price of consols was *at par,* and the interest of money on good bills two and a half per cent. After the passing of the Act, and towards the beginning of 1847, owing to the large speculations to which we have already referred, the amount of the precious metals gradually declined, until, on the 25th of October in that

year, it was reduced to £8,500,000. At the same time consols had fallen to
79¾, and the interest on first-class bills at the Bank of England was eight and
a half per cent. But now came the separation of the two departments into the
most perplexing operation. For whilst the bank of issue held specie to the
amount of £8,500,000, that of deposit possessed only £303,000, against
£20,500,000 of paper, and £14,000,000 of deposit, for which £34,500,000 it
was liable to be called upon any day or hour. But not one shilling of the
£8,500,000 held by its colleague could it touch to relieve itself, without an infraction of the Charter, which the necessity of the case compelled; for on the
25th of October a letter came from the chancellor of the exchequer to the governor and company of the Bank, as in 1797, authorizing them to extend the
issue of notes in the banking department, whereby the Act of 1844 was for the
time set aside.

But we have seen a more extreme case within the last few months, showing the folly and absurdity of this regulation. Owing to the vast extension of
our foreign commerce, and especially the imports, the exchanges have of late
been against the United Kingdom: and notwithstanding the enormous quantities of gold continually flowing into the Bank from the American and Australian gold-fields, the quantity held by that establishment has since 1852
been reduced from £22,000,000 (in July of that year) to about £7,000,000 on
November, 11th, 1857; the interest on first-class bills having, in the same period, risen from one and a half to ten per cent., and consols having fallen from
100½ to 88 per cent.

And now again occurred a specimen of the working of the separation of the
two departments. On this same 11th of November the amount of specie and
bullion in the issue department was £6,666,065, whilst the banking department absolutely had only £504,443, against £20,188,355 in notes, and
£19,103,078 in deposits, all liable to be instantly required to be made good in
cash; so that in fact, had not relief been afforded, the banking department must
have closed its books the next day, not having more than enough in specie to
pay about twopence half-penny in the pound! Such was the emergency, and
so critical the state of affairs in the deposit department, that the principals of
three of the leading firms in the monetary circle waited on Lord Palmerston,[3]
to represent the urgent necessity of taking immediate steps to afford relief, by
a temporary suspension of the Bank Charter Act. After some little hesitancy
on his part, his lordship consented, and a letter was immediately dispatched
to the 'governor and company' of the Bank, authorizing them to extend their
issue beyond the limits of the Charter, on condition that the *interest on bills
should not be reduced below ten per cent.* The argument that determined his

---

3. Lord Palmerston (1785–1865). Foreign secretary (1830–34, 1835–41, 1846–51) and prime
   minister (1858–65). Palmerston agreed to suspend the 1844 Bank Charter Act in 1857. [Ed.]

lordship to comply, is said to have been the declaration of one of the gentle-men, connected with a house of discount, that "he had a million of money lying at his bankers, but not one more bill would he cash until relief was granted."[4] And thus, a second time within ten years was the Act of Parliament set aside by the first minister of the crown; rendering it necessary to assemble Parliament at an unusual period, in order to obtain a bill of indemnity for this infraction of the Act.

This concession at once relieved the general commerce of the country, and people began to breathe freely; but it is evident that so far as the involvement of the Bank is concerned, it made things worse. Not only were the liabilities increased, but the bullion and specie continued for a time to decrease in spite of the stipulation on which the letter of licence was granted; for we find in the following week (Nov. 18th) that the amount of bullion and coin in the Bank was reduced to £6,484,096; and that the liabilities (notes and deposits) in the banking department had increased to £42,827,125, to meet which it held in specie only £404,501, or little more than twopence farthing in the pound; being of course the only portion of the assets available in case of a "run," sup-posing the Charter Act to have been peremptorily enforced.

Such is the position of the Bank of England at the present time; notwith-standing which, the credit of that institution cannot sustain any fatal shock, because, as we have already stated, it is so interwoven with the government in all its operations, that the latter stands deeply pledged to support it. This, how-ever, is not the question, but what is the influence the present Charter of the Bank has upon the prosperity of the country; and how far the two panics which have occurred since its existence have been aggravated by the restric-tion of the issue of paper to the amount of gold held by the Bank.

We must, in the next place, explain the position of the London joint-stock banks, and the private country banks of issue, whose interests have been ma-terially affected by the Bank Charter.

Previous to 1825, no joint-stock banks could be established in England. But in consequence of the panic in that year, and the numerous and extensive

---

4. During the panic of November, 1825, a gentleman belonging to a first-rate banking firm in the Eastern Counties applied to the Bank of England for an advance of £50,000. He was told it could not be granted; for that such was the pressure on the Bank, that it would have enough to do to meet it. The party then went to the firm in Lombard Street by whom their town busi-ness was transacted, and stated the case; upon which one of the partners returned with him to the Bank of England. "My friend here tells me," said the latter to the cashier, "that you de-cline to advance him what money he wants, to take home with him." "Yes," replied the cashier, "we dare not part with any more for the country." "Well then," rejoined the Lombard Street man, "if you do not let him have £50,000 before I leave this room, *I will go back to Lombard Street, and shut up my shop, and then—you shall shut up yours.*" This urgent ar-gument prevailed, and the money was advanced.

failures of private banks, an Act was passed the following year, (7th Geo. IV., cap. 46,) by virtue of which joint-stock banks and banks of issue were allowed to be established in England, *but not within sixty-five miles of London in all directions;* the Bank of England still maintaining the *noli-me-tangere* principle. But in 1833, when the Bank Charter was again renewed, this limitation was so far relaxed, that country banks, whether joint-stock or private, were allowed to have agents in London for the cashing of their notes, but without power to re-issue notes payable on demand. This commences the history of the London joint-stock banks, most of which, being confined in their operations to the routine of banking business, without the power of issuing notes, have succeeded; and some have had extraordinary success. They were even forbidden to accept bills at less than six months' date; and the Bank of England obtained an injunction to restrain the London and Westminster Joint-Stock Bank from doing so. But the law has been evaded, by the country bankers drawing upon the London banks, *"without acceptance,"* which practice, first instituted by the London and Westminster Bank, has since been adopted extensively by all the banks. The "Royal British Bank" forms an unfortunate exception to the picture of prosperity exhibited by most of the other London joint-stock banks, owing, not to the principle on which it professed to set out, which was that of the Scotch banks, but rather to the fraudulent conduct of some of the managers and directors, and the neglect of others; the former having lent the funds of the Bank to each other without adequate security, and the latter either conniving at it, or neglecting to look into the accounts; between both, the creditors and shareholders have been cruelly victimized.

It was, however, under the Joint-Stock Bank Act of 1844, (7 and 8 Vict., cap. 113,) that this latter bank was established; and we have now to show the operation of that Act upon the private and joint-stock banks respectively. The sections of the Act having special reference to country banks reach *seriatim* from the tenth to the twenty-second, and comprise the following regulations amongst others, viz.:—

1. That no new bank of issue shall be established in any part of the United Kingdom, nor shall any banker issue notes who was not lawfully doing so on the 6th of May, 1844.
2. That no banking company or partnership, which then consisted of *only six, or less than six, persons,* shall issue bank-notes at any time, after the number of partners shall exceed six.
3. Bankers having ceased to issue their own notes, whether by agreement with the Bank of England or not, cannot resume such issues.
4. Existing banks of issue to be subject to a fixed amount, ascertained by the average amount of notes in circulation during the twelve months preced-

ing the 27th of April, 1844; and at no time, after the 10th of October in that year, to have in circulation of greater amount, on the average of four weeks, than the amount so certified by the Commissioners of Stamps and Taxes; and the account to be published in the *London Gazette.*

5. If any banker shall issue notes exceeding in amount the authorized issue, he shall forfeit a sum equal to the excess.

6. The accounts of all banks of issue to be sent to the Commissioners of Stamps and Taxes, showing the amount of notes in circulation every day in the week, and the weekly averages to be published in the *London Gazette.* Any banker refusing or neglecting to comply with this regulation, is subject to a penalty of £100 for every such offence.

7. The mode of determining the amount of bank-notes in circulation, for the four weeks after the 10th day of October, 1844, is by dividing the number by that of days of business in such four weeks, and so on for every successive four weeks.

8. All bankers are compelled to take out a licence for every place at which their notes are issued, unless they had four such licences in force on the 6th of May, 1844.

9. The twenty-third section empowers the Bank of England to terminate all its agreements with bankers who had ceased to issue their own notes prior to the passing of this Act on December 31st, 1844; and to allow such banks a composition of one per cent. per annum on the average amount of Bank of England notes issued by such banks, and actually remaining in circulation, estimated on the amount of Bank of England notes delivered to such bankers within three months preceding some day in the month of April, 1845.

10. The twenty-fourth section empowers the Bank of England to agree with any banker entitled to issue his own notes under this Act. The same section provides, that in case any increase is made in the securities in the issue department, under an order in council, the amount of composition payable to such bankers shall be deducted from the amount payable by the bank to the public. By the twenty-fifth section, the whole of these compositions were to cease on the first day of August, 1856, or on any earlier day on which Parliament *may prohibit the issue of bank-notes.*

On these regulations, the importance of which to the public generally has induced us to give them in full, Mr. Ayres justly remarks, that "the main principle involved was the *ultimate extinction of country banks of issue,* or rather of their notes, and the substitution of Bank of England notes in their stead." The consequences of them already are, that up to the year 1855 forty-seven banks of issue have from various causes ceased to issue their own notes, to the extent of £712,623, apportioned as follows:—

			Authorized Issue
18 Private Banks closed			£217,146
11	ditto	become bankrupt	175,778
10	ditto	issue Bank of England notes	157,612
8 Joint Stock Banks dissolved			162,087
			£712,623

Looking at this result in twelve years after the passing of the Act, we will go further than Mr. Ayres, and say that *it is the interest* of the Bank of England to annihilate every bank of issue but itself in the kingdom, and that *it has the power in its hands to effect it.* Let the House of Commons look to this when the question of the Charter comes before it. We should like to hear an able financier show what would have been the consequences throughout the country, in a crisis like that of the 11th of November last, with no local notes in circulation, and the Bank of England compelled by its Charter to refuse an extension of its issues. We suspect the whole industrial energy of the country would have collapsed,—*died of inanition,* and its progress been thrown back for many years. As it is, houses of the first character for honour and respectability of dealing have been compelled to succumb, for no other cause than the operation of the Bank Charter Act, compelling the Bank to contract its issues when the circumstances of the country required a judicious extension.

We must next look at the Joint-Stock Banking Law of 1844, the most striking features of which are as follows. After recapitulating the process for obtaining the Charter of incorporation, and the routine of meetings, accounts, appointment of directors, &c., the terms on which a bank may commence business, &c., the Act provides a series of regulations, intended to protect the public as well as the shareholders from frauds, but which, in the sequel, have signally failed of their purpose. One of the most injurious clauses is that which confers upon the Court of Chancery a separate power from the Court of Bankruptcy, in case of a bank failure. The evils of this separate jurisdiction were strikingly exemplified in the case of the Royal British Bank, in which the squabbles between these two Courts for the power to have the handling of the rich legal booty that would accrue from the working of the insolvency, were most unseemly. We should like to know what the contest between these two rival blood-suckers cost the unfortunate creditors of the bank; for, of course, all the expenses were paid out of the estate: a notable illustration of the epigram,—

We lawyers, though so keen,
Like shears, ne'er cut ourselves, but what's between.

At the time of the passing of the Bank Charter Act in 1844, the amount of bank-notes issued by private and joint-stock banks, as authorized by the Act, was as follows:—

By 203 Private Banks	£5,153,407
” 72 Joint Stock Banks	3,495,446
Total, England and Wales	£8,648,853
Decrease by Private Banks £655,598	
Ditto Joint-Stock Banks 192,089	847,687
Present circulation	£7,801,166

The amount of notes of the Bank of England in circulation *against gold,* after the passing of the Act, was £15,400,000. On the 11th of November, 1857, it was only £7,170,508, making a decrease of £8,229,492. Add this to the decrease in the circulation of country bank-notes, and we find the amount to be:—

Country Notes, less	£847,687
Bank of England ditto, ditto	8,229,492
Total decrease	£9,077,179

Thus, whilst the foreign commerce of the country has doubled itself since 1844, and the internal trade has also largely increased, the circulation of paper-money is upwards of nine millions less than it was at that time; and that of private and joint-stock banks must necessarily continue to decrease under the present system, by which the Bank of England is endowed with the power of destroying any bank of issue, in order to replace its notes by its own,—the only way in which, according to the Charter Act, it can extend its issues beyond the prescribed limits.

We shall next consider the condition of the metallic currency, as having exercised a powerful influence in producing the late panic, both here and in America.

First, with regard to the United States. The discoveries of the gold-fields of California produced great excitement in the States of the Union; and under the impression that this sudden acquisition of wealth was about to cover the whole nation with an unebbing tide of prosperity, speculation was indulged upon the largest scale. In this category railways occupy the most prominent place, as having absorbed the largest amount of capital. It is estimated that the sum expended in these works up to the end of 1856 amounted, in round numbers, to £160,000,000 sterling, of which £16,500,000 have been subscribed by foreigners, the rest being raised in the States. It being impossible for the iron-masters of that country to furnish the rails and machinery, either *in time,* or at a rate of cost as low as those of England, most of the railway iron, as well as the machinery, was purchased or contracted for here. The United States, not having articles of export to exchange for it, were compelled to pay in specie or bullion. The consequence has been, that in six years from 1851 inclusive, the exports of the precious metals exceeded the imports by 213,115,399 dollars, or £42,623,080 sterling. This drain of specie had reduced the proportion held by the 1,273 banks of the Union to the ratio of 1 specie to $3\frac{1}{3}$ paper on the 1st of January, 1856; and this disproportion has largely increased since that period, and is now, we believe, as 5 of paper to 1 of specie; so that the Californian gold, which was to have enriched the States, and rendered them independent of foreigners, has been sent out of the country to pay for materials of undertakings, many of which are at present nearly useless, being driven into districts where there is no population to support a traffic, either in produce or passengers; whilst they involve the country in heavy expenses for their maintenance and management, without any adequate return.

We have no occasion to seek for other causes of the severe crisis under which the United States have been suffering. The whole circulation of the country has consisted of paper, which, whilst the credit of the banks by which it was issued remained unshaken, created no alarm. But the failure of one or two led to an exposure of the inadequacy of the means, to meet their liabilities *in cash,* of all the banks. A general run upon them ensued, in consequence of which the whole monetary system collapsed, producing the convulsion we have seen. Specie was demanded in every quarter, but none was to be had. Securities and property of all kinds fell to half their value; produce in the west could not be moved for want of the means for paying the transit expenses; all were sellers, but none could purchase; and at one period wheat was offered at Chicago at 1*s.* per bushel, but could not be disposed of. At New York, 4,000 failures took place; and it seemed as if the whole commerce of the place would become bankrupt. In this exigency, the whole of the banks came to a resolution to suspend cash payments; from which time, as a letter we received states, "the solvent merchants and traders began to breathe more freely." Confidence is gradually being restored, and the cloud which hung over the trading community of the States is passing away. But it will require years for the commerce of the country, notwithstanding its wonderful elasticity, to recover entirely the ground it has lost, and to reinstate it in the same degree of prosperity it previously enjoyed.

The shock of the American panic was necessarily felt severely in the United Kingdom, and was aggravated by the extraordinary drain of gold, to supply the continental nations, especially France. The non-receipt of the usual remittances from the United States led to increased demands on the Bank of

England, as well as private banks, for discounts, which were met by the former with a rise in the rate of interest, gradually increased, until it reached the unprecedented charge of 10 per cent.; and many of the first houses in the American trade, having their paper refused by the discount houses, were obliged to succumb. In the meanwhile, the drain of gold and silver—the latter chiefly for the East—from the Bank continued, as we have seen, and reached its maximum on the 18th of November. This extraordinary efflux of the precious metals demands more than this passing notice, connected as it is with the high rate of interest, the extreme caution exercised by the Bank of England, and the consequent embarrassment in the commerce of the country.

The railway panic of 1847 was of short duration. Enormous as were the sums that had been expended in a short space of time, the money had not left the country, being only transferred from one hand or class to another, and that only *pro tempore.* The openings for trade and commerce with the United States, California, and subsequently Australia, gave an impetus to every industrial interest, particularly that of railways, which in 1850 began to recover from the depression under which the panic had placed them. In the meantime, the gold from California found its way to our shores; the exchanges turned in our favour; and in 1852, as we have seen, the amount of bullion and specie at the Bank of England was £22,000,000, and the rate of interest $1\frac{1}{2}$ to $1\frac{3}{4}$ *per cent.* The gold-fields of Australia also now began to pour forth their stores of the precious metal, and everything looked promising for the financial condition of the country. Trade and commerce flourished to an unprecedented extent; almost every quarter's account from the Board of Trade exhibiting an increase upon the corresponding one of the preceding year.

Events, however, had transpired in France which materially changed the condition of the accounts of the Bank of England, and at last led to the monetary crisis which has just passed over the country. In 1851, the coup-d' état of Louis Napoleon placed him ultimately on the imperial throne of his uncle; and that sagacious prince saw at once that his interest and safety were bound up with that of the industrial classes of France. With this conviction, he originated a series of financial operations, which, whatever may be the opinions entertained by men acquainted with the subject, are calculated, so long as they continue, to give impetus and energy to all industrial employments. Amongst these, the most important are the *Société Générale du Crédit Mobilier,* for making advances upon moveable and transferable securities; and the *Crédit Foncier de France,* whose object is to advance money on mortgages of land, &c., repayable by means of annuities, extending over a period of fifty years, and consisting of the common interest, with the addition of an annual payment by way of sinking fund, which shall extinguish the debt in a period according to its amount. To these payments are added the expenses of the investment. We cannot go further into the details of these institutions, which, whilst they exist, are certainly calculated, if properly managed, to promote the interests both of the public and the shareholders. The *Crédit Mobilier* has been extraordinarily successful hitherto, having in 1855 paid the shareholders a dividend of 40 per cent. upon the capital, and in 1856, of 23 per cent. The *Credit Foncier,* the first three years of its existence, paid the more humble dividend of 7 per cent. per annum.

The war with Russia, in which Napoleon found himself involved almost at the instant at which he ascended the imperial throne, created, in conjunction with the financial movements we have referred to, and others, heavy calls upon the Bank of France for specie. Fortunately for the government of that country the supplies of gold obtained by the recent discoveries in California and Australia began at the very moment to pour into the United Kingdom and Europe, to minister to its wants. France has been for five years the chief purchaser of gold in the British and American markets. Since 1845 there has been coined in France £124,639,401 sterling, namely, £90,186,835 in gold, and £34,482,346 in silver. The chief portion of these amounts were purchased in England on account of the Bank of France, at a considerable premium[5] on the Mint price of £3. 17*s*. 9*d*. per oz. During the same period there has been coined in England only the sum of £65,507,379, namely, £62,117,784 in gold, and £3,389,595 in silver. The aggregate amounts in the two countries make up the sum of £190,146,780 sterling in eleven years, or an average of £17,286,071 per year.

When to these heavy drains upon the precious metals in England are added those for other nations of Europe, and to the East, (the latter chiefly in silver,)[6] we can be at no loss to account for the late decrease in the stock of bullion at the Bank. The amount coined in the United Kingdom was required by the large increase in the internal trade; and a full proportion of it is kept in active circulation, and is therefore lost to the Bank as to any permanent addition to its stock of specie. The Bank has, in fact, no more power to retain or reject the precious metals under the present system, than a sieve has to retain water; for, were it otherwise, the late rate of interest would have enabled it to do so. And

5. This was 1½ per cent. In October, 1855, the bullion in the Bank of France having fallen to less than ten millions sterling, that establishment resorted to a singular expedient to increase it artificially. It employed agents to purchase in the continental cities bills of *short date* drawn upon London, to send those bills for collection in London, and to instruct their correspondents to remit the proceeds *in gold coin or bullion* to Paris. It then bought up large parcels of bills of *long date* on London, presented them for discount at the Bank of England, or in Lombard Street, and conveyed the proceeds, *in bullion,* to Paris. This notable expedient to obtain a transient relief cost the Bank of France in fifteen months £410,000 sterling, the gold thus purchased amounting to £27,360,000, for which the premium paid was 1½ per cent.—*Tooke,* vol. vi., p. 85.
6. The quantity shipped to the East (China and India) in the six years, 1851–56, amounted to £41,500,000 sterling, namely, gold £5,000,000, and silver £36,500,000.

when specie continues to be in demand on the Continent, it is evident that no expense will be spared to procure it, and that the Australian and Californian supplies, however large, will still but touch our shores as a resting-place on their way to the continental nations.

We have thus endeavoured, very imperfectly, but as fully as time and space would admit, to point out what we consider to be the chief causes in producing those monetary convulsions which, since 1844, have produced so much disaster and distress in the commercial and trading communities, by deranging the currency, and reducing its amount at those periods when it most required expansion. Upon a review of all the facts we have stated, and all the collateral ones contained in Mr. Ayres's excellent and instructive work, but which we have been compelled in a great measure to pass by, we have drawn the following conclusions:—

1. That the Bank Charter Act of 1844–5 has signally failed of its intended purpose, namely, that of keeping steady the currency of the country; the government being compelled for that very purpose, on two occasions in ten years, to suspend the Charter Act, at periods, too, when, if ever, it ought to have displayed its utility.
2. That the separation of the two departments of issue and deposit is a commercial absurdity, anomalous in principle, and fatal, if carried out with rigour, to the interests both of the Bank of England and the public.
3. That the late panic, although precipitated by the American crisis, must have occurred at no remote period, owing to the aforesaid separation of the departments; by which all the responsibility of the Bank is thrown upon the deposit, whilst the means of meeting it are accumulated in the issue department, where it is not wanted.
4. That the three-fold interests of the proprietary of the Bank are inimical to the welfare of the community, because their private interests will naturally always be preferred to those of the public, whenever they are opposed to each other.
5. That the power bestowed upon the Bank by the Charter of extinguishing all other banks of issue, and which appears to have been the design of the legislature, or the promoters of the Act, is a monstrous injustice, incompatible with the British constitution, and tending to raise up the greatest and most injurious monopoly to which the country has ever been subjected; calculated to fetter and distress commerce by centralizing the circulating medium at one source of issue; the monopolists having private interests incompatible with those of the public, whilst they possess the power, by contracting their issues, to spread ruin and distress in every department of society.
6. That, taking all the circumstances into account, it becomes a question, now that the commerce of the United Kingdom, and consequently its financial

and monetary system, have so vastly increased in magnitude, and are so in-interwoven, by the operation of the free-trade principle, with those of the entire civilized world, whether it is consistent with justice or sound policy to intrust the management of the currency any longer to a public company possessing individually separate private interests, frequently interfering with those of the community at large; whether the system has not become too unwieldy by its magnitude for such a company; and whether, finally, a Chartered Bank, *in any* form, be not inconsistent with the new order of things, in which every other department of commerce is thrown open to the public.

We conclude our notice, which we have rendered a running commentary on the facts adduced by Mr. Ayres, with the following quotation from the work:—

In the facts which have been given of the progress of the Bank of England through a long series of years, there are ample materials for forming a comprehensive view of the monetary system of England, as it once was, and as it remains at present. It cannot be doubted that on the first establishment of the Bank of England, it was almost a necessity of the State, owing to the discredit which then existed, through the conduct of the Stuarts. And such was the position of the government of that day, that it was only by appealing to corporate bodies, holding out to them some peculiar privileges, that public credit could be restored. So far, therefore, the institution of the Bank became of national advantage, and the centre of the system around which all other banks revolved. In the course of the Bank's career, it had to encounter great difficulties, in the midst of which it has stood forward with great courage to defend the State, and maintain public credit. Time and circumstances have forced it to resign many of its privileges, which, however desirable in former days, could not now be permitted to exist. Further improvements still remain to be made; and like other institutions professing to be of public utility, it must submit to the reforms which conduce to the public welfare. The monetary system of this country is upon its trial. In the United Kingdom there is a great mixture of laws and regulations confounding and contradicting each other, all of which demand the most serious consideration of the country and the legislature. It is not intended in this publication to lay down any particular system, but to place before the reader such facts as will enable him to form correct opinions upon the subject; for it must be evident to those who have examined it in all its bearings, that any alteration, to be nationally beneficial, must embrace *the whole system* of the United Kingdom, and have no foundation but the public good.

We should not be doing justice to our author, if we omitted to state, that his work embraces a review of the financial routine of the whole civilized world, and consequently contains information of the first importance to the merchant as well as the statesman. And it is not the less entitled to the attention of *all parties,* that he has adroitly managed to merge his own private sentiments, whatever they may be, in the general question, so as to make it difficult to say, whether he was educated in the school of "one Tyrannus," the protectionist, or was brought up at the feet of "Gamaliel," the free-trader.

The rapid accumulation of bullion in the coffers of the Bank, and the equally rapid fall in the rate of interest from ten to two and a half per cent. in about three months, is a striking illustration of the working of the Bank Charter Act. In the meanwhile the heavy list of bankruptcies every three days proclaims the deadness of trade and commerce, and the utter exhaustion to which the late panic has reduced the industrial interests of the country. We shall look with interest and curiosity for the Report of the Committee appointed, during the short Session before Christmas, to renew the inquiry into the "Currency Question"; but we do not anticipate any alteration in the system, which is too convenient to the government, and too profitable to the Bank, to be either abandoned, or extensively modified, so as to meet the requirements of commerce.

A. J. WILSON

THE POSITION OF ENGLISH JOINT-STOCK BANKS[1]

FEW things are at present more striking than the apparent extreme prosperity of the joint-stock banks of this country. The complaints as to dulness of trade have been universal now for at least three years. You can hardly pick up a trade circular or a chairman's speech at some half-yearly company meeting without finding in it allusions to the depressed conditions of our national industries and the unsatisfactory character of the profits. In the iron and coal trades particularly, things have gone from bad to worse. Some of the largest smelting

A. J. Wilson, "The Position of English Joint-Stock Banks." *Fortnightly Review* 30 (August 1878): 284–302.

1. Since the above was written the London banks have for the most part published their mid-yearly balance-sheets, but they in no way affect the reasoning of this article. In almost all instances we find the amount of money invested in bills smaller than it was, and at the same time the profits are apparently larger. Deposits also in many cases continue to decrease, so that a certain wasting away in the available resources of the banking community is still more or less visible. Alongside this we must place the probability that more money may soon be wanted to sustain a new trade inflation. At present the stock markets alone have responded to the half-simulated and superficial return of political confidence. There has been a great rise in many descriptions of stocks, and that has already influenced the current value of money; but more is needed to bring the banks face to face with their position, and when trade speculation comes to be added to stock-jobbing "rigs," a banking crisis of the severest type is extremely likely to supervene.

works in the country have ceased to produce, and hundreds of smaller concerns either work along in great distress or disappear altogether, leaving little but debts to indicate that they ever existed. Prices in all departments of business almost have been falling continuously for many months, and therefore, although the bulk of the trade done may have been in some cases nearly as large as ever, it has often been trade conducted at a loss. There is, in short, undeniable evidences of strain everywhere, and business has in consequence been contracted wherever possible within the narrowest limits. We can hardly put our finger upon an industry of any importance the country through, and say,—this branch of trade at least is good; unless we consider the manufacture of instruments of destruction worthy of being taken into account. Sheffield languishes for lack of demands for its cutlery; Bradford is oppressed with an excess of manufacturing power for the "stuffs" which have at present no free market; Manchester warehouses are groaning beneath the weight of unsold and at present unsaleable cotton goods; the sugar industry has almost departed from Bristol; and at nearly all centres of raw silk manufacture stocks accumulate and prices sink. In the Black Country the stagnation is nearly universal; and even Birmingham hardware is not bought so freely as in former years. Everywhere almost there are at home signs of languishing, of the same reaction from over-production, and these are frequently aggravated by indications of increased foreign competition.

Such a state of things, one would naturally expect, must tell with instant force upon the position of our joint-stock banks. In their hands, for the most part, the trade of the country finds the means by which purchase and sale become possible. They have gathered the larger share of the surplus money possessed by the community into their hands, and have so developed the facilities for lending, for making and receiving payments, that the bulk of our trade hinges on them. We should, therefore, naturally suppose that if trade is languishing they would languish, and that only when it was active and yielding good profits would they prosper.

The case is, to all appearance, as near as may be just the reverse. If we except the London Joint-Stock Banks, to whose position further reference shall be made presently, the situation seems most prosperous. There is no diminution in dividends paid; on the contrary, they are higher in some instances than they were before 1873—the year when our trade prosperity may be said to have culminated. Reserves increase, and deposits appear to flow in until one wonders what can be meant by complaints about bad trade, declining profits, and industrial distress. So steady is the apparent growth of prosperity on the part of the country joint-stock banks in particular, that they frequently find it necessary to call up more capital in order to meet the demands of an extended business, and large dividends are paid on this capital with no difficulty whatever. Thus we learn from the *Banker's Magazine* for February last, that in the two years, 1876 and 1877, the net increase in the capital of the joint-stock banks of the country was over £4,000,000, including the premiums, in some cases very high, charged on the new issues of shares and placed to reserve funds, and the undivided profits also placed to reserve. This, to be sure, appears to include the Scotch and Irish banks, with which we are not now dealing; but the additions to capital made by them are small, and the bulk of the increased capital is to be credited to the joint-stock banks in England, mostly to those in the provinces. Of course all this increase does not represent money on which dividend is nominally paid, the premium being added to the reserve, on which there is no obligation to pay. But it may be considered that a full half of it does, and yet, as I have said, dividends do not fall off, except in a few isolated instances. It is a common enough event to find 20 and 22 per cent. per annum distributed on the paid-up capital, and anything under 10 per cent. is considered a very indifferent return.

I shall give a few averages for the last two years only in order to make this point evident, dividing the banks into (1) London banks proper; (2) London banks with provincial branches; (3) banks in provincial cities; and (4) banks having an important part of their business in agricultural districts. There are in the first category eight banks[2] in all, excluding the "Metropolitan," which does not pay a dividend on the whole of its capital, and is, in other respects, difficult to classify, and the average dividend paid to the share-holders of these eight banks during the last two years has been $10\frac{1}{8}$ per cent. per annum. This is a lower average than was customary just before the Collie frauds of 1875, the same eight banks having distributed in the years 1873 and 1874 an average dividend of fully $13\frac{1}{4}$ per cent. per annum, but it is none the less a remarkable yield.

In the second category we have five banks, excluding the Amalgamated Hampshire and North Wilts Bank, which has only recently come to London, and the Scotch and Irish banks with city offices. These five banks—the Consolidated, whose chief business is in Manchester, the London and County, the National Provincial, the London and Provincial, and the London and South Western—paid an average dividend of almost $13\frac{1}{2}$ per cent. per annum in the two years 1875 and 1876, which is much higher than the average of the London banks proper for the same period, and shows but little diminution upon the yield of the two years 1873 and 1874, which was only 14 per cent. per annum.

The third class of banks is a large one, and in some cases difficult to separate from the more distinctly rural banks. I have, however, taken thirty-one banks whose centres of business are in Birmingham, Liverpool, Manchester,

---

2. The names of these eight banks will be found at the head of an abstract of their accounts further on.

Leeds, Sheffield, Bradford, Halifax, and such like trading and manufacturing districts, and, avoiding those which have a considerable number of rural branches, have endeavoured to strike an average which shall tolerably closely represent the earnings of provincial city banks in the past two years. This average I find to be about 14 per cent. per annum; the dividends ranging from a mere 5 per cent., as in the case of the Nottingham Joint-Stock Bank, to the 30 per cent. paid by the Lancaster Bank. Considering the variety of conditions under which these banks carry on business, this average is remarkable, apart altogether from the question whether trade is dull or active. It shows that these banks, like the London banks with provincial branches, have large sources of revenue, and the condition of banking in provincial towns would appear at first sight to be much more favourable than in the City of London itself. No doubt this high dividend is in many instances paid on a relatively smaller paid-up capital than some of the London banks possess; but the country banks are in numerous instances facing increased disadvantages in this respect compared with those of London, inasmuch as they are the banks which we find continually augmenting their paid-up capital. They are doing this, it would seem, with impunity in the meantime, and in only a few instances, are the dividends paid for the last two years lower than those paid for the previous two years. Where this does occur, too, it is in the case of banks which have not added to their capital. Here also we have, therefore, an appearance of prosperity which is remarkable, explain it how we may.

But this prosperity is, if possible, more striking still with the banks I have selected as rural banks, that is, which do a large business in purely agricultural districts. Of these I have picked out twenty-nine, taking them as in the previous list, alphabetically from the list given in the *Investor's Monthly Manual,* and omitting only one or two very small banks, about whose rural connection I am doubtful. These twenty-nine banks have yielded an average dividend for the last two years whose figures have been published, of about 16 per cent. per annum. Some of them have not, up to the time of this writing, announced their dividend for the past year, so that the average does not compare strictly on all fours with the others. But here also the indications of falling dividends are few, and almost counterbalanced by instances in which the payment has been higher than in previous years. Such banks as the Yorkshire, the Wilts and Dorset, the Hampshire and North Wilts, the North and South Wales, and the Bury banks, pay steady dividends of from 17 to 25 per cent. with the greatest regularity and ease in the world; and, as a result, we have a general average for banks which we may consider at least partially rural, higher than for either banks in manufacturing districts or in London.

These figures are altogether startling, unless we could prove that the banks have taken advantage of the uncertainties of the trading community to exact higher terms for the money they lend. The superficial facts appear, however, to prove just the contrary, for the nominal value of money or the price of credit has seldom been so low as it has been in this country, and on every great money market in the world, since 1875. When bill brokers are thankful to discount good paper at the rate of ¾ per cent. per annum, as they have more than once been within the past three years, we can hardly say off-hand, that banking profits have been made out of dearer credit. What makes the dividend averages we have given still more remarkable is the curious increased ratio which they bear to the degree of prosperity enjoyed by the regions within scope of their operations. Thus, while the London banks pay a comparatively low average dividend, in spite of the greater scope for business which they enjoy even in dull times, the banks with agricultural connections pay the highest rate of all. Now agriculture has been an unprofitable occupation for years past in this country. We have had at least two bad harvests in succession; rents are nearly everywhere so unreasonably high, that in many instances landowners have been driven to relieve their tenants by making large reductions, and have frequently had farms left on their hands, because in times so bad no tenant would face the rent responsibility. Foreign competition in the supply of food of all kinds has at the same time been on the increase, and the farmers' old compensation for a bad year—high prices—can no longer be secured. He has thus nothing to relieve him from the full pressure of landlord monopoly and bad times. Yet, in spite of all this, the rural banks pay most flourishing dividends. How is all this to be accounted for?

To answer this question thoroughly, I should have to institute an examination of some length into the principles now supposed to govern English banking. In my view, few subjects are at present of more vital interest to the community, but I do not propose to enter at any length into such a discussion now. My object is rather to lay bare the immediate and visible causes of the apparent prosperity of our joint-stock banks than to examine the principles of banking in the abstract, and I shall therefore rest content with a reference to one or two general considerations which serve to show that, within certain limits, dull trade is, fairly enough, not without its compensations to the banker. This I shall do chiefly with a view to bring into greater relief the dangerous practices with which banks have so often eked out those compensations in times like the present.

And first of all it must be remembered that apart from the fact that nearly all banks earn interest on more money than the amount of their paid-up capital, dear or cheap money makes very little difference to the amount of profits they can get on a certain more or less important portion of their balances. Those banks whose "deposits" are large, can count on merely a margin between what they pay for the use of these deposits and what they can earn by them, whether the value of money be high or low. When money is dear, the depositors ask a larger interest on their balances, and when it is cheap they must perforce accept a lower. The banks get merely the difference. Hence, if they can employ the money at all, their profits may be almost as much on this class of balance when the Bank of England value of money is low as when it is high. Of course the floating balances on which no interest is paid will not yield so much, and in that respect the banks of large current account resources will stand at a disadvantage, a fact which no doubt helps to explain the lower earning power of the London banks in recent years. These also suffer severely from another and more permanent cause, inasmuch as they are subjected to much greater competition now than in former years by the large number of colonial, foreign, and Scotch banks whose offices in the City draw away from the City banks proper much business and money.

Another general consideration which relates rather more to country banks than to metropolitan is this: the ruling monetary rate quoted in the bill market or by the Bank of England, is to a considerable extent a fiction, because it is, for one thing, based upon a false standard of value. Custom has sanctified the usage which compels all banks to follow the Bank of England in its movement of the "rate for money." There is no real ground for this custom, and it does frequently as much harm as good, because the Bank of England is often moved by causes peculiar to itself, whether in raising or lowering this rate. The market rate is thus sometimes above and often below that of the Bank of England, and that bank is frequently compelled to place itself "out of the market" by a high rate, merely that it may protect the national store or reserve of bullion. But be this practice wise or the reverse, we should never forget that it is a practice which roughly determines the value of money for first-class merchants or bankers' bills alone. It does not establish, and only in a remote degree influences, the rate charged throughout the provinces for second-class bills or for advances with or without security. Even in London there is an enormous mass of small bill discounting done at 5 or 6 per cent. when the nominal Bank of England rate may be only 2 per cent., and the open market rate for the best paper barely half as much. This is not usurious discounting either, but the ordinary fate of fair trade bills, drawn probably by City merchants on the small retailers. In this class of business a time of so-called "cheap money" is consequently a time of high profits, for the banker is paying little for his deposits and getting much for their use, at the same time that the presence of dull trade is perhaps driving more of this kind of bills into the market. Throughout the provinces, where the bills circulating are on the average smaller than in London, this fixity of discount rate is of course much more customary, and the natural inference would be that in a time of dull trade banks could make a very good profit, provided always that they found steady employment for all their money. It is true, no doubt, that joint-stock banks in the country do not reap the full advantage of the difference between what they earn on money in times like these and what they pay for it, because they have probably always to pay rather more for their deposits than London bankers now do. The Bank of England rate is more a fiction with them at all times than it is in London, and their standard for interest payment on deposits is rather the yield on consols than "bank" rate. If they cannot allow some 3 per cent. on the money intrusted to them, their customers place it in the funds, so they are probably compelled in the dullest of times to pay about so much for the use of money. This is, however, only a partial drawback, as they are, on the other hand, able to command a higher price for their credits and discountings, and as these may tend to increase in bad times, their earnings are to a certain extent also legitimately higher.

These general observations might be assumed to have almost settled the point, did we not know that banking nowadays means much more than a mere discounting of bills. This is indeed but a small branch of the business of many banks, and in order to obtain some just conception of the position into which a period of dull business has brought them, I must now ask the reader's indulgence while I plunge into one or two statements of principles and figures. I shall try not to overload my pages with the latter, but a few are absolutely necessary.

Bankers nowadays are subjected to enormous temptations to travel beyond the line of their safe legitimate business, which may be briefly described as the business of borrowing for short periods on the security of their capital, in order to lend again for short periods upon mercantile securities at a profit. Their chief resources should thus be always *floating*. A banker has no business, for example, to lend money on the mortgage of a house which may not be realisable should necessity arise for calling in his money, and though less questionable, perhaps, the habit of lending on stocks and shares, may also turn out to be an extremely dangerous one. But stocks and shares and house property of all descriptions have multiplied so fast in recent years that the temptation to the banker to take these as "security" for loans made with his customers' money has proved irresistible. He lends heavily on such in brisk times, helps to "float" loans, backs adventures in railways, mining, house-building, and navigation on all hands, and in innumerable ways steps aside from his true position as mere go-between and auxiliary in ordinary commercial transactions, while in times of bad trade the temptation to make profit by such business is not to be resisted.

It may be justly said that a bank which allows itself to be drawn largely into speculations of any kind, involving great difficulty in the sudden realisation of its money, is a bank which, if it does not ultimately fail altogether, must suffer grievous loss. It is wise to invest guarantee funds in approved home securities, and it may be at times prudent to place a portion of the paid-up capital in the same position, but it is never safe for a bank to put any money belonging to customers into any security which is not continually as it were realising itself, a security where the risks of loss are small, and comparatively speaking, immediate. This I believe to be the one cardinal principle of sound banking, and now let us examine the present position of English joint-stock banks in relation thereto.

The task is less easy than it might seem, owing to the careless or indifferent fashion in which all joint-stock banks draw up their balance sheets. I have found the greatest difficulty in collecting the facts indicated in the statements of the various categories of banks whose figures I have examined, simply because these figures are often for practical purposes of no use at all. What shall be said, for example, of the practice which heaps all the items of a bank balance sheet—cash, securities, advances, bills, property, and overdrawn accounts, into a lump sum! Nobody can tell in the least how such an institution stands, yet this is the common practice with many provincial joint-stock banks. And where some details are given, they are rarely or ever minute enough to enable one to tell even approximately what the true position of an institution may be. "Cash in hand" and "cash lent at call or notice," are, for example, habitually lumped together, although the latter involves a risk of loss while the former does not; bills, advances, and over-drafts are also continually to be found swelling the same total, and country banks never, so far as I can discover, indicate that portion of their liabilities, which represents the mere contra of unsecured advances on current accounts; nor is there a bank within the United Kingdom which separates its liability on deposits bearing interest from the mere credit balances on current accounts, although the former is a liability of a kind quite distinct from the latter. A great reform is needed in this respect, but we shall probably have to wait for it till after the next collapse of banking credit in this country. Then with our usual zealous endeavour to redress wrongs and retrieve blunders, we will set vigorously to work to devise a perfect credit-checking machine when it is too late. The Government now looks after insurance companies, and compels them to publish returns which have at least the advantage of indicating whether an office is extravagant or the reverse. Why should it not compel all joint-stock banks to publish balance sheets which should at least enable the public to follow the changes which are continually taking place in the position of their accounts, and to see the character of their risks?

I shall leave that question to answer itself, and proceed to make the best of such figures as I have been able to procure, dealing first with those of the London banks. What strikes one most forcibly at first sight about these is the large decrease which has taken place in both their assets and liabilities between the end of 1873 and the end of 1877, the period which I have throughout chosen for comparison. I subjoin a table which will make this clear.

266 BANKS AND BANKING

London Banks Proper—Alliance, Central, City, Imperial, Joint-Stock, Westminster, Merchants' Metropolitan, and Union—Increases or Decreases in Their Working Resources and Liabilities

Assets

Cash in hand and at call	—	£620,849	net	Smaller banks, except City and Westminster, show increase.
Discounts and advances	—	10,395,314	net	Smaller banks again show increase.
Securities	—	186,123		
		£11,202,276		net decrease in the assets.

Capital and Reserves

Capital	+ £5,002	in Metropolitan alone.
Reserves	+ £16,754	Heavy decrease in London and Westminster, small in Union, the rest all increases.

Liabilities to the Public

Deposits	—	£9,029,944	Again increase in the smaller banks.
Acceptances	—	£2,463,685	Only Alliance and Metropolitan show increase; Joint-Stock and Central do not give their acceptances separately, but it is fair to assume that there has been a considerable falling off.
		£11,493,629	total decrease in the liabilities

These banks, it will be seen, have lost no less than £9,000,000 of their deposit in four years, and there has been a falling off of upwards of £10,000,000 in their discounts and advances. This, at first sight, seems a reduction out of proportion to the falling off in the dividends, inasmuch as it is equal to about a tenth of their total resources in deposits and acceptances; but to some extent, no doubt, the loss of deposits was a relief. The banks are to that extent delivered from the burden of money which they could not profitably use, and for much of which they had to pay interest. Their own action has, indeed, to some degree caused this reduction in their balance-sheet totals; for since they ceased to give interest on current account balances, the tendency of these balances has been to grow narrower. This, however, is not the chief cause of the change, much being due to the withdrawal of money by country banks.

And what of the actual diminution in the business done or indicated by the decrease of £10,000,000 in their discounts and advances? The figures do not give details enough to enable us to trace what this reduction consists in, but there is strong reason for believing that a paucity of trade bills and the keen competition already mentioned are the main causes. It is noticeable that the item "acceptances" is less by about two millions and a half, and that reduction should represent a decrease in pure mercantile business. Naturally, moreover, the more provident banks would curtail their advances on stocks, dock warrants, and other securities, in proportion as they lost their deposits, whether by their own free will, by the competition of other banks, or by the steady withdrawal of resources by the provincial banks, for whom the London banks act as agents. This last cause of reduction in the working resources of the London banks has been a most constant and powerful one, as we shall see when we come to examine the position of provincial banks.

On the whole, it may be safely concluded that the reduction in the available resources of the London banks, where they have not been caused by losses pure and simple, like the losses of the London and Westminster Bank in the Collie and other frauds, has not been an unmixed evil so far as their profits are concerned. Their stability ought certainly to be greater now than it was before. Unwieldy masses of capital are most dangerous possessions in times of mercantile depression. Could we then be sure that these banks have no hidden troubles, no safes full of bad or doubtful securities, no dangerously-extended credits, or deep involvements with mercantile firms whose trade is but a more or less frantic endeavour to retrieve the losses of the past, we should say their position is fairly sound and good. But these are just the points upon which no man can be sure until it has been seen how the banks pass through the first ordeal of very dear credit which shall succeed the depression of the past few years.

I must now ask the reader to look at the following table, giving an analysis of four London banks with provincial branches, similar to that given of the London Banks alone. The figures of the National Provincial, now probably the largest bank in the kingdom, were, when this was written, only available up to the 31st December, 1877; I shall therefore deal with them separately:—

Comparative Statistics of London Banks with Provincial Branches (Four Banks, Consolidated, London and County, London and Provincial, London and South-Western)

Assets			
Cash	+	£1,071,068	All show increases.
Advances	+	603,874	London and County alone decrease.
Securities	+	1,552,256	All increases.
		£3,227,198	net increase in assets.

Capital and Reserve

Capital	+	£386,920	Consolidated no change.
Rest	+	288,921	All increases, chiefly premiums on new shares.
		£675,811	

Liabilities to Public

Deposits	+	£6,531,953	All increases.
Acceptances	–	1,968,744	The London and Provincial does not state acceptances separately.
		£1,563,209	net increase in liabilities.

These figures are remarkably in contrast to those of the London banks proper. The resources of these banks are greater instead of less, and they would seem to have considerable difficulty in finding use for the money intrusted to them. Their cash on hand and lent at call has increased by over £1,000,000 in the four years, and it is clear that they find great difficulty in employing their money in discount, for the principal increase in their assets is under the heading "securities," and their acceptances are very much reduced. Amongst them, these four banks now hold no less than £3,800,000 worth of stock, independently of the amounts pawned to them by customers as security for advances and of which no indication is given. The London and County is driven most extensively to find this kind of employment for its money and has at the present time some £800,000, more than its capital and reserve together, locked up in investments. But the figures of the National Provincial Bank of England are the most striking of all. This bank has now deposits amounting to upwards of £26,000,000, and its money invested in stocks, probably exceeds £8,000,000 at the present date by a good round sum. At the date of the 1877 balance sheet the total investments was nearly £7,500,000, and this is how that balance sheet compares with 1873, or three years before.

The National Provincial Bank of England. Comparative Figures of the Balance-Sheet, 1873–1876

Assets

Cash . . . .+	£553,141
Discount and advance . . . .+	2,841,982
Securities . . . .+	2,204,290
Total increase	£5,599,413

Capital and Reserve

Capital . . . .+	£225,047
Rest . . . .+	300,000
Total increase	£525,047

Liabilities to the Public

Deposits . . . .+		£5,026,101
Acceptances . . . .+		153,036
	Total increase	£5,179,137

Here again we see that the increase in the resources of this bank has driven it more and more to seek a profitable use for its money in investments in stocks. Nearly half the increase in its deposits has gone in that direction, and thus, were we able to say what proportion of the £17,000,000 odd credited by it to "discounts and advances," was mercantile bills, what advances on various kinds of securities and pawned stock, we should probably see still more clearly how the great volume of business which this bank does is sustained and profitable. Although the acceptances of the bank are rather more, the increase by no means leads to the inference that mere mercantile business is flourishing in the provinces though stagnant in London. At the most we can only infer that this bank has succeeded in drawing to itself a better share of such good banking business as is to be had.

If the reader will bear the infliction of a few more figures relating to the provincial banks alone, we shall see evidence in plenty that mercantile bills of all kinds are not on the increase. In this case the balance sheets published vary from a mere statement of profits to details regarding cash, discounts, advances, &c., such as London banks do not give. The diversity compels me therefore to dispense with tables of figures, for I am unable to get a broad enough basis for comparison. There will be no difficulty, however, in arriving at some fair estimate of the position of the country banks by a strict analysis of the figures of isolated balance sheets taken from various parts of the country. I have worked out the results of some thirty of these and find them to be so striking as to require almost no elucidation.

Four things, for instance, stand out prominently in the comparisons of the balance sheets of the years 1873 and 1877: (1) an unprecedented increase in the "advances" to customers, upon security or on mere current account; (2) a heavy decrease in the amounts of trade bills held by the banks; (3) a decrease in the available cash; and (4) an increase in the capital and reserve. A fifth feature might be added in the shape of an increase in the stocks held, but that is almost a necessary offset to the falling off in the trade bills and the increase in the deposits, as also, perhaps, of the extension in the advances.

The augmentation in the advances of customers is often very startling. For example, Lloyd's Banking Company and the Birmingham Joint-Stock Bank have increased this item in their balance sheets by no less than £1,900,000 since 1873, and at the same time their discounts have fallen away £697,000. The position of Bradford, Manchester, and Liverpool banks appears to be the same, so far as I am able to trace their figures. And this, at all events, is certain, that wherever "advances" are stated separately, they showed unprecedented increases. It is the same too with banks that may be considered partly as agricultural. Thus I find that the Leicestershire Bank has increased its advances £459,000, its discounts being lower by £99,000, while Parr's Banking Company, in the same way, has extended its credits by £1,122,000, while its bills have fallen off £137,000. The Yorkshire and the Manchester City and County yield indications of the same kind, and it is only reasonable to conclude that in other instances, where the figures are too confused to enable me to draw a sharply defined conclusion, the larger totals are due to this identical process.

Now, while this expansion of credit has been going on for the past four years, the cash of these banks has been diminishing, and some of them have at the same time been making repeated and extensive calls upon their shareholders for more capital. Taking capital and reserves together, I find that eighteen provincial banks, out of some twenty whose balance sheets I have compared for the purpose, have increased their resources in this way by upwards of £2,500,000 in the four years. Of this total only a million is due to augmented reserves, a full half of which may safely be placed to the credit of premiums on share issues, so that we may say £2,000,000 has been added within the past four years to the paid-up capital of some eighteen banks alone out of the one hundred and twenty joint-stock banks altogether in England and Wales. It is hardly fair, perhaps, to take this as a sample of the average increase, seeing that there are a number of banks which have not resorted to this practice; but granted that only pushing banks in large business centres have thus acted, the necessity for calling up such large sums of money is surely very significant. They have found a use for the money, without doubt, because it is all employed, and they are now, it would seem, in need of more, but none the less is the circumstance peculiar and worthy of remark.

What, then, is the meaning of all these changes in the accounts of the banks? The key to it is very simple on the whole, and will be found, I believe, for the most part in an explanation of the apparent growth in the total liabilities of the banks on current and deposit accounts, for these also have swollen with few exceptions. At first sight the figures of this increase seem very satisfactory. This bank and that has increased its liability on deposits, &c., i.e. has to all appearance obtained money from its customers to the amount of a million, half million, or a few hundred thousands, more than it had four years ago. What could be more prosperous or more remarkable as a sign of the inherent soundness of the wealth of the country? The country banks, in short, appear to be in many instances overburdened with an excess of money.

Unhappily the reverse of this pleasing picture gives the true facts. The banks are not bursting with deposits, they are very poor, and their customers are very poor. So poor are the latter that they have had to come to the banks again and again for advances of cash, in order to carry on their trade—too often a losing trade—and it is these advances which swell the totals on the debit side of "deposit and current accounts." These seeming large increases in the deposits are, in other words, merely cross entries. A customer of a bank gets, say, a loan of £10,000 on "current account," i.e. is allowed to overdraw to that amount with or without security, and the bank immediately credits his account with the overdraft, which then appears in the balance-sheet of the bank as a "liability on current and deposit account." No practice could be more misleading than that which wraps up these advances in this fashion; but it is the fashion, nevertheless, and hence we see the curious phenomena of paucity of cash, increased capital, and smaller discounts accompanying an apparent swelling of the deposits and available resources of these banks.

Of course, for a time, this practice seems very profitable. In all probability the banks lending in this way do not charge less than 5 per cent. interest, and 1 per cent. commission on the amount of the overdrawn accounts. They may often charge more, and each half year the profits thus shown are added up and distributed as a big dividend to the shareholders. A further call on capital account is then made at a large premium, in order to provide further means for supporting these credits, and all goes swimmingly. But these banks are not, therefore, rich or sound; they may be just the reverse. Several of them are, indeed, at the present moment strained to the utmost to keep afloat, and it will, of course, depend on the nature of the securities they hold whether or not they can ultimately weather the storm which such financing is sure to breed.

The practice of thus dividing profits, which are in many instances nothing else than accretions to the debts due by their customers, is the exact financial counterpart of what a railway company does when it credits itself with interest on capital advanced to tributary lines, and distributes dividends upon this credit, although the lines may not have paid a penny of the money. I remember an instance of a company which did this at a time when the worked lines were not paying their working expenses, and the company came to grief in consequence. Some of the joint-stock banks appear to be coming perilously near this kind of dénouement.

I shall illustrate the situation by an example. Without giving their names, I take the balance sheets of two banks, one urban, and one with agricultural business, and combining their figures, place them before the reader:—

Abstract of the Combined Balance Sheets of Two Country Joint-Stock Banks

Assets		
	1873.	1877.
Cash	£1,623,000 .. £1,406,000 .... − £217,000
Securities	212,000 ... 1,073,000 .... + 861,000
Bills discounted	2,840,000 ... 2,114,000 .... − 726,000

Advances to customers .... 2,171,000 ... 4,747,000 .... + 2,576,000
Total .... £6,846,000 .. £9,340,000 . net increase £2,494,000

Liabilities

Deposits, credits on current account, &c £6,095,000 .. £8,112,000 .... + £2,017,000
Capital and reserves .... 625,000 ... 1,206,000 .... + 581,000
Total .... £6,720,000 .. £9,318,000 .... increase £2,598,000

I have omitted minor items such as the cost of bank offices, current profits, &c., and have given only the bare skeleton of the balance sheets. The figures are in truth sufficiently startling. Every available resource of these banks is absorbed in maintaining the swollen credits into which they have been drawn, and even were we to take the £8,000,000 of liabilities to the public at the end of last year as all real liabilities, which they are not, a large proportion being obviously the cross entry of advances representing, perhaps, the trade losses or locks-up of their customers—the position is not nearly so satisfactory now as it was four years ago. It will be seen that the apparent increase in the sum due to the public under various heads approximates to the augmentation in the advances, and that these advances together with the more extended investment in stocks absorb the increase in capital and the money set free by the diminished bill discounts, besides trenching on the cash in hand.

In judging of the soundness or otherwise of a bank, we have first of all to consider what proportion its most available assets bear to the liabilities. These assets are the cash and the trade bills discounted—the actual money, and the security most easily convertible into money immediately and without loss, or which is always in the ordinary course of business converting itself. If trade bills are good they should be equal to cash, less the price of discount, however bad the times. Now, in 1873, the cash and bills of these two banks amounted to upwards of 73 per cent. of the liabilities to the public, but at the end of last year they were equal to but about $43\frac{1}{2}$ per cent. These banks have therefore locked up their capital and available assets to an enormous extent in advances and in stock which may or may not be realisable. Now these balance sheets may, I believe, be taken as representative of a state of things which prevails all over the land, and the explanation of which is that although trade has been bad in nearly all its branches, merchants have gone on buying and selling, and the banks have hitherto sustained them under the losses incident to a narrower and a falling market. Farmers have suffered from short crops and low prices, and they in turn have been helped by their bankers in the hope that a better time will come when high profits will permit losses to be recouped. Manufacturers have kept their mills running in order to be ready for a revival of trade when it came. Miners have continued their output in the same way, and the net upshot of it all has been constantly falling prices and dwindling resources. The banks are therefore choked with pawned securities of all kinds—stocks and shares, mortgages on property, on manufactured goods, on raw produce, and are under advances without security in cases innumerable. The losses of the community from those and other causes have thus so far been buried in the banks. In all probability a large proportion of the advances which they have continued to make in this fashion will never be fully recovered, and the day may, therefore, be not far distant when many a bank shareholder may have to pay back the high profit he has enjoyed all through the years of depressed trade in calls to fill up yawning deficits which cannot otherwise be made good.

It may be said that the amount of bills and cash should not be taken as the only readily available resource possessed by the banks. Many of the securities they hold are good and realisable and ought therefore to be included in the assets which could be turned to account at a pinch. This is no doubt true in a sense, but even if we allow that the banks might be able to realise their Consols, for example, on an emergency, the position would not be materially altered. Consols form, in the majority of cases, the smallest of the securities which banks in this position hold, and it would be impossible to find a market even for Consols were many banks pressed to sell at the same time. Outside themselves there would be few buyers, and amongst those disposed to buy few could find the means without that banking assistance which, in a time of financial strain, is sure to be wanting. The truth of the matter is, as I insisted at the outset, that it is not in the long run prudent banking to lock up in mere Stock Exchange securities any portion of money which is liable at any time to be called for by its owners. That money ought to be in bills, in securities which represent commodities continually changing hands and undergoing realisation, securities which are therefore continually bringing the money back again to the banker's hands. If through dearth of these, or from any other cause, a banker buys interest-bearing stock to large amounts, or lends money on such stock pawned with him as security, he at once places himself in the position of having to face indefinite losses in the event of a forced realisation. He cannot always be sure of being able to realise when he wants to, and the more widespread the lock-up in such stocks the greater the difficulty of sale—the more certain the ultimate loss. For a banker by employing money intrusted to him in holding stocks contributes most materially to inflate the value of those stocks. The demand thus created is not natural, the outcome of private investment, but artificial, and the result is artificial prices which tell at once against the banker when his selling day comes. Especially is this the case where the price of certain kind of credit is abnormally low, for then the customers of a bank are only too ready to employ their deposit money in the same way, partly as "cover" for stocks bought and pawned with a view to secure a higher rate of interest than the banker chooses to allow. I cannot admit therefore that the position of those banks which have placed large sums of money out on advances, or into stock investment, is intrinsically sound, or that the test of bills and cash applied to their ability to meet engagements is other than a just one. But if one can hardly believe in the soundness of the banking which puts customers' money largely out into stocks, what shall be said of the immense credits which have been granted on the security of real estate, the huge loans on building speculations, the pawned leases and the innumerable instances where money has been advanced on personal security only? Can the banks stand a strain of credit with all these on their back? Without calling upon their shareholders I am sure that many of them cannot, and these imprudent commitments are in many instances alone sufficient to imperil the position of banks which now enjoy abundant credit and the repute of good management.

It is to be noticed, moreover, that even the strict test which I have applied is to some extent a deceptive one, so far at least as regards the "cash," for the figures which appear in the half-yearly balance sheets by no means represent the actual state of the till throughout the rest of the year. We know from the sharpness with which loans are called in just before the balance is struck, that banks make a regular practice of providing for a good show at the half-year's end, and consequently we may justly infer that much more money is in some shape out of hand throughout the year than appears in the balance sheet. Now money out on loan, even for a day, is money risked, and the barer banks keep their tills of cash, the greater the danger of sudden demands which a market by no means well supplied might be unable to meet. A process of denudation has been going on in respect to the cash at the best, which the fictitiously low rate for bill discounts in London has served to conceal. Country banks have, as we have noted, withdrawn much of their balances from the hands of their London agents, in order to help their country customers, and everywhere the disposition has been to work on as narrow a cash basis as possible. The Bank of England has been for some time gradually losing its store of gold, and its reserve of notes is at present hardly £11,000,000 with the discount rate at $2\frac{1}{2}$ per cent. and a liability on the part of the banks to the public of probably not less than £500,000,000, including the deposits in private banks. If, therefore, the little cash that banks do show in their balance sheets when compared with their liabilities to the public and with the balance sheets of four years ago, is to a considerable extent in the hands of bill-brokers, stock-brokers, speculators of all kinds throughout the year, may we not say that the position is beyond measure a dangerous one? It is bolstering all round. A fictitious level of value is maintained on mere windy credit, and when a pressure comes, tending to make things find their real level, there will be great danger of a general collapse. The cash which banks hold at the half-year's end is not their true available store all the year round. For the year, all but four or five days, they may run much shorter of mere till-money than their balance sheets reveal, and they do in fact so run. It will be said that this is surely a stupid and self-deluding way of conducting business, and no doubt it is, but so long as banks are permitted to publish such balance sheets as they please, and when they please, it is a practice that cannot be rooted out. All banks ought to be compelled to publish a weekly return, as was lately most appositely advocated in the *Statist, à propos* of the failure of Willis, Percival & Co., the private bankers in Lombard Street, who had carried on business for many years after they must have known perfectly that they were utterly bankrupt. But we shall not get this reform till the nation is stung to activity by the prospect of something like impending ruin.

In this view of the situation, nothing could well seem more absurd than the nominally low value of money; but the position of the joint-stock banks enables us to see without difficulty how it has been brought about. There are in fact two values of money ruling, as it were, side by side: one a matter of bargain between borrower and lender—the private loan made with or without security, for which the interest charged has been high—and the other, the open market rate for bills of exchange of the highest class. These latter have been a dwindling quantity, and as they have fallen off more rapidly than the surplus cash obtained by the bankers either from customers or shareholders was absorbed by the private lending and stock-jobbing, the interest obtainable for their negotiation has receded to a very low figure. But this low figure is not test whatever of the scarcity or abundance of money, except as regards its employment in a particular way, and hence the supplies of real cash kept in hand by bankers have been dwindling almost everywhere, at the same time that the floating balance available for discount purposes has been almost valueless. Banks are thus drifting towards a catastrophe, one may almost say without being aware of it. They have striven to make high profits in dull times and in channels not safe for bankers, and they have succeeded, but at a cost which only those who survive the next credit storm will be able to estimate.

That a storm of this kind is coming, I think there can be not the least doubt, and we can tell pretty clearly how it will come. Had this country rushed into war and begun to call up large sums of money on loan, that would have brought on a financial crisis almost at once. But it will come not less surely, though not perhaps so soon, should the world once more settle down to an uncomfortable armed peace. Trade will in that event make an effort at revival. It is showing some signs of life in this country now, but these I think are merely spasmodic— an outcome in part of the eager haste with which the Government spent most of its £6,000,000. Still trade will wake up a little now that peace is concluded, and with its revival there will be an immediate pressure on the floating capital in bankers' hands. More bills for large amounts will be drawn and offered for discount, and directly these reach a certain volume the bankers will find themselves without money to conduct their proper business. An effort will then be made to sell some of the securities held, or loans will be called in, involving sharp losses, and attempts will be made to get rid of mortgages, all with a view to find money for trade purposes. This will in the first place produce a heavy fall in Stock Exchange securities, and may induce something like a panic. Banks will then in some cases have either to face losses or to hold on to their securities and trust to weathering the storm, and the pressure for money may compel many of them to take the former alternative. For it will very soon be found that there is little or no available money to be got hold of, and as a consequence, few buyers of securities to be had. Private people will in fact want to sell as well as banks, in order to get cash for trade purposes. Depositors may then also begin to take alarm, and by asking for their cash force some banks to close their doors; the reserve of the Bank of England will become depleted, and we shall find ourselves, as usual, issuing a practically inconvertible paper currency in order to allay public apprehension.

At the same time, I am bound to confess that I think the majority of the English joint-stock banks will ride through the storm, at considerable cost to their shareholders perhaps, but still they will ride it through. Some of them are very strong, in spite of the bad times, and would be perfectly solvent even if compelled to shut their doors for a time; others are solvent though not strong; and nearly all of any consequence are backed by a proprietary capable in time of making losses good. What is really to be dreaded in present circumstances is the condition of the private banks, about which we know absolutely nothing with any degree of certainty, and of which therefore I have not spoken. We may safely conclude, however, that they have been in no way exempt from the errors and temptations of their joint-stock neighbours, and we can at least be sure that in many cases they are not backed as joint-stock banks are by a wealthy proprietary. There is, indeed, too much reason to believe that not a few of them are so poor as to be mere skeletons, and the failure of one large old private bank would be something more alarming, and fraught with deeper mischief, than almost anything else that could happen. I therefore think that the next financial crisis in this country will produce a radical change in the condition of all private banks, and perhaps seal the fate of many among them.

It will also, I hope, cause the introduction of several reforms which are very much needed in joint-stock banking. It should stop, for example, the present foolish race after preposterously high dividends, and introduce greater frequency, uniformity, and fulness in the published balance sheets. If the crisis at the same time reads the community a sharp lesson in regard to the practices which now prevail of using bank balances as a medium for gambling, and teaches bankers to be less ready to lock up capital which should be strictly "floating" in securities which, when the time comes, refuse to "float," the ultimate outcome must be good for the commercial stability of the country.

GEORGE RAE

PERSONAL CREDIT

> My meaning in saying he is a good man, is to have you understand
> that he is sufficient: yet his means are in supposition.
>
> —*Merchant of Venice.*

The leading subject of your daily education as a banker will be to learn whom to trust.

Given a certain individual as principal or surety in a proposed transaction, the question which you have to solve is—how many hundreds, or how many thousands, as the case may be, will he be "good for" to the Bank; at what figure can you safely put his individual responsibility?

To insure a reliable solution, you have first to ascertain what the man is "worth"—that is to say, what he would have remaining for himself, in money or money's worth, after clearing off the whole of his debts and other liabilities.

For the most part you will have to rely for this knowledge on hearsay and the opinion of others. You will consequently have to sift the information which you may gather as to the position of individuals with the utmost care, because on no other subject of daily gossip is there a greater tendency to exaggeration or mischievous credulity.

You will have early occasion to observe, amongst other things, that the opinions afloat as to the means and position of people are mostly of stereotyped character. The origin of these opinions is always more or less obscure: but when it once comes to be said—it does not seem to matter when nor by whom—that So-and-so is good for so much, his worth will pass current for that amount for years without challenge; until some day he collapses, to the ruin of some, the injury of many, and the wonderment of all.

When therefore you are confidently assured, by some one who professes to know, that Mr. Bounderby, for example, is worth twenty thousand pounds, put your informant to the question. Let him tell you in what form Mr. Bounderby's worth exists—whether in land, or houses, or business capital, or shares, or money lent, or otherwise, and whether his property, real or personal, is free of charge or incumbrance. The probability is that your informant can give you no such information; and that in that respect he is the mere echo of antecedent

George Rae, "Personal Credit." *The Country Banker, His Clients, Cares, and Work from an Experience of Forty Years.* 1885; rev. ed. London: John Murray, 1930. Pp. 6–13.

echoes. His opinion will be found in most cases to rest on that most unreliable of authorities—everybody. Everybody says so: therefore it must be true.

If he seek to cover a retreat from his first position by a flank movement in the direction, let us say, of Mr. Bounderby's expectations, and assure you that he will have a large amount at his father's death, your informant must still be put to particulars; because this reversion may not be absolute, it may be tied tightly up on Bounderby himself for life and go to his wife and children afterwards.

In matters of personal credit a well-regulated scepticism is the soundest frame of mind to cultivate. "Let the greatest part of the news thou hearest," says Quarles, "be the least part of what thou believest: lest the greater part of what thou believest be the least part of what is true."

Ask the first farmer you meet next market day what he considers Squire W—to be worth, and he will quote you a figure, in all likelihood, absurdly wide of the mark. You yourself know the Squire's rental to a pound, because he banks with you. You also know that the estate is strictly entailed and that his income dies with him, and therefore that the worthy Squire's reputed wealth is a popular delusion.

Ask your leading tradesman what he considers the means of his customer Colonel H—may be, and he will tell you that the Colonel must be rich, because he lives like a gentleman, and never owes his tradesmen a shilling. Nevertheless, when the good Colonel dies, would it surprise you to learn that he has lived up to his income all his life and left nothing?

When you are assured that Maltby has made ten thousand pounds in hops, do not believe it. Divide by ten, and in nine cases out of ten you will be nearer the mark. But register the fact in your memory, because if Maltby has made money this time, he has an equal chance of losing it next.

Be equally sceptical when you are assured that Bouncer has lost a "pot of money" in something else, until you have had the rumour verified; because a gain or loss in business, in these days, becomes magnified in passing from mouth to mouth to ridiculous excess, and is hardly surpassed in quickness of growth by Falstaff's men in buckram.

When any rumour reaches you, therefore, either to the credit or discredit of a man, have a care, before acting upon it, to sift it to the bottom: carefully weighing the probabilities for and against, and the evidence on which they rest, as if you were hearing a cause in a court of law. Business calumnies especially are of extraordinary vitality. You shall expose and stamp one out, as you imagine, and in a few months it will come back to you again from some distant quarter as fresh and brazen as if you had never crushed it under an angry heel. Whilst you have conceived it extinct and forgotten, it has been merely absent on a tour of the district.

But in many instances the only information which you will obtain will be of a nature which you cannot put to the proof. It will be of the vaguest kind and often contradictory. One informant will appraise a man as good for so much: another will value him at half the money. Either may be right—you cannot tell: or both may be wrong, and the truth lie midway between them: but it will be mere conjecture either way.

In such cases a prudential rule to find the measure of a man's safety, from a banker's point of view, would be to follow the method suggested in Maltby's case: given the popular estimate of a man's worth, divide by ten, and the quotient will be the result required.

You smile at this novel adaptation of the rule of division: but give the figures a personal application, and they will not perhaps look so entertaining. Given a man reputed to be worth £5000, but of which you have no actual proof, would you feel justified in lending him more than £500 without security out of your own pocket?

Never trust to a man's means or safety as seen through the telescope of rumour; you will find his truer diameter, as a rule, by reversing the glass.

As regards annuitants of all kinds, clergymen, naval or military officers, professional men and salaried officials of every degree, it has to be borne steadfastly in mind that their incomes die with them. If, therefore, they have laid nothing aside, and have no property beyond their life incomes to fall back upon, they are manifestly ineligible to a bank, either as borrowers on their own behalf, or as sureties for other people.

If they are living within their revenues, the balances of their accounts with you will always be in their favour: but if their accounts once get on the debtor side of your books, the means of repayment must be regarded as obscure, and the date of redemption as indefinite.

Take O—, for example, a most respectable man, but without property or means beyond his professional income which he spends in full: out of what conceivable fund is he to repay the several hundred pounds for which he has been allowed to creep into your debt without security? It cannot be the proper business of a bank to enable any man who is wholly dependent upon an income which terminates with his life, to anticipate and spend that income, or any portion of it, in advance, and thus assist in placing a burden upon a borrower's back—a veritable Old Man of the Sea—which he can never shake off.

In seeking to know whom to trust on the strength of hearsay, it has to be confessed that we have not found this source of knowledge to be altogether satisfactory or conclusive. But in the case of people who bank with you, you have in your ledgers a record which will enable you, in many cases, to check and rectify the estimate of their means and position which is current out of doors. A man's bank account will not necessarily disclose what he is worth:

but its entries, debtor and creditor, will serve as tracks to indicate with some degree of clearness the line of progress along which he is moving towards either failure or success. Your customers are unconscious diarists of a portion of their lives. Every account in your books is a record, more or less graphic, of the financial history and progress of the customer, contributed by himself.

In evidence of the teaching which your ledgers thus afford, let us take the account of your client, Mr. Giles Borax. He has recently retired from a lucrative business, and his wealth is popularly rated at any amount from a hundred and fifty to five hundred thousand pounds, according to the more or less fervid imagination of your informant. But the items on the credit side of his account will be a safer guide to the fact, than the most confident assertions of rumour. These items mainly consist of dividends on money in the Funds, or invested in leading railway and other shares or debentures. It will be an easy task to calculate from these the approximate value of Mr. Borax's property. If his revenue from all sources be £10,000 a year, you will not be far from the mark if you take it all round at twenty-five years' purchase, which would put his worth at a quarter of a million—less mortgages or other charges, if any, upon his property. Semiannual debits, identical in amount, to the same payees, will sufficiently indicate the existence of incumbrances, if there are any such.

If you are curious to know whether his net income exceeds or falls short of his expenditure, you have merely to compare the balance with which he commences the year with that with which he ends it, first excluding any transactions on capital account from your figures. He may have been laying money out on loan or investments, for example, or calling money in: in either case, these items would be excluded from your calculation.

It is, no doubt, possible, as you suggest, that Mr. Borax may not pass all his rents and revenues through his account, and that any estimate in that event, based upon its figures, would be defective. So much the worse for Mr. Borax; but the defect will be on the side of safety, so far as you are concerned. It will make him appear to be, by so much, less opulent than he really is.

You find serious difficulty, you say, in these occasional readings of accounts; because some of your customers draw their cheques in blank—that is, in favour of a number, or the initials of the payee, instead of his name. It does not follow, however, that cheques are thus drawn with intention to deceive. The parties may desire to keep their money transactions to themselves; and, if they are never in your debt in any form, they have a plain right to do so. But if they are debtors to the Bank, and especially if their indebtedness be uncovered by security, their right to work their accounts in the dark ceases, and the habit should be given up. If you trust them with your money, you have a right to at least a general notion of what they are doing with it. It is true that, even when an account is worked on the anonymous principle, it is easy to gather from the indorsements and other inscriptions on the cheques themselves much of what you desire to know: but that is no reason why the man who borrows the Bank's money should be allowed to work his account in cipher, and put you to the trouble of finding the cipher out. His cheques ought to reveal their object by proper mention of names or purposes, and not in the darkened speech of numerals.

In your reading of any account you have carefully to guard against a mere off-hand and superficial glance at the figures. As a case in point, let us take the account of Stokes & Co., by whom your Bank made a bad debt in the time of your predecessor, Mr. Littleworth. What misled Mr. Littleworth was the fact that the firm had always a substantial balance at their credit. He inferred from this that they had capital in their business even to overflowing, and his astonishment was great when they stopped payment one day, with some hundreds still at the credit of their cash account. Nevertheless it was so. Stokes & Co. were dealers in timber, bought it on six months' credit, and got immediate possession of the article. This they proceeded to dispose of to their customers, and drew upon them against sales, and the proceeds of the bills thus drawn they placed straightway to the credit of their bank account. They succeeded in this way with the greatest ease in keeping a good balance at their credit, seeing that they had always the produce of their sales in hand long before they had to pay for the timber themselves. By reference to the account, Mr. Littleworth might have noticed that the acceptances passed through it during the twelve months preceding their failure reached £20,000; and the acceptances having each six months to run, it followed that Stokes & Co. were constantly in debt some £10,000 for timber, the bulk of which, as it proved, they had sold to weak joiners and impecunious builders. When half a score of these came to grief, by reason of a collapse in building enterprise, the modest capital of Stokes & Co. vanished, and gave place to a balance deficient of many times the amount; whilst the £500 at their credit on your books still left the Bank to prove for an unpleasant amount on a batch of worthless bills.

You have to beware, therefore, of placing too much reliance on the balance usually at a man's credit as a test of his means, until you have first seen how the balance is created. If you find that he pays mostly by acceptance, and rarely in cash, you will conclude that his balance in your hands is merely fugitive, and virtually in pawn to other people. It is money placed with you in advance to meet coming liabilities. His trading position, in other respects, may be perfectly sound and solid; but the balance at his credit is not of itself conclusive evidence of the fact. It is, indeed, practicable for a clever rogue so to manage affairs as to be insolvent for years yet all the while maintain a respectable balance in his bankers' hands.

CHAPTER EIGHT

MONEY PRESSURES AND BANK FAILURES

THE LONDON TIMES
13 December 1825, p. 2

(FROM THE CITY)

An indescribable gloom was diffused through the City yesterday morning, by the knowledge of the fact, previously suspected, that the house of Sir Peter Pole, Thornton, and Co., of Bartholomew-lane, bankers, did not open for business. This house was among the most considerable in London, the firm being agents for no less than forty-seven provincial banks. As soon as the event was rendered certain, which was at nine o'clock, when the presentation of checks takes place, many persons assembled on the Exchange to inquire into the causes which led to it, and to learn if the credit of any other houses had been placed in danger. Some persons were base enough at this juncture to profit by the alarm which the countenances of the inquirers betrayed, to spread openly reports of other failures, mentioning without reserve the names of the most respectable firms, with the view of producing by the alarm a further depression of the funds; and such was the state of mind in which the hearers were placed, that no report, however absurd, failed to obtain implicit belief. At about eleven o'clock the alarm had reached its height, and so great was it, that men evidently felt as if all that was stable in the property of merchants or bankers was about to be involved in ruin. Some circumstances, however, transpired shortly afterwards, which tended very much to moderate the general agitation. Individuals who felt strongly inclined to doubt the truth of the reports, as applying to houses of established character, resolved on instituting

London Times (December 13, 1825):2.

a personal inquiry, the result of which inquiry justified those doubts, and the contradiction which they were thus enabled to give spread rapidly in all quarters. It was also given out that so great a competition had arisen among the London bankers to obtain the connexions of Messrs. Pole, Thornton, and Co., that it was hoped some arrangement would be made by which the customers would be protected in part from the loss which must otherwise fall upon them. The agency for some of the Scotch banks, in particular, is understood to be extremely valuable. The amount for which Messrs. Pole, Thornton, and Co. have failed has been variously stated, and there probably exist no data at present in which any just estimate can be formed; but we have reason to believe that their deficiency does not exceed 200,000l. Their customers in general are not supposed to have had very large balances in their hands.

It ought to be observed, since the declaration can no longer be injurious, that this is the house adverted to on a former occasion, as having received assistance from the Bank, on laying before the Directors such a statement of their affairs as was admitted at the time to be satisfactory. The amount advanced by the Bank is said to have been near 300,000l., and that sum, it was alleged, would be sufficient to secure the house against any future danger. In a week from that time, however, the firm has suspended its payments. It is but justice to say, that every effort was made by the house in question, that their unfortunate situation would admit, to make the blow as light as possible. It was recommended to persons holding draughts of the house on Saturday, in all cases wherein it could be done with propriety, to present them for payment, instead of passing them through their own bankers. At the clearing-house, the difficulties of the firm first became obvious, and their suspension of payments on Monday morning was soon foreseen to be inevitable. Much anxiety will naturally be felt as to the manner in which the affairs of so extensive a concern are likely to be wound up. We understand, on good authority, that there is no present probability of its terminating in a bankruptcy, but that trustees are to be appointed in the first instance, who will conduct the remaining business for the benefit of the creditors. Whether that course can be persevered in or not, depends upon the degree of solvency of the firm. One of the partners is well known to be a man of very considerable landed property. The decline of this house in credit is generally attributed to the anxiety felt by the partners at the time when the rate of interest was low, to make a profitable use of their capital, and hence they were led to employ it on securities capable of being realized only at a distant period, or of an inferior degree of credit. It is said that a great portion of their business will be transferred to the houses of Messrs. Smith, Payne, and Co.; and Messrs. Jones, Loyd, and Co. An attempt was made in the course of last week to prop up the house of Pole and Co., by the introduction of some men of property as partners, and by the exclusion of some of those who at present constitute that firm; but as time was necessarily required to obtain a full insight into the real state of its affairs, and as that could not be obtained, the arrangement came to nothing.

The letters from the country brought intelligence of two failures of provincial banks, but their circulation is said not to be extensive—that of Dobson and Co., of Huddersfield, and of Edmeads and Co., of Maidstone. The latter was one of the agency banks of Messrs. Pole, Thornton, and Co.

An extraordinary number of country bankers from all parts of England were in town yesterday, either for the purpose of procuring specie and Bank-notes as a protection against a run on them, or to ascertain by their own observations the state of affairs among their London friends. Several of them were to be seen in most of the leading banking-houses, anxiously waiting their turn for an interview with the principals. The heads of nearly all the London houses are as regular and constant in their attendance during this unsettled state of the money-market as any of their clerks, so frequent are the applications to them for supplies of specie and Bank-notes for the country.

This gloom without doors, and the events which produced it, were sensibly felt at the Stock Exchange. Such was the pressure to effect sales of Exchequer-bills, that those securities not only fell to an enormous discount, but the brokers who deal in them, who are few in number, became so much alarmed that they closed their books, and actually refused for a short time to engage in any transactions whatever. At that period the current quotations were 50s. discount, but some purchasers at that price having appeared in the market, the brokers took courage, and business went on as usual. The discount afterwards fell to 60s., and even on those bills for which money may be obtained at a day's notice at the Exchequer, the discount was 25s. in other words, a holder preferred receiving his 100l. *minus* 25s. to-day, rather than wait till to-morrow to receive his 100l. in full. India Bonds were at 45s. discount. Three per Cents. Reduced fell to 79, and $3\frac{1}{2}$ per Cents. to $31\frac{1}{2}$, sales being particularly pressed in those stocks, the books of which are still open for transfers. The same facility, however, was given at the Bank as was done on Saturday, in making transfers of 3 per Cent. Consols, and such transfers were effected to a large amount, though at a sacrifice of 1 per cent. or more, as compared with prices for the opening in January.

This state of things lasted so long only as was necessary to effect those sales to which persons having large money transactions to conduct, were necessarily compelled. The market then assumed a much more cheerful appearance. It was rumoured that the Directors of the Bank had met to meditate on the means of relieving the pressure for money out of doors, and that their councils had been reinforced by the arrival of no less a person than Lord Liverpool.[1] The latter fact proved to be untrue, and nothing transpired on the subject which had occupied the deliberations of the Bank Directors. It was also

---

1. Lord Liverpool (1770–1828). Tory Prime Minister (1812–17). [Ed.]

circulated, that a deputation of bankers was to wait forthwith on Lord Liverpool, to request that the Bank might be instructed to anticipate the period of the payment of the January dividends, but this soon fell to the ground, through the improbability that such a suggestion could either be made or listened to. Still later in the day a report was got up that a recommendation had been made by Ministers to the Bank Directors, that they should buy up a portion of the Exchequer-bills afloat, and this, though in all probability in no degree better founded than the other reports, really obtained such a degree of belief as gave an impulse to the price of Government securities generally. The discount on Exchequer-bills was diminished to 35s., and Consols for the account rose to $83\frac{1}{4}$, at which price business closed.

The Bank Directors, it is said, rejected very few of the foreign bills presented to them yesterday to discount. Such, however, is the extraordinary want of confidence without doors, that rich individuals accustomed to employ their money in discounts, refuse nearly all accommodation, even to first-rate paper, and the consequence is truly dreadful to those who hold that which possesses inferior credit. It is entirely useless to the owners, who would probably offer in vain 10,000l. in nominal amount to obtain the loan of 1,000l. It is common to hear of men worth 100,000l. asking the loan of 1,000l. or 2,000l. as a personal favour, on what would be termed at any other period but this, unexceptionable security. Indeed, in most cases it is not the character of the security which is considered, but the impossibility of procuring money at all. Next to the want of confidence, which has all along acted and is still acting most fatally, as a chief cause of the existing distress, may be classed the diminution of their resources by the London bankers to assist their country connexions, which makes them absolutely unable to give that assistance which their town friends have been accustomed to expect at their hands.

A dense fog pervaded the city during the whole of the day, according singularly with the dismal feelings by which most men's minds were influenced.

THE LONDON TIMES
14 December 1825, p. 2

THE MONEY MARKET

(from The City*)*

The agitation and alarm in the city have experienced as yet no abatement. At an early hour yesterday morning it was announced that another London banking-house, viz. That of Messrs. Williams, Burgess, and Williams, of 20,

Birchin-lane, had suspended its payments. This house, in common with other bankers, had to sustain, in the course of last week, a severe run upon it. But, according to the current rumours, the resolution to suspend payments was not definitively imposed on the partners of the firm till a late hour on Monday evening. The house of Messrs. Williams and Co., in Birchin lane, was beset during the whole day by a crowd of inquirers, anxious to satisfy themselves of the truth of the disasterous intelligence which had been announced. Some of the other houses in Lombard-street, and its immediate neighbourhood, were also besieged by crowds of people on some false alarm given—a manoeuvre which appears to have been adopted for the purpose of picking-pockets. In one instance, as we have heard, on Monday evening, a house which had closed its shutters on account of the reason, reported to have stopped payment. The house of Messrs. Williams and Co. had an agency for some country banks the number of which does not amount to more than 17g and we have been desired to mention that all notes and acceptances of Messrs. Cobb and Co., of Banbury, will be paid by Messrs. Jones, Lloyd, and Co., of Lothbury.

We understand that Mr. Robert Williams, who is the head partner of the firm in Birchin-lane, was not in town when the other partners found themselves under the painful necessity of suspending their payments, being detained at his seat at Moor-park, near Rickmansworth, in Hertfordshire, by the severe illness of one of his sons, whose situation is so precarious that Sir A. Cooper has been twice called from town to attend to him.

The failure of Messrs. Williams and Co. has led also to a suspension of payments by the banking-house of Sir Claude Scott, Williams, and Co., of Holles-street; but it appears by an advertisement in this day's paper that the house confidently expects to be able to resume payments at the latest, on Saturday next.

The difficulty of raising money on stock, bills, or any species of security, whether private or public, is entirely without example in the city of London. The rate of interest, wherever any species of accommodation is afforded, cannot in some cases be estimated at less than 50 per cent. As the usury laws form a bar to ordinary transactions of this nature, various plans are said to be adopted to evade their operation. For example, the current price of Consols for the January Account[1] being 83, any person wishing to convert that stock into ready money would not obtain offers for it at more than 79. At that rate the money is paid, and as soon as the transaction is completed, the purchaser can sell the same stock for the January account at 4 per cent. advance. He will receive his money for it in the middle of January, and thus gain more than 50 per cent. for its use in the intermediate period. In cases where the ultimate se-

---

1. One of the government's quarterly payment of dividends on the Consols, or shares of consolidated national debt. [Ed.]

curity is inferior to that of our Government securities, a rate even higher than that has been given. One natural consequence of this has been a great disproportion in value between those stocks which are transferable, and those which are shut for the dividend. The $3\frac{1}{2}$ per Cents., which, bearing $\frac{1}{2}$ per cent. more interest, are worth 11 per cent. more than Consols, were sold yesterday at the same price as that stock for the January account. The Three per Cents. Reduced being a more marketable stock on the whole than the $3\frac{1}{2}$ per Cents., were not more than four per cent. below the price of Consols. In Banks Stock, wherein there are very few jobbers, a peculiar difficulty occurred, so much so, that one offer for sale of a parcel of it amounting to 20,000l., (worth about 40,000l. in money) met with no bidders as purchasers:

The difficulty in obtaining money is not to be paralleled within the memory of the oldest merchants on the Exchange in London, who declare that the memorable epochs of 1797 and 1815 bear no resemblance to this.

The Bank Directors, who now assemble daily to deliberate on the means that may be in their power for stemming the present difficulties, came yesterday to the resolution of advancing the rate of discount to 5 per cent. instead of 4, and the new regulation will be in force this day. The following is a copy of the notice for that purpose, issued yesterday at the discount office:—

Bank of England, Dec. 13.
  Resolved—That from and after the 13th inst. No bills or notes will be discounted under 5 per cent. per annum.

Facilities for private transfers in Consols. continue to be given at the Bank. On Monday one transfer was made of 150,000l., and the number of transfers affected on that day and yesterday is little short of 100.

Shortly before the notice was circulated yesterday from the Bank of the intention of the Directors to increase the rate of discount, a report became current that the Directors would make loans on Bank stock in all cases wherein the holders could show that they would be compelled to make a great sacrifice on its present price by the sale; but we could not ascertain that any such resolution had really been adopted, and incline to the belief that the report is untrue. Loans were absolutely refused, we believe, on 3 per Cents. Reduced— Stock, for which accommodation application was repeatedly made yesterday to the Directors.

Expresses arrived in town yesterday from all parts for supplies of gold and notes for the country bankers. The town bankers, in general, refused all accommodation to their customers, and discounts could not be obtained to any extent on the best mercantile bills. We did not hear that the letters from the country communicated intelligence of the failure of any more local banks.

Accounts from the Continent of the state of the principal money-markets there are now looked for with much anxiety by the merchants, but in no quarter do they find that confidence is shaken in any thing like the degree which it has been in England. In Paris no scarcity of money at all proportionate to that of London exists, and the credit of the leading Paris merchants is for the most part unshaken. A letter from Paris of Saturday, adverting to the crisis here, says—"In this city we are not in a perfectly healthy state with respect to our circulation, but the malady is only skin deep, and may soon be cured, but yours is a deep wound, which it will require a long time to heal." In Amsterdam, transactions in money have scarcely deviated from the usual course. The current state of interest was five per cent. at the Bank of Amsterdam, but on commercial bills of the first order discounts were easily obtained at the rate of 4 per cent. Loans on stock paid 6 per cent. interest. At Hamburgh, the rate of interest was 8 per cent., but the evils arising from a scarcity of circulating medium are generally corrected there by their "free trade" in money, or the absence of all limitation on the rate of interest.

The fluctuations in the funds are indicative, as usual, of the general alarm and agitation. The $8^1/_2$ per Cents. Reduced opened at 85, fell to $82^1/_2$, and after several variations, closed at $85^1/_2$. The 3 per Cents. Reduced opened at $79^7/_8$, fell to 79, and closed at the same price, after having in the interval reached $80^7/_8$. Consols for the opening in January closed at $82^1/_8$; the highest price of the day being $83^1/_2$ and the lowest $81^7/_8$. Exchequer Bills left off at a discount of 38s., and India Bonds of 40s. Bank Stock was sold at 200s and left off at $202^1/_2$; but transactions in it to any extent could not be effected without difficulty.

JAMES WILLIAM GILBART

THE ADMINISTRATION OF A BANK DURING SEASONS OF PRESSURE

A pressure on the money market may be defined [as] a difficulty of getting money in the London market, either by way of discounting bills, or of loans upon Government securities. This difficulty is usually accompanied by an unfavourable course of exchange, a contraction of the circulation of the Bank of England, and a high rate of interest. These three circumstances have the rela-

---

James William Gilbart, "The Administration of a Bank during Seasons of Pressure." *The History, Principles, and Practice of Banking.* 1882; rpt. New York: Greenwood Press, 1968. Vol. I: 309–25.

tion to each other of cause and effect. The unfavourable course of exchange induces the Bank of England to contract her circulation; and the contraction of the circulation, by rendering money more scarce, increases its value, and leads to an advanced rate of interest. The removal of the pressure is in the same order:—the foreign exchanges become favourable—the Bank of England then extends her circulation—money becomes more abundant, and the rate of interest falls. The degree to which the exchanges are unfavourable is indicated by the stock of gold in the Bank of England; and when this is at its lowest amount the pressure may be considered to have attained its extreme point; for as the amount of gold increases, the Bank will extend its circulation, and the pressure will subside.

If we take a review of all the recent pressures on the money market, we shall find they have always been preceded by the following circumstances:— First, by abundance of money; secondly, by a low rate of interest; thirdly, by some species of speculative investments. The principal pressures that have occurred of late years, have been those of 1825, 1836, 1839, 1847, 1857, 1866, 1875, and 1878.

The following is Mr. Horsley Palmer's[1] opinion of the causes of the pressure of 1825, as stated to the Bank Committee of 1832:—

Will you state to the committee what, in your opinion, was the nature and the march of the crisis in 1825?—I have always considered that the first step towards the excitement was the reduction of the interest upon the Government securities;[2] the first movement in that respect was, I think, upon £135,000,000 of five per cents, which took place in 1823. In the subsequent year, 1824, followed the reduction of £80,000,000 of four per cents. I have always considered that reduction of interests, one-fifth in one case, and one-eighth in the other, to have created the feverish feeling in the minds of the public at large, which prompted almost everybody to entertain any proposition for investment, however absurd, which was tendered. The excitement of that period was further promoted by the acknowledgment of South American republics by this country, and the inducements held out for engaging in mining operations, and loans to those governments, in which all classes of the community in England seem to have partaken almost simultaneously. With those speculations arose general speculation in commercial produce, which had an effect of disturbing the relative values between this and other countries, and creating an unfavourable foreign exchange, which continued from

---

1. John Horsley Palmer, deputy governor of the Bank of England (1820–30), governor of Bank of England (1830–33), who was responsible for formulating the "Palmer Rule," which allowed the currency to fluctuate in relation to the Bank's specie. Palmer argued that bankers should have greater discretion over the size of the currency. [Ed.]
2. In 1823, the British government reduced the interest it paid on the Consols. This, along with another reduction the following year, drove many investors out of the market for government securities and into the riskier market of foreign loans. [Ed.]

October, 1824, to November, 1825, causing a very considerable export of bullion from the Bank—about seven millions and a half. Commercial speculations had induced some bankers, one particularly, to invest money in securities not strictly convertible, to a larger extent than was prudent; they were also largely connected with country bankers. I allude to the house of Messrs. Pole and Co.—a house originally possessed of very great property, in the persons of the partners, but which fell with the circumstances of the times. The failure of that banking-house was the first decisive check to commercial and banking credit, and brought at once a vast number of country bankers, which were in correspondence with it, into difficulties. That discredit was followed by a general discredit throughout London and the interior.

With regard to the pressure of 1836, there was in the beginning of that year no appearance of distress; but, on the contrary, every symptom of prosperity, attended by its usual concomitant, a readiness to engage in speculative undertakings.

The following description of this period is taken from the speech of Mr. Clay,[3] on introducing his motion respecting Joint-Stock Banks, May 12, 1836:—

To what extent the operations of the joint-stock banks may have contributed to create the present state of excitement in the commercial world, must, of course, be mere matter of conjecture. That they have had some considerable influence is probable, from the fact that the excitement and rage for speculation is greatest in those parts of the kingdom where the operations of those establishments have been most active. London has been comparatively unmoved, but Liverpool and Manchester have witnessed a mushroom growth of schemes not exceeded by the memorable year 1825. I hold in my hand a list of seventy contemplated companies, for every species of undertaking, which have appeared in the Liverpool and Manchester papers within the last three months. This list was made a fortnight or three weeks since, and might probably now be considerably extended. It is impossible also, I think, not to suspect that the facility of credit, and consequent encouragement to speculation, to which I have alluded, cannot have been without its effect in producing the great increase of price in almost all the chief articles of consumption and raw materials of our manufactures. That increase has been enormous—not less than from twenty to fifty, and even one hundred per cent. in many of the chief articles of produce, of consumption, and materials of our manufactures.

These appearances continued with little alteration until the month of July, when the Bank of England raised the rate of discount to four-and-a-half per cent. It then became known that there had been a demand upon the Bank for

---

3. Member of parliament for Tower Hamlets. [Ed.]

gold from the preceding April, and this measure was adopted by the Bank as a means of rendering the foreign exchanges more favourable. This being found ineffectual, the Bank in September raised the rate of discount to five per cent. Besides raising the rate of interest, the Bank adopted other measures for increasing the value of money. A large amount of American bills upon first-rate houses had been offered for discount and rejected. A high degree of alarm was immediately spread throughout the community. The dread of a panic similar to that of 1825 almost universally prevailed. Those who had money were unwilling to part with it—trade became suddenly stagnant—the prices of all commodities fell considerably, and numbers of commercial houses, chiefly of the second class, suspended payment. Many railway and other projects now fell into oblivion.

The alarm that existed was kept up by the monthly accounts of the bullion in the Bank of England. The public returns showed a gradual decline from April, 1836, to February, 1837. It was therefore supposed that the Bank of England would be under the necessity, for its own safety, of still further contracting its issues, and thus increasing the existing pressure. This apprehension caused all persons who had money to retain it in their possession, and bankers and others withheld accommodation they would otherwise have been disposed to grant.

This state of alarm was considerably augmented by the publication of the Report of the Secret Committee of the House of Commons upon Joint-Stock Banks. This committee had been appointed on the motion of Mr. Clay, the Member for the Tower Hamlets, whose speech on the occasion might be termed a bill of indictment. The joint-stock banks had rapidly increased; they had issued small shares; they had large nominal capitals; they had circulated an excessive amount of notes; they had promoted speculation. These were the charges brought against them; and they had greater weight from being advanced by a member who was known to be friendly to joint-stock banking. The report of the committee appeared to sustain all Mr. Clay's accusations. This report was highly creditable to the talents and industry of the committee, but marked by a decided hostility of tone. While it enumerated all the actual or possible imperfections of the joint-stock banks, it ascribed to them scarcely a single excellence. At the same time, the committee deferred to the succeeding session the proposal of any measures for their improvement; thus the public were led to suppose that in the following session some stringent measures would be adopted with reference to joint-stock banks, but what they would be none could conjecture.

Had the report appeared at any other period it might possibly have done good; but as its appearance was contemporaneous with a pressure on the money market, and a high state of alarm, it unquestionably tended to weaken public confidence, at a time when it required to be strengthened. Persons who were unfriendly to joint-stock banks seized the opportunity of dispraising them, and believed, or pretended to believe, that the banks were unsound, and would certainly stop payment. Others, who were friendly, were apprehensive that the banks, being still in their infancy, would be found too weak to withstand the storm now raised against them. But though this alarm began with respect to joint-stock banks, it did not end there. It was soon foreseen that if a few joint-stock banks were to stop payment, the private banks in their neighbourhood would be put to a severe trial; and if the banks should even be compelled to withhold their usual advances to their customers, the credit of individuals must suffer. Hence the private bankers and the merchants, as well as the joint-stock banks, made preparations to meet any event that might occur, and by thus increasing the pressure on the London money market, occasioned still farther apprehensions.

The alarm was augmented by the stoppage of the Agricultural and Commercial Bank of Ireland, in the month of November, and the demand for gold which that stoppage occasioned in Ireland. The joint-stock banks of England now became subject to increased suspicion; the accommodation they had been accustomed to obtain by the rediscount of their bills in the London market was considerably restricted; and in the beginning of December, the Northern and Central Bank at Manchester, a bank having a paid-up capital of £800,000, with above 1,200 partners, and forty branches, applied for assistance to the Bank of England. This was afforded upon condition, in the first instance, that they should wind up all their branches, except that at Liverpool; and afterwards farther assistance was granted, upon condition they should discontinue business after February, 1837. Soon afterwards, the old and respectable London banking-house of Messrs. Esdaile and Co. received assistance upon similar terms.

The pressure which existed in England rapidly extended to America. A large amount of American securities, consisting chiefly of bonds of the respective States, had been remitted to the agency houses in England. This circumstance, in connection with the exportation of gold to America, attracted the notice of the Bank of England. A large amount of bills drawn from America upon first-rate London houses was rejected. In America the pressure became severe—money was wanted to remit to England to meet the drafts that had been drawn upon England, either upon credit or against securities that could not now be sold. The rate of discount at New York rose to two, and even to three per cent. per month.

From the pressure upon the money market, and from the great fall in the price of American produce, the cotton and other commodities sent from America to meet drafts upon the English agents could not be sold except at a ruinous loss. And other remittances not having arrived, several houses in the

American trade, who were said to have given extensive credit to parties in America, applied for assistance to the Bank of England.

Such was the character of the pressure of 1836. We next proceed to the pressure of 1839. The pressure of 1836 may be said to have commenced from the month of May in that year. From that month the stock of gold in the Bank gradually and uniformly declined until February, 1837, when it reached its lowest point of depression. From this point it uniformly advanced: the lowest point of the circulation was in December, 1836, though even then it was not lower than it had been in the preceding January. The Bank raised the rate of interest from 4 to $4^{1}/_{2}$ per cent. in July, and to 5 per cent. in the following September. During the whole of the year 1837 the amount of gold in the Bank of England continued to increase; the Bank extended its circulation, and after the payment of the July dividends, money became very abundant, and the market rate of interest experienced a considerable fall. The foreign exchanges continued to be favourable during the early part of 1838, and gold accumulated in the coffers of the Bank of England. In the spring of that year the directors of the Bank of England sent nearly a million of gold to America. Money became increasingly abundant, and the rate of interest fell. In February the Bank reduced their rate of discount to 4 per cent., and the interest on the loans granted during the shutting of the funds was reduced in March to $3^{1}/_{2}$ per cent. The low rate of interest caused large sums of money to be invested in American securities. Bonds of all kinds issued by the Bank of the United States, by the various States in the Union, and by numerous private undertakings, were poured upon the English market, and found eager purchasers. Several of the directors of the Bank of England, in their individual character as merchants, became agents for the distribution of these securities. About July the exchanges became unfavourable, and in the latter part of the year some symptoms of uneasiness were apparent in the money market; but as the stock of bullion in the Bank of England was considerable, and the directors granted their usual loans in December at $3^{1}/_{2}$ per cent., public confidence was not shaken. In the beginning of the year 1839 the exchanges became increasingly unfavourable, and the monthly returns of the Bank showed a gradual diminution in the stock of gold. The price of corn rose so high as to admit of foreign wheat at the lowest rate of duty. This occasioned a further demand for gold to be exported. The stock of gold in the Bank of England rapidly declined, until, in the month of October, it was no more than £2,525,000, while the liabilities of the Bank upon notes amounted to £17,612,000, and upon deposits to £6,734,000. The Bank directors were very anxious to stop this demand for gold. With this view, they raised the rate of interest on May 16th to 5 per cent., on June 20th to $5^{1}/_{2}$ per cent., and on August 1st to 6 per cent.; and they charged the same rate upon their short loans. They are supposed to have sold large amounts of Government stock and exchequer bills, and on July 13th they announced that they were ready to receive proposals for the sale of the dead weight. None of the offers, however, met their approbation. Finding these measures not speedily effective, an arrangement was made with the Bank of France for a loan of £2,500,000. Messrs. Baring and Co.[4] drew bills on account of the Bank of England upon houses in Paris for this amount, which the Bank of France undertook to discount. The directors also determined to refuse to discount any bills drawn or indorsed by any private or joint-stock bank of issue. Notwithstanding these measures, the stock of gold in the Bank continued to decrease until the 18th October, when it reached the lowest point of depression. From this point it continued to advance, and the pressure began gradually, but slowly, to subside.

It may be useful to notice the differences between the pressure of 1836 and that of 1839. If we measure the intensity of the pressure by the difference between the largest and the lowest stock of gold in the Bank of England, the former pressure will range from £7,801,000 to £4,032,000, and the latter from £10,126,000 to £2,525,000. In the pressure of 1836, one joint-stock bank, a London private bank, two country private banks, three large American agency houses, and a great many respectable merchants, stopped payment. In the pressure of 1839, there was scarcely a failure until the month of December, and then only among the second class of traders. In the pressure of 1836, the prices of nearly all commodities fell considerably, and almost immediately. In the pressure of 1839, the prices of most commodities remained for a length of time nearly the same. In 1836, the Bank of England did not raise their rate of interest above 5 per cent. In 1839, the rate of interest upon both discounts and loans was raised to 6 per cent. In 1839, the Bank gave notice that they were willing to sell the dead weight, and they made arrangements for borrowing £2,500,000 sterling from the Bank of France. In 1836, the Bank adopted neither of these measures. In 1836, the Bank of England rejected all bills drawn or indorsed by joint-stock banks of issue. In 1839, they rejected also all bills drawn and indorsed by private banks of issue.

It would appear that a season of pressure is always preceded by one of speculation; and hence it follows that a banker who wishes to be easy in a time of pressure must act wisely in the previous season of speculation. It requires no ordinary firmness to do this. To act wisely in a season of speculation is far more difficult than to act wisely in one of pressure. But unless a banker acts wisely in the previous time of speculation, his wisdom will probably be of little avail when the pressure arrives.

---

4. Merchant bank, specializing in finance to foreign countries. This important bank almost failed in 1889 but was saved by an agreement among the Bank of England and the major London banks. [Ed.]

While, therefore, money is still abundant, the public funds high, and other bankers liberal in accommodation, he should be doubly cautions against taking bills of a doubtful character, or making advances upon irregular securities. He should not suffer the desire of employing his funds, or the fear of offending his customers, to induce him to deviate from sound banking principles. He should also take this opportunity of calling up all dead or doubtful loans, and of getting rid of all weak customers. He should also, under any circumstances, avoid making advances for any length of time, and investments in securities that are not at all times convertible, or the price of which is likely to sustain a great fall on the occurrence of a pressure. The discount of first-rate commercial bills having a short time to run, or short loans on stock or other undeniable security, however low the interest received, seem to be the most safe and advantageous transactions.

When the aspect of affairs seems to threaten that money will be in demand, and the failure of a number of merchants and traders may consequently be apprehended, it behoves him to prepare for approaching events by avoiding all discounts of bills of an inferior class, and by keeping his funds in an available state. With a view to these objects, he will review all his loan and discount accounts, call up his loans of long standing, where it can be done without injury to the interest or reputation of his bank, avoid all overdrawn accounts, and reduce the amount of discounts of the inferior class of accounts. In performing these operations, he will exercise due judgment and discretion, making proper distinctions between his customers, and reducing chiefly those bills which are not of a business character, or which are drawn upon doubtful people, or upon parties that he knows nothing about; he will also mark particularly those accounts which require large discounts, but keep no corresponding balance to the credit of their current accounts.

As the pressure advances, he will find that there are three demands upon his funds. First, his customers will reduce their balances, and keep less money in his hands. Money lodged at interest will be taken away, because the parties can make higher interest elsewhere, or they will be tempted by the low price of stock to invest it in Government securities. Secondly, he will have a greater demand for loans and discounts, not merely from weak people whom he might not care about refusing, but from persons of known wealth, whom it is his interest and his inclination to oblige. Thirdly, he will think it prudent to guard against sudden demands by keeping a larger amount of bank notes in his till. To meet all these demands he will be compelled to realize some of his securities, and he will realize those first on which he will sustain no loss.

If a banker has money lying at demand with a bill-broker, he will now have occasion to call it in. If he has money lent at short periods at the Stock Exchange, he will, as he has occasion, take in the money as the loans fall due. If he has discounted brokers' bills, he will receive the amounts when due, and discount no more. Should these operations not be sufficient to meet the demands upon his funds, he will then sell his stock or exchequer bills, or borrow on them in the money market. A country banker who has kept his reserve in bills of exchange will be anxious to re-discount them, and will think himself lucky if he can do so readily and at a moderate rate of interest.

It will be useless for a banker to attempt to call up dead loans, or to reduce his discounts, after the pressure has commenced. He should have thought of these matters in the previous season of abundance. As he cannot get in any outstanding advances, he had better not ask for them, but merely charge the parties an increased rate of interest. If he demand the money, he will not get it, and he may give rise to a surmise that he is short of funds. This season of pressure is, however, a good opportunity for calling up advances, or getting rid of connections that he would, on other grounds, like to be without. The "scarcity of money," the "pressure on the money market," are capital reasons to assign for refusing applications which, even otherwise, he would refuse, and for calling up loans which, under any circumstances, he would like to see repaid.

During a pressure, a banker will have to give a great many refusals, and some discretion will be necessary in the form of giving these refusals. Let him refuse in what way he may at such a season, he will be sure to give offence. And the party refused will possibly publish the refusal, and, from motives of ignorance or malignity, represent the refusal as having arisen from want of means, and possibly may circulate a report that the banker is about to stop payment. Hence rumours about banks are always rife in seasons of pressure, and they add to the general want of confidence which then prevails.

During a pressure, a banker will have offers of new accounts to be transferred from other bankers, provided he will consent to make certain advances. Some caution must be exercised in this matter. It is quite possible that some perfectly safe parties, having large accounts, may be disposed to remove in consequence of their present bankers not being equal to the supply of their wants. In this case, the banker will be regulated by the value of the proposed account and the extent of his own means. On the other hand, it is equally possible that weak people, to whom their present bank might not, in any case, have given advances, may use the "scarcity of money" as a pretext for making application to a new banker, stating their belief that their old banker was unable to meet their requirements. It behoves a banker to use much discretion in such a case, especially if it be a large account. If he errs at all, he should err on the side of caution.

It will rarely be wise for a banker in a season of pressure to attempt to get away the customers of other bankers by offering them greater accommodation. The best way of getting new connections is to treat well those that he has.

It is better for a banker to employ his funds in supporting his old friends than in attempting to get new ones. If his funds are so ample that he can do both without inconvenience, very well. But caution is necessary in taking new accounts at this time, and he should be doubly cautious in making applications to parties. Unless he has the most ample and satisfactory information as to their circumstances, he had better wait until they apply to him. It would then devolve upon them to satisfy him that he would be justified in making the advances required.

During the pressure, a banker will find that some of his wealthier customers, who, when money was abundant, took their bills to be discounted by a bill-broker, because he would cash them at a lower rate, will come back, and expect to have discounts from their banker. This is no fault of the bill-brokers. People put money in their hands avowedly for temporary purposes. In seasons of abundance the bill-brokers are glutted with money. When the pressure commences this money is withdrawn. The consequence is, that in seasons of abundance the bill-brokers will discount at a lower rate than the bankers, and when money is scarce they discount at a higher rate, and in many cases will not discount at all. Sharp-sighted people, who are acquainted with the London money market, will, when money is abundant, take all their first-rate bills to a bill-broker, and send to their banker all their inferior bills, which a bill-broker would not take. Now, if a banker has occasion to curtail his advances in seasons of pressure, he should begin with people of this sort. But if he has ample means, and the parties are wealthy, he may deem it worth his while to take their bills, charging a high rate of interest, and gently reminding them of their former delinquencies. Exhortations to good behaviour have always a greater effect when administered in seasons of affliction. And reproof at this time to a party who has thus wandered may induce him to pursue in future a more righteous line of conduct.

During a pressure, a banker will find that some of his customers will get into difficulties, and will apply to him for assistance. He will often be at a loss to decide whether he should or should not grant the assistance required. This hesitation will arise from his doubts as to the extent to which he can prudently rely upon the calculations and anticipations of his customer. The party states that he must immediately stop payment unless he has assistance; but he has abundance of property, and his difficulties arise only from not being able to realize it. If he has a certain sum he can then go on comfortably. The banker grants him this sum. After a while, he comes again, and states he must now stop unless he has a farther sum. The banker hesitates, but ultimately gives him this farther sum. He comes a third time, and states he has not yet got enough; and not being able to get more, he then stops, leaving the banker at best with a large lock-up, and probably with an ultimate loss.

During a pressure, those banks that allow interest on deposits will be asked for a higher rate of interest.[5] It is quite right that those parties who have had deposits at the bank for some time, should receive a higher rate of interest, proportionate to the increased value of money. But it may be questioned whether it is worth while to receive farther lodgments, during a pressure, at a high rate of interest, unless they are lodged for a fixed period. For, should the pressure increase, these sums are sure to be withdrawn, or else applications will be made for a higher rate of interest than the banker can prudently give. Nor must it be forgotten that it is not wise for a banker to give, during a panic, an extravagant rate of interest. Should he do so, he will give rise to an opinion that he is short of funds, and this may cause more deposits to be withdrawn than he would obtain from his high rate of interest.

During a pressure, a banker will pay considerable attention to the published returns of the Bank of England. The increase or diminution of the gold and silver in the issuing department will show the progress of the pressure. As these increase, money will become less scarce, the rate of interest will fall, and the pressure will subside. In this department, it is the progress of increase or diminution, more than the actual amount, that should be the main object of attention. The banking department resembles any other bank. Its means are the paid-up capital—the real or surplus fund—the public deposits—the private deposits, and the seven-day bills. These means are employed in public securities, private securities, and cash in the till. Its ability to make advances, at any given time, depends on the amount of cash in the till. The diminution of this amount shows the increase of the pressure, and the banker will act accordingly.

As far as past experience goes, all panics or pressures have resulted in a subsequent abundance of money. It would be a grand thing for a banker if he could know beforehand at what precise point this change would take place. But this he cannot know, and he had better not speculate on the subject, but just follow the course of events as they occur. When, however, the point is fairly turned, he will act wisely in investing all his surplus funds in such convertible securities as are likely to advance in price, from the increasing low rate of interest. Exchequer bills are most likely to be the first affected, and then the public funds. He will, also, be more liberal in granting discounts, and other advances, and he will lower the rate of interest at which he takes deposits. At the same time, he will be cautious in the bills he discounts. For,

5. The rate of interest allowed on deposits by the banks in London and throughout the country generally is regulated by the Bank of England rate for the time being, and is, as a rule, one per cent. below that rate. But in special instances, when money is scarce and the bank rate high, or plentiful and the bank rate low, one and a half per cent., and even more than that, below the bank rate, is frequently the rate allowed for deposits.

though money may be abundant, yet trade may be depressed, and the effects of the previous panic may be the failure of a great number of persons in the middle class of society. The banker will therefore be cautious in extending his discounts, except on bills of an undoubted character.

We will observe, lastly, that, in a season of pressure, it is peculiarly necessary that a banker should pay regard to the state of his own health, and to the discipline of his own mind, so as to guard against any morbid or gloomy apprehensions with regard to the future. He should attempt to form a cool and dispassionate judgment as to the result of passing events; endeavouring so to arrange his own affairs as to be prepared for whatever may occur, but taking care not to increase the present evil by predicting greater calamities. If he suffer a feeling of despondency to get the mastery of his mind, he will be less able to cope with the difficulties of his position. He will then, probably, refuse reasonable assistance to even first-rate customers, realize securities unnecessarily at a heavy sacrifice, and keep in his till an amount of unemployed treasure excessively disproportionate to the extent of his liabilities. This will increase the pressure. Fear, too, is always contagious. A banker of this melancholy temperament will impart his apprehensions to others, and thus the panic will become more widely extended.

THE MONEY MARKET, COMPANY LAW, AND FINANCIAL FRAUD

The first two selections included here provide a variety of perspectives on the heart of the financial system, the money market—that transfer of value, typically in the form of credit, from various lenders to borrowers through financial institutions like the securities market, the banks, and the London discount houses. D. Morier Evans's essay, which forms part of his popular collection of financial articles, *Speculative Notes and Notes on Speculation,* shows how financial information, which seemed mysterious and boring when he was a child, acquired all of the intrigue of sensational crimes when Evans became a City reporter. In this and other essays contributed by Evans to various newspapers and periodicals, we see how financial reporters constructed the money market as romance, peopled by its own heroes and fueled by its own fantasies. Like Evans, Walter Bagehot composed his essay on the money market during a period of easy credit, but his is a more cautionary voice than Evans's. Bagehot's discussion of the discrepancy between credit and cash reminds readers that the romance of the market is based on trust and image rather than the solid backing of gold. By mentioning the international context in which the British financial system operated, Bagehot hints that arrangements that linked one nation to another, like the exchange rate and the balance of trade, lay beyond Britain's control. Note too that Bagehot refers once more to the question of how to figure a bank's "reserve." Like the essays collected in Chapter 3, Bagehot reminds us that decisions about how to represent "money" were as critical to the well-being of the system as was the amount of gold actually held in the Bank of England's vaults.

Chapter 10 includes essays that focus on the results of two of the most important financial developments of the century: the passage of limited liability legislation in 1856 and 1862 and the collapse of the great discount house, Overend, Gurney, & Co. in 1866. D. Morier Evans's essay, which was published before the extent of company fraud was revealed, is cautiously optimistic about limited liability and the company promotion it had already begun to spark. His references to the failure of some early joint-stock banks and to international finance companies sound ominous notes to those who read with hindsight, for joint-stock banks were the companies most likely to fail, and international finance companies became notorious for offering high-risk, poorly secured, long-term loans. Although Evans could not have known this when he wrote this essay, the collapse of Overend, Gurney, & Co. was to bring down nearly all of the international finance houses based in London. Writing in the wake of the crash of the great "Corner House," Bagehot touches on two important issues: the wisdom of suspending the Bank Act of 1844 (also known as "Peel's Act") so that the Bank of England could help alleviate the monetary crisis that followed Overend, Gurney, & Co.'s collapse; and the difference between the "credit panic," which swept through the money market late in 1866, and the capital panics and bullion panics that had erupted earlier in the century. In his treatment of the decision to suspend the Bank Act, Bagehot reveals that financial writers had begun to represent such suspensions as normal consequences of the 1844 Act. In his discrimination among kinds of panics, Bagehot suggests the level of analytic sophistication that financial writers had begun to claim by 1866. As observers began to name the features of panics, commentators tried to reassure readers by depicting the orderly sequence that every panic followed and by assigning panics to a clear typology. Bagehot's hints that some observers of the money scene had long known that Overend, Gurney, & Co. was operating in a financially, if not legally, dubious manner also seems to have been intended to reassure readers of the *Economist,* which was widely recognized as a respected financial guide by 1866.

Laurence Oliphant's "Autobiography of a Joint-Stock Company (Limited)" reveals the dubious machinations of company promotion, finance, and winding-up in scintillating detail. Based on the actual case of Albert Grant, the promoter who created the notorious finance company, the Credit Foncier and Mobilier of England, in 1864, this essay was heralded by contemporaries as being true in every particular. Like the "Biography of a Bad Shilling," included in Part 1, this essay personifies and gives voice to the financial instrument (in this case, the company, most of whose "life" takes the form of various kinds of paper). This strategy enables Oliphant to expose the various stages of fraud that lay behind the company's formation while generating some sympathy for the company promoter (Grant), whom he calls "Captain Hawk." As Captain Hawk finds his original idea hijacked by Mire, the German Jewish financier, and other members of the sponsoring syndicate, Oliphant implicitly asks us to appreciate how difficult it is to attribute agency to a single individual or to adequately apportion responsibility for such a company's collapse. Oliphant suggests that the financial penalty Mire is ultimately required to pay falls short of the damage he has wreaked on the public trust when he notes that the financier's tombstone is engraved with the clause of the Companies Act Mire violated. Captain Hawk, meanwhile, escapes, to promote another company under the lax provisions of the limited liability acts.

CHAPTER NINE

THE MONEY MARKET

D. MORIER EVANS
❊❊❊

THE STATE OF THE MONEY MARKET
FROM A FRESH POINT OF VIEW

I remember well, when I was a tiny boy, the strange feeling of dread inspired by my father, who was a fund-holder, emphatically desiring me, as fathers can do, to look under the head of money market, and read to him the two or three first paragraphs respecting the state of the stocks. This command was usually made at breakfast-time, as I was the first to rush to the newsman when his short, sharp tinkle of our bell announced his arrival; and if I was deeply engaged in perusing the horrors of that frightful discovery, the murder of Maria Martin in the Red Barn, and the further particulars of the apprehension of Corder, taken, as I well recollect he was, while cooking eggs at his own fireside, my annoyance was increased, because to wade, as I then thought, through a dreary column devoted to facts and prices, was an ordeal second only to that of returning to school after the customary month's vacation.

But although not immediately yielding with the best grace, yet I knew that if my father desired it, the most pleasant course was to comply, and get out of my misery with the least delay, since, notwithstanding he was an affectionate parent, there was not the slightest utility in endeavouring to evade his imperative request. Little did I dream at the time—now more than thirty years ago—that I should ever have been thrown so completely head-over-heels, as

D. Morier Evans, "The State of the Money Market from a Fresh Point of View." *Speculative Notes and Notes on Speculation, Ideal and Real.* 1864; rpt. New York: Burt Franklin, 1968. Pp. 84–92.

it were, into this maëlstrom of financial life, or that this same heavy, dreary column, would become the bread and cheese of my every-day existence, serving to support Paterfamilias, with a numerous family, whose wants and requirements are not of the most insignificant kind.

Well do I remember how greatly I used to wonder at the old gentleman being so solicitous about whether the Three per Cents. were up or down—whether Long Annuities had moved or not, and if any notice was taken of the next red-letter day at the Bank. To me it was wearisome in the extreme to have to plod through these miserable figures to satisfy paternal curiosity, particularly if, by a furtive glance of the eye, I could see on the next page, an interesting narrative of Mr. Green's balloon ascent from the royal property, Vauxhall, or the narrow escape of the Duke of Brunswick when he accompanied Mrs. Graham. Still the duty had to be done, and I accomplished it in the best spirit I was able, and being the youngest of a family of five, my inclinations on the subject were neither studied, nor respected.

In course of time, as I grew up, I became more accustomed to the quaint, crabbed phraseology of the markets, and finding that my father used occasionally to tell my mother, when the prices were going down through rumours of war, or political differences, that it was the right period to "buy in," I discovered that there was some pecuniary reason at the bottom of all these diurnal investigations. I did not fail to shortly put a few interrogations to my mother, and being slightly a favourite, I was informed of the nature and importance of the money market, the position and interest-bearing capacity of the funds, and promised, if I were a very good boy, a trip with my father to take his dividends.

Although no doubt my poor mother, a clever, sensible woman, gave me a clear, intelligible account in her own way of the Government connection with the Bank, the rise and progress of the Debt, and the difference between Consols paying three per cent. and the Long Annuities returning almost six, my mind was of too errant a cast to at once appreciate the information; and when she told me that the neighbourhood of the money market was the Bank, the Royal Exchange, and the great lottery establishments, which loomed out in Cheapside and Cornhill, with their prominently emblazoned boards of Bish, Hazard, Goodluck, and the other singular names imported to give weight to their transactions, I became more confused than ever.

According to my notion, as I then saw by the best light I was able, the money market ought to have assumed an eminently practical appearance, and I expected, as I told her, to see when I went round the Bank, and the other localities, bank-notes, gold, and stock offering for sale, as you would see articles of merchandize exhibited in other trading places. She was not long, however, with the assistance of my father, in explaining that although this was not so in actual matter of fact, it really was the case in effect, through the intervention of bankers and brokers, who made it a special business to deal in these things. When I grew older, my father, to redeem the promise made on his behalf, took me with him to receive his dividends, and then much of the hazy film, which had previously covered my young and inexperienced eyes, was suddenly removed.

There through the ancient rotunda, the resort at that time of a great body of the jobbers, I dragged my way with difficulty, following close to the "governor," and I soon became enlightened as to the manner in which some of the transactions of the country were conducted. The calling of the name from the books, the check and issue of the dividend warrants, their conversion into bank-notes and gold, and most of all, the apparently careless shovelling up of the heap of glittering coin placed before the clerks, riveted my attention, and from that date to the present, I have been a close observer of the course and current, of our principal financial operations.

From that point of view I will dismiss all considerations of the money-market, and now look at it from a different one. It will be understood, *in limine,* that I am now directly interested in the state and fluctuations of the rate of discount, in the position and change of the various investments and enterprises, not as an operator or dealer, but in the character of a daily chronicler of facts and events. I am therefore thrown into association with the leading bankers, the chief discount establishments, the principal money and stockbrokers; in short, with almost every one who has anything to do with capital or finance.

With my matured light and experience, I should now as soon think of visiting the gorilla country or Japan, as reading a murder or a balloon ascent, in preference to at once diving into the financial columns of the press. I scarcely imagine I should be able to sleep at night, without I was well posted in the latest price of Consols, French Rentes, and knew the closest price of money, both at the Bank, and in Lombard Street.

What an avalanche of sorrow should I be immersed in, if the Bank directors ever raised the *minimum,* and I was not acquainted with the circumstance! Surely I should never recover the shock, and it might probably terminate in a financial suicide. What are the best oratorical excitations of Mr. Gladstone and Mr. Disraeli if they are not associated with revenue and expenditure, fiscal and other alterations, producing an impression in Mincing or Bartholomew Lanes? And do I not loudly asseverate against their want of compression in dealing with facts and figures, so as to bring their information within manageable compass and ready comprehension? What I used to think an intolerable bore—what a great number of other people still think an intolerable bore—a City life, is to me now, a paradise of delight, and I move through its shifting scenes and its circles, much in the old-fashioned manner of a horse in a mill, who rarely leaves the centre of his operations save to take his rest and his corn, and does not seem after all much the worse for wear.

The only close stickers to the collar like myself are the money brokers of the present day—and when I say the money brokers, I mean those who are really money brokers, not the discount brokers, or those identified with general financial transactions, who do their business in ordinary course—but the type of the staid old school, whose very looks and appearance are capital itself, and whose simple word for £100,000 would be taken quite as readily as their signature or their cheque.

The body as a class, are not so numerous as they were; the two principal representatives of the firms who take the lead in this kind of business—and they rank in name according to the two first letters in the alphabet—B, perhaps, in point of importance in this instance, taking precedence of A—having brought nearly the whole of these particular operations into their own hands. The sober seriousness of both these active, intelligent gentlemen, the weightiness of their engagements being impressed upon their visages, the bustling progress of the one, with the alert walk of the other, indicating how fully they enter heart and soul into the nature of their calling. The knowledge that the house of one has been nearly a century occupied in the same absorbing pursuits, and that the firm of the other, can go back upwards of half a century in close relations with most of the great money firms, will at once account for the division of the business between them, in so far as relates to special departments.

Both occupy extremely important positions in their respective walks, and being like myself City pedestrians, through the nooks and corners surrounding the Royal Exchange, Birchin Lane, and other various outlets and inlets associated with monetary engagements, it seems to me in some respects a lost day, if I have not encountered either of them in my route. As they constitute the great "go-betweens" in the banking and discount community and the Stock Exchange, turning over frequently a half or three-quarters of a million a day, they in the course of conversation acquire a vast fund of intelligence, and by reason of their actual transactions, can trace the causes and effects of the several mutations in the money-market. These are the parties acting for such firms as Messrs. Glyn, Mills, and Co., Messrs. Overend, Gurney, and Co., the National Discount Company, the Joint-Stock Discount Company, and other large institutions having the command of the floating balances of the day, for use at the Stock Exchange, or among the bankers and brokers themselves.

If money is to be provided, in consequence of heavy sales of securities by the Government, or the Court of Chancery, and the bank-notes current in the market to meet the requisite demands run short, it is usually one, or both of these gentlemen, who have, by arrangement, to obtain loans by which the proper supply is secured. Sometimes, in similar transactions for the large Insurance Companies, or the Scotch Banks, the supply being restricted in the market, and the means of these individuals temporarily exhausted, applications have to be made to the Bank itself, and then the pressure being comparatively great, the quotation increases.

It may be fairly estimated that the chief of these establishments, enters into operations ranging over some five or six millions a week, the other at least four to five. As illustrating the importance of these engagements, it may be safely asserted that at the period of the Turkish Loan of 1862, when the enormous deposits were made on account of that transaction at Messrs. Glyn, Mills and Co., one of these money brokers dealt with nearly £2,000,000 in the course of a day, having to employ it, to the best advantage he could, in his several channels. Such an influx into the general market, naturally at once largely influenced the rate, and then it was, that the terms for short periods averaged about 1½ per cent. To use my friend's smart and practical expression in relation to such an extent of business, "It was indeed something like a day's work, and the commission represented a pretty penny."

Marvellous must be the sums passing through their hands from year to year, particularly in connection with establishments like Messrs. Mullens, Marshall and Daniell, Hitchens and Harrison, Lawrence, Pearce and Son, P. Cazenove and Co., G. E. Seymour, Hill, Fawcett and Hill, and the other old-established, and leading Stock Exchange houses.

Let me suppose I am going my diurnal round. I am passing through Lombard Street between 11 and 12 a.m., I meet the great money broker B—; he is just coming out of one of the banks. I ask if there is anything fresh. He says he hardly knows. The market is not in condition yet, not having gone the whole of his circuit. Perhaps in half an hour or an hour, I encounter him again, either coming from "the house at the corner,"[1] or one of the discount companies. "Money, money, eh! what is it?" There is a good supply; he has been able to get large sums, and the rate he thinks ought to be quoted from day to day about 2 to 2½ per cent.

Later again, perhaps, I meet him with a blue bag containing securities, India bonds, Exchequer bills, and other first-class descriptions, the value of which if divided by ten, would, he graciously assures me, make either of us comfortable for life. The market meanwhile has fluctuated. There has been a diminished or increased supply, and the rate has varied in accordance with the wants of the moment.

Another day I meet him rushing, driving along: scarcely time to exchange a word. He is in and out, of banking houses, discount houses, stockbrokers' offices; he pulls up people in the open thoroughfare; he exchanges a word and

---

1. Overend, Gurney, & Co. Founded (as Richardson, Overend, & Co.) in 1805, this had become the most important bill-broking firm or discount house in London by 1840. The house collapsed on May 11, 1866. [Ed.]

hurries on. I see him; he sees me; it is not convenient to speak to him, and knowing that I shall be in the same circle for several hours, I bide my time to obtain my information.

At length, in the afternoon, we fall across each other. I then discover, what I had previously anticipated from the course of events during the day, that great stringency had been experienced at the Stock Exchange through the calling in of loans, and that owing to this shortness of supply, he has been up to his chin in re-arranging his engagements, altering the rates, curtailing amounts in some quarters, and carrying them on in others.

Thus his daily avocation requires unremitting attention, and either for himself or his competitor in the same kind of business, little time is left for recreation, save what can be snatched from the end of Saturday to the beginning of Monday. But they work on steadily and well, and prosper, making position and profit in due proportion to their untiring exertions. I only hope that their successors—for the time must come when this constant wear and tear will have to be relinquished—may be as popular, and as deserving of support, and that their transactions may prove equally lucrative and extensive.

WALTER BAGEHOT

THE MONEY MARKET, NO. 1
What the Money Market Is, and Why It Is So Changeable

The design of the present series of articles is peculiar. We wish to bring together in a continuous series those facts and those arguments which are most necessary to explain the peculiarities of the money market. The present time almost *requires* something of the sort. The enormous growth of trade, the vast increase of credit, the quickness and the ease with which capital is sent on loan from country to country, and especially from England, where it is so rapidly saved, the altered condition of consols and exchequer bills in the face of new investments, the frequent changes in the value of money, the high rate of discount which, on the whole, has prevailed during the past year, and has not yet ceased—these new facts, and others which might be mentioned, make a new outline of the subject necessary. Our new experience *ought* to have taught us much, and we ought to take stock of what it has taught us. The changes in

Walter Bagehot, "The Money Market, No. 1: What the Money Market Is and Why It Is So Changeable." *Economist* 22 (May 12, 1866): 1105–7.

the value of money are forcing the practical study of the money market much more than of old upon men of business. Money is not, as formerly, always to be had at 5 per cent. The investment of the large savings now made from business incomes is also a serious matter. The money market, like all other markets, is a matter of business, and any man of business who will really attend to it will comprehend it; but it *needs* real attention and consideration. You cannot keep a ledger in a hurry, and you cannot understand the money market in a minute; and, therefore, we wish by a continuous series of articles to aid its study and consecutive consideration.

It is not only in England that such subjects have now an extended interest. There is an *Economist* in several countries in Europe. The growing wealth of the whole Continent gives an interest to the manner in which wealth may be secured, and in which it may be made the most of. In France, the attempt of M. Pereire, by the aid of the forgotten privileges of the Bank of Savoy, to invade the privileges of the Bank of France, has elicited a crop of pamphlets like those on the "Act of 1844." A review of these questions though principally from an English point of view, will, we hope, have therefore its interest for our continental readers.

The money market is best described by a French phrase. It is an "organisation of credit," by which the capital of A, who does not want it, is transferred to B, who does want it. It is a vast borrowing machinery, composed of many links, and in which a vast number of persons give a surprising trust to one another. The machinery is so familiar and so useful that we forget that it is in the last degree refined. A Somersetshire farmer pays five sovereigns into a Somersetshire bank; no more trivial act, few less important people, can be conceived. Nor, indeed, has an individual act any importance. But the sum total of such acts has an indefinite importance. If the agricultural community stopped "paying in", London would be bare, Lombard Street would be ruined, and the whole exchanges between England and foreign countries would receive a shock to be remembered for fifty years. The mode in which Lombard Street is supplied, and the use of its being supplied, is this. A vast number of districts in Great Britain cannot employ their own yearly accumulations. You cannot *create* new trades, new manufactures, new wealth, upon a large scale, in a stagnant rural district. On the other hand, large districts like Lancashire or the West Riding of Yorkshire have a chronic craving for capital. They could continually employ half as much again as they have, if only they had it. An energetic man of business continually feels "what a business he could do, if only he had money enough." The machinery of the money market gives him or tends to give him this money. The savings of rural districts—the small savings, especially, which those who saved them could not employ on the spot— are deposited in local banks, are sent by them to London, are deposited at notice or at call with the bill brokers, and invested by them in the discount of bills from the *go-ahead* districts—from Lancashire and the West Riding of

Yorkshire. Whatever trade is most prosperous bids highest for this spare money, and *gets* it.

The principle is just the same, though the machinery is a little different, if the money be lent on securities upon the stock exchange. Persons who have no present use for their money leave it with a banker; persons who wish to buy or hold "securities"—that is, shares or *parts* of actual undertakings—railways, canals, gas works, etc., come to the banker and ask for a loan. He lends them the money his depositors lent him; he is the medium by which the money of the inactive class is divided and distributed among the enterprising class.

The curious point which strikes a cursory observer of Lombard Street is that everything is done on *credit.* If you deposit five thousand pounds with Messrs. Overend or the National Discount Company, you deposit it by cheque, which is only a piece of paper; and when they repay you, it will be by another piece of paper. In a very few cases bank notes may be used, as where securities have to be parted with to those whose credit is not good, and the holder of these securities says, "I will part with them to you when you bring me bank notes and not before." But even these bank notes are only, as Mr. Huskisson said, "circulating credit"; they are only promises to pay—*believed* promises; and on a large scale in London no coin—nothing *not* credit—no intrinsically valuable medium, is ever seen or thought of.

Persons who have had to do with some of anglo-continental banks have had great difficulty in making foreigners comprehend the safety of this state of credit. In many countries bankers do not like to take money to be paid by cheque—money at call, because they think they could not safely use it. They think it would be asked for, and then they should not have it. Even in Paris the timidity of bankers is amazing to Englishmen; but the answer of the Parisian banker is intelligible. "Ah!" he says, "You do not know what 1848 was in Paris; *I do.* If you knew how suddenly a revolution may come, and how much money it makes people ask for, you would be cautious *as I am.*" We are so familiar with all this trust and confidence that we do not know how rare and exceptional in commercial history it is, how marvellous it seems and must seem to nations less advanced in mercantile organisation.

This vast organisation of credit has, unquestionably, a most solid basis—it is based on the bullion in the Bank of England. This (putting aside the reserves which Scotch or Irish banks may be compelled by Sir Robert Peel's Act to keep, and other minor exceptions), speaking broadly and practically, the whole of this great machinery of credit is based on the bullion in the vaults of the Bank. A *good* cheque, in the last resort, means that, if the holder wishes, he can have an equivalent amount of *that* gold and take it home with him. His cheque may be on the London and Westminster Bank or a country bank, and these banks can by law compel him to take *from them* Bank of England paper.

But this difficulty is a difficulty of one step only. He can take that "paper" to the Bank, and there get change for it. Most people have a little small change about them, all bankers have coin for daily purposes in their till, but no banker and no common person keeps at hand more coin than he can help; people like to make something of their money, and coin is "barren." The bullion in the Bank of England is the sole accumulated reserve, the sole come-at-able reserve of intrinsic wealth out of which our promises, if paid, must be paid, on the faith of which our credit, while good, is good.

In former times it was difficult to illustrate the dependence of the public upon the bullion store in the Bank of England. The accounts of other bankers were so secret that they could not be used to explain anything. But the success of the joint stock bank system has changed all this. The Union Bank, for example, has the largest amount of liabilities of any private, of any *non*-national bank in the world. What is its reserve? It is as follows:

	£	£
Cash in the till	721,343	
Cash at the Bank of England	751,546	
Cash lent at call	1,044,000	
		2,516,889
Investments in general stock, exchequer bills, debentures, etc.	1,266,080	
		3,782,969

—a very large reserve, but of this great aggregate only £721,343 is money, is coin, and of that not a sixpence could probably be spared. The whole of it is doubtless wanted for the requirements of the day's business. The rest is money at the Bank, money at call, money invested in government securities: that is, money which is *lent* to someone. Out of the £19,500,000 of the Union Bank's liabilities, there is only £721,000 of actual coin, of money unlent to anybody. What is true of this great bank is true of smaller ones, as far as they go: their reserve, too, is lent or invested somehow. The bullion in the Bank is the only uninvested, unlent, *tangible* reserve in Great Britain.

This reserve is the fund—the only fund—we have to meet *exchange* payments to foreign countries. If the balance of trade goes against us—if, as is now common, we make cash loans to foreign countries—this single reserve in the vaults of the Bank is the one store, the sole accumulation, we have to pull upon.

It is very remarkable that, vastly as our credit augments, enormously as our trade develops, this cash balance, this sole available unemployed fund, does not increase. In September 1844, the first account under Sir Robert Peel's Act, the bullion at the Bank of England was

	£
September 7	15,209,060
— 14	15,207,771
— 21	15,158,964
— 28	15,022,256

whereas the last return is only £12,980,033, or *two millions less than twenty years ago.*

In this time, who can tell how the liabilities of the banking system of Great Britain—the liabilities against which this reserve is held—have augmented? We cannot estimate with accuracy those liabilities, either as they were in 1844 or as they are now; but we have a test which, though not perfect, is at least approximate, and may suggest an idea sufficiently true:

	£
In 1844—deposits, etc., London and Westminster were	2,676,741
— — London Joint Stock	2,245,330
— — Union	1,591,200
— — London and County	1,231,412
....	7,744,683

And we showed last week that the liabilities of these same banks were now £65,162,292, or nine times as great. Doubtless these banks have gained in part by aggression upon others. Yet *it is said,* by people who should know, that the aggregate liabilities of the present London bankers are much greater than they were in 1844; and undoubtedly so it is with the Scotch and the English country banks. We do not, therefore, hesitate to say that the credit of the country has augmented *manifold* in twenty years, and yet the basis of that credit, the cash balance, has not augmented, but has diminished.

We need not show at length how the trade of the country has increased since 1844:

	£
The exports of the produce and manufactures from the United Kingdom, were in 1844	58,584,292
Ditto ditto in 1863	146,489,768

—a business of *treble* the amount in the last year that it was in the first.

No wonder, therefore, that our money market is delicate, now that we understand what it is. The basis of credit has not diminished, and yet that credit has multiplied no one can say how manifold. And trade has grown, and as it grows, this demand upon our store of bullion, upon this basis of our credit, must of necessity grow too. We have to pay a *balance* of trade, and if the trade gets larger, if it deals in immensely bigger figures, the possible difference in any one year between exports and imports is augmented, and the amount of bullion to be paid in consequence is augmented likewise. Who, therefore, can wonder that our money market is delicate when he sees that in the last twenty years the store *to be* attacked has not increased, but diminished, while the attacking force has during the same period increased so portentously and wonderfully?

CHAPTER TEN

COMPANY LAW AND FINANCIAL FRAUD

D. MORIER EVANS

WHITHER IS LIMITED LIABILITY LEADING US?

Significant indeed is the fact, that limited liability has become "a power among men." It was not supposed that the Act, in its general acceptation, would have been received with such favour, when first it obtained the sanction of the Legislature. Vaunting, as were its authors, of its adaptability to the wants of the mercantile and financial community, it was several years before its privileges were made available; and when they were originally brought into operation, they did not shadow forth its advantages in the most encouraging light.

The early attempts to introduce its privileges—much as they were spoken of—eventuated, as it might be supposed they would, in the most lamentable failures; and then it was distinctly asseverated that so little were they suited to English taste, and English convenience, that they fell still-born, leaving the public dissatisfied with the experiment, and willing to abandon the new system for the old and better-working machinery of the general Joint-Stock Act. For a somewhat lengthened period "limited liability" was, so to speak, a dead letter, and notwithstanding provincial experience was rather more favourable to the development of the principle, it was difficult to get a metropolitan proprietary to organize undertakings, which should give it a proper or extensive trial.

Disheartening as were the prospects which were associated with the

D. Morier Evans, "Whither Is Limited Liability Leading Us?" *Speculative Notes and Notes on Speculation, Ideal and Real.* 1864; rpt. New York: Burt Franklin, 1968. Pp. 228–36.

progress of the movement, a few companies with small capitals were started, which essayed to give vitality to the Act; and though these could not be looked upon as more than additional crude experiments, they made progress, and finally rendered the public familiar with what was before considered a partially impracticable dogma.

Although appeals were made to transatlantic knowledge, where the elements of success were so unmistakeably apparent, like every new notion based upon theory rather than practice, our countrymen were most slow to take the initiative. Into operation, however, the principle came at last, and notwithstanding it was but by steady and sure degrees, the multitude, when it was fairly recognized, were only too ready and eager to adopt it. The earlier undertakings that acknowledged its influence, and made its provisions subservient to their purposes, were those of a manufacturing description; and though even after the first great break-down there were occasional difficulties through mismanagement, they were ultimately counterbalanced by the more legitimate results arising in other channels from this kind of co-partnery.

Nevertheless, doubts were still entertained if "limited liability" would turn out the great boon that had been predicted by its most ardent admirers, and none were more averse to the new form of arrangement than the Joint-Stock Banks and Private banking interests. Strange to say, as is very frequently the case, and as if some foreshadowing of such a change were approaching, the Joint-Stock and the Private Banks have probably more than any other class, been affected by the revolution. The "limited liability" rage made its first step in Manchester, and there attacked the financial community in its stronghold, by converting an old and influential bank to the tenets of the bill. Liverpool followed, and, with a prescience acknowledged in the locality, it was not long before Birmingham, refusing to be behindhand, did not wait for old banks to recognize the principle, but started one on this basis, which has since, although a creation of only a few years, proved one of the most thriving in the neighbourhood.

But people shook their heads, looked sombre, and were not then prepared to admit that there was the slightest prospect of the Act taking substantial root in London, or ever becoming thoroughly acknowledged. A short time, however, only elapsed before the plethora of money, occasioned by the curtailment of trade through the American war, opened a new field for the inventive genius of those, who considered themselves specially adapted to promote joint-stock enterprise, and they at once sought to make its principles subservient to their plans.

The dividends of the half-yearly meetings in 1861 and 1862 had been very favourable; capital was seeking an outlet for employment; and though the supply of banking accommodation was large, it was nevertheless believed that it might he extended. The effects of unlimited responsibility were discussed, but notwithstanding they were considered the best applicable to banking, both as giving confidence to the public and customers, promoters themselves found that "limited liability" was more suited to their prospects and arrangements, and at a very opportune moment the vessel with the new name, showing new colours, was launched, not without, however, a little fear and trembling.

The period, it was soon ascertained, was propitious, the current ran smoothly; and though occasional cries of breakers ahead were heard, they never in reality appeared. Two banks were originally started, but the names of the directors in either case being scarcely, in City parlance, strong enough to float such institutions, arrangements were made for effecting an amalgamation. Before this one bank, under its altered appearance, and with a strengthened board, could make its preliminaries perfect for commencing business, the prospectuses of two others appeared for public support—not, it is true, simultaneously, but following closely on each other's heels. One, in the shape of share subscriptions, was a most decided success; the other speedily secured its capital, but, measuring its worth by the market price, it was not so great a favourite, either with the speculative, or the investing public as its competitor.

Previously to this, it should be mentioned, Discount Companies had been started, with the same inscription on their business banners, but in more prosaic terms, and they were regarded for a period as banks in disguise, though events subsequently showed the contrary. But it was a partial struggle for them to succeed, and when the great failures in the leather trade took place, predictions fatal to the lengthened existence of these institutions, were freely uttered. Their losses, it was certain, were large, in common with the various banks and discounting establishments, which suffered through the enormous mass of accommodation paper, put into circulation through the agency of Lawrance, Streatfeild, & Co., and accruing when they were least able to bear them, caused their balance-sheets, when printed, to exhibit a discouraging appearance.

The principal company stood their ground bravely, the managers worked well and vigorously, and in the space of two half years re-established their position, much to the satisfaction of the proprietors, who manifested throughout, complete confidence in their directors. The other unfortunate company, guided by a timid board, and assaulted by shareholders who, purchasing stock at a depreciated value, found on investigating the accounts, a profitable amount of assets to divide, failed to recover its *status,* and it was not long before it was determined to liquidate its affairs, which was gradually and successfully accomplished. This was a blow to the development of the principle of "limited liability" in the financial circles of the Metropolis; and, until the inauguration of the new banking movement, was the great argument always employed by the anti-limited liability party.

But when it was so readily perceived that, with a decided plethora in the money market, a revived taste among the public for speculation, and encouraging prices for shares, that limited liability would be accepted even among the banking community, and that the experiment would not be adopted on an unimportant scale, scarcely any bounds were placed to the animation which now ensued, and "limited liability" soon became not only patronized by banks, but by every other conceivable kind of financial and industrial undertaking.

Not only, however, was the principle rendered applicable to banking in London and the provinces, but organizations were formed for extending its usefulness to the more distant quarters of the globe. Hindustan and China, Brazil and Portugal, Austria and Italy, the Cape of Good Hope, Australia and New Zealand, were very speedily accommodated, and in several of the more important instances with every prospect of success. Even the nearer relations of the United Kingdom were not neglected: France, Belgium, and the Netherlands being at the same time completely supplied. The effect, as might be supposed, was also to introduce those large and important finance credit companies[1] which have since been raised, with capitals more extended than those of the banks. These again, striking into new paths and new channels, have been accompanied by those exchange establishments, which are entering upon domains in the territory of finance, before occupied alone by the leviathan capitalists, whose names have been passwords throughout Europe and the world, for wealth and resources, almost defying competition.

It will be several years ere the true success of these institutes will be established; but, regarding them as agents working in circles, where they must come in contact with the connections and operations of their great predecessors, they will doubtless attempt to wrest from their grasp, a portion of the enormous returns and profits, they have hitherto exclusively appropriated to their own benefit. Whether these private leviathan houses will have to succumb in the open hostilities, which may now be considered to have been declared between themselves and the limited liability undertakings, cannot be immediately determined; but it is reasonable to suppose that they will have to encounter strong competition—stronger probably than was originally imagined.

But it is not in this direction solely that limited liability is putting forth claims for universal support. Everywhere now the adoption of the principle is encouraged, and from the highest to the lowest enterprise, no other kind of foundation is permitted. Bold would be the individual who dared in these days to propose to start an undertaking on the unlimited system, holding the share-

---

1. Innovation in finance companies created in the 1860s. Based on the French Crédit Mobilier, these companies specialized in long-term (hence risky) loans to mines, railway companies, and other large ventures. Most of these companies lent recklessly in the period between 1862 and 1866, and all but one failed in the wake of the collapse of Overend, Gurney, & Co. [Ed.]

holders, as in the case of many existing institutions, responsible "to his last shilling, and his last acre." That which seven or eight years ago was considered an experiment—and an experiment of a very dangerous character, even as applied to the most ordinary adventures, has at length become so popular, that it bids fair to over-ride antecedent interests, joint-stock and private, and throw them wholly into the shade. Indeed, it may be said to be an analogous expansion to that experienced in the period of railway history, when every route, every highway, or every canal, was to become auxiliary to the new interest, and be finally absorbed.

In the present instance the adaptation of the principle to the whole class of projects seeking popular support, leaves no chance for any other system to be developed, and when we see that vested interests, which were previously furious against the alleged innovation, ready to recognize its value, it may be fairly considered that limited liability possesses claims which cannot be altogether ignored. It would be all very well to say that the new principle might be regarded as an experiment, if its application were strictly confined to undertakings which were ushered into existence during the last two or three years; but when we discover, apart from this, that old and wealthy establishments—several of undoubted reputation and position—are making arrangements to dissolve their private partnership character, and array themselves in the apparel of the Hon. Mr. Lowe's Act,[2] it must be allowed that either we are again in the midst of a most speculative epoch, or that the privileges offered, deserve to be fully tested.

Of course "limited liability" may in its extended form be carried beyond due bounds; it may, like the railway system, be so expanded that the recoil from the shock may be felt detrimentally in some quarters when a collapse takes place; but although this may occur sooner or later, it does not follow that "limited liability" as a principle will not turn out a success, and stamp encouraging traces of its handiwork upon many of the recently established financial and commercial institutions. The very excess of the preponderating influence, which has brought forward the late large crop of industrial enterprise, must at no distant date be relieved by reaction; but although this will come, and its effect will be exhibited in a variety of localities, the result will not for ever prejudice the vitality of the principle.

Limited liability has at length made itself a name, and a position in the land; and though there may still be failures, and mischances in individual cases associated with its working, it will not be an easy task to divert it from its recognized channels. Limited liability, it has been jocosely remarked, has become our banker, our credit and finance purveyor, our armourer, our hotel-keeper, our brewer, our baker—not as yet our butcher, though there is no great

---

2. 1856 Act proposed by the Whig Robert Lowe (1811–92) establishing limited liability for company owners. [Ed.]

reason why eventually this may not be the case—our bootmaker, our dairy supplier, and caterer for our most ordinary wants.

With this dominant tendency the power of the Act, now it has been so fully brought into play, must be severely felt, particularly by those who have hitherto endeavoured to stem the tide of its operation, and disinclined, as they even now may be, to receive its proffered assistance, they will not eventually escape its gradually absorbing powers. Limited liability is, therefore, established as a great principle; it may have its weak points, and defective arrangements will, in all probability, occasionally bring its development into disgrace; but, as a principle, it will outlive any such drawbacks as these, and finally extend its influence, if possible, even more widely than at present.

WALTER BAGEHOT

THE PANIC

We may congratulate our readers, and we own that we rejoice ourselves that the Friday on which we write is not like last Friday. Last week, Lombard Street looked more like a country fair than its usual self; most people were asking, will the Act[1] be broken? What will Mr. Gladstone[2] do? Several people stated to us, *on their own knowledge,* that the Act had been broken hours before it had been, or even before there had been any serious consideration of breaking it. But though this week is not one of acute agony like last week, it is the more fit for careful thought, and the recent history of the money market gives ample room for thought. There are four questions to be asked. First,

WHY WAS THERE A PANIC?

for many people looking back feel that they hardly know why they suffered such extreme fear, though that they did suffer it is most certain. The answer is that this panic is, more than any other which we remember, a *credit* panic. Credit, as we all know, and as has been explained over and over again in these pages, is to the last extent delicate. In this country, rightly or wrongly, reserves

Walter Bagehot, "The Panic." *Economist* 24 (May 19, 1866): 581–83.
1. The 1844 Bank Charter Act. [Ed.]
2. William Ewart Gladstone (1809–98). As chancellor of the Exechequer, Gladstone introduced independent audits of the Exchequer accounts. As prime minister (1868–74, 1880–85, 1886, 1892–94), he was the head of a coalition of Whigs, radicals, and Peelites that were known as the Liberals. [Ed.]

are used up to the last limit. The promises which we have given to pay gold on demand could not be performed by many thousand times as much gold as there is in the country. And when this is the case our whole mercantile system must always be easily injured by causes comparatively slight. Lately credit has been far more delicate than usual. It has been well known that a portion of our loanable means has been applied to inconvertible securities, and perhaps to unprofitable undertakings. "Financing"means this: it means that those who ought to have used their funds in convertible securities have employed them in things for the moment wholly unsalable, and very often permanently worthless. A great deal of this bad business was lying on the market, and no one knew in whose hands it was. Many people were a little suspected, and almost everybody shared in some infinitesimal distrust. Just then the house which had the greatest and oldest name for credit—Overend, Gurney and Co.—failed. In London it was well known that their management had long been bad; that the affairs of the old firm had been disastrous; that the operations of the new company had not, and could not, retrieve them.

In consequence the country world, which always trusts the London world largely, became frightened. It was disconcerted beyond example, and it did not know what to do. Even in London itself the effect, though mitigated in some degree by previous preparation, was very great. It was like a spark falling upon tinder. The diffused though slight discredit caused by the known bad finance speculations, and the uncertainty who might be mixed up in them, was at once aggravated into malignant fear. Last Friday no one knew who was sound, and who was unsound. The evil was not an over expenditure of capital such as at other times, as in 1847, has caused a panic; nor a drain of bullion which, except for admirable management, in 1864 would have caused one, but a failure of credit from intrinsic defect. Suspicion got abroad not because our whole reserve of bullion was too low to support the credit of the country; not because our annual expenditure had dangerously surpassed our annual saving; but because the lenders of money were *suspected* of misusing it; because the most celebrated of old houses evidently had misused it; because no one knew who else might not be to blame; because all persons under obligations to pay on demand felt they must strengthen themselves because the floating peril might come their way, and if they did not they might perish. The panic of 1866 was, to speak strictly, a credit panic—not a capital nor a bullion panic. And this is why there was such need for

THE SUSPENSION OF THE BANK CHARTER ACT

The whole mercantile community quite assent to the infraction of the Act; indeed, if it had not been broken this month, it would have been repealed next. The matter resembled what Mr. Lowe so happily said of the cattle plague report. He remarked that all the press wrote down the recommendations of the commissioners, but the disease "took the matter" into its own hands, and showed that they were right. Just so the "panic" took the matter into its own hands and proved that the Act could be no longer maintained—proved it not to theoretical minds or by fine argument, but to the great bulk of ordinary men, and by the palpable argument which strikes the massive common sense of the world. People do not indeed precisely understand *why* the Bank Charter Act ought to be suspended, but they plainly perceive that somehow it must have been.

The advantage of an expansive clause in Sir Robert Peel's Act for which we last week contended was never so evident. If it is not inserted soon, the Act will be repealed soon. The present evil is that many persons think we have committed some sin, not a great one perhaps, but still a little one. They are like people who have told a "white lie"; they do not think they have done much harm, but still they have done what they do not like much to remember, what they would not wish to do again, what rather puzzles their mind and plagues their morality.

But in a time of discredit, such as we have described, the suspension of that Act is not contrary to economical theory, but is the precept of that theory. On many points of currency doctrines there is much dispute, but on this there is scarcely any. Lord Overstone,[3] for example, is the best of all witnesses when it is a question of breaking the Act of 1844. He observed, and he has over and over again said the same thing, that "there may be action upon the circulation arising from accidental causes, a panic, and therefore not controllable by principle, which the Act cannot regulate, and which must, if they run to an excessive extent, therefore be reached by some extraordinary power." If ever they ran to an excessive extent, it was last Friday.

We showed the reason last week, and it is a reason which may be recognised by all schools of currency, whether Peelite or anti-Peelite. The ordinary bank note circulation is supported by a great mass of auxiliary circulation, by a credit circulation of a more refined sort. Cheques in all ordinary times supply without fear or danger a medium of communication far more easy, much more convenient, infinitely more used than bank notes. But in extraordinary times their efficiency is disturbed. Every country bank all over England, whether a bank of issue or not, lately strengthened itself because it could not be satisfied that the usual routine of banking would be continued. The efficiency of the auxiliary credit money was destroyed, and therefore a large amount of the simpler credit money, the note, was required to take its place.

It is to be observed that the bullion reserve of the country has been quite

---

3. Samuel Jones Lloyd (1796–1883). Financier, politician, and leader of the Currency School, which argued that coin and paper money are tangible and thus altogether different from credit, which is insubstantial. [Ed.]

enough. The French fancy we have suspended cash payments, but this is a total misconception. We have only done what the Bank of France could have done without breaking any law at all; if Peel's Act be broken, the constitution of our Bank will be exactly like the constitution of theirs. The suspension of our Act in a panic is a simple substitution of one sort of credit currency for another; it is a replacement of the more complicated form of that currency by the more simple. But the French mistake is a powerful argument against having, in case of panic, to break a law. It *looks* like a breaking of contract, though it is not. If our machinery worked more easily, if it did not appear like an action of the executive government to break faith between debtor and creditor, the Continent would not be puzzled, and the discredit which now deranges the exchanges would in great part be spared us. And not only was the suspension of the Act required by the most plain, if we may so say by the most Peelite, theory, but it was palpably necessary. We can understand its being argued that the Bank of England *ought* to manage so as always to keep a reserve sufficient to meet such times as last Friday; but we do not at all understand how it could be argued that on last Friday the Bank of England had such a reserve.

We believe that just before the suspension of the Act, no bank was—*considering the nature of its liabilities*—in so much danger as the Bank of England. It had a reserve of only £3,000,000 in town and country, and from all parts of the country demands on that reserve were pouring in every hour. Country bankers felt they must either get more notes and more sovereigns, or give up their business; London bankers were pressed upon not only by their country customers, but by a kind of oscillating run which now went to this bank and now to that. In such a state of things the banking department of the Bank of England could not with such a reserve be safe. Hardly any reserve, perhaps no reserve which could in the limits of probable practice be kept, would make it so. Our system of credit is so intertwined that no one bank can stand when all other banks fall. Some people say that the Bank should have stood firm and let everyone else go down. It should, they say, not have increased but have decreased its discounts; should have let its bills run off and so increased its reserve. But the bills would not have run off, for they would not have been paid. They are paid in general by the discount of other bills, and last Friday those "other" bills would not have been discounted except by the Bank. The Bank of England could not have increased its reserve by letting its bills "run off"; for they would not have "run off" but have accumulated unpaid in its bill case. The Bank of England could not have increased its means, and over its present means it had no power. The London bankers' deposits are understood in general to amount to between three and four millions, and on Friday last must have amounted in the aggregate to a larger sum than the London reserve. These bankers would not—and we believe some of them plainly used such language—allow the Bank of England to go on while they failed. Nothing is so imitative as panic, and if one or two large bankers had drawn their balances, all the rest would have followed like sheep, and the banking department of the Bank of England *must* have been left bare.

Whether it be a desirable thing that one bank should keep the reserve of the country may well be doubted; we have often said that, starting de novo and speaking in theory, it would be undesirable. But this question is not to the purpose now. The *aggregate reserve,* taking the banking department of the Bank by itself and supposing Peel's Act to be still in force, was insufficient. Everybody was pressed upon, and the banking department of the Bank more in reality than any. In figures its reserve looks larger than that of its competitors, but only because it includes that of its competitors. It was at least as badly off as they, for it existed on their sufferance.

In some influential quarters it has been said that the Act would have worked better if no notes had been issued on securities, but if there had been five sovereigns in the issue department for every £5 note issued from thence. But this is a mistake: the Act would have worked just the same. We wanted, and wanted so much, notes in the banking department, not bullion in the issue department. There was already quite enough of the latter; piles more bullion on the wrong side of the Bank would have been useless. If there had been 15,000,000 of sovereigns or bullion in the issue department instead of £15,000,000 securities, being so much futile treasure, they would not have discounted a London bill or sent a pound more into the country.

We have argued this question, as it will seem to most of our readers, at very needless length; but it is of great importance to confute, not by mere generalities which leave no trace, but by pointed arguments of detail, the erroneous notion that the suspension of Peel's Act in a panic is a misdemeanour in the eyes of *any* recognised school of political economy as well as in the eyes of the law. We pass to the

CONDUCT OF THE BANK OF ENGLAND

since the issue of the letter of liberty. As far as we can judge, with a single exception, their policy has been sound, cautious, and admirable. They have given mercantile and banking accommodation, as their accounts show, to an unprecedented extent, considering the shortness of the time under consideration and the rapidity of events within it; and as Mr. Gladstone stated in Parliament, and as is confirmed by the voice of Lombard Street, they have not departed from their usual care, discrimination, and caution in the selection of securities. We have called Mr. Gladstone's a letter of liberty; it was intended to be so, not a letter of license.

The exception of which we speak was the hesitation, the trifling hesitation, to lend upon government security. We say the trifling hesitation, because after the statement of Mr. Gladstone last night that they had lent £2,800,000 on such security, and after what has lately been notorious in Lombard Street, it would be a grave error to speak of a rare and occasional delay as if it had been a direct or common refusal. But we own that the slightness of the difficulty interposed is a reason for thinking that no difficulty should have been interposed. There was no wild speculation in the consol market which required check or suggested reprobation. As a moral hint, the measure was needless, and as a precautionary measure it was worthless. It was expressly said that sound, respectable, non-speculative people should upon government security receive accommodation, and there was (as we believe) nobody else at that moment to be found with government security. The real drain was, so to say, a respectable drain, and if that was to be permitted to continue, a casual speculation in consols might have been pardoned even if it had happened; it would not have emptied the Bank till of £1,000. But probably the present policy has emptied it. The mere statement of a doubt—we are speaking of matters which we know—caused an uneasy feeling both in London and at a distance, and led all persons who had consols to see if *they* could have advances on them, and, if they could, to take them while they were going. A slight discouragement seemed to many a premonitory symptom of future denials. So far from lessening advances on consols, the occasional hesitation certainly tended to augment, and we consider, in fact, augmented them.

It appears from Mr. Gladstone's statement that the Bank said they would not advance on consols because they could be sold in the market, whereas a mercantile bill could not be so sold. But the fact is otherwise. No considerable amounts of consols can be sold at moments when the Bank is for such purposes the only lender, and when it refuses to lend. The jobbers in stock are men of means, but they are not masters of secret hoards of *ready money*. It is not a question of price but a question of cash. How is a jobber on the stock exchange to create bank notes or sovereigns to buy stock with? In ordinary times if stock comes forward in unusual quantities for sale, he can with ease borrow on it, or dispose of other securities to purchase it. But in a panic these "other" securities are probably unavailable, and if the Bank of England hesitate to lend, the other resources of the market are very scanty. *If* the Bank were, in a panic, absolutely to refuse to lend on consols, they would not be salable for cash.

The object, too, with which the Bank have been acting during the week should be considered. They have been making advances to allay a panic which as much as anything was a country bankers' panic. But of all terrific events to a sound country banker, the worst is that consols may not be salable. He has been bred in the idea that they can, as he says, "be sold on a Sunday". But if there is a doubt about them, all his notions are overturned, and his apprehension becomes excessive. If, too, you try to replace the auxiliary credit of the country by the bank note (and we have shown that this is the principal object of suspending the Act of 1844), advances on consols are especially suitable to that purpose, because the best bankers who supply and support that auxiliary credit are the very persons who hold that kind of security. They relinquish high interest to be safe and keep in good credit, and if *any* credit is to be maintained theirs surely ought to be so.

But the most interesting point is

WHAT WILL HAPPEN NOW?

And of course on this point prophecies of detail are not possible. But some general conclusions are very certain. We believe and hope that from this time our improvement will be gradual; but still it must be interrupted by painful events, and cannot be healthy if it is too rapid. "Finance" paper too often means bad investments, and while so much of it is held about the market, credit must be tender, uncertain, and liable to vicissitudes and shocks. Of course this applies rather to money lending credit than to mercantile credit. A merchant is a borrower, not a lender; he will not have taken finance paper: if his business is good, and except in particular branches of speculative trade (as cotton, or pig iron, or the ship dealing and owning fostered by Barned's[4]) English commerce was hardly ever sounder.

The foreign exchanges show that there has been considerable distrust and alarm abroad at the state of English credit. And when Overends fail, and Peto[5] fails, and an Act is done which foreigners confound with a suspension of cash payments, no one can wonder that there is anxiety. But the appearances of the last two days indicate that this fear is mitigating; there are new orders for long-dated English bills from abroad, and on the whole there is every appearance that, though the immediate future must be chequered and painful, the worst bitterness of the panic is already spent and past.

LAURENCE OLIPHANT

THE AUTOBIOGRAPHY OF A
JOINT-STOCK COMPANY (LIMITED)

In a few days my brief and stormy career will finally close. I can calmly, and even thankfully, contemplate this premature extinction of an existence which has ruined reputations, shattered fortunes, and carried want and misery into

4. A Liverpool bank that failed in 1866. [Ed.]
5. Peto, Betts and Co. was a company that ceased payment in 1866. [Ed.]

Laurence Oliphant, "The Autobiography of a Joint-Stock Company (Limited)." *Blackwood's Edinburgh Magazine* 120 (July 1876): 96–122 (excerpt).

hundreds of humble homes; for I am wearied and worn out with the effort it has caused me to achieve these deplorable results, and utterly disgusted with the advanced state of civilisation which has made me the victim of its immoral tendencies. As far as my exhausted and feeble condition will allow me to feel anything, I think I can honestly say I am conscious of being in a repentant frame of mind.

What philosopher can explain to me the nature of the causes of which I am the vile effect? It was not my own fault that, like those who first hatched me, I was conceived in sin and shapen in iniquity, and became almost immediately the means of demoralising every one who came into contact with me, of deceiving those who trusted in me, and of crushing those who opposed me, until my own turn came, and I fizzled out in a gutter of fraud like a bad squib. Depraved though I am, I regret to say that, knowing as much as I do of the merits of the other members of my fraternity who still exist and flourish, I may yet hope that a process of natural selection is in progress, and that joint-stock companies, like the human race, are to rise into new and better conditions through the "survival of the fittest." At the same time, I know that I am not altogether bad; for I always found myself in sympathy with the few honest men upon my board. Now and then I experienced the novel and delightful sensation of awakening conscience, forming good resolutions—which at one time I intended to keep; and I looked forward to a calm and serene old age, soothed by the reflection that thousands would be rendered happier by my existence, and that my own health and well-being would be a source of amiable anxiety to numbers of respectable shareholders.

How the moral element thus temporarily infused into my system was afterwards expelled, and my whole nature became even worse at the end than it was at the beginning, is part of the thrilling story of my life to which I invite the attention of the reader; and I address myself to all without distinction, for all will be the wiser by the perusal of this most timely and instructive warning. I address myself to you, my innocent clerical friends in remote country parishes—for I know of no more ignorant and confiding class of investors—and though you may not think that the life and fortunes of a joint-stock company (limited) can interest you whose vocation lies in such a very different direction, as long as you have little earnings which you blindly invest on the faith of neatly-addressed circulars and prospectuses, you are interested, deeply interested, in the story I have to tell. I address myself to you, fair readers, especially widows and spinsters; for however capable you may think yourselves of enjoying the franchise, I am able from my own knowledge to declare that you are utterly unfit to manage your own money-matters, and I should never have been able to enter upon my fraudulent career had it not been for the powerful support I derived from the trusting contributions of confiding or speculative female investors; and now, in such solemn tones as I find it possible to command, reclining as I am at this moment in the arms of my official liquidator, with but a feeble spark of vitality still left, I warn you to read carefully this melancholy history. Believe me, it concerns you deeply. Such of you as have invested in me, I shall endeavour to remind of my gay and misspent youth, by providing you, by means of the officer legally appointed for that purpose, with infinitesimal dividends, extracted at long intervals from my miserable and shrunken remains—Bless you!

I address myself to you, rich landed proprietors, who never meddle with City matters, or investments, or "that sort of thing," but leave it all to your men of business, and I ask you whether you have had reason to be satisfied with the results of their advice this year? Don't you think you had better try and understand a little where your money is, and where it is not? And you men of business, who advise your clients, no doubt with the best intentions, have you had reason always to be satisfied with the advice you have given them? Clever though you are, and honest though you may be, it will do you no harm to read my narrative. And you, impecunious connections of the aristocracy, who have neither brains nor experience, but think you know enough to combine West-end fashion with East-end financing, if you ever read anything, read me, that you may avoid having your purses—which, indeed, at best are trash—stolen, and your good names filched. Alas! I fear that those I seek to reach are just those who will think I don't concern them. The parsons, the widows, the orphans, the officers on half pay, the rich squires, the titled dupes—the sponges, in fact, whom I want to warn against the squeezers, will pass me by, while the squeezers themselves will chuckle over my adventurous career, as thieves read the police reports, partly on account of the affectionate interest they take in the profession, and partly in the hope of picking up a wrinkle or two for future use and guidance.

Having taken the liberty, with a frankness which I regret formed no part of my original character, but which my approaching dissolution has suggested to me as expedient, to address these and all other classes of my readers, I will now endeavour to convey to them some idea of the process of my inception. I wish it, however, to be distinctly understood, that while I carefully veil the mystery of my identity, I am not altogether a mythical character;[1] that the facts of my existence are real, and not imaginary; and that there is nothing I am about to relate which has not actually occurred: at the same time any attempt of the most experienced promoter or knowing broker to discover exactly who I am, or rather was, will be utterly futile, so artful is the disguise behind which this record of my varied fortunes has been concealed.

Disdaining to take refuge in a fictitious name, and scorning the subterfuge

---

1. This essay fictionalizes Albert Grant's promotion and founding of the Credit Foncier and Mobilier of England in 1864. By 1877, Grant was bankrupt and disgraced. [Ed.]

of a sham prospectus, I will merely say that I first received the rude outlines of my subsequent shape in the ingenious brain of a needy and adventurous speculator. This gentleman, who had passed through the various phases of an officer in the army, a member of the House of Commons, and a broker on the Stock Exchange, from all of which he had, in one form or other, been practically, if not by any formal process, expelled, had been driven to earning a precarious livelihood by taking up what he called one "little business" after another. He was popularly known as the "Captain"; and in consideration of his natural predatory habits, I will venture to introduce him to my readers as Captain Hawk. His style of "little business" consisted in arranging for concessions, acting apparently as principal where it was too dangerous for the real principal to appear; playing the part of spy or detective between business friends at the request of either, or both; dealing in horses and carriages; trying to obtain contracts for large contractors; and introducing people who had "good things" to sell, or valuable ideas to impart, to capitalists likely to invest in them, and vice versa: on all which transactions he received commissions varying in amount— sometimes, indeed, very trifling—or was remunerated in other underhand methods well known to the craft. I don't think he was originally a dishonest man, and he still possessed many amiable and generous traits—such, for instance, as that of freely lending his friends the money which did not belong to him, and being always ready to put them into "good things," a service which they rarely returned. The fertility of resource and ingenuity of invention with which this worthy was gifted was something amazing; and I shall never forget the first time I saw myself in manuscript. He was in very low water at the time, and lived in a small lodging in a street off the Strand; but he shared the peculiarity of other members of the same fraternity, of rising and sinking with extraordinary rapidity and facility. There never was anything to equal his elasticity in this respect. The contrast between his gay and jaunty appearance when he was dashing down Piccadilly behind a pair of high-stepping bays, when his luck was good—and the seedy sort of swagger with which, a few months after, in an almost starving condition, he would secretly visit financiers who were ashamed to see him openly,—was a perpetual marvel to me. His external appearance was that of a somewhat dissipated "plunger." Heavy sandy moustache, from which volumes of smoke perpetually issued, concealed a not unpleasant mouth; and as he wrote me out impregnating me with his filthy tobacco, I remember looking up with astonishment into his calm blue eyes, and wondering how such an apparently vacuous countenance could ever have imagined such a complicated and incomprehensible prospectus as I felt myself, even in that first dawn of consciousness, to be.

Poor man! he deserved to get something for his trouble; for the effort of producing me cost him hours of concentrated thought, six tumblers of brandy-and-water, and as many cigars; and, though of course I cannot say I have any recollection of it, I have a dim sort of consciousness that I had, so to speak, been incubating in his brain for many weeks before I saw the light.

At last, after innumerable corrections, modifications, and final polishings, I was folded up, put into his pocket, and entered upon the next stage of my still infantile existence.

This gentleman is known in the phraseology of finance as my *Promoter;* and in spite of his many bad habits and general laxity of morals, after an extensive experience of city men engaged in providing investments for the public and managing them after they have been provided, I am proud to say that I can think of him with a certain feeling of filial tenderness, and even respect, for he did not conceal unknown villanies under the guise of respectability: having no profession he certainly made none; he was contented to live on the outskirts of the society to which he really belonged, instead of forcing his way into the society to which he did not belong—and rather picked up the remnant after the leaders of the profession had robbed the public, than stole from them himself.

Although I naturally did not know where I was going to, or what the next feature of my existence was to be at the time, it will make it clearer if I explain, which the light of my subsequent experience enables me to do, the plan of my Promoter. In order to give me any real value, it became necessary for him to obtain certain concessions and permissions from foreign Governments and municipalities—for I was a vast conception with ramifications all over Europe, and my success depended upon the construction of divers works involving contracts; in fact, there was a great deal of money to be made out of me by my Promoter, if he was only careful in his manipulation of me in my early stages. The first difficulty, and indeed the one, poor man, with which he had most frequently to contend through life, was impecuniosity.

He now stood in need of cash with which to pay his travelling expenses, and which should enable him to deposit the necessary caution money. Now there were two courses open to him: he could either go to a capitalist, explain the merits of the scheme, and go as his agent, having to give an account of his expenses, and receiving a stipulated sum; or he might take a partner from among the unwary youth of the West End.

The objections to the first course were obvious. The City capitalist would use him and throw him aside with a beggarly remuneration when he had no further need of him. The poor Captain knew this from bitter experience; but the obstacle in the way of the other course was, that the Captain had exhausted the tribe of fast and rich young men whom he had known in his fashionable days. He could only think of one man with whom he had a chance in this direction; if this failed, he would have to do the best he could in the City. A few weeks before, he had observed in the papers the death of a rich baronet, who had made his fortune in trade, and whose son had been a cornet in my Promoter's regiment, where he was noted for his weakness of intellect and extreme vanity. This youth had now become Sir Twig Robinson; and to him with a sanguine and even triumphant air my Promoter addressed himself, though I could feel the sinking presentiment of failure agitating his breast as I pressed against it.

Inexperienced as I then was, I was literally thunderstruck at the skill with which my Promoter flattered, tempted, and cajoled Sir Twig. That young gentleman, inflated with the newly-acquired consciousness of great wealth, was dazzled by the prospect of his name being connected with the brilliant and gigantic enterprise which my Promoter expatiated upon with extraordinary eloquence. Not only was there great profit, but there was great credit to be got out of it; and if the truth is to be told, with management, there really was both. Sir Twig was, after all, not by any means such a fool for taking me up, as he has been since on many occasions; and he exhibited a certain degree of cunning in the tenacity with which he insisted that if he advanced the whole of the capital necessary for these preliminary expenses, the concessions should be taken out in his name alone. The Captain was afraid of exciting his suspicions if he objected too strongly to this: so it was finally settled, that in consideration of my Promoter undertaking the by no means simple task of securing the concessions and permissions, Sir Twig was to find the money requisite, and the profits were to be equally divided; or, as he elegantly expressed it, "We'll go halves in the pull."

I am obliged, in order not to prolong this veracious history to undue limits, to deprive the reader of the exciting narrative of my adventures in various foreign capitals. Indeed I have some excuse for this; for although I was generally in his pocket, they were not so much my adventures as my Promoter's. He it was who lingered and gambled at Monaco, and justified it afterwards to Sir Twig on the plea that he was obliged to go there in order to meet a lady who was supposed to exercise a paramount influence over a certain well-known minister who dispensed concessions. An admirable linguist, my Promoter was eminently qualified for the duty on which he was now engaged. His easy assurance secured him a favourable reception in society; and although he was somewhat shyly regarded by our own embassies and legations, he succeeded in winning access to the authorities with whom he had to deal, generally by means of his popularity with the fair sex. My readers would indeed be surprised to learn the names of certain distinguished foreign dames to whose powerful advocacy the Captain owed more than one concession, and whom he, in consideration thereof, allowed to "stand in" for a certain number of fully paid up shares in the Company when formed. For more than six months did my Promoter dine, bribe, flirt, and intrigue, to his own great content; for he spent Sir Twig's money as freely as if it had been his own, while he graduated his bribes with a most delicate discrimination. It takes a great deal of patience and diplomatic skill to secure a concession; for any small employé can put a spoke in the wheel if he is not "squared" in some shape or other, and they know their power but too well. But my Promoter was more than a match for them, and returned triumphantly just as Sir Twig was beginning to take a gloomy view of things, and to think that the whole affair was a *ruse* of the Captain to live luxuriously abroad at his expense. It was with a surly grunt, then, that he received my Promoter, as the latter, in faultless attire purchased with Sir Twig's money, and with a radiant smile, burst into his room one morning to announce his success.

"I thought you were never coming back," growled Sir Twig. "I suppose you thought there was no occasion to hurry, considering that I was paying the piper. I kept writing to tell you to come back, but you took no notice of my letters; and now you have got these precious concessions, I don't believe they are worth anything. Who is going to buy them? People who know about these things tell me the public are shy of going in for a thing of this sort, and that there is not a chance of its going down."

"Of course it won't go down, my dear Twig," said the Captain, with a delightful impudence.

"Then why did you get the concessions, and what do you propose to do?"

"Form a syndicate, to be sure,—what else should I do?"

"A syndicate! what's that?" asked Sir Twig.

"I'll explain in a moment," replied the Captain; "but before we go any further, we have a little business to settle between us. You will observe that all these concessions are, as you stipulated they should be, taken in your name. Now I want you to sign a little agreement to the effect that whatever money is given for the concessions, if we sell them, is to be equally divided between us. This is only fair, you know—an ordinary matter of business routine. After you have done that, I'll explain to you the nature and functions of a syndicate."

Sir Twig had a vague feeling that it was never safe to sign his name, but he could see no valid objection to this proposal of the Captain's; and, moreover, he felt himself in his ignorance so completely in that plausible gentleman's power, that he did as he was told, with a sigh.

"Now," said the Captain, with a glance of amiable compassion, "I will proceed to teach this young idea how to shoot. We have an invaluable packet here of concessions and permissions. The great object is to induce the confiding country investor to think that his or her future happiness and prosperity depend upon their obtaining possession of them. Now if you or I were to offer them for sale, their reputation for value would be ruined, because the public never look into the intrinsic value of the article to be purchased, but are influenced entirely by the manner in which it is presented to them, and the financial standing of the persons who offer it for sale: a poor, honest man will utterly fail to sell them a good thing in a straightforward way, while they will jump greedily at a bad thing, dangled skilfully before them by a rich rogue. The first thing for us, therefore, to find, is the rich rogue. He will become the syndicate manager. And his business is to induce a number of gentlemen of the highest standing he can find to become the directors of the new Company, and an eminent contractor to engage to carry out the works, upon the certain assurance that money will be found; and at the same time to induce the public to subscribe the money upon the no less certain assurance that the directors and contractor have been found. This looks like a vicious circle, because you can only obtain one essential condition on the distinct understanding that the other has been already secured."

"And how do you manage to get out of it?" asked Sir Twig.

"Why, we offer the scheme in the first instance, not to the public, but to an influential combination of capitalists called a syndicate."

"But why should the capitalists take the shares which the public will not take?"

"Because," replied the Captain, "they will get them much below their nominal price; and by being only a few holders, and all known to each other, they can put up prices on the Stock Exchange, and easily rig the market, and then clear out at a profit."

"Excuse my stupidity," said Sir Twig; "but how do they rig the market?"

"That is very simple. A says to B, don't sell your shares under ten per cent premium. I will buy them publicly at that price through a broker, if you will privately give me back my money afterwards, and take back your shares. The next day B buys from A, and so on. This keeps up the price on the official quotations on the Exchange, and the outside investor comes in and buys; then the syndicate can quietly unload."

"I see," said Sir Twig, with more humour than I gave him credit for; "it seems to me that this syndicate, as you call it, is itself the 'vicious circle' of which you were talking just now; but where shall we find a syndicate who will be sufficiently respectable to inspire confidence, and yet be guilty of such practices."

"My innocent Twig, have you lived so long in this world," said the Captain, with calm superiority, "and not found out yet that confidence in matters of finance is not inspired because a man deserves it, but because he has accumulated vast wealth by a long and successful career of fraud? Leave this to me—I will find the syndicate: they will pay for the concessions; and whether they are afterwards 'stuck' with the shares, or succeed in palming them off on the public, surely does not concern us."

"And how much shall we ourselves make out of it?" asked Sir Twig, with an eye to the main chance.

"Can't say. We shall ask £250,000, and probably take £50,000, which makes £25,000 each. However, put yourself unreservedly into my hands, my dear Twig, and you won't have any reason to complain." Saying which, the

Captain nodded in a reassuring manner, took up his hat, and swaggered off, soliloquising thus as he went along. From my advantageous position in his breast-pocket I could hear him plainly.

"This little matter looks tolerably healthy. I shall get £25,000 for my half of the concession. Considering I deposited no caution money, and I bled Twig pretty freely in the matter of expenses, I shan't lose on that. If I introduce my syndicate man to a good contractor, the latter will have to pay me at least one per cent commission on the contract price, which certainly does not concern my Twig. After all, he has only paid £15,000 in caution money and expenses, and he will make, without any exertion of brain, £10,000 on that, which, considering that he has no brains to exert, ought to satisfy him."

I wondered, as we went along, where my Promoter was going to, but was soon enlightened, as he turned in to some handsome offices, and I observed the names of Chisel Bros., the well-known contractors, on the door. Mr. Chisel was engaged; but my Promotor waited patiently to see the great man, who was evidently in no hurry to see him, and made him a cold, suspicious bow, as he offered him a chair. "What I am about to say," remarked the Captain, with the bold assurance of one about to confer a favour, "must be considered absolutely private and confidential. A certain friend of mine, who is of the highest respectability, and moves in the first social circles—in fact I may tell you, under the pledge of secrecy, that he is a baronet, is the possessor of certain most valuable concessions"—here the Captain explained in general terms their nature, and went on,—"Now I have come to tell you that some City friends of mine, a most powerful combination of capitalists—men, I need scarcely say, of first-class financial standing, as you would yourself acknowledge if I was permitted to divulge their names—are inclined to take up the scheme. I thought that the project was one which would just suit you, and that if you felt inclined to undertake the contract, it would be useful to you to be introduced to the capitalists interested. I should be glad to present you to them; but in order to be able to talk to my friends, I should be happy to know what your prices are for carrying out the proposed works."

Mr. Chisel here fixed my Promoter with his eye, and asked him bluntly for the names of his financial friends. With an air of profound secrecy, but with an appearance of absolute bona fides, the Captain as steadily returned the glance, as he replied, "I have already said I am not at liberty to give you their names; but if you keep it entirely secret, I may say this, that one of the partners of Cash, Bullion & Co. is interested in the matter." I literally trembled in his pocket as my Promoter uttered this unblushing falsehood; but he evidently knew his man. The name of the firm, combined with the imperturbable calm of the Captain's manner, seemed to affect the contractor; and with a furtive side glance at him, he said, as he carelessly turned over the leaves of a book on the table, "Do you want our prices net, or will they include any commissions?"

"They will include one per cent commission for me," replied the Captain, coolly, but firmly.

Mr. Chisel seemed prepared for this, and quietly dismissed his visitor with the assurance that he would soon hear from him, and that he would make an estimate of the prices.

My Promoter instantly hurried eastward, murmuring, as he went, "Chisel bites—and so he ought, for there has not been a sounder or a better thing put on the market this long time; now the only thing is to find the powerful combination of capitalists I told Chisel I had found already. I suppose there is not a chance of Cash, Bullion & Co. going into it. But, confound it! when he pressed me so hard, I had to give some name, and under those circumstances there is no reason why one should not give the best; but I must see them first, just to save appearances if Chisel ever calls on me to explain my statements." And to Cash, Bullion & Co. he accordingly went. A frigid reception and still more frigid refusal was all he got there; but he seemed rather to enjoy the joke than otherwise, and, with a chuckle to himself, proceeded in quest of that less scrupulous class amongst whom he knew that his powerful combination could alone be found. [. . .]

I was surprised at the number of his acquaintances: without describing them seriatim, I may give a general outline of our mode of procedure. We always seemed desirous to shun observation, and to approach the great man we were in quest of as quietly as possible. The very clerks seemed to entertain a certain feeling of contempt for us, and knowing looks passed between them as my Promoter's card was taken to the sanctum of the millionaire. At first I used to feel this humiliation; but as I saw my inventor was perfectly stolid, I soon ceased to feel sensitive on the subject. On no one occasion that I remember were we at once admitted, but generally kept waiting in some dingy little back room for an hour or two, during which time my Promoter was preparing his part. I now, to my great delight, became aware, by the contrast which his manner presented to the personages to whom I was submitted for inspection, that my Promoter was a gentleman. There was a delicate combination of dignity, mystery, and reserve which struck me as very effective; and I used to wonder how any one could resist the low persuasive tones and explicit definitions with which my great advantages were described. I even myself really believed that I should be the means of making the fortunes of all who had anything to do with me; and felt quite irritated at the cold suspicious manner in which my merits were treated, the objections which were raised to me, and the evident doubt with which I was often regarded. The peculiarity of all these magnates seemed to be that they were very purse-proud, very grasping, very overbearing, and generally more or less vulgar; the richer they were, and the more convinced they became that I really was of some intrinsic value, the more unreasonable they seemed to get, and I quite sympathised with my poor Promoter's repeated disappointments. By degrees he dropped from the eminent financier to the eminent stockbroker, from the eminent stockbroker to the doubtful financier, and from the doubtful financier to the German Jew; and it was amongst this latter fraternity that at last he found a man willing to take me up. His name was Mire. He was a person of great activity, great perseverance, parsimonious habits, grasping in his transactions, and one who, although possessed of a great affection for all the members of his family scattered about in various countries, was not averse to cheating them when he could realise a respectable margin thereby. He took me up coolly at first, but grew warmer and warmer over me as he spent some time in considering my merits. Finally, he told the Captain that he would give him an answer on the following day; as he wanted to consult his solicitors, the eminent firm of Twister, Wriggle, Sly & Wriggle.

The Captain occupied the interval by seeing Chisel's manager, explaining to him that Mire had taken up the affair, and that circumstances had arisen in consequence which made it advisable that Cash, Bullion & Co. should not be mixed up in it; and he received from the manager the prices which had been promised, and a great deal of technical information, primed with which he kept his appointment with Mire. That gentleman began by making difficulties, said that the public were not ripe for enterprises of the sort, that the capital wanted was very large, the state of the market very bad (the Captain happened to know that the market had never been more buoyant), and that it would be difficult to find a good contractor willing to take it up. At this point the Captain interrupted with great effect, and poured out his recently-acquired knowledge with a volubility which somewhat disconcerted Mire, to whom he explained that for certain technical reasons connected with the nature of the works, there was in fact only one contractor in England who was really competent to carry out so magnificent and gigantic an enterprise, but that he fortunately was prepared to undertake it practically without making his legitimate profit, as it was indispensable to him to crush a rival firm, who were seriously threatening his pre-eminence in that particular line. Mire gave a deliberate wink, as if he distrusted this latter piece of intelligence; but his intense desire to get a good bargain overruled his better judgment, and he relented. After a prolonged negotiation, in which some very pretty fencing took place, showing great wariness, coolness, steadiness of purpose, and self-control on both sides, Mire agreed to take up the matter and to form a syndicate, on condition that he should be syndicate manager. The following terms were agreed upon: The contract was given to Messrs. Chisel Bros. Mire here asked, "What is the price net?" The Captain replied, £1,500,000. "I understand you," said Mr. Mire, "to say this is absolutely net?"

"Absolutely," said the Captain, with a calmness which caused me a painful feeling of distress, well knowing as I did that it included one per cent commission to himself. After a long and searching look into the Captain's inscrutable physiognomy, Mr. Mire seemed evidently satisfied, and said, with a knowing look, "My dear sir, have you mentioned this price to anybody but me?"

"I have not," rejoined the Captain.

"Then," said Mire, "Let us tell the contractors they must ask for £1,515,000. I must have something for my trouble."

"I presume," blandly remarked the Captain, "one-third of this will go to me."

Mire seemed to undergo a convulsion; he sprang from his chair and violently paced the room. "I thought, sir," at last he remarked, planting himself firmly before the Captain, "that you acted on behalf of the concessionaire, and you will have to look to that gentleman for your remuneration."

"Very well," drily remarked the Captain. "As nobody knows what the contractor's net price really is, if you make any difficulty about my standing in, I shall take care that the contractor will refuse to ask for a higher price than the one he actually receives. Indeed, although I am aware that this practice is not uncommon with other contractors, it will be difficult in this case, anyhow, to induce so respectable a firm to consent to it."

Finally, it was arranged as a first condition that the Captain would agree to overcome the contractor's scruples on this point for a percentage of one-sixth of the commission to be given by the contractor to Mr. Mire. Second, that Mr. Mire should be syndicate manager, which post, as it afterwards turned out, involved a variety of commissions. Third, that the concessions of Sir Twig Robinson should be bought for £50,000. On this point there was also considerable haggling, the Captain having begun by asking £150,000 for the concessions. "The little business" being so far settled, Mr. Mire produced a box of cigars and a bottle of capital sherry; and, fifteen minutes later, the Captain left the office in high spirits, with the promise of an interview with Mr. Mire on the following day at his solicitor's. From all of which you will perceive, O my investing readers, how much trouble it takes to prepare the gaudy fly by which you are ultimately to be hooked. Nobody knows what running about, and worry, and meetings, and appointments, and disappointments, and wrangling, are involved in the promotion of a company—what patience it requires, what constant watchfulness, lest by one false move the labours of months are neutralised, and the profits swept away by a stroke of sharp practice on the part of a friend and a brother. My Promoter's anxiety of mind during this trying period involved a perpetual recourse to stimulants, and he almost lived in Hansom cabs.

His next interview with Mire was in the office of the eminent solicitors already alluded to. There he met a small closely-shaved gentleman, with sharp pinched features and an oily manner—Mr. Wriggle, to wit; and there also were present several of Mr. Mire's powerful financial friends, whose names are of no importance. For many successive days did this little group meet in close conclave, their principal duty being to write to, and produce their correspondence with, their financial friends abroad, whom they had urged to join them in the enterprise, and become members of the syndicate, and who wished to be informed in regard to sundry details. At one of these meetings the contractor and his solicitor appeared on the scene. The contractor insisted that the whole of the capital of the intended Company should be "taken firm" by the syndicate before the prospectus was issued; which, I find out, means, that the various financial gentlemen who form the syndicate are required to sign a letter, which is called a syndicate letter. The skeleton of this letter ran as follows:—

The X. Y. Z. Co. (Limited).

(Of course my real name was given here.)

To be incorporated under the Companies Acts 1862 and 1867.

Capital £———, in one hundred thousand shares of £— each.

To the Manager of the Syndicate.

Sir,—We authorise you to place our name on the syndicate for raising the cash capital of this Company for a subscription of £—. We understand that Sir Twig Robinson, Bart., is prepared to sell several valuable concessions from foreign Governments and municipalities for the sum of £———, and that Messrs. Chisel Bros. are prepared to enter into a contract for the construction of. . . . . at a total contract price of £——— in cash, and £——— in fully paid up shares of the Company. We guarantee to the extent of our subscription the raising of the whole of the above-mentioned capital of £———; and further, that if the whole of such capital shall not within one month from the date hereof be otherwise applied for, the members of the syndicate will themselves subscribe for a sufficient number of shares to make good the deficiency; on the understanding that, by way of remuneration for our trouble and influence in establishing and bringing out the Company, and in raising the capital, and as a consideration for our entering into the above-mentioned undertaking, Messrs. Chisel Bros. will pay to bankers to be agreed upon on behalf of the syndicate, a sum of £———, which is equivalent to seventeen per cent of the capital of the Company, that sum to be appropriated as follows: Two per cent on the capital or the sum of £———, to be paid to the syndicate manager for syndicate management and expenses, and the remaining fifteen per cent or £——— to be divisible pro rata among the members of the syndicate.—We are, Sir, your obedient servants.

This somewhat complicated document was printed and shown to the eminent financiers assembled, in a guarded manner, as productions of this sort are of too delicate a character to leave the hands of the initiated few who are promoting the Company. Its real purport only became clear to me after I had overheard the following explanation of it by the Captain to Sir Twig, to whom he showed a copy of the letter, the intelligence of the hon. baronet being quite unequal to grasping its meaning on a bare perusal.

"My dear fellow," said Sir Twig, after having laboriously endeavoured to master its contents, "you might as well have expected me to understand an Egyptian papyrus as this long-winded yarn. What does it all mean?"

"Well, Twig, it becomes plain enough when you have had as much to do with promotion work as I have. We want to be paid for the concession; it is an essential preliminary to this that the capital of the Company be found: if you advertise the prospectus, the public may or may not subscribe to it. To make it a certainty, we find a small lot of financiers first, which, as I before explained, is called a Syndicate, to subscribe for the whole of the shares. The shares are then offered to the public for subscription. Whatever amount is applied for by the public is allotted to them at par; whatever amount remains is taken up by the members of the syndicate, in the proportion of their original subscription, so that a man who figures in the syndicate as a subscriber for one-tenth of the capital has to take one-tenth of the shares which have not been subscribed for by the public. In consideration for this risk he receives a syndicate commission of, say, fifteen per cent on the whole of his original subscription in the syndicate; so that if he has subscribed £50,000, and the public take all the shares, he receives £7500 for having affixed his name to a syndicate letter, and without having disbursed a farthing. If the public subscribe half, he receives the same commission, but has to take up £25,000 worth of shares, and so on."

"That is clear so far," said Twig; "but I don't see who is to pay them the fifteen per cent. Who do they get it out of—the public?"

"Of course out of the public in the long run, but in the first instance out of the contractor. It is clear that the Company cannot openly allot shares to the public at par, and to the syndicate at 85. That would be illegal. The situation therefore has to be turned. This is easily managed by sticking the syndicate commission secretly into the contract price, which appears in the public prospectus; and the contractor equally secretly hands back this commission to the syndicate when he receives his first instalment from the Company."

After many days spent in negotiation and preliminary haggling over further details too minute and complicated for me to go into here, and sundry financial firms had risen freely at the tempting bait offered to them, some boldly dashing at it, others shyly coquetting with it, a certain number were sufficiently firmly hooked to be brought to the point of signing; and a meeting was held of all those intending to become members of the syndicate with the contractor, the Promoter, Mire's solicitor, who was to become the solicitor of the Company, and the contractor's solicitor.

The syndicate was to consist of upwards of seventy members, of whom, however, only thirteen attended, acting for themselves and their friends. Mr. Mire had in the meantime prepared and finally settled the memorandum and articles of association of the future Company—a contract for the conveyance of the various concessions of Sir Twig Robinson to the new Company, and the contract to be entered into between Messrs. Chisel Brothers, on the one part, and Mr. Mire, acting on behalf of and for the future Company, on the other part, and a deed of transfer of such contract from Mr. Mire to the future Company.

Printed copies of all these documents were profusely scattered over the table. Their backs were neatly lined with red tape, as though to impart an air of respectability to their contents.

While they were assembling, these gentlemen collected in groups and talked finance until they were called to order by a sort of admonitory cough from Mr. Mire, who took a chair which happened to be at the top of the table, and addressed the meeting as follows:—

"Well, gentlemen, you are all aware of the nature of the business which has brought us together today: the valuable concessions of Sir Twig Robinson, who is represented by our friend Captain Hawk, are to be taken over by the Company which we propose to form. Mr. Wriggle, the deeds of transfer are, I presume, in order?"

Mr. Wriggle nodded assent. "The contract with Messrs. Chisel Brothers," pursued Mr. Mire, "has been in your hands, for the past week, and I should be glad of any observations referring thereto which any of you, gentlemen, might desire to make."

At this moment a funereal-looking individual in a suit of black, gaunt and scraggy, with high cheek-bones and a sanctimonious expression of countenance, interposed and said in unctuous tones, which seemed rather more appropriate to a meeting in a dissenting chapel than of a syndicate Committee:—

"It appears to me that the 45th clause of the contract does not sufficiently provide for the penalty to be incurred by the contractor in case of the completion of the works being delayed for more than two days beyond the time specified in clause three. I observe that the contractor is not bound to pay any forfeits, not only in the case of an interference by *force majeure,* to which, of course, nobody amongst us could object," and he threw a glance reverently upwards, "but also in the case of a strike amongst his workmen; it appears to me that in a Christian country like ours, it is utterly unnecessary if not injurious to public morality to secure the contractor against a contingency which cannot arise if he chooses his workmen only among converted and God-fearing men."

The contractor maintained that this observation was founded on a fallacy, and that his experience had proved to him that workmen were pretty much alike when it came to the question of a rise in their wages, no matter what their professions might be.

The contractor's solicitor here interfered, and produced a number of similar contracts entered into with other companies which all contained the same clause, and to which no such objection had ever before been taken. It was finally overruled. The gaunt gentleman observed that there were a great many other points in the contract to which he could not assent, and he proposed therefore to take the contract clause by clause. As his name was down on the syndicate list for by far the largest amount, no serious objection could be raised to this. It would weary the reader, as it certainly did the syndicate, were I to attempt to enumerate the objections raised by this perverse and pious millionaire to almost every point contained in the contract. He was only finally interrupted by a portly and jovial-looking personage declaring he felt faint, and that it was time to adjourn for lunch. At this meal the contractor managed cleverly to sit next the lugubrious objector, whose name was Sarmist, and a whispered conversation took place between them, which I managed to overhear, and which resulted in a secret offer from the contractor of a commission of two per cent on the contract price if the scruples of that high-minded man could be overcome on all the points raised by him, and the contract could be admitted as it stood now. Mr. Sarmist rejoined that two per cent was not enough, and that he could not possibly waive his scruples for less than three. I now understood the motive which had prompted his obstructive conduct throughout. The contractor refused absolutely to accede to this, feeling sure that the other was only "trying it on," and would ultimately take two.

The sherry at luncheon seemed to have a salutary effect upon the transaction of the business, for Mr. Sarmist retained an attitude of dogged silence during the subsequent proceedings, while the jovial gentleman was smoothing away difficulties and winning over waverers whose natural dispositions were not so sanguine as his own, until, as the day closed in, the meeting was adjourned, and everybody seemed to feel a certain amount of relief in the reflection that matters had been nearly brought to a head, and that one more sitting would at last give me definite existence, crown the hopes of my Promoter, and line the pockets in various proportions of the gentlemen who so kindly and disinterestedly invented for the public its latest want, and now modestly undertook the means of supplying it.

It was proposed to meet again on the following day. Mr. Sarmist, however, with an expression of profound regret, announced that a meeting at Exeter Hall[2] demanded his presence, and begged those present, in solemn tones, to adjourn reassembling for two days. This was agreed to. With a light and buoy-

---

2. Founded in 1829 as a meeting-house for religious and charitable societies, especially the Evangelical opponents of the Anti-Corn Law League. Located on the Strand. [Ed.]

ant step my Promoter wended his way homewards. He calculated as he did so what this, his last venture, was likely to prove worth to him. The schedule which he worked out in his mind, if put on paper, would read thus:—

Price of concession,	£50,000
Old Twig out of pocket,	15,000
Leaves to be divided,	£35,000
Half of that for me,	£17,500
One per cent on contract price,	15,000
One-sixth of old Jew's commission,	2,500
Total,	£35,00

As this figure presented itself to his imagination, a radiant smile overspread his countenance, and I felt his heart beat faster with the throb of pleasant anticipation. For a moment, but only for a moment, this feeling was checked by the sad recollection of the numerous former occasions on which a cup equally overflowing had been rudely dashed from his lips; but he regained confidence as he recalled the instant when his sharp eye detected the contractor in secret conversation with Mr. Sarmist, and the change which it affected in that pious gentleman's subsequent demeanour.

I must here remind my reader that having been printed in so many forms, I now filled the pockets of all the syndicate members, and that it was owing to this circumstance that I overheard the following conversation in Mr. Mire's office.

That gentleman was engaged in affixing his valuable signature to sundry invoices for a large cargo of tallow, when Mr. Sarmist's name was announced by a seedy-looking junior clerk with a hooked nose. Mr. Mire quietly turned on their faces all the letters which happened to be lying open before him on his desk, and signified his willingness to receive his visitor.

"I have come to speak to you, Mr. Mire," said that gentleman, with whom it had been my misfortune to be present at the meeting which we had just quitted at Exeter Hall, "about the contracts to be entered into for the X. Y. Z. Co. I have received distressing information this morning that several of my Continental friends have changed their minds about joining the syndicate, as they first intended. This would entail (if the Company for which we are working is to succeed) the contractor's taking a certain amount of his price in fully paidup shares. From confidential inquiries which I have had made, it appears that Chisel Brothers, though excellent contractors, have already rather more paper than they like, and that they would hardly be in a position to take anything but a cash contract. I have called, therefore, on Messrs. Gouge & Co., limited, who are willing to execute the works for £1,350,000 in cash, and £250,000 in shares."

"This is about £100,000 more," Mr. Mire replied, "than Messrs. Chisel Brothers have asked; and as to their taking part of the contract price in shares, I have no doubt whatever that they could make as favourable terms as Gouge & Co.; besides, Mr. Sarmist," he added, with a grave countenance, "it would be hardly fair and business like—and certainly injurious to my reputation for straightforward dealing—to throw over at the last moment a contractor with whom we have gone so far."

After a good deal of skirmishing, Mr. Sarmist, who seemed to have good reason for preferring Messrs. Gouge & Co., limited, drew his chair close up to Mr. Mire's, and having assured himself that the door was locked, said to him—

"I may tell you, my dear sir, that in point of fact their price is rather lower than Chisel's, being only £1,250,000 in cash, and a quarter of a million in shares—£100,000 being available for distribution amongst their friends."

"In cash, or in shares?" asked Mr. Mire.

"In cash," replied Mr. Sarmist, watching the effect that this announcement would produce upon his antagonist.

"Well," said Mr. Mire, "this looks like business: how much of that would go to me?"

"Half," responded the other.

"Done," said Mire, unhesitatingly.

My heart sank when I thought of my poor Promoter's schedule, and heard this nefarious bargain struck. The two worthies then engaged in minute calculations as to the distribution of the funds. It was found absolutely necessary to reduce the price of the concession to £25,000. This gave me another pang on the unlucky Captain's behalf; and for the first time I became aware that the *concessionaires* were practically powerless, and that those who had most capital at their backs really divided the spoil, and dictated their terms to everybody else. After a long and close confabulation, a schedule was drawn up and agreed to between Messrs. Mire and Sarmist.

This version of the schedule was, as a matter of course, kept perfectly secret between the two gentlemen, who, with a smile of mutual respect, congratulated each other upon "standing in on the ground-floor," as they significantly expressed it. A second schedule was then prepared for the benefit of the syndicate and *concessionaires,* to be submitted to them at the meeting on the following day. This body was only to be allowed to stand in on the next floor, and of course knew nothing of what took place on the ground-floor. And lastly, a third schedule was prepared to form the basis of the prospectus which was to be offered to the bona fide investors among a confiding public, who naturally were not to be allowed to stand in on any floor.

I give the three schedules side by side for the better edification of this last class of my readers, who will appreciate their position on the tiles.

The X. Y. Z. Company, Limited

Capital £2,000,000

Schedule for Mire and Sarmist (*ground floor*)	Schedule for Syndicate (*first floor*)	Schedule to be used for public prospectus (*on the tiles*)
Contract price shares £250,000	Contract price shares, £250,000	Concession, ...£25,000
" cash, 1,250,000	" cash, 1, 350,000	Working
£1,500,000	17% on £1,750,000, . . 297,500	capital, ...45,000
Wanted in cash—	Prel. Ex.—	Contract, ...1,930,000
17 on £2,000,000	Making	£2,000,000
Less 250,000 shares.	market, . . . £20,000	
£1,750,000 . . .£297,500	Law, ... 2,000	
Contract, ... 1,250,000	Brokerage, . . . 3,000	
X X X, ... 100,000	Press, ... 2,000	
Working Capital, ... 45,000	Advertising, . . 5,000	
Concession, ... 25,000	Contingencies . . 500	
Making market, ... 20,000	£32,500 . . 32,500	
Law, ... 2,000	Concession, ... 25,000	
Brokerage, ... 3,000	Working Capital, ... 45,000	
Press, ... 2,000	£2,000,000	
Advertising, ... 5,000		
Contingencies, ... 500		
£1,750,000		
Shares, ... 250,000		
Capital, ... £2,000,000		

Fair female investor, youthful scion of nobility, confiding officer on half—pay, gentle curate, dull squire, do not turn from an examination of this dreadful-looking sheet of figures because it is dry and complicated, but try and understand the explanation I am now going to give of it. You will see from the first column how a company is started with a capital of £2,000,000 to get works done which only cost £1,500,000, to acquire concessions which cost £25,000, and to retain a working capital of £45,000. The difference of £430,000 is spent as follows: £100,000 are absorbed by what Mr. Sarmist delicately styles X X X, in order not to do violence to his own religious sentiments, but by what is called, according to the individual tastes of financing men, "loot," "plunder," "faux frais" (an expression used by the more travelled and cosmopolitan financiers), "pull," "swim," and "margin." In the particular instance you are investigating, the Jew and the Christian each stole half of this amount, which rightfully belonged to my shareholders.

From this example you will perceive that the highest aim of every financier engaged in work of this description is "to stand in on the ground-floor." £297,500 were spent in a syndicate commission, the nature of which my Promoter has already carefully explained to Sir Twig; £20,000 were spent in "making a market"—a swindling process also I hope made clear to you. Lawyers, brokers, advertising agents, and a small contingency fund, absorbed legitimately enough £2000, £3000, £5000, and £500 respectively; and £2000 were distributed among the gentlemen of the independent press, in order to impress them favourably with my undoubted merits. The greater part of this sum, however, was refused by all the more respectable members of journalism, and Mire and Sarmist of course pocketed what remained. The second schedule only differs in so far from the first that the contract appears to be £100,000 higher, as this amount, which has already been secretly appropriated by the two gentlemen living on the groundfloor, could not be disclosed to the lodgers on the floor above. The third schedule differs very widely from the two former, as it only contains what can in common decency be mentioned to the public. The contractor here appears as taking for his contract, and for preliminary expenses, a sum which exceeds his real price by exactly £430,000; and many a time, when his friends congratulate him upon his gigantic enterprises and advantageous contracts, he mournfully thought to himself how little of the first instalment of his nominal price ever found its way into his banker's account. However, he had no reason to complain, because when my works came to be made I found to my surprise that they really did not quite cost a million. So that, for doing work which, in fact, scarcely cost a million, and for holding his tongue about what happened to the other half million, he was paid a million and a half.

Hence my total capital came to be two millions.

On the following day, the powerful influence of Mire and Sarmist carried their scheme. The syndicate did not raise much objection to the change of contractor, as they got their seventeen per cent. The poor Captain, who neither got his one per cent from Chisel Brothers nor his part of Mire's commission from the same firm—they having been dropped at the eleventh hour—and who only got at last £25,000 instead of £50,000 for the concessions, saw his bright dream of £35,000 vanish, and found himself a winner of only £5000 on the whole transaction. Sir Twig, of course, received the same, but immediately lost it at the next Derby. Chisel never forgave himself for having gauged his man so badly, and not having been more wary in his dealings with one so profuse in Christian profession as Mr. Sarmist; and his former antagonism to Gouge & Co., Limited, has derived a bitterness all the more intense because he so nearly carried off the prize himself.

This practically terminated my existence as an embryo. I shortly after saw the light of day, and received my formal name at the hands of the Register of Joint-Stock Companies.

One more step, however, had to be taken on my behalf before I could be introduced in a complete shape to the investing British public. My Board had not yet been constituted, and my success now mainly depended upon the air of respectability which might be imparted to me by the names of the gentlemen who could be induced to sit on it. Messrs. Mire and Sarmist were, of course, among the number; but unfortunately their names inspired no confidence in the City, and were utterly unknown anywhere else. It became necessary to find persons who possessed the two rare and valued attributes of a director—a high social standing, and an entire ignorance of business: this latter somewhat negative quality being thought indispensable by Mire and Sarmist, to enable them to exchange their functions as members and managers of the syndicate, for the equally dignified and not less lucrative position of wire-pullers—in other words, they wished to retain in their own hands the control of the Company's fortunes for the purpose of manipulating its operations with a view to their own private aggrandisement.

The process of forming a Board has been so recently revealed in the columns of the daily press, that it is not necessary for me to go into any detail in regard to it. I was no exception to the general rule. A noble lord, an ex-Minister of a foreign State, a Right Honourable, a General K.C.B., and four Members of Parliament, were secured mainly by the exertions of a well-connected young man of fashion, who received the usual commission; and duly qualified themselves by accepting a present of the necessary number of fully paid-up shares, in return for the dazzling effect which it was confidently and not unreasonably anticipated their names would produce upon the country public. It is due to these gentlemen to say that they were so firmly convinced of their own value, that it did not occur to them that there was anything wrong in selling themselves in this way; and I have always felt that any reflection upon their honesty was most unfair. It is natural that a duped public should be indignant with every one connected with the cause of their disasters, but let me assure you that nearly all these gentlemen sinned purely through ignorance and indiscretion. I found them invariably struggling to be honest all the time they were on my Board, and vainly attempting to comprehend and thwart the nefarious schemes of Mire and Sarmist. That they did not succeed, and ultimately drew upon themselves the anathemas of an exasperated public, was the result of being tempted by a plausible touter, with the prospect of increasing their limited incomes, into engaging in matters of which they had no experience, and of a certain fascination which the idea of directorial responsibility and dignity exercises upon certain weak minds.

A prospectus setting forth my merits in the most glowing terms, and promising a return of unheard-of dividends, was now printed in all the papers, and freely circulated through the means of an advertising agency, which had a list of all the names of unhappy shareholders in other companies. So well was my prospectus drawn, so overwhelming was the brilliancy of my Board, that my shares were greedily subscribed for; and I found myself established in handsome offices, with a board-room which became a favourite lounge with sundry of my directors, and a manager, secretary, and an array of clerks and officials which made me the envy of my neighbours. I need scarcely say that my manager was the nominee of Mire and Sarmist. This gentleman possessed an invaluable physique; his flowing grey locks, and general air of matured sagacity and intense respectability, which he heightened by wearing a white tie, produced an invariably reassuring effect upon shareholders. But he lived in a perpetual thraldom, for he was bound with chains which had been dexterously thrown round him by the two cunning intriguers to whom he owed his position, and who, while they never allowed him to forget the debt of gratitude he was under, had taken care to place him still more absolutely in their power by the loan of one thousand pounds, which his extravagant habits made it impossible for him to think of repaying. [. . .]

The sober, and as it would appear to the world the legitimate work of the undertaking of which I was the embodiment, now commenced. The works were executed one by one, as the shareholders were informed at the first public meeting, in the most brilliant and satisfactory manner; but frequent discussions between the contractor and my Board convinced me that the former was endeavouring to do as little as possible for the price, and was attempting to put on "extras" whenever opportunity offered. A period of about a year and a half was thus spent, at the expiration of which time my works were completed, and I entered upon my functions as a public benefactor. My operations were a decided success, in spite of the high remuneration set aside for the directors' services, and of the appointment of a numerous staff of ignorant connections and nominees of the directors, irreverently termed by the really efficient employés "Directors' puppies." My intrinsic merits were so great that large receipts were taken, and there was every prospect of a high dividend being paid at an early date.

I was surprised to find that my anxious shareholders were by no means well informed by my Board as to my excellent prospects, but that profound secrecy was maintained in regard to my actual position. From the frequent conversations which I overheard between my manager and sundry gentlemen who rushed in and out of his office gaily dressed, and with a noisy and impudent air—whom I, by degrees, discovered to be brokers—I became aware, to my intense regret, that my shares were being freely knocked up and down in the market; and after having listened to frequent extraordinary conversations carried on in the slang peculiar to all engaged in Stock Exchange transactions,

I finally realised that Mire and Sarmist were ultimately becoming what they styled "bulls" or "bears" of my shares. They carried out their operations by spreading rumours sometimes detrimental, sometimes favourable to my interests. They never failed to take advantage of the turn of the market which had thus been influenced by them. Their best coup was made immediately prior to the declaration of my first dividend. My earnings had been so large that a high dividend should have been paid. Mire and Sarmist, however, obstinately insisted upon the absolute necessity of laying by a large reserve fund; and so strongly objected to what they termed "stuffing shareholders with dividends," that for some time it really appeared that only a low dividend would be declared. This prospect, of course, soon finding its way into the Stock Exchange, depressed my shares considerably. Mire and Sarmist thereupon bought largely, and relented at the next Board meeting in their objections to a high dividend, which was eventually declared. My shares flew up with a bound, and the clever pair cleared out with a large profit.

Up to this time my career had, although not free from the influence of all the refined forms of swindling which our advanced civilisation makes possible, and almost encourages, been one of unbroken prosperity. Indeed my success was so palpable that rumours soon reached me of a competing company being promoted. My old friend the Captain easily overcame the scruples of Messrs. Gouge & Co., who at first thought it unfair to assist in starting an opposition company to the one out of which they had made so much profit; and after the usual sharp practice, and the many vicissitudes of promotion had been successfully encountered, my competitor was at last fairly started.

The state of terror which was now created amongst my Board was pitiable to behold; while Mire and Sarmist experienced the most intense indignation at anybody's daring to invade what they considered their private field of enterprise. These two worthies, however, eventually consoled themselves when they found a congenial friend on the Board of the rival company in the person of Sir Verrikute Trimmer, who made common cause with them, furnished them with all possible information regarding my young enemy in return for being well supplied with the latest news about my own health and circumstances; and they all three operated cleverly in harmony, so as effectually to plunder the shareholders in both companies. When my competitor's works were completed a brisk competition ensued. My rival's Board addressed themselves to the public in the capacity of general benefactors—the same work which had been performed by me at a remunerative rate to my shareholders was to be done by my newborn rival much more cheaply. The effect of this was a great loss to both of us, and a consequent fall in our shares; this went on for some time; everybody connected with either of us, whether shareholder or director, felt profoundly miserable. Even the very managers, who, as enjoying fixed salaries, cared little for the amount of the dividends earned, began to yield to the general feeling of gloom; only the recently-constituted triumvirate of Mire and Sarmist on my Board, and Sir Verrikute on the other, chuckled and rubbed their hands in an unostentatious and modest sort of way as they agreed upon one move after the other, which had the effect of still further depressing our revenues, and proportionately drove down our shares. All this time the three conspirators were heavy "bears," and made large amounts.

It was during this period that I for the first time understood what it meant to be a bear. The process of operation is as follows: Sir Verrikute, for instance, operating for joint account as a bear, calls into his sanctum in his City abode, one fine morning, one of his junior clerks. "Mr. Jones," says the chief, "will you send for one of the partners of Contango, Backwardation, & Margin, and tell them to sell £100,000 of X. Y. Z. for you." Mr. Jones, who is a rosy-cheeked, guileless youth, with a flower in his button-hole, drops his not over-intelligent countenance very considerably indeed. "Beg your pardon, sir; sell what?" "Send for the broker," says Sir Verrikute, gruffly; "I want *you* to sell a bear." The broker arrives, and Mr. Jones tells him—having been ordered to do so by his chief—to sell for him, Jones, £100,000 worth of X. Y. Z. shares, wondering all the time how on earth he could sell such a fortune in securities of which he never owned a single pound's worth in his life. Nor had his principal the shares either in his possession. The intelligent transaction simply consisted in this: Sir Verrikute sold through an impecunious clerk, who acted as nominee, £100,000 of X. Y. Z. shares which he did not possess. The purchaser paid £100,000 for them. The shares would, in the ordinary routine of business, have to be delivered about a fortnight hence or later; and Sir Verrikute knew well that by that time he might buy them for £90,000, as he was running them down in conjunction with Mire & Sarmist by proceedings injurious to both companies, but justified by them on the ground of exigencies of competition, public convenience, and so on. So, at the last moment, he bought himself for delivery at £90,000 what he had sold fourteen days previously for £100,000 thus getting the advantage of the unwary purchaser, who was, of course, not "in the swim," to the tune of £10,000.

At last the ruinous effects of competition began to tell so severely upon both companies that the directors resolved to open negotiations for an amalgamation. This, again, was done in the most secret way; and while terms were being negotiated which could not but raise the price of my shares enormously whenever they should become known, Mire, Sarmist, and Sir Verrikute were buying shares, to the full extant of their available cash balances, at a low figure; and, as it afterwards turned out, again realised largely when the amalgamation was consummated and the shares rose in consequence.

It must not, however, be imagined that all the proceeds of their enterprising speculations went into their own pockets. It was necessary to "square" other directors, to "put them in for a call" of shares; in short, the weak and respectable fractions of both Boards had to be persuaded that they ought to agree to certain measures—hold their tongues, and participate in the illicit plunder, as it was "a sort of thing which every business man did."

My chairman, who was elected to that office chiefly through Sarmist's efforts, because he was a noble lord, and because he had the qualification, still more important in Sarmist's eyes, of the most charming and absolute ignorance of business, was, shortly before the completion of the amalgamation, confidentially taken into a corner by Sarmist.

"It will be necessary, my lord," Mr. Sarmist said, "that our company should increase its capital and create new shares. The new shares will be given in exchange for the shares of the opposition company. This it will be easy enough to carry at a general meeting of shareholders. Our capital being two millions, and that of the other company one, we should require to make ours three millions; but I should strongly recommend that it should be made six."

"What!" exclaimed the noble lord; "six!—what for!"

"Well," said Sarmist, complacently smiling, "it will halve the dividend—that is, our shareholders will receive £200 of share certificates for every £100 invested, and their dividends will apparently look only half as big as they are, and this will deter further competition."

The noble lord was not quite able to follow the argument; he rather thought there was something wrong about it, but the idea of doing away with further competition, and the business authority of Sarmist, at last made him yield.

Thus my competitor was bought; my capital was first increased to a sufficient amount to represent the shares of both companies, and the joint capital doubled, or, as they called it on the Stock Exchange, "watered," and we jogged on unitedly as one concern, and yielded half our former dividend.

My shares now became very much the instrument of gambling on the Exchange, and I am afraid that my directors gradually began to assume a less and less dignified position, as my shares passed into the hands of speculators far more knowing than the majority of them were. In vain Mire and Sarmist, who were no doubt "up to all the dodges," attempted to keep my Board as well in hand as they had them formerly; the disastrous results of their general malfeasance and of the "watering" of my stock were only too perceptible. The high figure at which my capital now stood made "market operations" in my shares safe, and therefore attractive, and the bold speculator began to divide the controlling power with the wire-pulling.

A violent struggle now took place between a powerful combination of speculators; who bought large quantities of my shares, and Mire and Sarmist, as to who should control my destinies. The latter soon found that they would have to appropriate a very much larger amount of their own capital than they cared to lock up towards purchasing my shares, if they wished to retain their hold upon me. In order to meet this danger, and to find large sums of money belonging to other people which could be used for their own purposes, they conceived the brilliant idea of starting a trust company. The capital of this company was fixed at three millions. It was set forth in the prospectus that the trust company would exchange its own certificates against the certificates of various other companies at a given figure calculated upon the average market price of each security. The holder of one trust certificate would by this means become a part-proprietor, in a large shareholding concern which owned a variety of securities, receiving their dividends and paying to its own shareholders the average on all the dividends it had taken. It was very plausibly urged that even the smallest investor would by these means always obtain a fair return for his outlay, no matter whether some of the companies, the shares of which were owned by the trust, were paying well or not. Mire, Sarmist, and Sir Verrikute naturally made themselves directors of the trust, completing their Board from the ranks of the necessary fashion and ignorance. The new trust was readily taken up by the public; large quantities of all the shares which had been selected as eligible for the trust were exchanged for the new certificates. Mire and Sarmist, by pointing out how very low my shares stood at that moment in the market, considering my intrinsic merits, easily induced their colleagues to sell the best of the securities which had been tendered for exchange by the public, and buy with the proceeds of the sale large quantities of my own shares. Before long, half a million sterling was invested by the trust in me. This practically gave to the trust—or, in other words, to the three directors who controlled it, once more an overwhelming influence over my fortunes. This was the culmination of the power of the triumvirate. They again were in a position to bull and bear my shares with an almost absolute certainty of success; and whenever adverse circumstances or unforeseen difficulties upset their calculations and involved loss, they immediately represented themselves to have undertaken the speculation on behalf of the trust, and "stuck" that unhappy company with the transaction. Their purse-proud arrogance and insufferable insolence at this period procured them great consideration in commercial circles, which unfortunately even extended to fashionable society in the West End. While my directors were thus triumphantly magnifying my stability and grandeur, I myself was becoming painfully conscious of the seeds of incipient disease; the water seemed to be pressing upon all my vital functions. My works were allowed to fall into disrepair, and every consideration of prudence in management was sacrificed to giving the shareholders the highest possible dividend. My reserve fund was little more than nominal, and it was very evident to me that additional capital would soon be required to renew my already decaying system and make good my numerous deficiencies. At the moment when I was regarded with envy by my enemies, with pride by my friends, and was encircled with a general halo of respect, I began to feel myself tottering on my swollen limbs, and to have a dark presentiment of the final crash.

Meantime Messrs. Chisel Bros. had not been nursing their vengeance in vain. Following with a watchful eye my rising fortunes, their quick experience soon detected the internally rotten condition I have just described; and they suddenly appeared as contractors of a rival company, which had been financed with unusual secrecy and honesty. Chisel himself was averse to the fraudulent dealings in which he had nearly become involved in my case, and determined, in order the more effectually to crush me and my contractors Gouge & Co., to content himself with moderate profits. The consequence was, that the A. B. C. Co. started with a capital of only one million, and with works almost as extensive as mine. It was utterly unable, however, to contend against the overwhelming forces which Mire and Sarmist brought to bear against it; they invoked the aid of their influential shareholders, of the Peers and Commoners who had assisted at my banquet, and, above all, of the Press. Many baser members of the journalistic world wrote up those gentlemen and their enterprises on every possible occasion, and opened upon my rival with a chorus of slander like a pack of hounds on a hot scent. Every disgraceful transaction of which they had themselves been guilty, Messrs. Mire and Sarmist darkly insinuated was practised by the Directors of the A. B. C. Co. These latter gentlemen did not happen to have been obtained by the same method as mine; but were quiet business men—not much known either to the world of fashion or of finance—their praises had not been sounded at banquets, nor had the public been made familiar with their names in articles written in their laudation. The consequence was that the poor A. B. C. Co. had a very rough time of it, and was generally regarded as one of the most dishonest, gambling, stock-jobbing concerns in the city—an impression which certain of the less reputable members of my own Board found it easy to produce, by getting up "rings" to bull and bear its shares, heaping discredit upon it thereby, while they at the same time filled their own pockets. Another favourite device was that of spreading false reports about it; and when they were found to be false, they accused the A. B. C. Directors of having invented them in order to "rig" the shares. I knew the A. B. C. Co. intimately; and I used to tell it that I felt like a skunk who squirted its own vile odour all over it, and then cried aloud to the passers-by to shun it on account of its noxious effluvium. So successful were these tactics, that for a year or two the poor A. B. C. Co. scarcely got business enough to pay its working expenses. In the meantime, Mire and Sarmist could not shut their eyes to the danger which was slowly but surely threatening—not my existence alone—for which after all they cared very little—but their position as wire-pullers of a large joint-stock company, which had enabled them to accumulate so much ill-gotten wealth. They ceased, therefore, to be content with slandering the A. B. C. Co., but intrigues were secretly set on foot for the purpose of acquiring it. In this case, however, my competitor was not so easily absorbed as on the former occasion. No congenial friend was found on the Board who was willing to go halves in the plunder. The negotiations between the Boards failed. The un-principled attempts of broken-down speculators, who at the command of Mire & Sarmist, and with their money, bought shares in the A. B. C. Co., and ap-peared at that body's public meeting in the characters of distressed share-holders, and insisted upon the necessity of coming to terms with me—the powerful rival—were frustrated by the firm attitude of the A. B. C. Board; and even the threat of the still powerful Trust Company to acquire a controlling influence in the A. B. C. shares and extirpate that Company's Board, unless they came to terms, was of no avail with my rival, and practically never car-ried out by the Trust Company for want of funds.

A feeling of intense irritation now took possession of Mire and Sarmist; but the despondency to which, for a moment, they almost succumbed, was succeeded by a reaction to their old arrogance and self-confidence; and with a boldness which was characteristic of their palmy days, they determined to infuse new life into me by supplying me with new works. This had, indeed, become absolutely necessary; for the contrast between my efficiency and that of the A. B. C. Co. was dawning even upon the outside public.

With feverish anxiety they rushed a resolution through my Board for the raising of additional capital. With agitated anticipation my prospectus was placed before the public, inviting that never failing source of money to sub-scribe to my seven per cent first mortgage debenture bonds. This time, alas, the appeal was made in vain. Just as my prospectus appeared, a serious finan-cial crisis had shaken the confidence, not only of the money circles in the city, but of the investing public at large. As a last resource, my shareholders were called together, and a piteous appeal was made to them by the noble lord who occupied the chair. My shareholders, however,—who had been in a fool's par-adise up to this time, and only looked forward to receiving dividends, instead of being called upon to furnish additional capital,—indignantly demanded further explanations from the chairman, which the utter want of knowledge, on the part of that nobleman, of my affairs prevented him from affording in a satisfactory manner; and eventually a stormy meeting was brought to a close by the adoption of a resolution, moved by a powerful speaker, that a commit-tee be elected from amongst the shareholders to inquire into the Company's position.

Now, for the first time, I became perfectly aware myself of my utter want of vitality. The weak and credulous part of my Board was even more aston-ished than I was myself at the revelations which were the result of this inquiry. On the second day of these investigations large defalcations were discovered, and upon summoning the elderly and highly respectable manager to account for them, it was found that he had not yet arrived in his office. The day passed without this functionary making his appearance—indeed, it has since been as-certained that he spent the afternoon in a passage to Boulogne, and is to this day a subject of interesting but fruitless inquiry to the police. Sick at heart were the unhappy shareholders when they understood the real position of their fine property, and even Mire and Sarmist were crushed in spirit when they saw the proud Temple of Gambling, which they had reared to themselves, about to crumble to dust. It was some consolation to them doubtless to reflect upon the thousands they had made out of me, but even of this they were soon to be deprived. The Committee's report was submitted to a second meeting, recommending my immediate liquidation; and the necessary legal steps were at once taken, which landed me in that bourne from which no company returns—the Court of Chancery.[3]

Inexorable fate, which had already overtaken me through the agency of Chisel Bros. and their friends, who had started my triumphant rival, dealt the final blow at the hand of my old friend and promoter the Captain. With the *cœur léger* which characterised that gentleman, he had applied at the outset for a few of my shares, which he retained through my varied fortunes; and now he appeared in a court of law in the since famous suit of "Hawk *v.* Mire and others," claiming to be reimbursed the purchase money for his shares, on the ground that a certain sum was paid to Mire and Sarmist, being directors, by Gouge & Co., being contractors, under a contract which was not disclosed in the prospectus, and which contract related to the X X X or plunder money with which my readers are already familiar. This revealed the whole of the fraudulent transaction I have narrated. The high-minded judge who presided on the occasion ruled that Mire and Sarmist should repay to the shareholders the sum of £100,000; and he expressed himself in unequivocal language as to the corruption which had crept into a certain class of the commercial community of London.

My melancholy history is now closed. If I have wearied you, my patient readers, and still more patient investors, my apology must be that it would have been quite impossible for you ever to have obtained the valuable information which has been disclosed in this veracious history, excepting through the medium of an abstract being like myself. I now bid you farewell with that feeling of remorse akin to tenderness which those in their last moments are generally supposed to entertain towards persons whom they have irretrievably ruined in purse and character. I look mournfully for the last time upon the Captain as he dashes past the office in which I am now lying, behind his high-stepping bays, bent on the promotion of a new Company. Only yesterday I overhead Sarmist say to the official liquidator in greasy tones that he had been sorely chastened by Providence, but that he intended to kiss the rod and profit by the lesson he had received, by which I understood him to mean that for the

---

3. The Court of the Lord Chancellor of England, the highest court in the nation next to the House of Lords. [Ed.]

future he would take proper precautions to see that X X X was so contrived that the law could not lay hold of it. Mire, I am informed by the remains of the Trust Company now lying under liquidation in the next room, took to his bed when the decision of the high-minded judge was communicated to him, at the fearful prospect of having to disgorge several millions of pounds, under the precedent just created by the said decision. He sunk gradually and never rallied. He now lies in the cemetery of a synagogue not far distant, and on his tombstone, engraved in choice Hebrew, is a correct translation of the thirty-eighth clause of the Companies Act (1867), 30 & 31 Vict. cap. 131.

N.B.—The 38th clause runs as follows: "Every prospectus of a Company, and every notice inviting persons to subscribe for shares in any Joint-Stock Company, shall specify the dates and the names of the parties to any contract entered into by the Company, or the promoters, directors, or trustees thereof, before the issue of such prospectus or notice, whether subject to adoption by the Directors, or the Company, or otherwise: and any prospectus or notice not specifying the same shall be deemed fraudulent on the part of the promoters, directors, and officers of the Company knowingly issuing the same, as regards any person taking shares in the Company on the faith of such prospectus, unless he shall have had notice of such contract."

Glossary

acceptor   An acceptor receives a bill of exchange as payment.

agiotage   Speculation, especially in stocks or company shares.

animadversion   Notice.

annuitants   Holders of annuities, which were guaranteed yearly incomes.

auriferous   Containing or yielding gold.

bankocracy   The de facto rule of an economy and, by extension, of a nation by the arrangements that accompany banking and the establishment of a national bank in particular.

beaks   Slang for magistrates or justices of the peace.

bearing   This stock-market practice involved decreasing the price of shares by contracting to sell at a future date and at a rate below market price, with the expectation that this agreement would force the price of shares down so that the bear could repurchase the shares at a rate lower than the one for which he had contracted to sell. **Bears** were individuals who attempted to lower the price of shares in this way.

bimetallism   The system of currency valuation based on both silver and gold.

Bourse   Term for the exchanges or markets in Paris and Amsterdam.

branch establishments (branch banks)   Auxiliary, provincial banks that serve as extensions of the main bank. These were initially formed for the Bank of England, which had twelve branches by 1834. Branches enhanced the flow of funds from place to place, especially to and from London. After midcentury, joint-stock banks were more likely to have branches than were private banks.

broker   A broker bought and sold shares for investors on the stock exchange.

bulling   Bulling referred to the stock-market practice of increasing the price of a stock by buying shares at a rate greater than market value, with the expectation of selling when the price surpassed the purchase price. **Bulls** were individuals who attempted to raise the price of shares, typically by such speculative purchases over market price.

capital   In general use, any money that is used to make money. In Karl Marx's theory (*Capital,* vol. III, chapter 48), capital is a social relation, which appears as money or as things. Capital is "the means of production monopolized by a certain section of society, confronting living labour-power as products and working conditions rendered independent of this very labour-power, which are personified through this antithesis in capital."

cipher   A secret or disguised manner of writing.

conveyancer   A lawyer who prepares documents for the conveyance of property and who investigates titles to property.

credit associations   Finance companies willing to back ventures traditionally viewed as too risky because of the lengthy period of the loan.

dealer   A dealer on the stock exchange was a jobber who would "go uneven," which meant that he would pay for and hold securities until the price was right.

defalcation   Misappropriation of funds; monetary deficiency created through mismanagement or fraud.

denudation   Divesting, as when banks deplete their cash reserves.

depreciation   Lowering of value; a fall in the exchangeable value of money or a negotiable instrument.

direct taxation   Direct taxes are taxes on wealth or income.

discount accommodation   The willingness to give cash for bills of exchange or debt (accommodation) at a particular rate of interest (discount).

dock warrants   Certificates given to owners of goods warehoused in a dock. These could also be traded as if they were stocks.

drawer   A drawer is the person who drafts a bill of exchange against his account, generally in a bank or with a merchant.

export premiums   Fees imposed upon goods that are exported.

expropriation   Forcing someone from the land or depriving someone of property. In Karl Marx's theory, expropriation is the forcible removal of peasants from common lands and small leasehold farms.

fixed capital   Value lodged in durable things, such as machinery or buildings, that remain in the owner's possession.

flimsies   Slang for paper banknotes.

fly   Slang for savvy, informed.

franchise   The right to vote at public elections.

fusible assets   Liquid assets, assets that can be converted to money.

green un   Slang for a naïve, usually young, initiate.

gross produce   The total or the entire amount of produce.

gross revenue   The total revenue.

guano deposits   Deposits of bird droppings, which were valued as a natural manure.

hap'orth   Slang for "a half-penny's worth"; in the negative, slang for "not in the least."

hedges   Slang for edges.

hypothecate   To give or pledge as security.

inalienable   Not subject to transfer to another person.

indirect taxation   Indirect taxes are principally customs levied on imports and exports and passed along to the consumer at the point of purchase. Indirect taxes are regressive, in the sense that they tax the poor disproportionately to their wealth.

These taxes were very extensive in the period, including (in England) taxes on soap, land, candles, beer, malt, newspaper advertisements, glass, carriages, coats of arms, bricks, windows, horses, dogs, salt, sugar, raisins, tea, coffee, and tobacco. In India, indirect taxations were imposed on an even greater number of commodities.

indorse   Another form of "endorse": To sign one's name on the back of a bill or cheque. The signature makes the bill or cheque payable. An indorser accepts the bill or cheque by signing the back of the bill.

Issue Department   One of the two departments of the Bank of England created by the 1844 Bank Charter Act. The Issue Department issued banknotes and thus controlled the nation's currency. The Banking Department conducted all the Bank's other business.

Jacobites   Supporters of the House of Stuart (James II) after the Glorious Revolution of 1688.

jobber   A jobber acted as an intermediary between brokers on the stock exchange or bought and sold shares independently, on speculation. A jobber squared his books every day, which meant that he had sold whatever he had agreed to buy and bought whatever he had agreed to deliver.

net profits   The amount of profits after deductions, such as expenses or taxes.

net revenue   The total revenue after expenses, taxes, and so on have been deducted.

nobby togs   Slang for fashionable or respectable clothing.

nominal value   The face or name value, as opposed to the actual or real value, which is dictated by market conditions.

political economy   The science of wealth. Although most often linked to Adam Smith, whose *Wealth of Nations* established the principles of economic liberalism, or classical political economy, the term first appeared in Antoyne de Montchretien's *Traicte de l'oeconomie politique dedié en 1615 au roy et la reyne mère du roy,* which emphasized the role that the state should play in governing a national economy.

premium (selling at a premium)   Selling shares above their face (nominal) value.

prigged   Slang for taken.

protective duties   Taxes imposed upon imported goods.

quondam allies   Former or previous allies.

railway debentures   Bonds or securities issued by railway companies in order to raise money at a fixed rate of interest.

reversion   The return of an estate to an heir. When the reversion was not absolute, legal provisions imposed conditions that limited the inheritor's right to sell any part of the property or to use it as security for a loan.

savings banks   Banking facilities intended to encourage saving by possessors of small amounts of capital. Depositors were paid £3 interest a year for every £100 deposited. No more than £30 could be deposited each year, up to a total of £150. These banks were established by the Trustee Savings Bank Acts (1817–80). The government-sponsored post office savings banks were established in 1861.

seignorage   A duty levied on the coining of money to cover the expenses of minting and to raise money for the government.

sinking-fund A fund formed by periodically setting aside revenue to accumulate at interest in order to reduce the principal of the national debt.

stag Slang coined in the 1840s for a person who buys shares on the stock exchange solely for the purpose of selling them immediately.

stone-pitcher Slang for prison.

strictly entailed A legal provision governing the transmission of property. A strict entail required the estate to pass intact (that is, not subdivided or diminished through sale) to a single heir, usually the eldest son.

suffrage The right or privilege of voting.

surplus-value The profit produced by the difference between the cost of maintaining the laborers and machinery that produce goods and the amount received by the capitalist who owns the machinery and employs the workers. According to Karl Marx, surplus-value results from the exploitation of workers.

syndicates Combinations of capitalists or financiers assembled to finance an enterprise requiring a large amount of capital.

troy The standard system of measure used for precious metals and precious stones.

unmarketable paper Bills of exchange, I.O.U.s, and other promises to pay that cannot be sold to a third party or used as securities.

usury Lending money at interest, typically at rates of interest considered exorbitant. The usury law, which prohibited interest rates above 5 percent, was repealed in 1833.

vellum Calf-skin parchment.

warehouse-warrant A form of receipt for goods deposited in a warehouse. The title to the goods could be transferred (used as money) by signing this document over to someone else.

work'us Slang for the workhouse, the state-run home for the indigent. A more extensive system of workhouses was established by the New Poor Law of 1834.

Contributers' Biographies

Ameer Ali, Syed (1849–1928)   Ameer Ali, the first Muslim to receive a M.A. from the University of Calcutta, studied law in England, then returned to Calcutta to practice and teach. He soon became a leader of Muslims in India, founding the first political organization of Indian Muslims in 1877. He became a member of the Bengal legislative council in 1878, one of three Indian members of the governor-general's council in 1883, and a member of the high court of Calcutta in 1890. In 1904 he retired to England, where he was appointed to the Privy Council five years later.

Aytoun, William Edmondstoune (1813–65)   A lawyer and member of an old Scottish literary family, Aytoun became a contributor to *Blackwood's* in 1836, then a staff member in 1844. His most popular work was his collaboration with Sir Theodore Martin on the paraodic "Bon Gaultier Ballads" (1845). Aytoun's solo work includes several books of poetry and the printing of *Ballads of Scotland* (1858). He was also a popular teacher at the University of Edinburgh.

Bagehot, Walter (1826–77)   Bagehot was born in Somersetshire, where he became a vice-chairman of a bank. From 1860 to 1877, he was the editor of the *Economist*. Bagehot was considered an expert in banking and finance and advised the government in times of crisis. His publications include *The English Constitution* (1867), *Physics and Politics* (1872), and *Lombard Street* (1873).

Blanchard, Sidney Laman (1827–83)   Son of Samuel Laman Blanchard, member of the young Charles Dickens's literary circle. When his father committed suicide in 1845, Sidney Laman Blanchard and his siblings were supported by a fund raised by Dickens, Thackeray, Bulwer-Lytton, and Cruikshank.

Cobbett, William (1762–1835)   Cobbett, the self-taught child of Surrey peasants, repeatedly moved between England and the United States in an often unsuccessful attempt to avoid imprisonment for sedition. In the early 1800s, his politics shifted from anti-Jacobin to radical. In 1802, he founded *Cobbett's Weekly Political Register,* which remained an influential working-class journal until his death. He also founded the *Parliamentary Debates* in 1803, passing them on to Hansard in 1812.

He collected his essays about the condition of rural workers in the book *Rural Rides* (1830). An advocate for reform, he won a seat in Parliament after reform was passed.

Evans, David Morier (1819–74)   Evans began his journalist's career as the assistant city correspondent to the *Times,* but he left to direct money articles for the *Morning Herald* and the *Standard.* He also contributed to the *Bankers' Magazine,* the *Bullionist,* the *Stock Exchange Gazette,* and the *Bankers' Almanac and Diary.* His books include *The Commercial Crisis, 1847–48* (1848); *City Men and City Manners* (1852); *History of the Commercial Crisis, 1857–58, and the Stock Exchange Panic, 1859* (1859); *Facts, Failures, and Frauds: Revelations Financial, Mercantile, and Criminal* (1859), and *Speculative Notes and Notes on Speculation Ideal and Real* (1864).

Fawcett, Henry (1833–84)   Despite being blinded during a shooting accident in 1858, and holding unpopular radical beliefs, Fawcett became professor of political economy at Cambridge in 1863 after publishing a *Manual of Political Economy* (1863). He entered Parliament in 1865 as a radical, supporting parliamentary reform, abolition of religious tests at universities, extension of workers' protection to agricultural workers, and the preservation of commons. He became best known, though, for his dedication to protecting the people of India from poverty and official exploitation; in fact, he was often called the "member for India." After years of attacking the Liberal Party, he accepted the office of postmaster-general under Gladstone where he instituted numerous reforms. When Fawcett died, a national subscription paid for a monument in his honor in Westminster Abbey.

Gilbart, James William (1794–1863)   Gilbart combined careers in banking and writing about banking. He was clerk for a London bank that stopped payment during the 1825 panic, then went on to serve as a cashier for a Birmingham firm and as manager for branches of the Provincial Bank of Ireland. His first book, *A Practical Treatise on Banking* (1827), was followed by more than a dozen additional books and numerous periodical articles. In 1833, Gilbart became manager of the London and Westminster Bank, the first joint-stock bank established in London.

McCulloch, John Ramsay (1789–1864)   Born in Scotland, McCulloch is best known as the popularizer of classical political economy, the author of *A Dictionary of Commerce and Commercial Navigation* (1832), and the editor of the *Wealth of Nations* (1828). McCulloch also contributed influential essays to the *Edinburgh Review.* He was an original member of the Political Economy Club, for which he collected and published a two-volume edition of scarce and curious tracts on money and commerce. A prolific and controversial champion of political economy and statistics, McCulloch was said to have "possessed in great degree the inflexibility of the old Roman character."

Marx, Karl (1818–83)   Born at Trier, Marx was a socialist theorist and political agitator. In 1844, he began a collaboration with Freidrich Engels, which lasted until Marx's death. In 1864, the International Association was founded with Marx as a leading participant. Marx published the first volume of his most famous work, *Das Kapital,* in 1867; the second volume was edited by Engels and published in 1885; the third volume appeared in 1894.

Oliphant, Laurence (1829–88)   Before he was thirty, Oliphant had traveled widely in Europe, Asia, and North America as a war correspondent and diplomat, always publishing about his experiences. In 1867, he joined a cultlike community in the United States led by Thomas Lake Harris. Oliphant finally broke with Harris, managed to recover some of his property, and then lived in Constantinople and Haifa where he hoped to support Jewish colonization of Palestine. Oliphant was remarkably prolific, writing political satires, spiritualist tracts, and countless travel and war memoirs, in addition to his work as a journalist.

Patterson, Robert Hogarth (1821–86)   Born in Edinburgh, Patterson was educated as a civil engineer. He began his career in publishing in 1852 as editor of the *Edinburgh Advertiser,* a position he left in 1858 for London. He went on to edit, and occasionally own, a number of newspapers both in London and Glasgow. On the basis of his periodical writing, he gained a reputation as a financial expert. Eventually, he was consulted by both the Bank of England and the Bank of France and was elected a fellow and then a member of council of the Statistical Society. Among his books are *Essays in History and Art* (1862), *The Economy of Capital; or Gold and Trade* (1865), *The Science of Finance* (1868), *Railway Finance* (1868), *Gas and Lighting* (1876), and *The New Golden Age and the Influence of the Precious Metals upon the World* (1882).

Rae, George (1817–1902)   Rae entered banking at the age of twenty, when he joined the North Scotland Bank. He was chief manager of the North and South Wales Bank from 1845–65 and Chairman of the Board of Directors of that bank from 1873. In addition to the *Country Banker,* he also published "Bullion's Letters to a Bank Manager."

Richardson, R. J.   A self-described "poor man," Richardson contributed a series of articles on banking to the Chartist newspaper *Northern Star.* He also describes himself as the author of the "Red and Black books."

Shand, Alexander Innes (1832–1907)   In 1867, Shand, a lawyer, began to write for a short-lived conservative paper, the *Imperial Review,* which quickly led to contributions to the *Times, Blackwood's,* and the *Saturday Review.* Shand also published some twenty books: novels, biographies, war journalism, travel sketches, and even a book on food.

Sidgwick, Henry (1838–1900)   Sidgwick spent his entire career in philosophy at Cambridge University, where he also was influential in its governance. Perhaps most prominently, he was an important supporter of women's education at the university. He helped found what became Newnham Hall in 1876 (the second college for women at Cambridge), and he helped win admission of women to university examinations in 1881. His major works, almost all of which were greatly influenced by J. S. Mill, include *The Ethics of Conformity and Subscription* (1871), *Methods of Ethics* (1874), *Principles of Political Economy* (1883), *The Scope and Method of Economic Science* (1885), *Outlines of the History of Ethics* (1886), and *Practical Ethics: Addresses and Essays* (1898).

Wilson, Alexander Jonathan (1841–1921)   In 1878, Wilson published a collection of statistics entitled *The Resources of Modern Countries: Essays Towards an Estimate of the Economic Position of Nations and British Trade.* He also published other works on economic subjects, including *Banking Reform* (1879), *Reciprocity, Bi-Metallism, and Land Tenure Reform* (1880), and *The National Budget* (1882).

Suggestions for Further Reading*

<u>COINS AND CREDIT INSTRUMENTS</u>

Nineteenth-Century Sources

Jevons, William Stanley. "Postal Notes, Money Orders, and Bank Cheques." *Contemporary Review* 38 (July 1880): 150–61.

McCulloch, J. R. "Credit." *A Dictionary Practical, Theoretical, and Historical of Commerce and Commercial Navigation.* 1832; rev. ed. London: Longmans, Green, and Co., 1871. Pp. 475–79.

McCulloch, J. R. "Discount." *A Dictionary Practical, Theoretical, and Historical of Commerce and Commercial Navigation.* 1832; rev. ed. London: Longmans, Green, and Co., 1871. P. 496.

McCulloch, J. R. "Laws of Bills of Exchange." "Exchange." *A Dictionary Practical, Theoretical, and Historical of Commerce and Commercial Navigation.* 1832; rev. ed. London: Longmans, Green, and Co., 1871. Pp. 596–99.

Newmarch, William. "Bills of Exchange in Circulation, 1828–47." *Journal of the Statistical Society of London* 14 (1851): 143–183.

Palgrave, R. H. Inglis. "Guinea." *Dictionary of Political Economy.* London: Macmillan and Co., 1900. II: 270–71.

Modern Sources

King, W. T. C. *History of the London Discount Market.* London: George Routledge & Sons, 1936.

Kynaston, David. *The City of London.* Vol. I. *A World of Its Own, 1815–1890.* London: Chatto & Windus, 1994.

Pool, Daniel. *What Jane Austen Ate and Charles Dickens Knew: From Fox Hunting to Whist—The Facts of Daily Life in 19th-Century England.* New York: Touchstone, 1993.

---

* Attributions of authorship for nineteenth-century periodical articles from *Wellesley Index to Victorian Periodicals.*

COUNTERFEIT COINS

Nineteenth-Century Sources

Binny, John. "Coining: Coiners" and "Coining: Forgers." In Henry Mayhew, *London Labour and the London Poor.* 1861–62; rpt. New York: Dover Publications, 1968. IV: 377–83.

Evans, D. Morier. "The Frauds and Forgeries of John Sadlier, M.P. and Late Lord of the Treasury." *Facts, Failures & Frauds: Revelations Financial, Mercantile, Criminal.* 1859; rpt. New York: Augustus M. Kelley, 1968. Pp. 226–67.

McCulloch, J. R. "Forgery of Coin," "Laws as to the Counterfeiting, &c. of Coin": "Coins," sections 8 and 9. *A Dictionary Practical, Theoretical, and Historical of Commerce and Commercial Navigation.* 1832; rev. ed. London: Longmans, Green, and Co., 1871. P. 333.

Palgrave, R. H. Inglis. "Forgery." *Dictionary of Political Economy.* London: Macmillan and Co., 1900. II: 120.

Wills, W. H. and Charles Dickens. "Two Chapters on Bank Note Forgeries, Chapters I and II." *Household Words* 1 (September 7, 1850): 555–61; (September 21, 1850): 615–20.

Modern Sources

Brewer, John. "Commercialization and Politics." In *The Birth of a Consumer Society: The Commercialization of Eighteenth-Century England.* Eds. Neil McKendrick, John Brewer, and J. H. Plumb. Bloomington: Indiana University Press, 1982. Pp. 197–262.

MONEY

Nineteenth-Century Sources

Forrester, Charles Robert. "The Philosophy of Money." *Bentley's Miscellany* 11 (April 1842): 396–405.

Grenfell, Henry R. "What Is a Pound?" *Nineteenth Century* 9 (June 1881): 937–48.

Lowe, Robert (Viscount Sherbrooke). "What Is Money?" *Nineteenth Century* 11 (April 1882): 501–9.

McCulloch, John R. "Treatise on Money." *Treatises & Essays on Subjects Connected with Economical Policy, with Biographical Sketches on Quesnay, Adam Smith & Ricardo.* 1853; rpt. New York: Augustus M. Kelley, 1967. Pp. 1–79.

McCulloch, J. R. "Money." *A Dictionary Practical, Theoretical, and Historical of Commerce and Commercial Navigation.* 1832; rev. ed. London: Longmans, Green, and Co., 1871. Pp. 893–95.

Montagu, Samuel. "Dangers of Modern Finance." *Fortnightly Review* 57 (March 1892): 322–36.

Palgrave, R. H. Inglis. "Money." *Dictionary of Political Economy.* London: Macmillan and Co., 1900. II:787–96.

Modern Sources

Collins, Michael. *Money and Banking in the UK: A History.* London: Croom Helm, 1988.

Dutt, Romesh. *The Economic History of India in the Victorian Age.* Vol. II. *From the Accession of Queen Victoria in 1837 to the Commencement of the Twentieth Century.* 1904; rpt. New York: Augustus M. Kelley, 1969.

Singh, V. B. *Economic History of India: 1857–1956.* Bombay and New York: Allied Publishers, 1965.

HISTORY AND MAGNITUDE OF THE NATIONAL DEBT

Nineteenth-Century Sources

Grellier, J. J. *The History of the National Debt from the Revolution in 1688 to the Beginning of 1800 with a Preliminary Account of the Debts Contracted Previous to That Era.* 1810; rpt. New York: Burt Franklin, 1971.

McCulloch, John R., ed. *A Select Collection of Scarce and Valuable Tracts and Other Publications on the National Debt and the Sinking Fund.* 1857; rpt. New York: Augustus M. Kelley, 1966.

McCulloch, J. R. "Three per Cent. Consols, or Consolidated Annuities." "Funds," II, section 2. *A Dictionary Practical, Theoretical, and Historical of Commerce and Commercial Navigation.* 1832; rev. ed. London: Longmans, Green, and Co., 1871. P. 622.

Palgrave, R. H. Inglis. "Market (on the Stock Exchange)." *Dictionary of Political Economy.* London: Macmillan and Co., 1900. II: 697.

Modern Sources

Dickson, P. G. M. *The Financial Revolution in England: A Study in the Development of Public Credit, 1688–1756.* London: Macmillan, 1967.

Ferguson, Niall. *The Cash Nexus: Money and Power in the Modern World, 1700–2000.* New York: Basic Books, 2001.

Hargreaves, E. L. *The National Debt.* London: Frank Cass, 1930.

INVESTMENT AND SPECULATION

Nineteenth-Century Sources

Bagehot, Walter. "Investments." *Inquirer* 11:526 (July 31, 1852): 482.

Duguid, Charles. *The Stock Exchange.* London: Methuen & Co., 1904.

Evans, D. Morier. "Review of Some Extraordinary Operations." *Speculative Notes and Notes on Speculation, Ideal and Real.* 1864; rpt. New York: Burt Franklin, 1968. Pp. 14–28.

Evans, D. Morier. "The 'Reign of Terror' in the Share Market." *Speculative Notes and Notes on Speculation, Ideal and Real.* 1864; rpt. New York: Burt Franklin, 1968. Pp. 294–300.

Gale, Frederick. "The Railway Bubble." *Cornhill Magazine* n.s. 7 (December 1886): 585–95.

Hall, John Parsons. "Speculation: A Tale of a Bank." *Bentley's Miscellany* 21 (February 1847): 166–75.

Hyndman, H. M. *Commercial Crises of the Nineteenth Century.* London: Swan Sonnenschein & Co., 1892.

May, Henry. "The London Stock Exchange." *Fortnightly Review* 44 (October 1885): 566–80.

Modern Sources

Alborn, Timothy L. *Conceiving Companies: Joint-Stock Politics in Victorian England.* London and New York: Routledge, 1998.

Ferguson, Niall. *The Cash Nexus: Money and Power in the Modern World, 1700–2000.* New York: Basic Books, 2001.

Michie, Ranald C. *The London Stock Exchange: A History.* Oxford: Oxford University Press, 1999.

INTERNATIONAL IMPLICATIONS OF INVESTMENT AND DEBT

Nineteenth-Century Sources

Broadfoot, William. "Australia and India: Their Financial Conditions and Mutual Relations." *Blackwood's Edinburgh Magazine* 154 (July 1893): 64–73.

Campbell, George. "The Finances of India." *Fortnightly Review* 25 (April 1876): 514–35.

Fawcett, Henry. "The Proposed Loans to India." *Nineteenth Century* 5 (May 1879): 872–89.

Hyndman, H. M. "Bleeding to Death." *Nineteenth Century* 8 (July 1880): 157–76.

Laing, Samuel. "The Crisis in Indian Finance." *Nineteenth Century* 7 (June 1880): 1065–1077.

Morley, John. "The Impoverishment of India Not Proven." *Fortnightly Review* 30 (December 1878): 867–81.

Pratt, E. "India and England." *Westminster Review* 148 (December 1897): 645–53.

Modern Sources

Ambirajan, S. *Classical Political Economy and British Policy in India.* Cambridge: Cambridge University Press, 1978.

Davis, Lance E., and Robert A. Huttenback. *Mammon and the Pursuit of Empire: The Economics of British Imperialism, 1860–1912.* Cambridge: Cambridge University Press, 1986.

Dutt, Romesh. *The Economic History of India in the Victorian Age.* Vol. II. *From the*

Accession of Queen Victoria in 1837 to the Commencement of the Twentieth Century. London: Kegan Paul, 1904; rpt. New York: Augustus M. Kelley, 1969.

Edelstein, Michael. *Overseas Investment in the Age of High Imperialism: The United Kingdom, 1850–1914.* London: Methuen, 1982.

Jenks, Leland H. *The Migration of British Capital to 1875.* London: Jonathan Cape, 1938.

Platt, D. C. M. *Finance, Trade, and Politics in British Foreign Policy, 1815–1914.* Oxford: Clarendon Press, 1968.

Singh, V. B. *Economic History of India: 1857–1956.* Bombay and New York: Allied Publishers, 1965.

PRINCIPLES OF BANKING

Nineteenth-Century Sources

Bell, G. *The Philosophy of Joint-Stock Banking.* London: Longman, Brown, Green, and Longmans, 1855.

Dalton, J. *The Banking Clerk, Comprising the Principles and Practice of Banking.* London: C. Knight, 1843.

Gilbart, James William. "The London and Westminster Bank: Its Principles." *A Practical Treatise on Banking.* 1829; rev. ed. Philadelphia: G. D. Miller, 1855 (3rd American from the 5th London ed.). Pp. 259–70.

Gilbart, James William. "The Moral and Religious Duties of Banking Companies." 1846; rpt. *A Practical Treatise on Banking.* 1829; rev. ed. Philadelphia: G. D. Miller, 1855 (3rd American from the 5th London ed.). Pp. 387–422.

Gore, Catherine. "The London Banker." *Bentley's Miscellany* 14 (December 1843): 598–604.

Grenfell, Henry. "Banking and Commercial Legislation." *Nineteenth Century* 5 (March 1879): 534–46.

Price, Bonamy. "What Is a Bank? And What Does It Deal In?" *Fraser's Magazine* 21 n.s. (May 1880): 668–82.

Rae, George. "Personal Credit." *The Country Banker, His Clients, Cares, and Work from an Experience of Forty Years.* 1885; rev. ed. London: John Murray, 1930. Pp. 6–13.

Rae, George. "The Testimony of a Balance Sheet." *The Country Banker, His Clients, Cares, and Work from an Experience of Forty Years.* 1885; rev. ed. London: John Murray, 1930. Pp. 14–26.

Modern Sources

Capie, F. H., and A. Webber. *Profits and Profitability in British Banking, 1870–1939.* London: City University, 1985.

Clapham, Sir John. *The Bank of England: A History.* London: Macmillan, 1945.

Collins, Michael. *Banks and Industrial Finance in Britain, 1800–1939.* Cambridge: Cambridge University Press, 1995.

Collins, Michael. *Money and Banking in the UK: A History.* London: Croom Helm, 1988.

Kynaston, David. *The City of London.* Vol. I. *A World of Its Own, 1815–1890.* London: Chatto & Windus, 1994.

MONEY PRESSURES AND BANK FAILURES

Nineteenth-Century Sources

Anon. "The Panic of 1866." *Bankers' Magazine* 26 (1866): 637–41.

Bagehot, Walter. "History of 'the Crisis.'" *Bankers' Magazine* 26 (1866): 645–55.

Ewen, Robert. "Banking Abuses and Banking Uses." *Westminster Review* 141 (February 1894): 133–38.

Newmarch, William. "The Failure of the City of Glasgow Bank and Its Lessons." *Fortnightly Review* 30 (December 1878): 882–901.

Patterson, R. H. "Bank Failures and their Remedies." *Blackwood's Edinburgh Magazine* 125 (June 1879): 750–66.

Rae, George. "Deposits and Runs." *The Country Banker, His Clients, Cares, and Work from an Experience of Forty Years.* 1885; rev. ed. London: John Murray, 1930. Pp. 125–34.

Modern Sources

Ferguson, Niall. *The Cash Nexus: Money and Power in the Modern World, 1700–2000.* New York: Basic Books, 2001.

Kindleberger, Charles P. *Manias, Panics, and Crashes: A History of Financial Crises.* Rev. ed. New York: Basic Books, 1989.

THE MONEY MARKET

Nineteenth-Century Sources

Evans, D. Morier. "The North and South American Coffee-houses." *City Men and City Manners. The City; or, the Physiology of London Business, with Sketches on 'Change, and at the Coffee Houses.* London: Groombridge & Sons, 1852. Pp. 116–31.

Palgrave, R. H. Inglis. "Money Market." *Dictionary of Political Economy.* London: Macmillan, 1900. II: 796–98.

Patterson, Robert H. "The City of Gold." *Blackwood's Edinburgh Magazine* 96 (September 1864): 367–84.

Modern Sources

King, W. T. C. *History of the London Discount Market*. London: George Routledge & Sons, 1936.

Kynaston, David. *The City of London*. Vol. I. *A World of Its Own, 1815–1890*. London: Chatto & Windus, 1994.

COMPANY LAW AND FINANCIAL FRAUD

Nineteenth-Century Sources

Anon. "Clearing the Ground." *Bankers' Magazine* 26 (October 1866): 1165–68.

Anon. "John Skeeme, The Promoter." Part I: *All the Year Round* 24 (October 5, 1867): 342–46; Part II. 24 (October 12, 1867). 376–81.

Anon. "The Law of Bankruptcy." *Westminster Review* 52 (January 1850): 419–35.

Bagehot, Walter. "What a Panic is and How it Might be Mitigated." *Economist* 24 (May 12, 1866): 554–55.

Dickens, Charles. "Convict Capitalists." *All the Year Round* 3 (June 9, 1860): 201–4.

Dickens, Charles. "Very Singular Things in the City." *All the Year Round* 3 (July 14, 1860): 325–26.

Evans, D. Morier. "The Rise and Fall of Mr. George Hudson, M. P." *Facts, Failures & Frauds: Revelations Financial, Mercantile, Criminal*. 1859; rpt. New York: Augustus M. Kelley, 1968. Pp. 6–73.

McCulloch, J. R. "Bankrupt and Bankruptcy." *A Dictionary Practical, Theoretical, and Historical of Commerce and Commercial Navigation*. 1832; rev. ed. London: Longmans, Green, and Co., 1871. Pp. 134–37.

Newmarch, William. "The Recent Financial Panic." *British Quarterly Review* 44 (July 1866): 125–40.

Modern Sources

Alborn, Timothy L. *Conceiving Companies: Joint-Stock Politics in Victorian England*. London and New York: Routledge, 1998.

Baskin, Jonathan Barron, and Paul J. Miranti, Jr. *A History of Corporate Finance*. Cambridge: Cambridge University Press, 1997.

Edwards, J. R. (ed.). *Legal Regulation of British Company Accounts, 1836–1900*. 2 vols. New York: Garland, 1986.

Hunt, B. C. *The Development of the Business Corporation in England, 1800–1867*. Cambridge, MA.: Harvard University Press, 1936.

Lester, V. Markham. *Victorian Insolvency: Bankruptcy, Imprisonment for Debt, and Company Winding-Up in Nineteenth-Century England*. Oxford: Clarendon Press, 1995.

Robb, George. *White-Collar Crime in Modern England: Financial Fraud and Business Morality, 1845–1929*. Cambridge: Cambridge University Press, 1992.

Index

accommodation bills, 11
accounting, 234, 265, 271
The Administration of a Bank During Seasons of Pressure (Gilbart), 288–299
advances
    evils of, 279
    increase in, at provincial banks, 269–270
    prudent behavior, 267
    true nature of, 270–271
advertising, 4, 26
Afghanistan, 207–209
agriculture, 115–116, 262
Ameer, Ali—*The Rupee and the Ruin of India*, 111–121
Anonymous
    The Bank Charter, and Commercial Credit, 242–258
    Facts for Enquirers: The National Debt, 125–126
    Stockbroking and the Stock Exchange, 149–173
Australia, 71–72
Austria-Hungary, 190–191
The Autobiography of a Joint-Stock Company (Limited) (Oliphant), 327–356
Ayres' Financial Register, 257
Aytoun W.E.—*The National Debt and the Stock Exchange*, 127–148

backwardation, 164
Bagehot, Walter
    on the *Economist*, 29
    The Money Market, No. 1, 310–315
    The Panic, 321–327
    qualifications, 101
    The Singularity of Indian Finance, 201–205

balance of payments, 88
balance of trade, 211–212
balance sheets, 271–272
banks
    bills of exchange on, 53
    with branches, 233, 267–269
    business extensions, 264–265
    business principles, solidity, 182
    characteristics, 231–233
    customer movement, 296–297
    deposit magnitude, 102–105
    failure, domino effect, 286, 292
    failure reports, 282–288
    failures in 1856, 292
    government oversight, 265
    incorporation ease, 16–17
    in India, profitability, 180
    joint-stock ventures, 20
    lending practices, 19
    limited liability acceptance, 318
    limited liability opposition, 317
    London, reduction in business, 266–267
    National Debt investment, 13
    and national debts, 222
    profits, 263, 271
    provincial, 269–270
    prudence in bad times, 295–296
    prudence in good times, 294–295
    reserve example, 313
    rural traditions of, 57
    security for loans, 273–274
    selecting, 234–235
    soundness, judging, 272
    transfers to country banks, 287
    United States, run on, 253
    use of, persuasion, 233–234
    user guidelines, 235–236